J.E.H. MacDONALD UP CLOSE

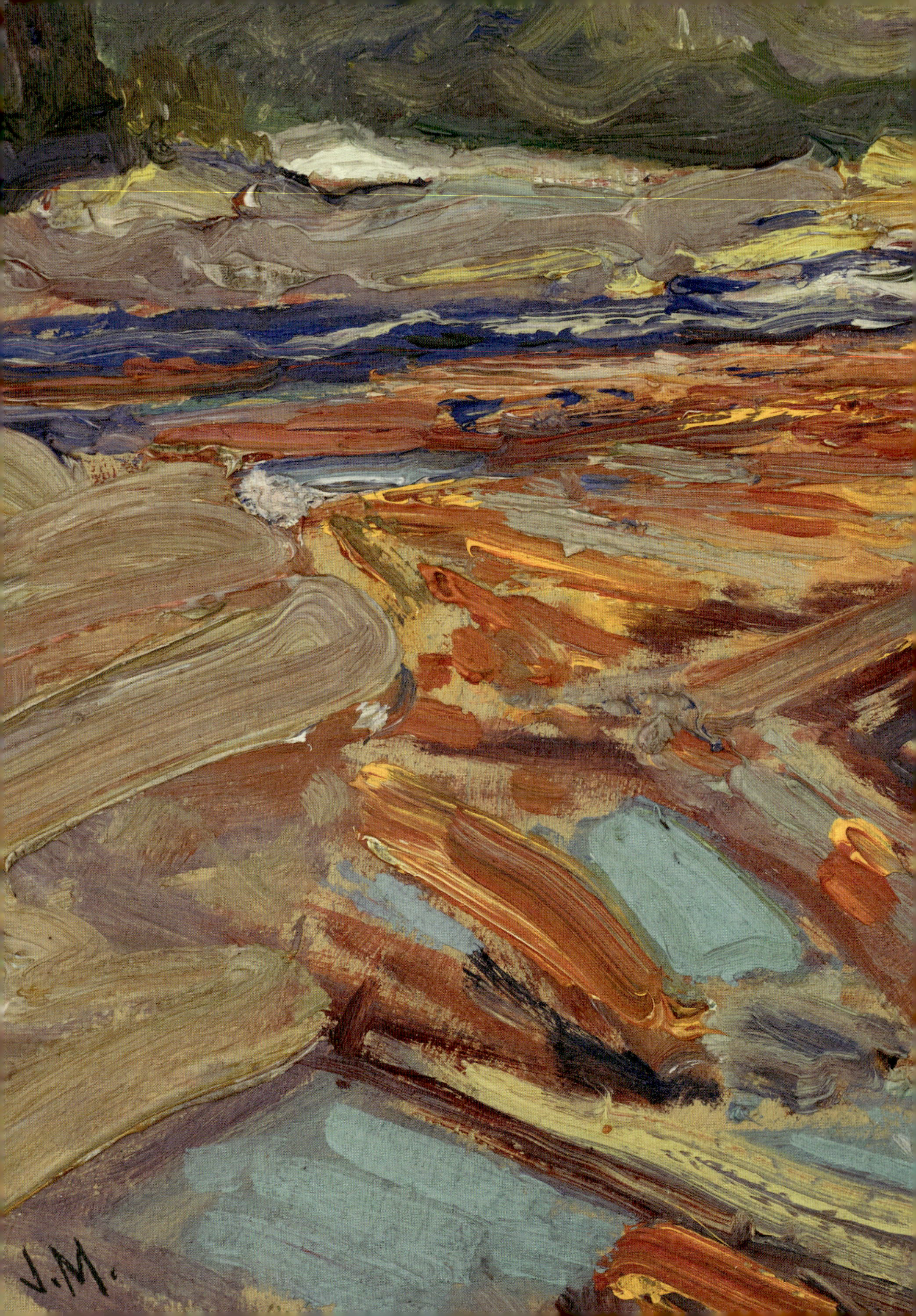
J.M.

J.E.H. MacDONALD
UP CLOSE

The Artist's Materials and Techniques

KATE HELWIG and ALISON DOUGLAS

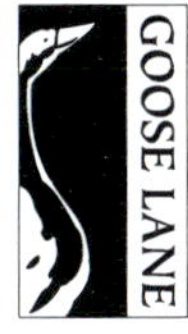

Edited by Margaret Gracie, Canadian Conservation Institute, Government of Canada.
Cover and page design by Julie Scriver.
Photographs courtesy of Art Gallery of Ontario; Canadian Conservation Institute, Government of Canada; McMichael Canadian Art Collection; National Gallery of Canada; National Gallery of Canada Library and Archives; anonymous private collector; Vancouver Art Gallery; and Whyte Museum of the Canadian Rockies.

Cover image: Detail of *The Tangled Garden*, 1916, National Gallery of Canada, Ottawa. Photograph by Germain Wiseman, Canadian Conservation Institute, copyright © Government of Canada.
Image below: Detail of the palette in J.E.H. MacDonald's Madderton paintbox, private collection. Photograph courtesy of the owner.
Printed in Canada by Friesens.
10 9 8 7 6 5 4 3 2 1

Library and Archives Canada Cataloguing in Publication

Title: J.E.H. MacDonald up close : the artist's materials and techniques / Kate Helwig and Alison Douglas.
Names: Helwig, Kate, author. | Douglas, Alison (Art conservation expert), author.
Description: Includes bibliographical references
Identifiers: Canadiana 20230553109 | ISBN 9781773104157 (softcover)
Subjects: LCSH: MacDonald, J. E. H. (James Edward Hervey), 1873-1932—Criticism and interpretation. | LCSH: Painting, Canadian—20th century.
Classification: LCC ND249.M25 H45 2024 | DDC 759.11—dc23

Goose Lane Editions is located on the unceded territory of the Wəlastəkwiyik whose ancestors along with the Mi'kmaq and Peskotomuhkati Nations signed Peace and Friendship Treaties with the British Crown in the 1700s.

Goose Lane Editions acknowledges the generous support of the Government of Canada, the Canada Council for the Arts, and the Government of New Brunswick.

Goose Lane Editions
500 Beaverbrook Court, Suite 330
Fredericton, New Brunswick
CANADA E3B 5X4

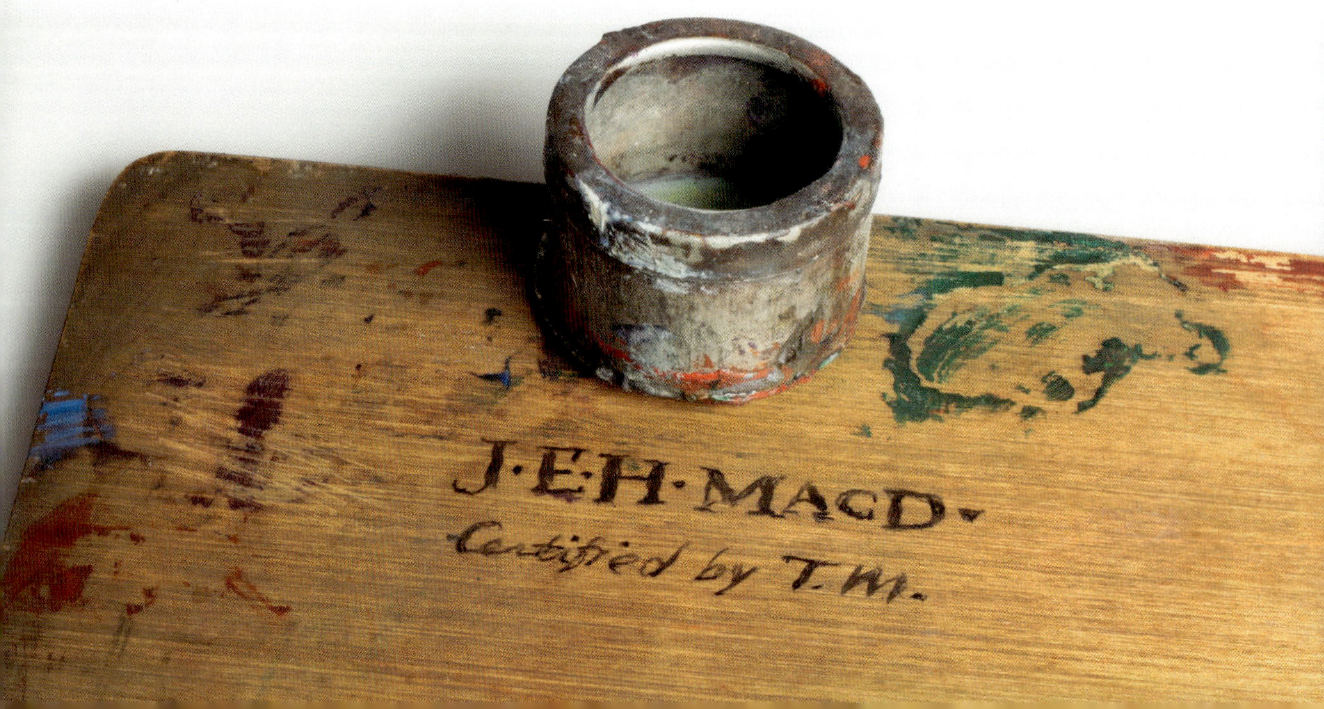

To Claude, with love.
– Kate Helwig

For my lovely mum, Jean, a firm believer that the arts made life worth living.
Her inspiring example and unwavering support helped light my artistic path.
And for my dad, Ron, who is steadfast in his strength, determination,
work ethic, and love of the mechanics of getting things done.
– Alison Douglas

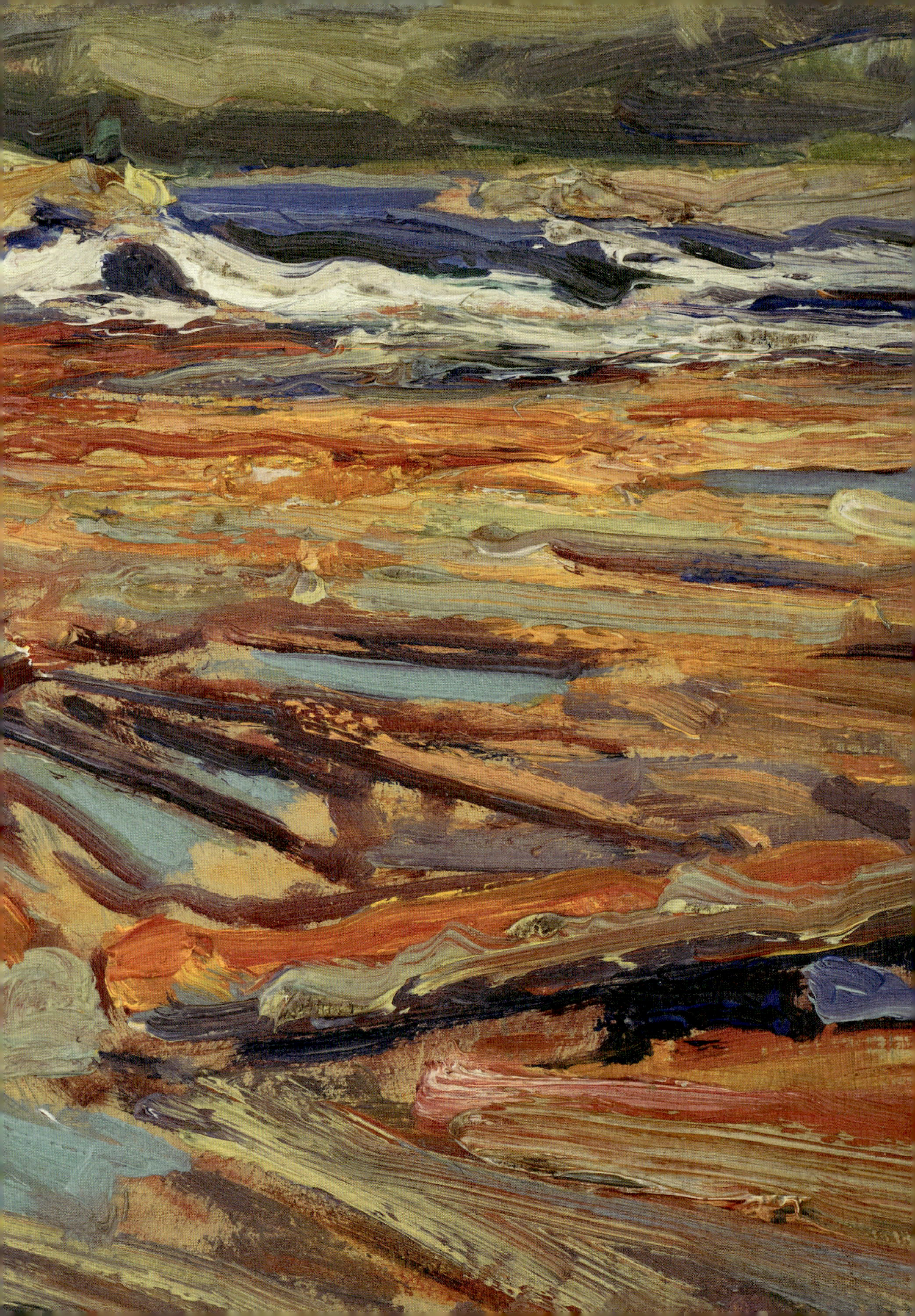

CONTENTS

(opposite and p. ii) Detail of *Logs on the Gatineau River*, 1914, McMichael Canadian Art Collection, 1981.85.5. Photo: McMichael. (see p. 23)

LIST OF ABBREVIATIONS

AGO	Art Gallery of Ontario
AMDIS	Automated Mass Spectral Deconvolution and Identification System
CCD	charge coupled device
CCI	Canadian Conservation Institute
CNE	Canadian National Exhibition
COSAD	Central Ontario School of Art and Design
EI	electron ionization
eV	electron volt
FTIR	Fourier transform infrared
GADDS	General Area Detector Diffraction System
GC-MS	gas chromatography-mass spectrometry
ICDD	International Center for Diffraction Data
IR	infrared
IRUG	Infrared and Raman Users Group
kV	kilovolt
mA	milliampere
MCT	mercury cadmium telluride
NFS	not for sale
NGC	National Gallery of Canada
OCA	Ontario College of Art
OSA	Ontario Society of Artists
PDF	powder diffraction file
PLM	polarized light microscopy
RCA	Royal Canadian Academy of Arts
SEM/EDX	scanning electron microscopy/energy dispersive X-ray spectrometry
TASL	Toronto Art Students' League
TMAH	tetramethylammonium hydroxide
TSP	thermal separation probe
UV	ultraviolet
VAG	Vancouver Art Gallery
XRD	X-ray diffraction

FOREWORD

THERE IS NO QUESTION of the important role that J.E.H. MacDonald played in the history of Canadian art as a designer, painter, educator, and co-founder of the Group of Seven. The landscapes that he rendered in such vibrant and diverse ways are iconic scenes from across the country that continue to inspire Canadians. Indigenous peoples observed and lived in harmony with those lands for thousands of years before MacDonald's awestruck observation led to his painted works. Those landscapes that once stirred poetry and images in J.E.H. MacDonald will continue to stir newcomers who choose Canada to be their new home.

The extensive study of the sketches and paintings presented in this book allows us to better understand J.E.H. MacDonald's choices as an artist, his exchange and dialogue with fellow painters, and the travels in Canada and abroad that so impacted his life. The characterization of artist materials and the meticulous documentation of their use over time helps to paint a picture not only of the scenes depicted, but of the artist's life.

The Canadian Conservation Institute (CCI) has studied and published the findings of the materials of Canadian artists for several decades. This important work has enriched our knowledge of the artists and their working methods. In addition, observation and scientific investigation into the materials and their current state of conservation help to identify deterioration, alterations, and past interventive treatments. The research can inform the most opportune future conservation treatment as well as the optimal conditions for a work's storage and display. On occasion, these studies also serve to authenticate a work and to cast aside any doubt that may surround an artist's oeuvre. The findings presented throughout this book serve as a material representation of MacDonald's writings on art. They shed light on the manufacturers and distributors of a bygone Toronto and other locales. They help tell the story of how MacDonald's style evolved over time.

CCI undertakes comprehensive technical studies of an artist's work in partnership with other heritage organizations. We are truly grateful for the fruitful collaboration with the McMichael Canadian Art Collection to further the knowledge of J.E.H.

MacDonald and his work. Years of curiosity, dialogue, research, and exchange of expertise have culminated in the publication of this book. I would like to thank, in particular, conservator Alison Douglas and conservation scientist Kate Helwig for leading this extensive study and for guiding its publication in such an accessible format.

Whether an art historian, a seasoned conservator, an aspiring curator, or simply a lover of art, the following chapters will reveal a wealth of information through stories about MacDonald's life, stunning images of graphic detail, and rich appendices of scientific data. I am pleased that this collaborative work between heritage organizations is now available to the public, and I hope that it will benefit many more organizations and interested readers in the years to come.

DR. KENZA DUFOURMANTELLE, Senior Director
Research, Conservation and Scientific Services
The Canadian Conservation Institute

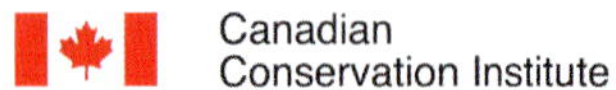

Canadian Conservation Institute
Institut canadien de conservation

...

BY ANY MEASURE, J.E.H. MacDonald is one of the towering figures of Canadian art. It is usually pointed out that he was "the oldest member" of the Group of Seven, as if age had anything to do with it. He was a founding member of that group because of the quality, dynamism, and modernity of his vision. The exhibition of his paintings held at the Arts & Letters Club on Adelaide Street East in 1911 may be said to be one of the seminal moments in the inexorable march towards the eventual founding of the Group in March 1920. Yet the path to becoming a professional painter was, for him, not an easy one. Not for him the stringent academic training enjoyed by many of his colleagues. MacDonald apprenticed to a lithography firm soon after his arrival in Canada at aged fourteen from his native England. He somehow managed to learn his craft, attending Saturday and evening classes where possible and studying other painters' techniques wherever the opportunity arose, while nearly always having to earn a living, either through commercial art or, later, through teaching.

Art historians rely a lot on biography, the timeline of crucial events and facts marking the passage of that life to match against its creative output. They note stylistic changes, incoming influences, and emotional crisis points to help us understand the art. Then there is connoisseurship – all too often (not always, of course!) a form of snobbery dependent on belief in a superior eye. The connoisseur sometimes feels empowered to question, with the aid of their magic eye, the quality, date, or even authenticity of an artist's particular work, and art history, frankly, is littered with their mistakes, misattributions, and dodgy value judgments.

But the scientific story embedded in the objects themselves provides another kind of history to consider. Analysis of the works elicits patterns of technique, idiosyncrasies of process, technical revelations as to materials used and much else that provides us with a body of invaluable and measurable evidence to add to the art historian's trained eye and mastery of historical fact and the connoisseur's honed instinct. Here lies the work of the scientist and conservator.

I was fortunate in 2018 to be able to use a sneak preview of some of this fascinating material in an exhibition I mounted at the McMichael Canadian Art Collection (the McMichael) that drew on the deep resources of MacDonald's work held in our permanent collection. Our visitors were given the opportunity to take a deep dive into the technical information available for a handful of the paintings on view in that show, and that opportunity immeasurably enhanced the experience for curator and public alike.

We are privileged, indeed, to have Alison Douglas on our team as conservator at the McMichael. She and her colleague Kate Helwig, conservation scientist at CCI, have spent years getting "Up Close" to J.E.H. MacDonald. Their truly important collaboration finally allows us to trace his artistic development through the materials and techniques he used.

May 2023 marked 150 years since MacDonald's birth in Durham, England, in 1873. What better way could there be for us to celebrate the sesquicentennial of J.E.H. MacDonald, one of Canada's most beloved artists, than the publication of this book?

IAN A.C. DEJARDIN, Executive Director
McMichael Canadian Art Collection

McMichael
CANADIAN ART COLLECTION D'ART CANADIEN

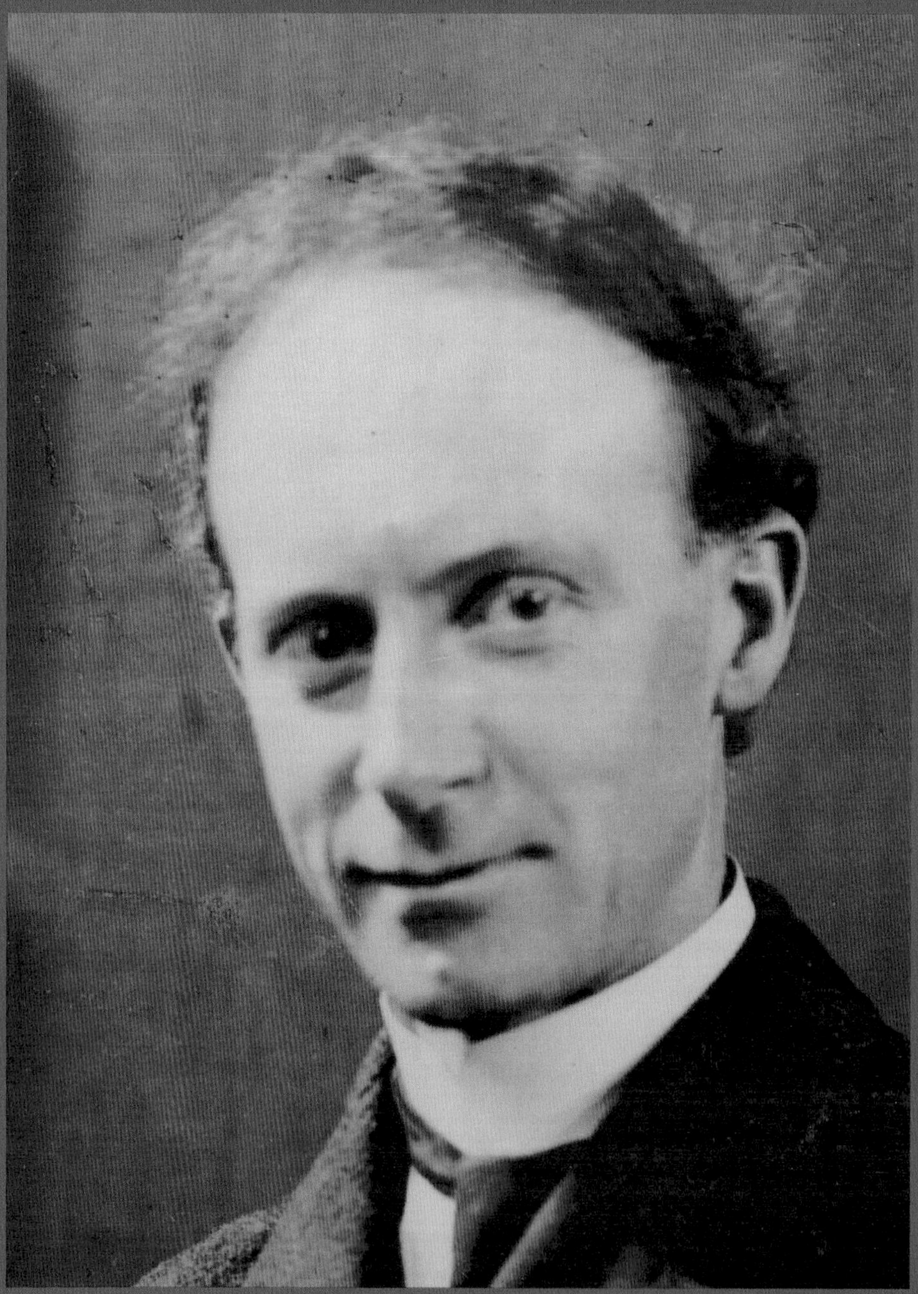

J.E.H. MacDonald, 1913. Photograph by M.O. Hammond.
National Gallery of Canada Library and Archives. Photo: NGC.

AN INTRODUCTION TO THE RESEARCH

As part of exhibition planning at the McMichael Canadian Art Collection (the McMichael), leading up to the one-hundredth anniversary of the Group of Seven, we had the opportunity to study a large collection of paintings by J.E.H. MacDonald. This book, the result of a joint research endeavour between the McMichael and the Canadian Conservation Institute (CCI), describes what we learned about MacDonald's artistic practice by combining close visual examination with rigorous scientific analysis of his painting materials.

James Edward Hervey MacDonald (1873–1932), a distinguished Canadian artist of the early twentieth century and one of the founding members of the Group of Seven, has been the subject of several biographies and exhibitions. Here, we present a new interpretation of MacDonald's artistic development, focussing on his painting materials and methods. Our investigation produced in-depth information about how MacDonald created his artworks: his choice of painting support, his use of preparatory layers, his preferred pigments and mixtures, and many aspects of his technique. Exploring the interface between art history and science, we studied exhibition and artists' materials catalogues, as well as MacDonald's diaries, letters, and lectures, to provide socio-historical context for the scientific results.

Although MacDonald's commercial design work is an important part of his oeuvre, our study concentrated specifically on his oil paintings. These paintings are principally landscapes and views of nature that embodied his vision of Canada in the early twentieth century. They consist of mid- to large-scale works that he produced in his studio as well as small-scale paintings, referred to as "oil sketches." These oil sketches or "little pictures"[1] are about the size of a standard sheet of paper or smaller. They were executed rapidly and were usually created outdoors through direct observation of nature.

The research included a detailed visual examination of 160 oil sketches and 14 studio paintings from the collections of three institutions that collaborated on the project: the McMichael, the National Gallery of Canada (NGC), and the Art Gallery of Ontario (AGO). MacDonald was a master of plein-air sketching, and his small, outdoor oil sketches constitute a major part of his artistic legacy. The oil sketches were a focus for the study, particularly because initial results suggested a well-defined chronological pattern in their dimensions, support type, and preparation.

A smaller group of works, comprising 21 oil sketches and 11 studio paintings, was chosen for scientific analysis of the painting materials. This is, of course, only a small proportion of MacDonald's artistic output. He is estimated to have made between 600 and 800 oil sketches and on the order of 100 to 150 larger paintings.[2] While limited in number, the works chosen for scientific analysis are representative of MacDonald's painting career: the selected paintings cover his active years from 1909 to 1932 and include works made on a variety of support types.

The oil sketches in the study group included several early works, such as a small sketch from 1909 that he painted in High Park, Toronto. Examples from MacDonald's sketching trips to the Algoma region of Ontario, to Nova Scotia, and to British Columbia are also represented, as are works painted closer to home, such as in his Thornhill garden. The latest sketches in the study were painted in 1932 on a trip to Barbados during the final year of his life.

Throughout his career, MacDonald chose certain of his oil sketches as the basis for larger-scale paintings that he worked up in his studio. The mid- to large-scale paintings chosen for analysis include works dating prior to 1918, representing MacDonald's early and Thornhill periods, as well as six oil paintings on canvas inspired by his Algoma sketching trips. Finally, several later paintings based on sketches made in the Rocky Mountains were included, notably, *Goat Range, Rocky Mountains* from 1932, one of his last completed works.

After an introduction to MacDonald's life and art in chapter 1, the research results are presented in the order in which he created his works. Chapter 2 describes his choice of support for both oil sketches and paintings. This chapter also outlines how MacDonald prepared his supports before painting. In chapter 3, we uncover MacDonald's painting process. This includes how he applied the paint, how he built up the composition, and how his technique changed and matured over the course of his career. Chapter 4 provides technical information about MacDonald's materials: his choice of pigments, the combinations of paints he used to produce different shades, and what is known about his paint brands. These chapters are illustrated throughout with photographs taken through a microscope, providing an up-close, visual record of MacDonald's working methods. While the main part of the text includes general observations, the appendices provide tables of the results and a comprehensive description of the analysis methods.

The book presents MacDonald's materials and methods in an accessible way for the general reader with an interest in art and art history. The detailed data compiled in the appendices is intended for a more specialized audience, such as art conservators who need to make decisions about appropriate treatment of paintings by MacDonald and his contemporaries. The data will also be valuable to scientists, curators, art historians, and collectors when questions arise about authenticity. Chapter 5 describes several examples that illustrate how knowledge of MacDonald's materials and methods can add to authentication research, to dating of his works, and to understanding the condition issues observed on some of his paintings.

There was even something of the quietist about him, something that made him unwilling to force his gifts, something that kept him from saying all he knew and made him wait and not meddle with himself. Such men are not easy to know.

– Barker Fairley on J.E.H. MacDonald, 1937.

The strongest influence in his life was his inherent honesty, and his greatest teacher was nature.

– E.R. Hunter, 1940, p. 2.

1. LIFE AND ART

As with any painter, J.E.H. MacDonald's life story, including his education, travels, friends, and key experiences, is a backdrop for his art. This chapter outlines the major aspects of MacDonald's biography that provide context for his paintings and their materials. Selected oil sketches and studio paintings that were included in our study are illustrated within their historical framework throughout.

Artistic Beginnings: 1873–1907

James Edward Hervey (J.E.H.) MacDonald was born near Durham, England, on May 12, 1873, to an English mother and a Canadian father. MacDonald's father was a cabinetmaker and was likely an influence in developing his son's proficiency in craftsmanship, which included carpentry and artistic wood carving.[1] Although little is known of MacDonald's early years, he has been described as a thoughtful, quiet child, and perhaps a bit of a dreamer.[2] In his adulthood, these same traits were expressed in his poetic sensibility and complex inner life. Family and friends have described him as reserved, sincere, and gentle, with the "essential loneliness" of an introvert. However, there was another side to MacDonald; he was also known for his spirit, strong opinions, and quick wit.[3]

Although he was an avid reader with a natural love of learning, MacDonald's formal education ended just before his fourteenth birthday, when his family emigrated from England to Hamilton, Ontario. After the move to Canada, MacDonald left school to become an apprentice at a lithography firm, and, in his spare time, attended evening classes at the Hamilton Art School.[4]

By 1890, his family had moved to Toronto and MacDonald had begun apprenticing at the Toronto Lithographing Company. He had also started taking evening and Saturday classes at the Central Ontario School of Art and Design (COSAD) under George A. Reid and William Cruikshank.[5] While these instructors were certainly important in his early development as an artist,[6] to a large extent, MacDonald learned his painting technique without formal training. Biographer E.R. Hunter has said of MacDonald that "the strongest influence in his life was his inherent honesty, and his greatest teacher was nature."[7]

During the 1890s, MacDonald belonged to several clubs and associations where he met fellow artists and practised drawing and painting both indoors and out. One important group was the Toronto Art Students' League (TASL), active from 1886 to 1904.[8] MacDonald later credited many of the TASL members, along with other artists, such as his early teachers at COSAD, with being important influences, both for himself and, more generally, for the development of Canadian art in the early part of the twentieth century.[9]

By 1895, MacDonald had joined the Toronto-based commercial design firm Grip Printing and Publishing Co. (Grip), where he worked until moving to England in late 1903. Through his friendship with fellow Grip employee Lewis Smith, MacDonald met Joan Lavis, whom he married in 1899. Their son, Thoreau, who was also to become an artist and later a strong supporter of his father's artistic legacy, was born in 1901.[10]

While some of MacDonald's drawings and watercolours from this early period are represented in public collections, including works made during summer visits to Smith's home in Nova Scotia, there are no known oil paintings. Certain passages from an 1898 letter to Smith, however, suggest that MacDonald was, in fact, working on developing his oil painting technique. For example, he wrote, "If one can *see* colour he'll soon learn how to mix it and put it on canvas." Later in the letter, he added, "Mr. Reid gave me a good criticism today, one that made me see something. He did something he never did before – painted in a piece of work and then scraped it out with the palette knife. I'd like very much to see some of his early work. I'm sure it would help to contradict my discouragement."[11]

In 1903, several of MacDonald's TASL colleagues invited him to join Carlton Studios, a design and illustration company that they had founded in London, England, a few years before. MacDonald left Toronto alone in December 1903 and initially lived in a London boarding house with one of his Carlton Studios associates. After about a year, he returned to Toronto and brought his wife and son back to England with him. The family moved into a flat in Loughton, Essex, on the edge of Epping Forest.[12]

MacDonald produced primarily book and jacket designs while working at Carlton Studios,[13] and in his free time, he visited galleries and painted in both watercolour and in oil. Among known works from this period is a small watercolour of Epping Forest, dated circa 1905.[14] An August 1905 entry from his wife's diary provides direct evidence that he was also painting in oil: "J. went up to London to the Tate Gallery. This afternoon he made a sketch at home in oils. Moonlight – elms and water."[15] The 1908 catalogue of the Canadian National Exhibition (CNE) includes an entry for a painting by MacDonald entitled *Nightwind – Near Epping Forest, England*, presumably either painted while he lived in Loughton or inspired from sketches made during his time there.[16]

It is possible that MacDonald first became aware of the Cambridge Colours oil paint brand while he was living in Loughton, since this small town in Essex was the location of the paint factory that produced it.[17] As outlined later in the book, chemical analysis of MacDonald's paintings showed that Cambridge Colours was one of the brands that he used throughout his career and is the source of the particular white pigment that is so characteristic of his palette, as well as the palette of a number of his fellow painters, including Tom Thomson.

The Cambridge Colours were produced by the British firm Madderton & Company, beginning in 1891.[18] Their factory in Loughton, Essex, which began as an Arts and Crafts–inspired collective, with artists and artisans working and living nearby, would certainly have been of interest to MacDonald. According to a Loughton historian, the chance of an artistic resident like MacDonald not knowing of Madderton's factory would have been small; both the founder, A.P. Laurie, and the manager, Vincent Nello, were well-known local figures.[19]

That MacDonald began using Cambridge Colours during his time in Loughton, and perhaps introduced the brand to his painting colleagues in Toronto upon his return, is an intriguing hypothesis but remains to be proven. Future research may uncover evidence, either through the analysis of oil paintings from his Loughton period or from documents showing that he used this brand or visited the factory while living in England. Of course, it is also possible that MacDonald learned about this paint brand after returning to Canada. As described in chapter 4, the Cambridge Colours were sold in Toronto as early as 1906.[20]

Early Oil Paintings: 1908–1913

In late 1907, MacDonald left Carlton Studios and returned to Toronto where he rejoined Grip as a senior designer. It was through Grip that he met Tom Thomson, as well as future Group of Seven members Arthur Lismer, Franklin Carmichael, and Frank Johnston. MacDonald was painting in oil regularly by this time and often sketched in High Park near his home on Quebec Avenue.[21] *Snow, High Park*, the earliest work in our study group, is a small, postcard-sized oil sketch from this period, painted in 1909 (Fig. 1.1). He exhibited paintings at the Ontario Society of Artists (OSA) Exhibition and the Canadian National Exhibition (CNE) for the first time in 1908 and continued to show his works regularly at these venues in the years following.[22]

Like many of his male contemporaries in Toronto with literary or artistic inclinations, MacDonald was closely associated with the Arts & Letters Club, which had been founded in 1908. It was at the Club that he first met Lawren Harris as well

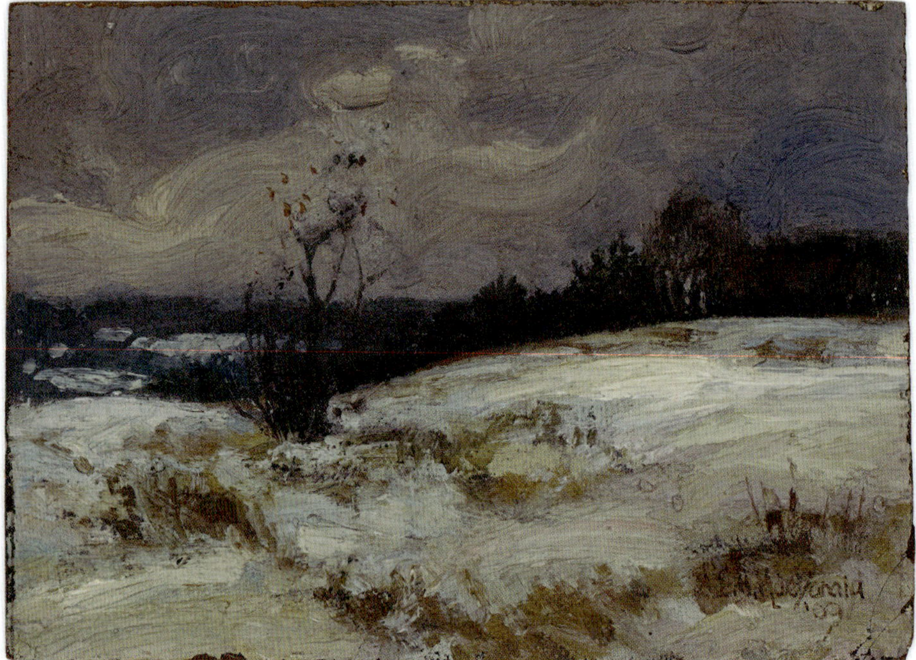

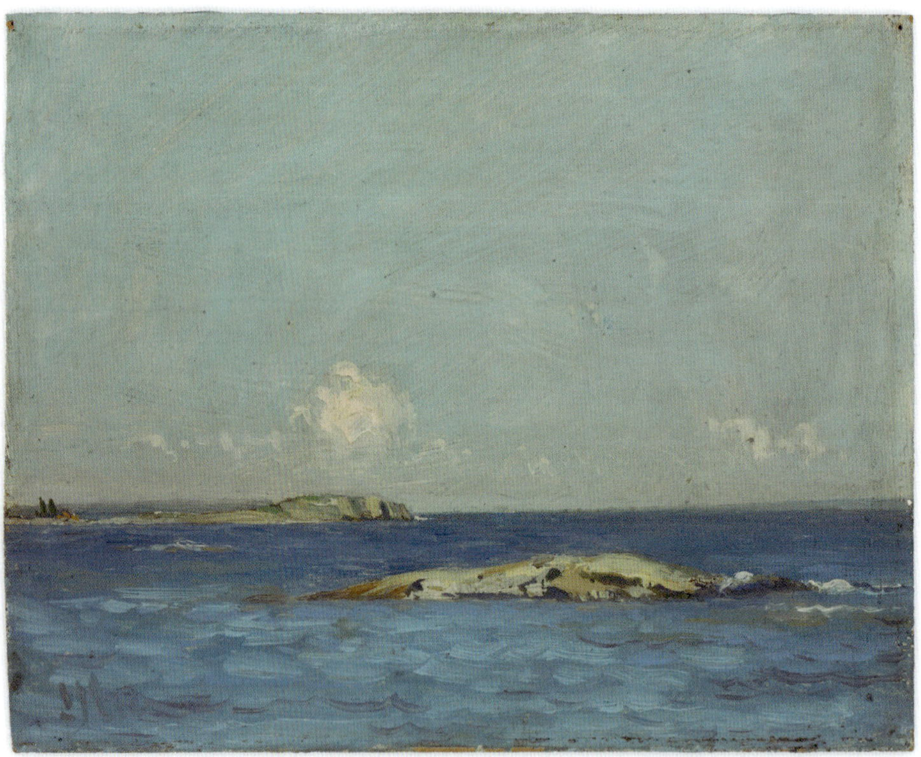

(top to bottom)
Fig. 1.1: *Snow, High Park*, 1909, 12.6 × 17.6 cm, oil on paperboard, McMichael Canadian Art Collection, 1981.24. Photo: McMichael.

Fig. 1.2: *View from Split Rock*, 1912, 18.0 × 22.8 cm, oil on paperboard, National Gallery of Canada, Ottawa. Photo: NGC.

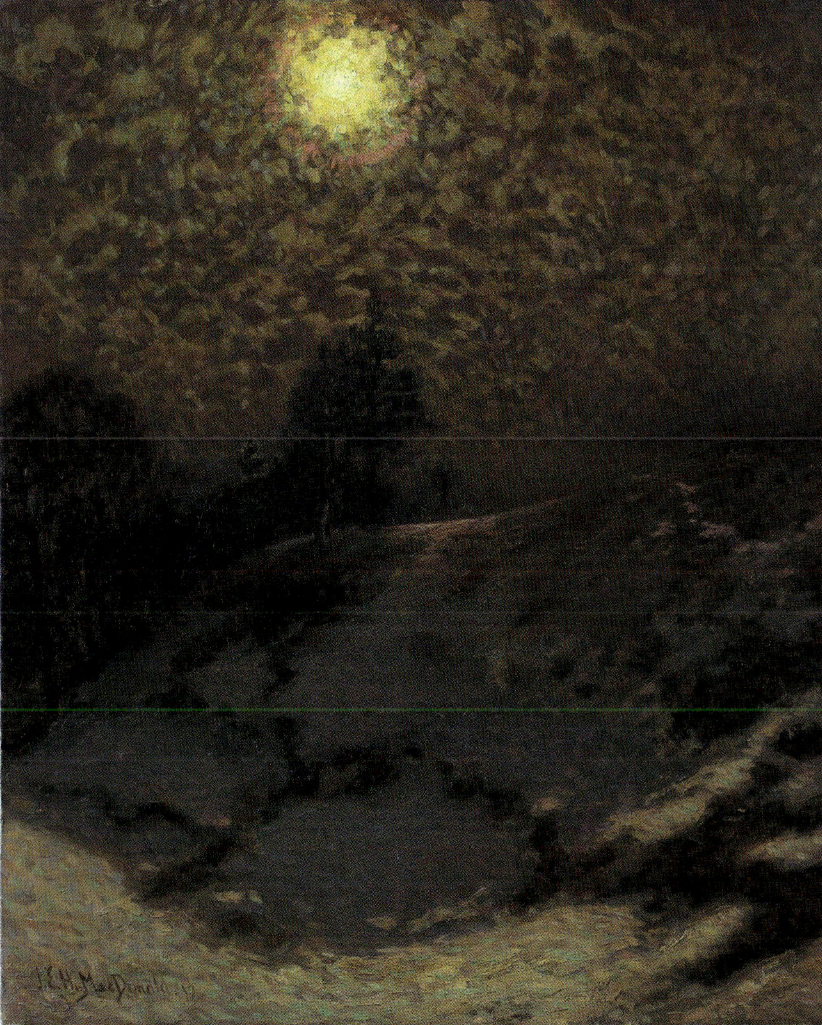

Fig. 1.3: *Early Evening, Winter*, 1912, 83.8 × 71.1 cm, oil on canvas, Art Gallery of Ontario. Photo: © AGO.

as Dr. James MacCallum, art patron and particular supporter of Tom Thomson and the future Group of Seven artists. MacDonald was elected as a member of the Arts & Letters Club in early 1911, and in November of that same year, it was the venue for his first solo exhibit of oil sketches.[23] The positive response to this exhibition,[24] along with the encouragement of friends and colleagues, especially Harris and MacCallum, convinced MacDonald to leave his position at Grip to focus on painting.[25]

MacDonald went on several sketching excursions in the spring of 1912, including a trip to Burk's Falls and Magnetawan River, Ontario, an area that he had visited regularly, beginning in 1909.[26] That summer, he made his first trip to MacCallum's Georgian Bay cottage, located on an island in Go Home Bay.[27] He painted a series of small sketches at Go Home Bay in the summer of 1912; one of these, *View from Split Rock*, is illustrated in Fig. 1.2. MacDonald exhibited several larger oil paintings on canvas at the OSA and CNE in 1912, including *Early Evening, Winter* (Fig. 1.3) and *Tracks and Traffic*, his well-known painting of an industrial area of Toronto.[28]

He was gaining recognition as an artist by this time: in 1912, he was named associate of the Royal Canadian Academy of Arts (RCA) and had his first painting purchased by the NGC.[29]

During 1913, as well as taking painting trips together to Mattawa, Ontario, and to the Laurentians in Quebec,[30] MacDonald and Harris travelled to Buffalo, New York, to see an exhibition of Scandinavian art. In a lecture given near the end of his life, MacDonald described how this exhibition was a tremendous inspiration that influenced the future course of his art. In this lecture, he explained how the Scandinavian artists depicted the specifics of their national landscapes with bold painting, remarkable colour, and rich design inspired directly from nature, repeating several times that his overall impression was that "this is what we want to do with Canada."[31]

Thornhill: 1914–1917

In January 1914, MacDonald began to rent space in the newly completed Studio Building, located at 25 Severn Street in Toronto. Lawren Harris and Dr. MacCallum financed the Studio Building with the aim, as Harris put it, of building a "workshop for artists doing distinctly Canadian work."[32] During the early years of the Studio Building, many of the future Group of Seven painters and artists associated with them worked there. The first tenants of the building were J.E.H. MacDonald, Lawren Harris, A.Y. Jackson, Tom Thomson (who shared Jackson's studio that year), J.W. Beatty, Arthur Heming, and Curtis Williamson.[33]

The Studio Building was a hub for discussing ideas about their new vision of Canadian art. In his autobiography, Jackson described it as "a lively centre for new ideas, experiments, discussions, plans for the future and visions of an art inspired by the Canadian countryside."[34] The artists would also have conferred on more technical aspects of their paintings, and there is evidence that they sometimes shared materials. For example, Harris had a large roll of jute sent to him from New Jersey and shared it with his painting colleagues.[35]

The Studio Building painters would have had easy access to artists' materials from Alex G. Cumming, manager of the Art Metropole, who rented space in the building from about 1916 to 1918.[36] At that time, the Art Metropole, located at 149 Yonge Street, was a leading supplier of artists' materials in Toronto, with Winsor & Newton being their primary oil paint brand.[37] As well as selling art supplies to many Toronto painters, Cumming was also willing to barter, since some artists were regularly short of cash. He is known to have traded oil paints and other supplies to Thomson, for example, in exchange for paintings.[38] As described in the next chapter, the commercial label on the back of one of MacDonald's 1912 sketching boards provides evidence that he purchased materials from the Art Metropole.

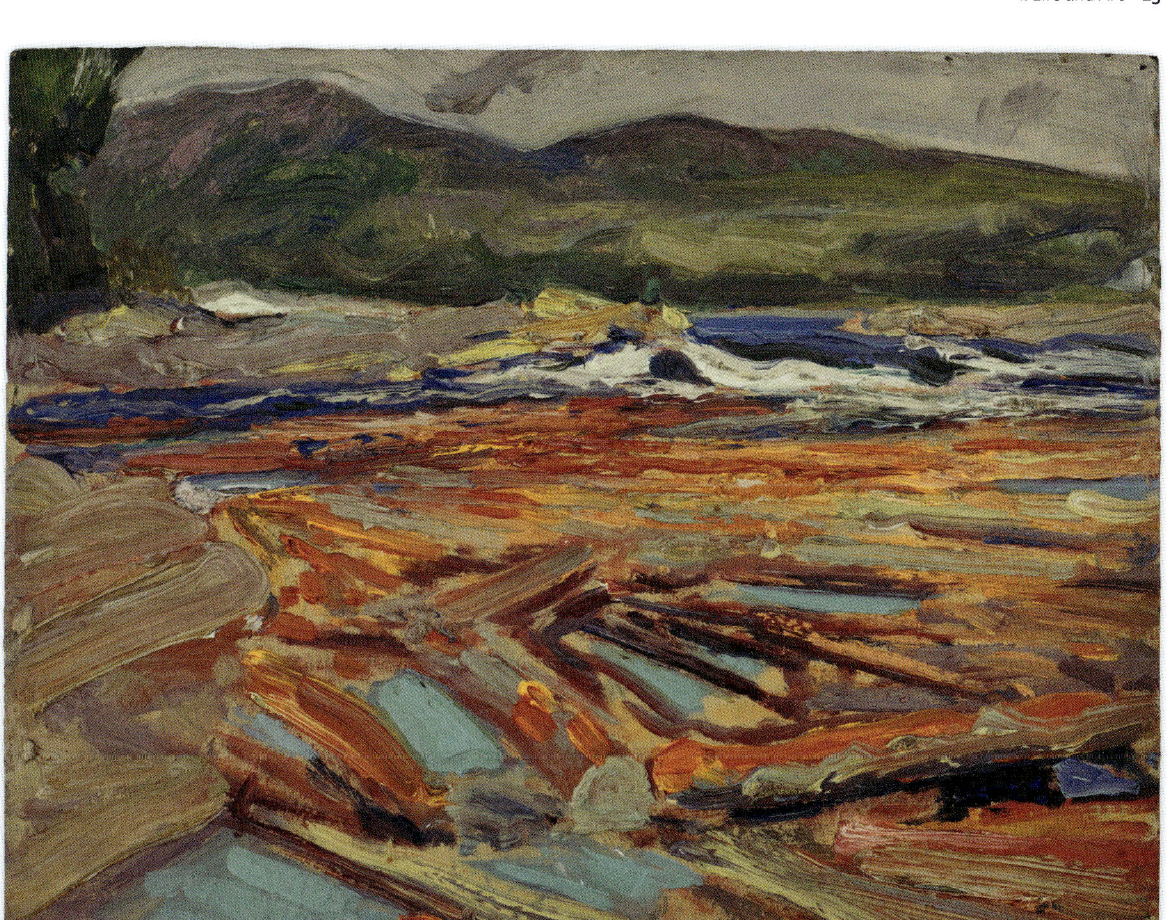

Fig. 1.4: *Logs on the Gatineau River*, 1914, 20.3 × 25.4 cm, oil on paperboard, McMichael Canadian Art Collection, 1981.85.5. Photo: McMichael.

In March 1914, soon after they became neighbours in the Studio Building, MacDonald and Beatty travelled to Algonquin Park for a winter sketching trip, where they met up with Jackson, who had arrived several weeks earlier. Later that year, MacDonald made a sketching trip to Western Quebec, in the Gatineau region, with Harris.[39] *Logs on the Gatineau River* (Fig. 1.4) was made during this trip.

MacDonald moved with his family from Toronto to Thornhill, Ontario, in 1913. They purchased a farmhouse at 121 Centre Street about a year later.[40] The Thornhill property, which they named "Four Elms," was the inspiration for numerous sketches and paintings. *The Tangled Garden* (Fig. 1.5), one of MacDonald's best-known paintings, is based on sketches made in his Thornhill garden during the late summer of 1915. This includes two sketches of the full composition as well as a study of a sunflower, *Sunflower Study, Tangled Garden Sketch*, that may represent the original idea for the painting.[41] *The Tangled Garden* was first shown at the 1916 OSA exhibition, along with four other paintings, including *The Elements* (Fig. 1.6), another key work of this period.[42] While the composition for *The Elements* was inspired primarily by sketches made during his 1915 visit to the MacCallum cottage,

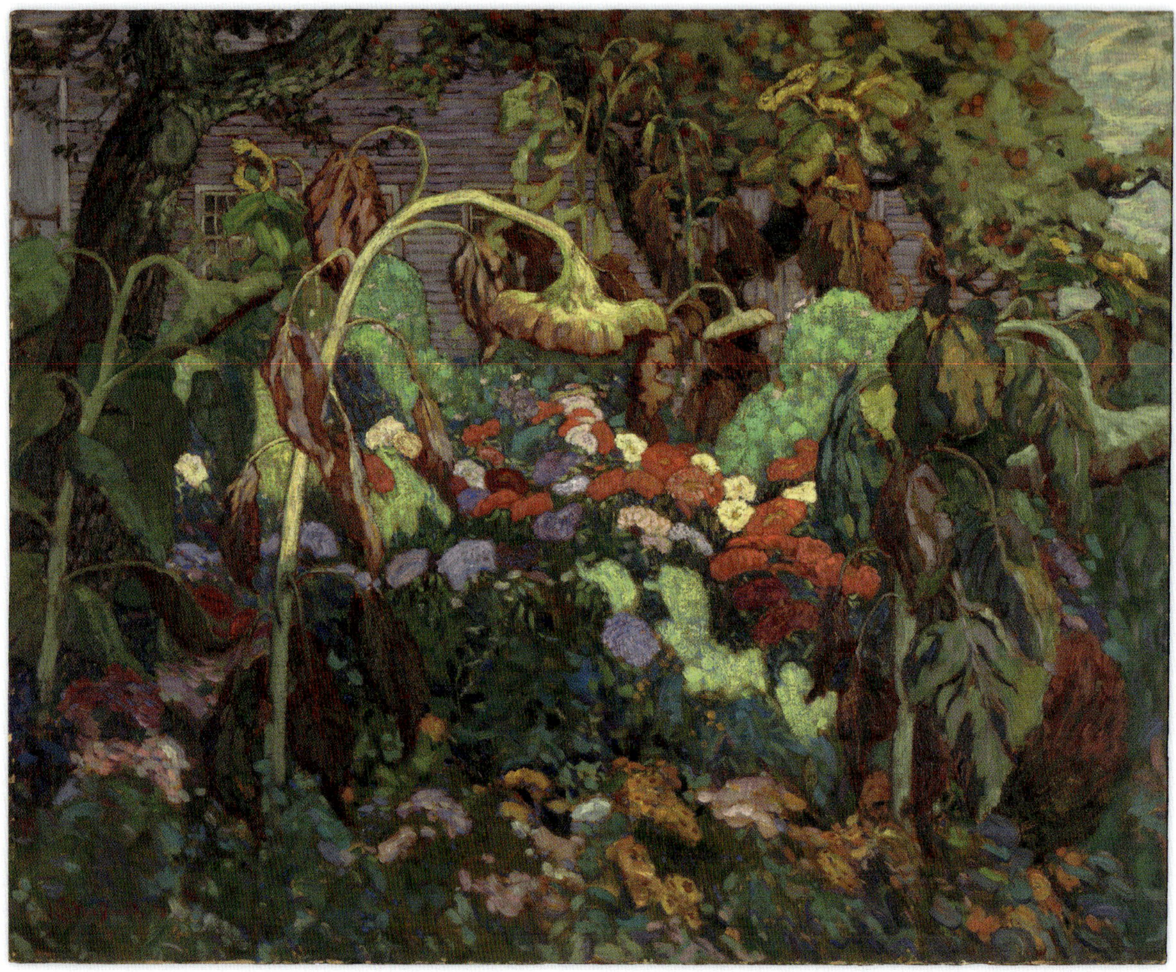

Fig. 1.5: *The Tangled Garden*, 1916, 121.4 × 152.4 cm, oil on beaverboard, National Gallery of Canada, Ottawa. Photo: NGC.

the sky is based on *Storm Clouds*, an earlier sketch painted in the Laurentians.[43] The fact that MacDonald used multiple oil sketches as inspiration for *The Elements*, as well as for some of his other large-scale paintings, is a notable aspect of his working process.

Although they are now highly regarded for their innovations in the use of colour and composition, *The Tangled Garden* and *The Elements* were harshly criticized by reviewers when they were first exhibited. The work of some of the painters who espoused a new kind of Canadian art had been criticized before,[44] but the response to the 1916 OSA exhibit was especially unkind and singled out MacDonald's paintings specifically.

In one of the most cutting reviews of the exhibition, the critic Hector Charlesworth stated that "the chief offender seems to be J.E.H. MacDonald, who certainly does throw his paint pots in the face of the public."[45] Charlesworth went on to say that *The Elements* might just as well have been titled "Hungarian Goulash," while another critic described *The Tangled Garden* as "a huge tomato salad." A few days later, the artist Carl Ahrens said that MacDonald and his fellow painters in the

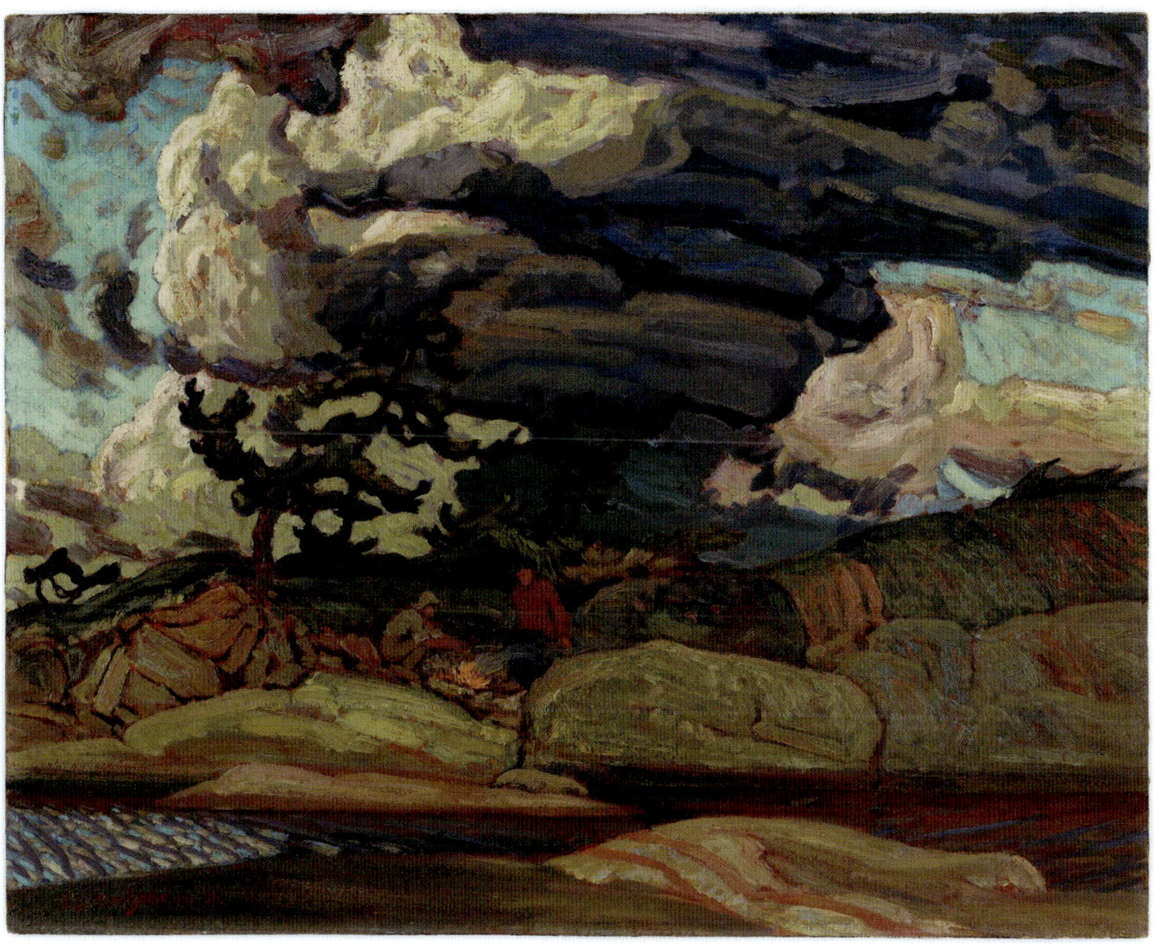

Fig. 1.6: *The Elements*, 1916, 71.1 × 91.8 cm, oil on wood-pulp board, Art Gallery of Ontario. Photo: © AGO.

exhibition would "gain a much higher standing before men if they gave their now mis-spent efforts to the destruction of the Hun."[46] As Charles C. Hill pointed out in the exhibition text for *Pictures That Can Be Heard: J.E.H. MacDonald's "The Tangled Garden,"* MacDonald was affected by these reviews because not only did the critics fail to appreciate or understand his work, but they also implicitly questioned his and his colleagues' patriotism during a time of war.[47]

As described more fully in the next chapter, MacDonald painted *The Tangled Garden*, as well as some other works from the 1915 to 1918 period, on beaverboard – a type of wallboard produced for the building trade – rather than on a traditional canvas support. MacDonald appears to have begun using beaverboard in 1915, the same year that he started work on a series of decorative murals painted on this type of panel. Dr. MacCallum commissioned these murals on beaverboard for the living room of his Georgian Bay cottage at Go Home Bay.[48] The commission would have provided a helpful source of income; as an artist and freelance commercial designer, MacDonald often had financial difficulties, and these difficulties were exacerbated during the war years.[49]

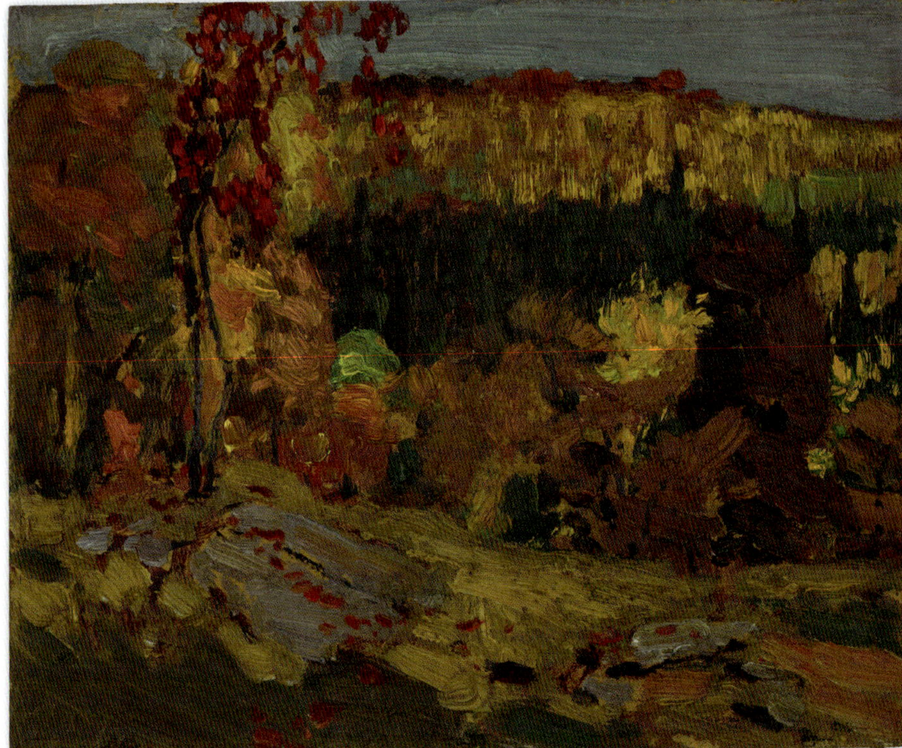

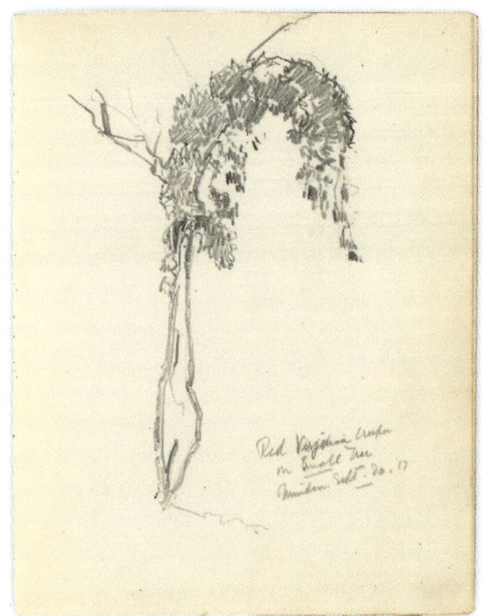

(top to bottom)
Fig. 1.7: *Near Minden*, 1916 or 1917, 20.3 × 25.4 cm, oil on paperboard, McMichael Canadian Art Collection, 1966.15.12. Photo: McMichael.

Fig. 1.8: *Red Virginia Creeper, Minden*, 30 September 1917, graphite on wove paper, 23.5 × 18.8 cm, National Gallery of Canada, Ottawa. Photo: NGC.

MacDonald made a trip to the Go Home Bay cottage in the autumn of 1915 to take measurements for the murals. The panels were then prepared and painted by MacDonald, Lismer, and Thomson in their Toronto studios during the winter of 1915–1916. MacDonald returned to the cottage in the spring to install the murals.[50] He made several sketches during his 1915 and 1916 trips to the McCallum cottage, including one of the preparatory sketches for his 1917 painting *Wild Ducks*.[51]

As well as his visits to Georgian Bay for the mural project, MacDonald took part in several other sketching expeditions during this period, including a September 1915 trip with Harris to Western Quebec and to Minden, Ontario. The two friends returned to Minden in the autumn of both 1916 and 1917. After travelling to Minden in 1917, they extended their trip to the Laurentians, sketching around Saint-Jovite, Quebec.[52] During the 1916 to 1917 period, MacDonald also visited Coboconk, in the Kawartha Lakes region of Ontario, staying at the cottage of a former co-worker at Grip and sketching in the countryside nearby.[53]

The oil sketch entitled *Near Minden* (Fig. 1.7) is thought to be from MacDonald's 1916 trip to the area, based on an inscription on the back of the painting.[54] However, the strong similarity of the small tree in the foreground of the sketch to a dated pencil drawing in one of MacDonald's sketchbooks[55] inscribed "Red Virginia creeper in small tree, Minden, Sept. 30, 1917" (Fig. 1.8) suggests to us that the oil sketch may, in fact, date from the following year's trip.

The drowning death of his close colleague Tom Thomson in Algonquin Park in July 1917 was a heavy blow to MacDonald. It added to the emotional burden that he already felt due to the war and his financial worries. Jackson wrote to MacDonald that August: "I know how keenly you will feel his loss. You had very much in common. Tom, I know though he was a man of very few words, often expressed to me his confidence in you and in the future of your work, and without you he never would have associated himself with our little school."[56]

In October of 1917, MacDonald accompanied Beatty to Canoe Lake in Algonquin Park to erect a memorial cairn for Thomson, which included a plaque of MacDonald's design. An oil sketch of Canoe Lake, which MacDonald likely painted during this trip, is shown in Fig. 1.9. MacDonald's 1917 sketches from Algonquin Park would have been among the last works that he painted before suffering a serious physical collapse, believed to be a stroke, in November of that year. This event took place the day after a move from Thornhill to York Mills, and it is thought to have been caused, at least in part, by a combination of the stress of the move with all the other difficulties of the preceding few years.[57]

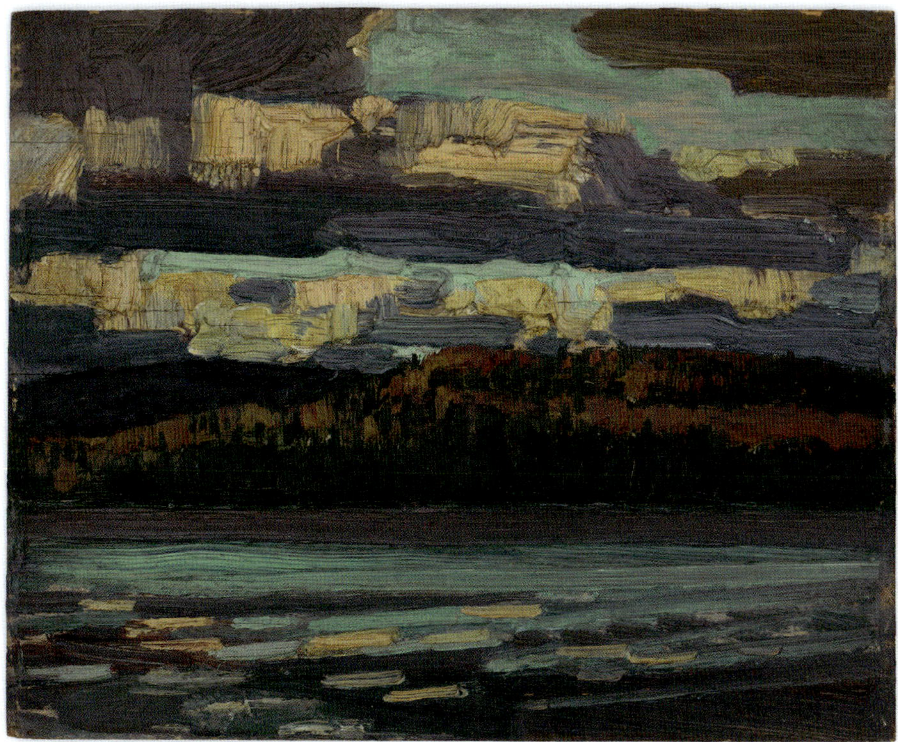

Fig. 1.9: *Canoe Lake*, circa 1917, 20.2 × 25.3 cm, oil on plywood, McMichael Canadian Art Collection, 1978.34.1. Photo: McMichael.

Algoma: 1918–1923

The day before his November 1917 collapse, MacDonald had moved his family from Thornhill to a house next to Ussher Farm in York Mills. The move was made, in part, for financial reasons, but also because his wife felt isolated in Thornhill.[58] The MacDonalds lived in the York Mills house, which belonged to Mrs. Lucille Taylor, a friend of Joan MacDonald's, for about 18 months.[59] The farm adjacent to their York Mills rental house was used by the Arts & Letters Club for wartime gardening during the growing seasons of 1917 and 1918.[60]

Over the winter of 1918, MacDonald slowly recovered his strength and, while unable to paint, spent time writing poetry and essays. Barker Fairley, a scholar and a strong supporter of the Group of Seven who spent time with MacDonald during this period, wrote about it evocatively: "I remember him best as he sat up in bed day after day during a long winter's illness ... writing verses about maple bloom and moonlight and March wind and an old horse and a grist mill and suchlike, all in an easy natural way as if this were only what a man would do who was temporarily prevented from painting."[61]

MacDonald was well enough to begin painting again during the spring and summer of 1918. During this period, he produced some sketches, for example *Arts and Letters Club Farm, York Mills*, along with a few larger paintings.[62] He also taught that summer, replacing J.W. Beatty as an instructor at the Ontario College of Art (OCA) summer school in York Mills.[63] During MacDonald's convalescence, his son, Thoreau, who had just turned 17, took on an important role in assisting his father, particularly with his commercial design work.[64] Thoreau continued to work alongside his father until MacDonald's death in 1932: as well as design work, Thoreau helped with the preparation of sketching supports, with the building of wooden frames for some of MacDonald's larger paintings, and with architectural commissions.[65] As a counterpoint to other accounts that focus on MacDonald's sometime physical frailty, Thoreau's notes and recollections emphasize that his father was quite capable in practical work. He remembers how MacDonald felled trees on the property surrounding their first home, did carpentry around the house, and was a skilled woodworker.[66]

In September 1918, MacDonald made the first of three important sketching trips to the Algoma District of northeastern Ontario, north of Sault Ste. Marie. This was a prolific and important period in his career, and his Algoma works are among his most highly regarded. In a tribute to MacDonald shortly after his death, A.Y. Jackson wrote that "what Thomson was to the Algonquin country, MacDonald is to Algoma" and that his depictions of Algoma "take a permanent place in the history of Canadian art."[67] MacDonald's trips to this region, one each year from 1918 to 1920, were in September to October, and the paintings are filled with autumn colour, or as MacDonald described it, "the great farewell decoration of the woods."[68]

For the 1918 Algoma trip, the group, which included MacDonald, Lawren Harris, Frank Johnston and Dr. MacCallum, used an Algoma Central Railway boxcar as their home base. It was Harris who organized the trip and invited MacDonald to join. In a letter to MacDonald prior to their departure, he wrote: "Your only real essentials, as I see it now, are blankets (lots of them), warm clothes and sketching outfit.... We leave Toronto the evening of Tues. the 10th or Wed. the 11th of Sept., arrive Soo next day – board our car and stay therein and thereout for three weeks or so, having supplies, mail, etc. left us by passing trains every second day or so."[69] Although the artists would have brought most of their required painting materials with them, this letter shows that they could also have had supplies delivered during the trip.

The artists departed Toronto by train and arranged for the boxcar to be left at Agawa Canyon station. After about a week, it was moved to Hubert, and finally, for the third week, to Batchewana.[70] MacDonald was immediately struck by the Algoma landscape. A panoramic view of Lake Superior visible from the train inspired him to write that he had "never seen anything so impressive as the half-revealed extensiveness of the lake. There was a sharpness in the air which merged the horizon with the sky and that smooth shimmering infinity of waters was like a glimpse of God himself."[71] Upon his return from Algoma, MacDonald displayed 36 sketches from the trip, about a dozen from each of the three locations, in an exhibition with Harris and Johnston at the Art Gallery of Toronto (now the AGO).[72]

In September 1919, MacDonald joined Harris, Jackson, and Johnston on a second boxcar trip, which included the same three stops as the previous year.[73] In a lively account of the 1919 expedition, MacDonald described searching out sketching locations on foot, by handcar, or by canoe; the challenges of the weather ("The weather took an adverse critical view of Canadian art in Arcadia."); and humorous anecdotes about their daily life. He also described how, after a day of sketching, the painters would critique each other's works in the evening.[74] MacDonald returned with the same group for his third, and final, visit to Algoma in the autumn of 1920. For this third trip, rather than saying in a boxcar, they rented lodgings near Mongoose Lake.[75]

MacDonald's time in Algoma was very productive: based on the number of sketches he exhibited from the 1918 trip, his total output for the three expeditions would have been a hundred or more. Many of MacDonald's Algoma sketches are not signed or dated on the front. And while there are numerous sketches with inscriptions on the back, the date is not always included. For works without a date on the front or back, the painting year can sometimes be estimated based on factors such as the style, the location depicted, the exhibition and provenance history, or the date of an associated studio work. In other cases, dating a sketch to a specific Algoma trip may not be possible. Figures 1.10 to 1.12 illustrate three of MacDonald's Algoma sketches: *Autumn Leaves, Batchewana, Algoma*, painted during one of the boxcar expeditions, along with *Algoma Hills* and *Moose Lake, Algoma* from his 1920 trip to the Mongoose Lake area.

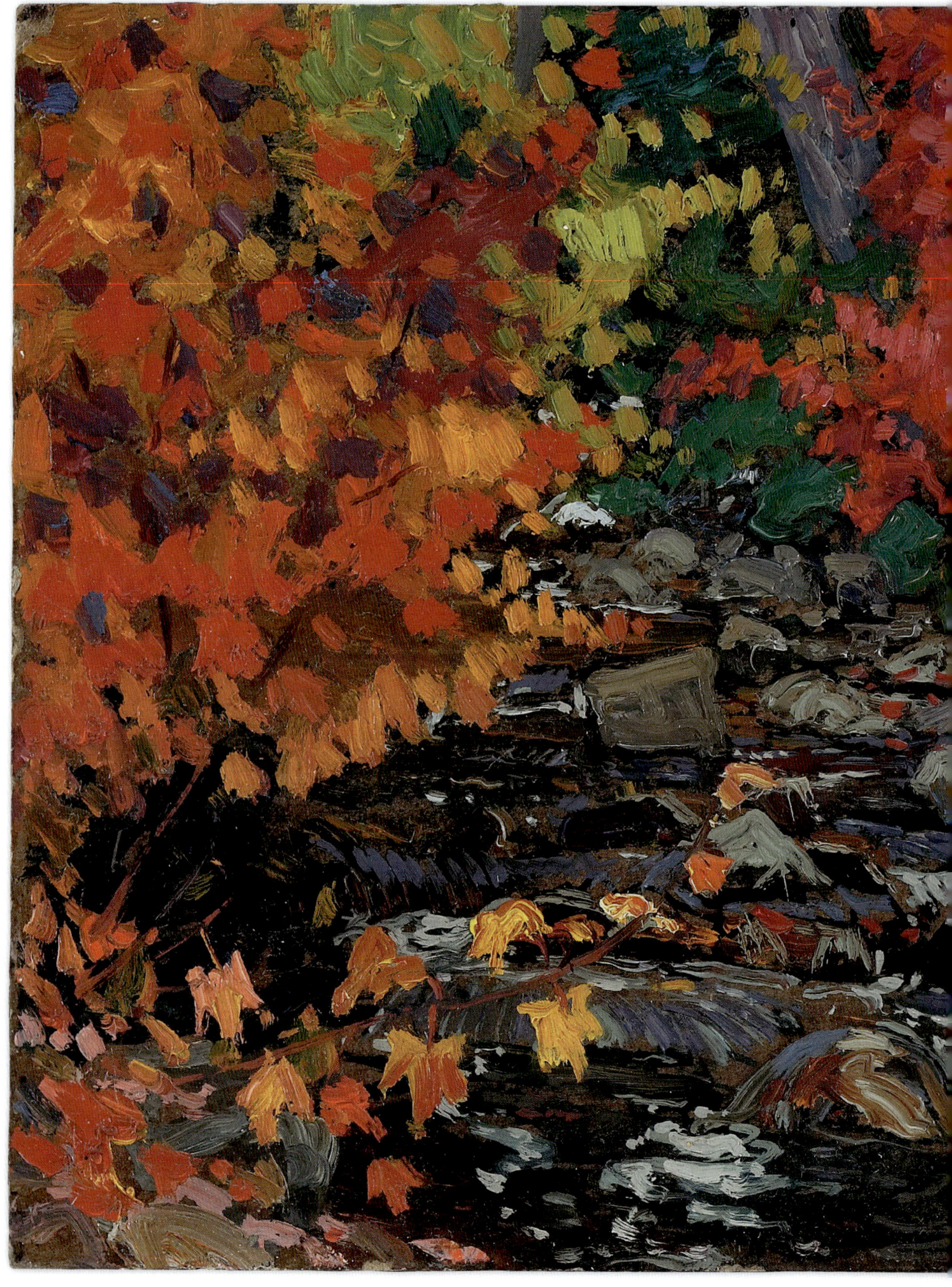

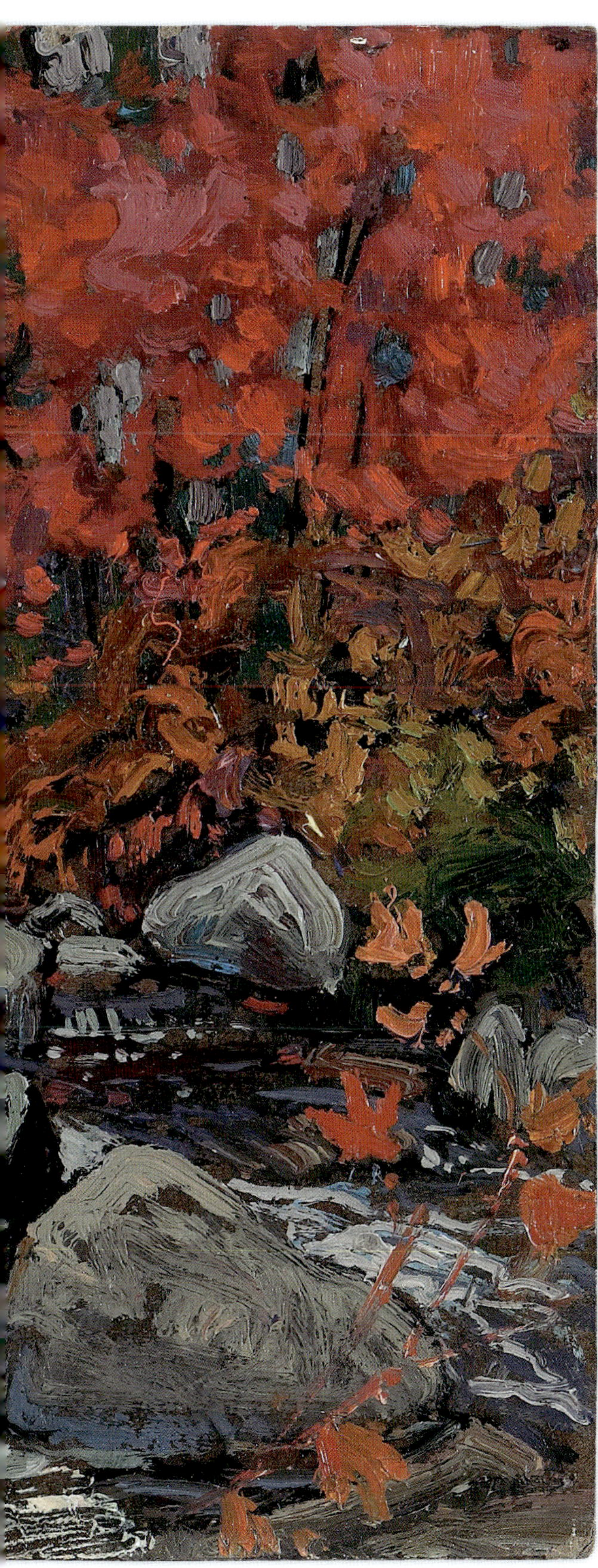

Fig. 1.10: *Autumn Leaves, Batchewana, Algoma*, circa 1919, 21.6 × 26.7 cm, oil on paperboard, Art Gallery of Ontario. Photo: © AGO.

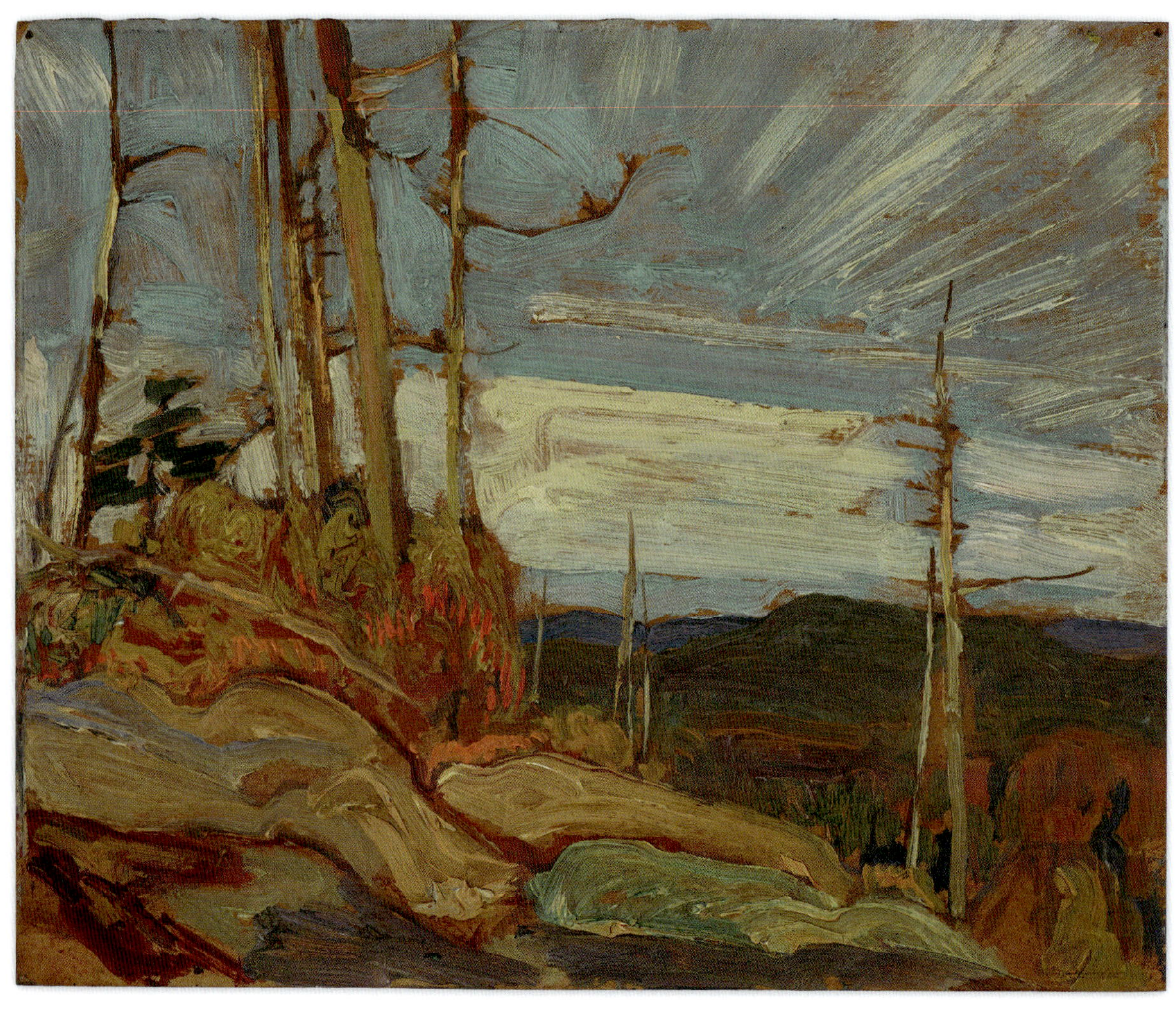

Fig. 1.11: *Algoma Hills*, 1920, 21.4 × 26.4 cm, oil on paperboard, McMichael Canadian Art Collection, 1966.15.6. Photo: McMichael.

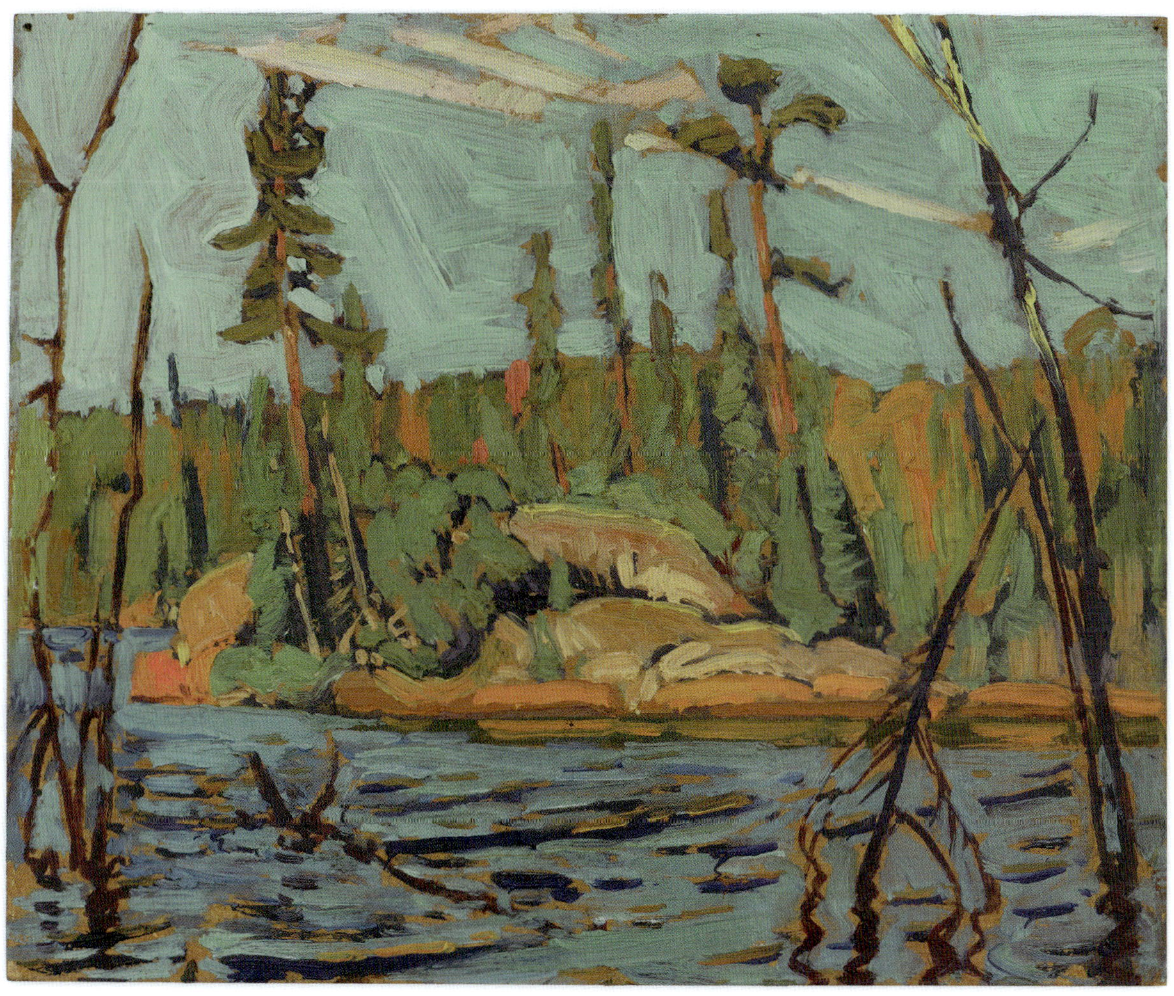

Fig. 1.12: *Moose Lake, Algoma*, 1920, 21.5 × 26.6 cm, oil on paperboard, McMichael Canadian Art Collection, 1966.15.4. Photo: McMichael.

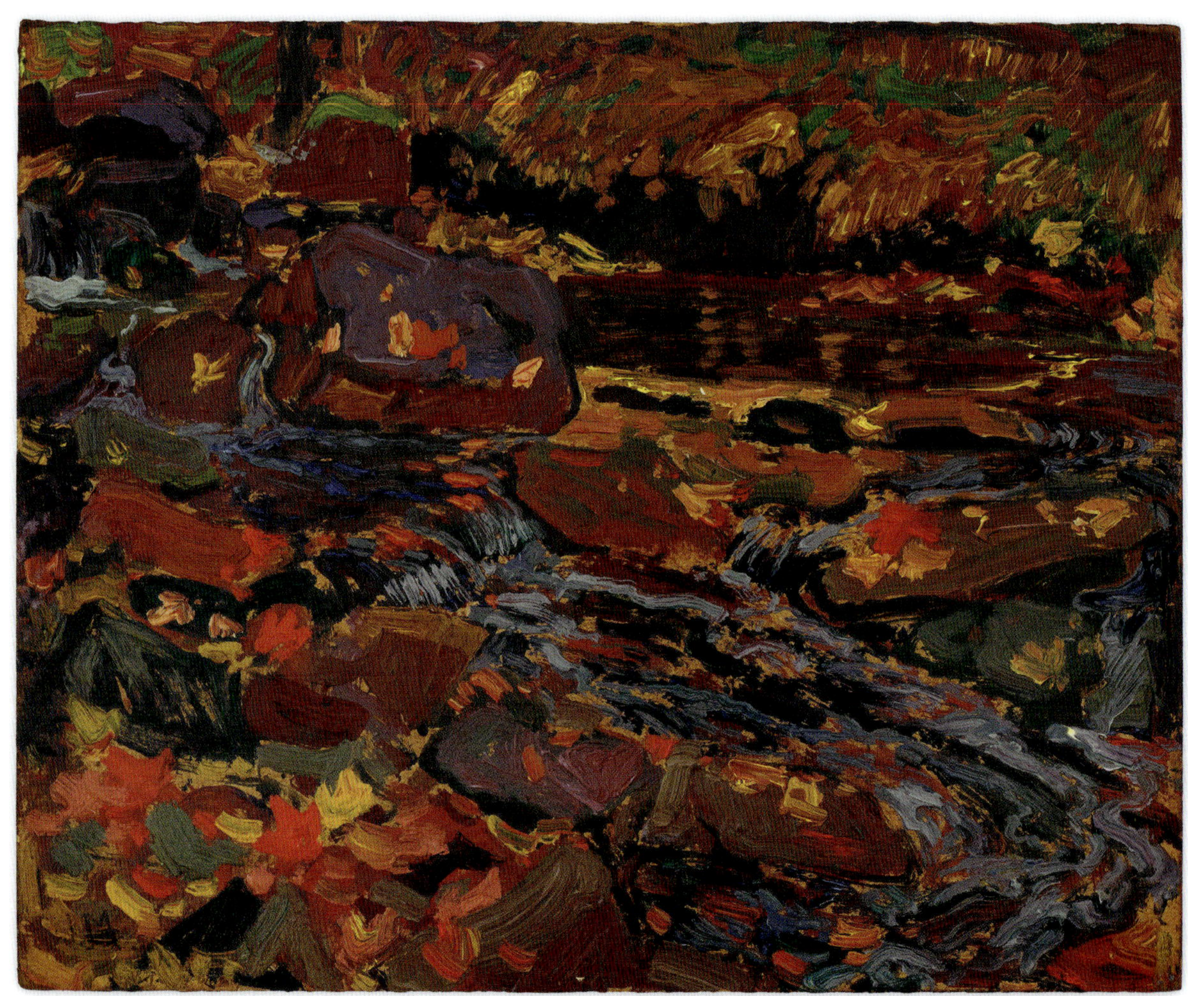

Fig. 1.13: *Leaves in the Brook* (sketch), circa 1918, 21.3 × 26.6, oil on paperboard, McMichael Canadian Art Collection, 1966.16.35. Photo: McMichael.

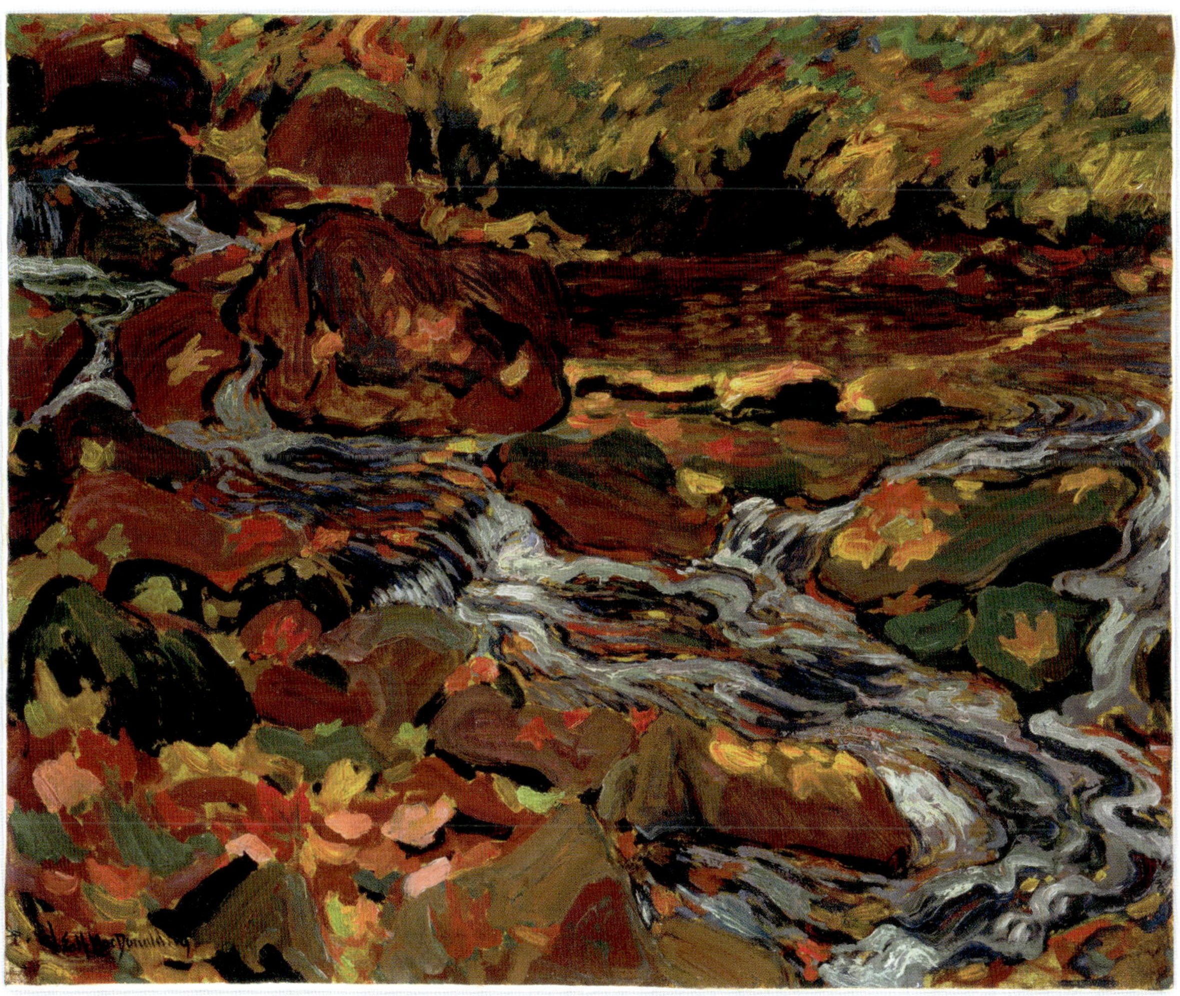

Fig. 1.14: *Leaves in the Brook*, 1919, 52.7 × 65.0 cm, oil on canvas, McMichael Canadian Art Collection, 1966.16.32. Photo: McMichael.

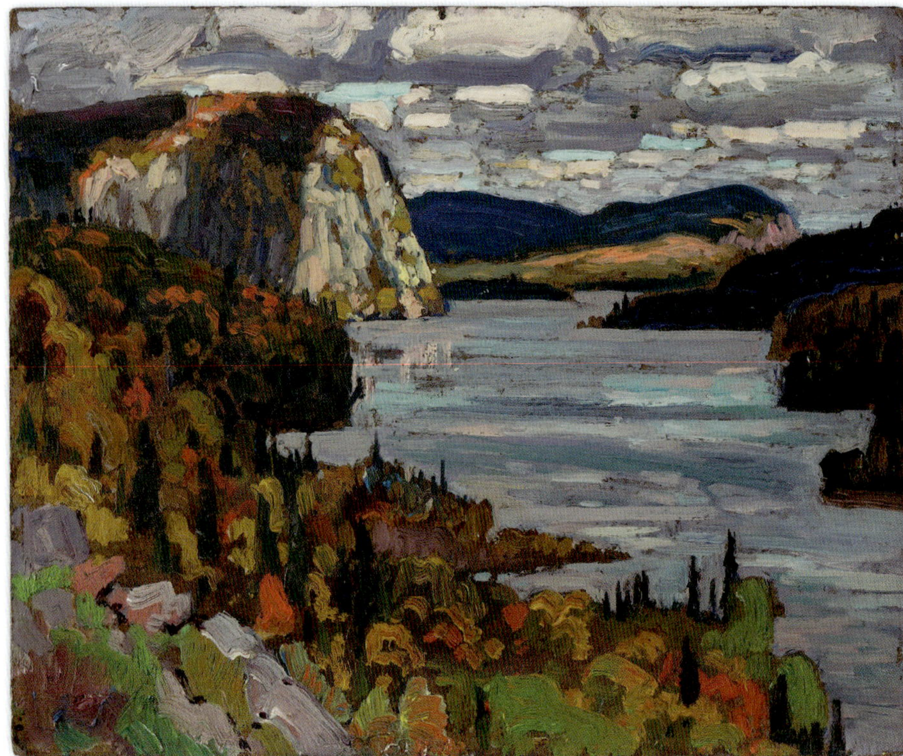

Fig. 1.15: *Solemn Land, Algoma* (sketch), circa 1919, 21.6 × 26.7 cm, oil on paperboard, Art Gallery of Ontario. Photo: © AGO.

Between 1919 and 1922, MacDonald produced a number of larger oil paintings on canvas that were based on certain of his Algoma sketches. He worked on these paintings in the Studio Building in Toronto, where he continued to rent space. For two of MacDonald's Algoma compositions, *Leaves in the Brook* (Figs. 1.13 and 1.14) and *The Solemn Land* (Figs. 1.15 and 1.16), both the plein-air sketch and the resulting studio painting were included in our research. The sketch for *The Solemn Land* shown in Fig. 1.15 is one of three known preparatory works by MacDonald of this composition, which depicts a panoramic view of the Montreal River Valley.[76] The resulting large-scale canvas painting is considered one of his greatest achievements. The NGC purchased this painting after the spring 1921 OSA exhibit where it was first shown.[77]

Another well-known Algoma painting on canvas included in the study is *Forest Wilderness* (Fig. 1.17) from 1921. Measuring 1.2 × 1.5 m, this painting shares the same ambitious scale as *The Solemn Land*. These paintings, as well as some other of MacDonald's Algoma studio works, are painted on coarse jute canvas. As described later in chapter 5, MacDonald's use of jute has caused deterioration in some of his paintings.

In March 1920, several months after MacDonald's final trip to Algoma and during planning for a spring exhibition, the Group of Seven painters was officially formed. MacDonald and Harris are often described as the main motivators for the creation of the Group. Along with them, the original members included A.Y. Jackson, Frank

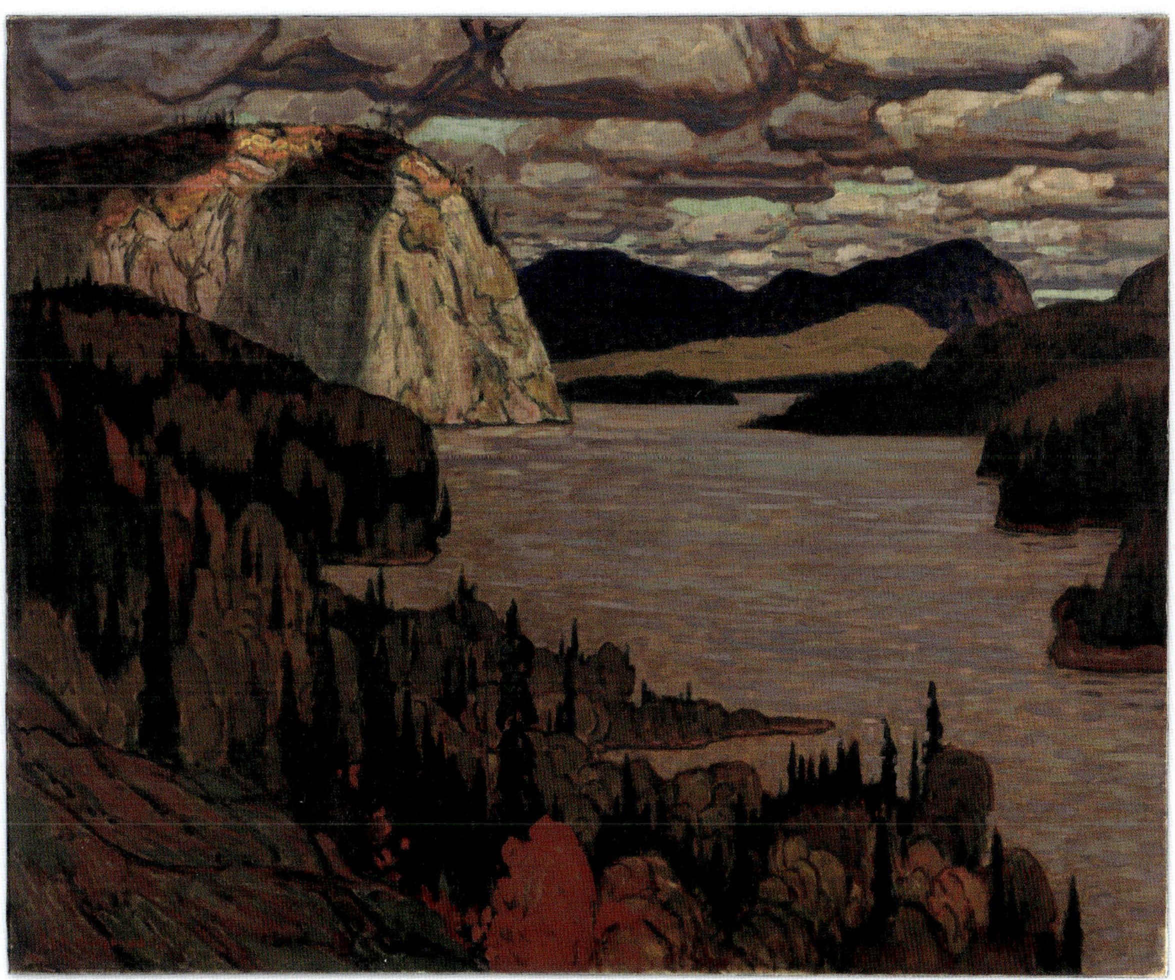

Fig. 1.16: *The Solemn Land*, 1921, 122.5 × 153.5 cm, oil on canvas, National Gallery of Canada, Ottawa. Photo: NGC.

Fig. 1.17: *Forest Wilderness*, 1921, 122.0 × 152.0 cm, oil on canvas, McMichael Canadian Art Collection, 1968.7.1. Photo: McMichael.

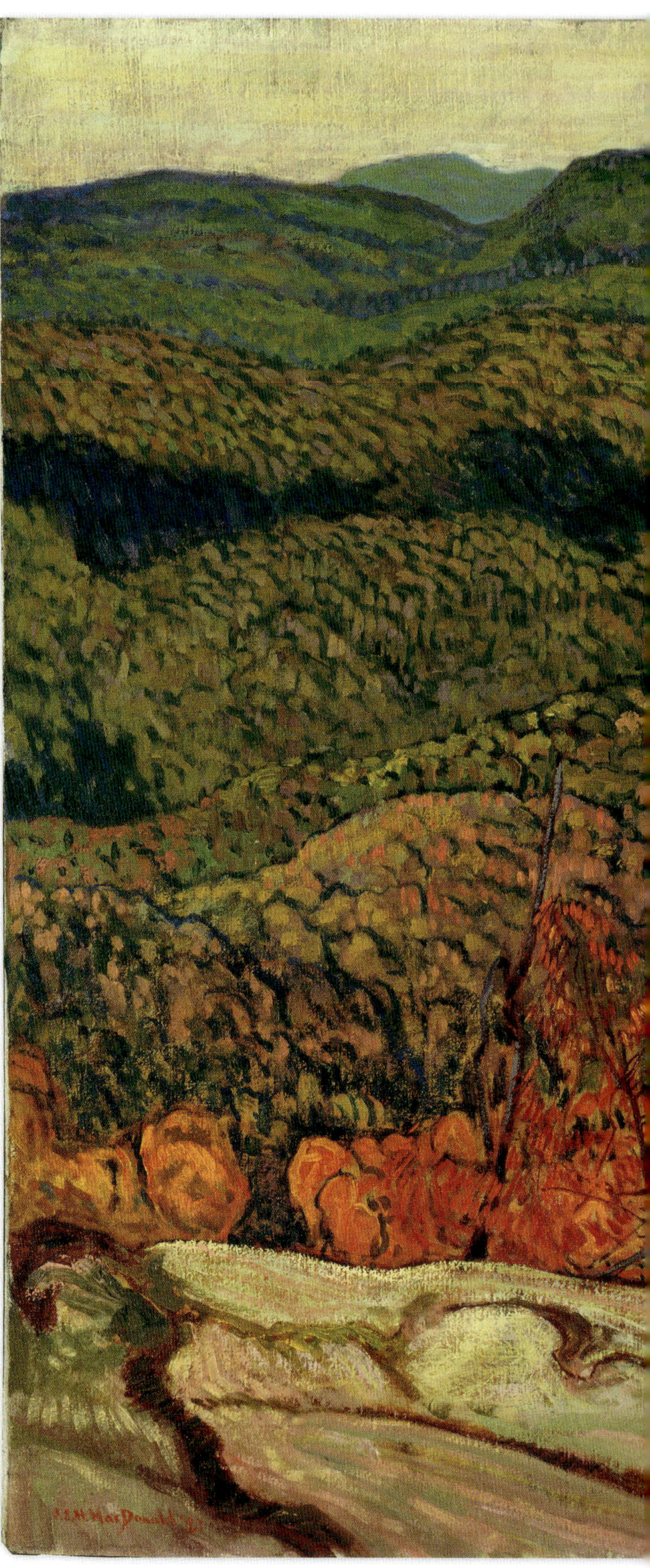

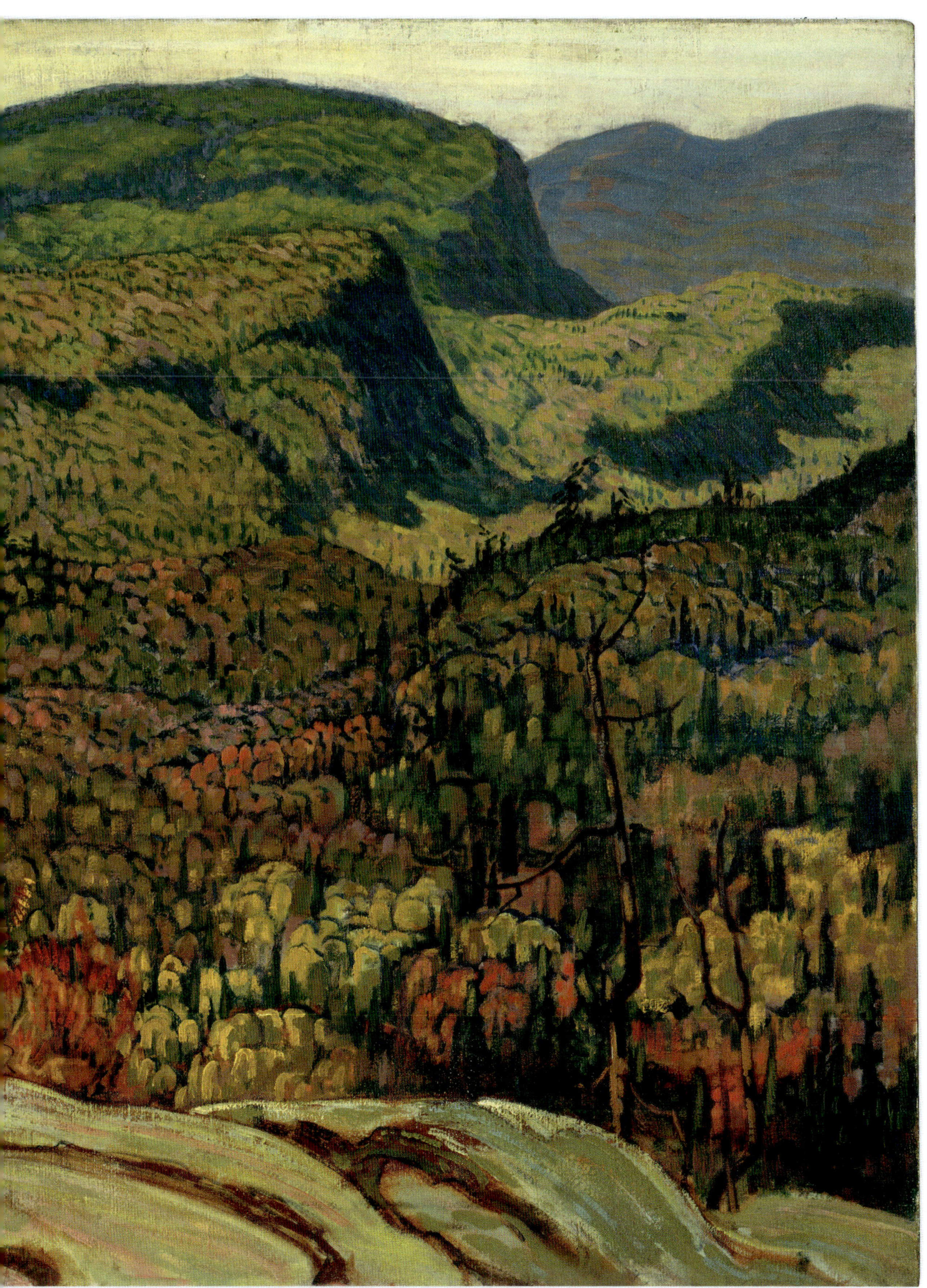

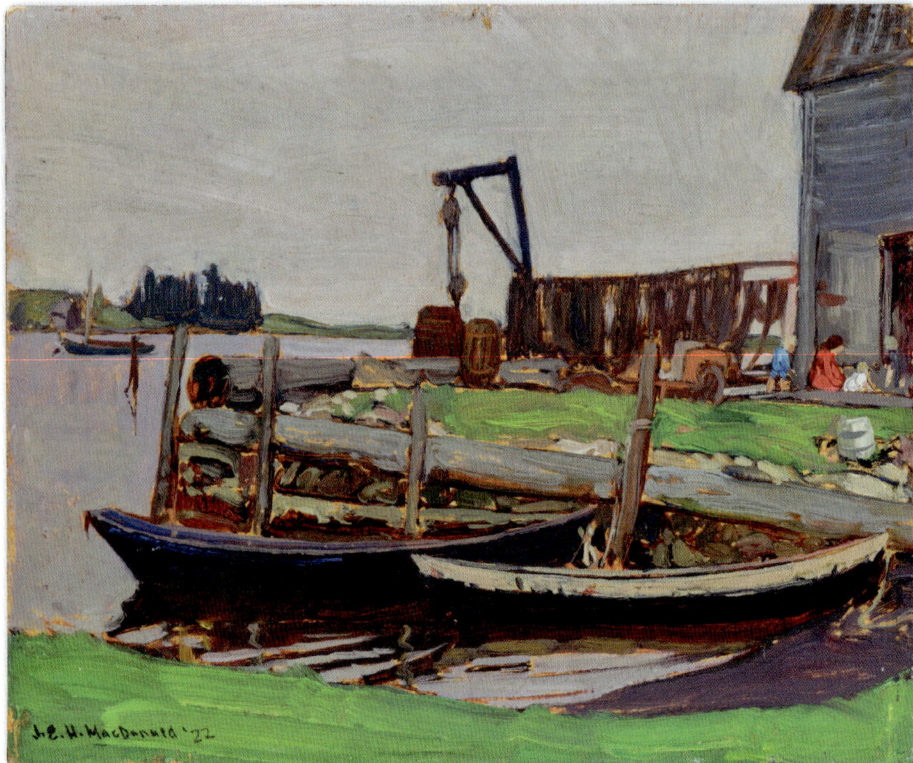

Fig. 1.18: *Old Dock, Petite Rivière, Nova Scotia*, 1922, 21.4 × 26.4 cm, oil on paperboard, National Gallery of Canada, Ottawa. Photo: NGC.

Johnston, Franklin Carmichael, Arthur Lismer, and Frederick Varley. While the Group of Seven was a loose alliance, and not meant to replace any of the existing artists' societies, its establishment did formalize the shared interests and philosophies of its member painters. The Group exhibited for the first time in May 1920 and continued to organize shows together, although with some changes in membership, throughout the 1920s.[78]

Beginning in 1921, the need for a stable source of income compelled MacDonald to take on a permanent teaching position at the OCA,[79] and consequently, he had less time to devote to painting. Although he never returned to Algoma, MacDonald did make shorter sketching trips in the early 1920s, including to Lake Simcoe, and in 1922, a summer visit to the home of Lewis Smith in Nova Scotia. Figure 1.18 shows one of his Nova Scotia sketches, painted at Petite Rivière. As he had done in previous years, MacDonald also travelled to Coboconk, Ontario, several times during the early 1920s, staying at a friend's cottage and producing sketches at nearby Gull River and Little Turtle Lake.[80]

In addition to painting, teaching, and freelance graphic design work, MacDonald undertook several architectural commissions during the 1920s. The most important of these was the decoration of St. Anne's Church in 1923. Although MacDonald rarely wrote about his painting technique, his description of the St. Anne's church commission, published in the *Royal Architectural Institute of Canada Journal*, provides insight into some of his ideas about design, as well as colour choice and mixing.[81]

The Rockies: 1924–1932

During the last decade of his life, much of MacDonald's time and energy was taken up by his work at the OCA. After assuming the role of full-time instructor in 1921, he later became the head of the department of graphic and commercial art, and finally, from 1929 until his death in 1932, the principal of the college. While he sometimes begrudged the time that his work at the OCA took away from his painting, MacDonald was known as a thoughtful instructor and mentor to younger artists.[82] The painter Carl Schaefer, who was one of MacDonald's early students and later his assistant, wrote admiringly about his wide-ranging lectures, calling him an "inspired teacher."[83]

Despite his academic responsibilities, MacDonald continued to create art. Although he had little occasion to paint during the school year, between 1924 and 1930, he was able to make seven annual sketching trips to Yoho National Park in the Rocky Mountains in British Columbia.[84] His diaries from these trips are an important record of his travels, as is the article "A Glimpse of the West" that he published in the *Canadian Bookman* soon after returning from his first expedition in 1924.[85]

Each of MacDonald's sketching trips to the Rockies took place in August and September and lasted about three weeks. These trips were a highlight of the latter part of his painting career. Even the travel itself was an adventure: the 3000 km train trip from Toronto through Ontario and the Prairies took several days, and after reaching the Wapta Lake railway station, MacDonald would then embark on a 14 km horseback ride to arrive at Lake O'Hara.[86]

According to his son, MacDonald's "enthusiasm for the mountains was unlimited and for weeks after each trip he spoke of little else."[87] His diaries show that he was interested in everything; he recorded engaging descriptions of the animals, the plants and trees, and even anecdotes about other visitors. But what attracted him the most, and had the most impact on his art, were the colours and the quality of the light, which were so different from anything he had seen before. Describing his first view of a mountain lake, MacDonald wrote, "Here was blue Wapta Lake, or is it malachite or emerald, or rainbow-green? These are the terms people use. Let any one of them conjure up the finest color your mental eye can picture, you cannot overdo it. Rainbow-green seems to me the best. It has a soft quality of light and change and variation of intensity which come the nearest to the feeling of the mountain lake color."[88]

The geological structures and patterns of the mountains, or "mountain architecture" as he called it, also made a strong impression; several diary entries describe his thoughts about trying to capture their essence. For example, in September 1930, he wrote, "After lunch took on another trouble, rock pattern, ridges and fissures, small shrubbery, etc. Meant to express 'mountain architecture' but failed in the solidity that had attracted me."[89]

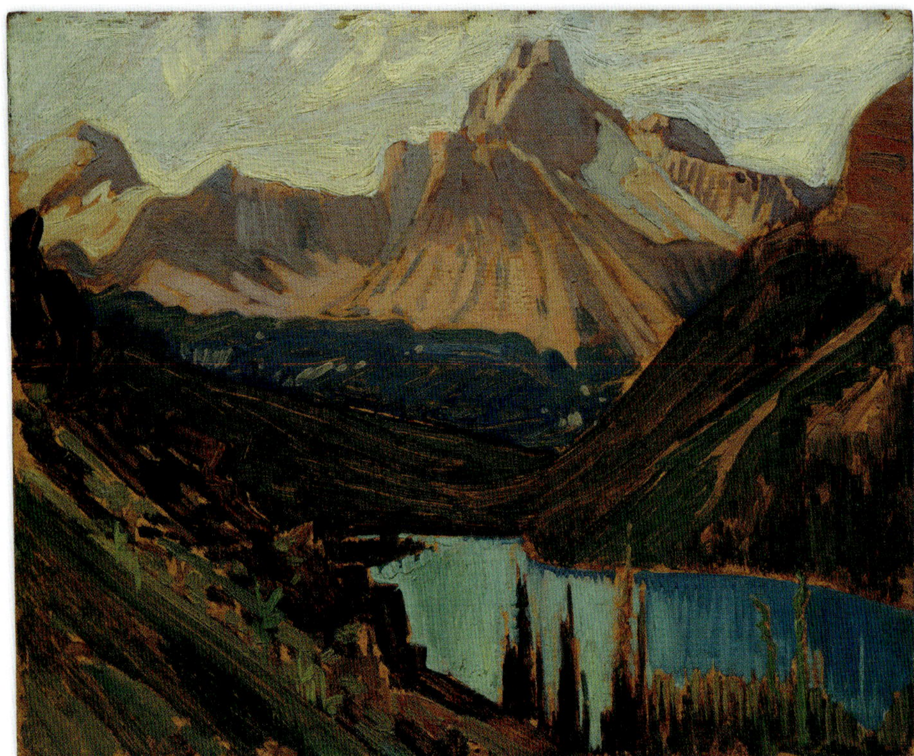

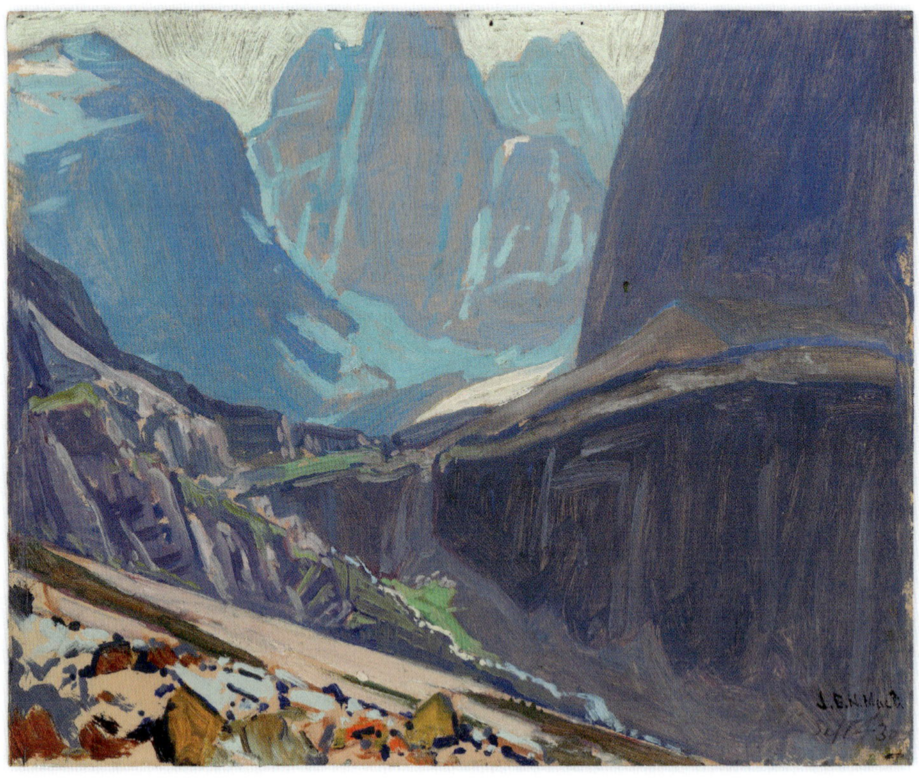

(top to bottom)
Fig. 1.19: *Cathedral Peak and Lake O'Hara*, 1927, 21.4 × 26.6 cm, oil on paperboard, McMichael Canadian Art Collection, 1966.15.9. Photo: McMichael.

Fig. 1.20: *Near Lake Oesa, Abbot's Pass*, 1930, 21.5 × 26.6 cm, oil on paperboard, National Gallery of Canada, Ottawa. Photo: NGC.

MacDonald discovered his mountain subjects during day hikes, sometimes alone, other times with guides, fellow hikers, or sketching enthusiasts. He is known to have sketched with Aldro Hibbard, a well-known plein-air painter from Massachusetts, as well as with Peter Whyte, a younger, aspiring artist from Banff. In a letter from 1928, Whyte wrote, "There is an artist here from Toronto, Mr. J.E.H. MacDonald, and we always seem to come here at the same time, about the second week of September. He is a lovable old Scotchman [sic] with red hair, a remarkably fine painter. We get along fine together and tramp and paint together all day."[90] In 1930, Whyte and MacDonald were joined on their sketching excursions by Whyte's wife, Catherine, also a painter, and by Tommy and Adeline Link, mountain enthusiasts and dedicated trail builders at Lake O'Hara. The group called themselves the "Opabin Shale-Splitters," and they spent many days together during MacDonald's final trip to the Rockies.[91]

MacDonald would have produced more than a hundred sketches from his seven trips to the Rockies. Two of these are illustrated in Figs. 1.19 and 1.20: *Cathedral Peak and Lake O'Hara* dated to 1927 by an inscription on the back, and *Near Lake Oesa, Abbot's Pass* from his final trip in 1930.

Some of MacDonald's mountain sketches are difficult to assign to a specific trip. As in the case of his Algoma sketches, when a date is not present on the work, the year can sometimes be estimated based on the painting style, an associated studio work, a diary entry, or research on exhibition history and provenance. The depicted view is also sometimes helpful; however, this is complicated by the fact that MacDonald often returned to favourite locations, discovering different vantage points and subjects each time. In his diaries, he mentions leaving supplies behind at comfortable and well-situated sketching spots for later use. For example, in a diary entry from 1930, he describes lighting a fire with wood he had left two years ago in the same spot while sketching Mount Lefroy.[92]

Even with the demands of his position at the OCA, MacDonald was able to develop some of his mountain sketches into larger paintings. He first exhibited several of these, including *Mount Goodsir, Yoho Park* (Fig. 1.21), at the January 1925 Group of Seven exhibition at the Art Gallery of Toronto. The stylized, decorative approach that MacDonald used in these studio paintings received mixed reviews when they were first exhibited.[93] The more natural effect in several of his late paintings, such as *Goat Range, Rocky Mountains* (Fig. 1.22) from 1932, suggests that, at the end of his life, MacDonald was moving towards a new way of expressing his vision of the mountains.[94]

In addition to his yearly expeditions to the Rockies, MacDonald managed a few shorter sketching trips during the latter part of the 1920s. Several dated sketches from Gull River and Little Turtle Lake indicate that he returned to the Coboconk area in 1926 and 1927.[95] He also revisited Georgian Bay late in his career. *Windy Sky near Pointe au Baril* (Fig. 1.23) dates from his 1931 sketching trip to this region. He

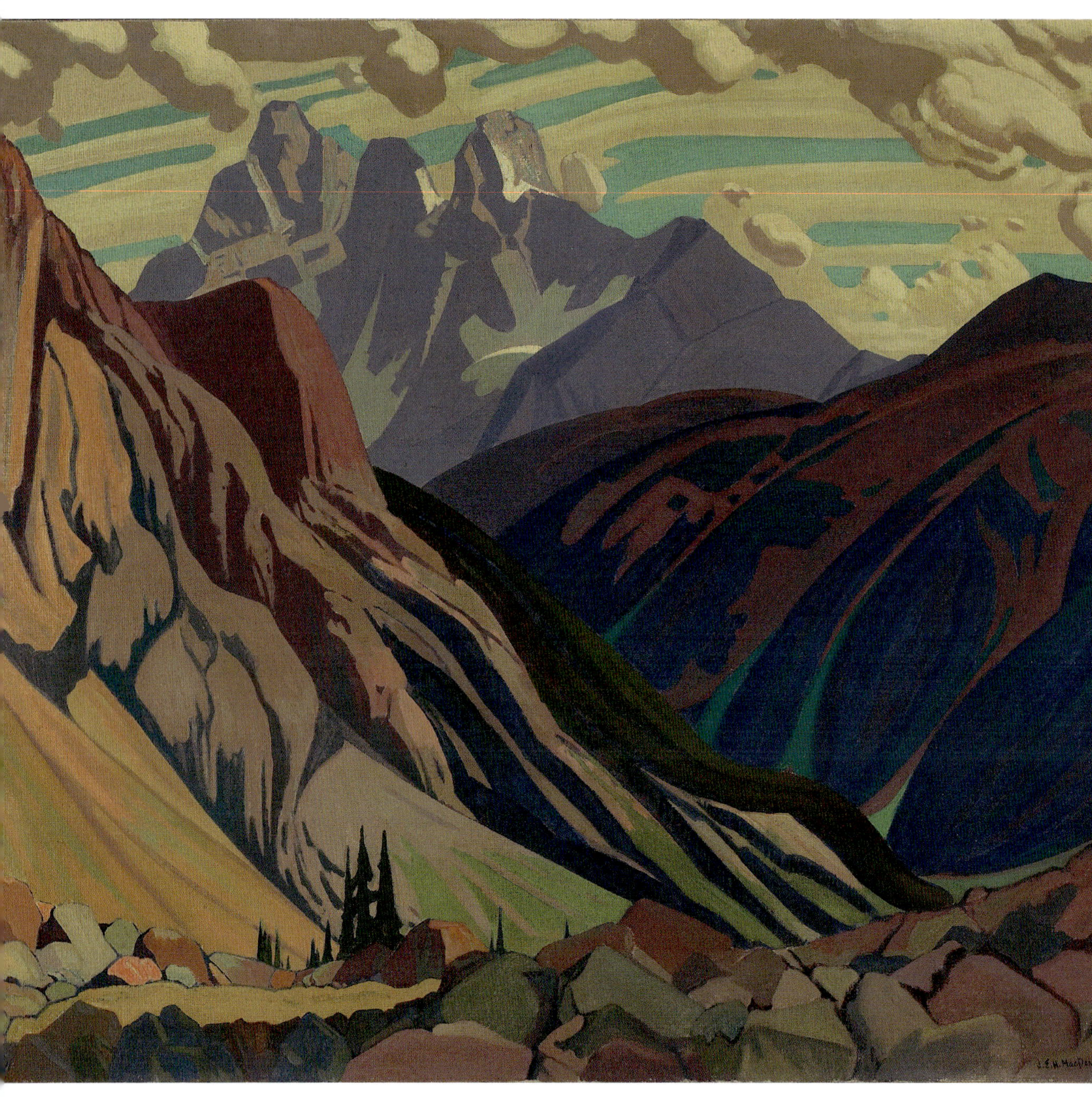

Fig. 1.21: *Mount Goodsir, Yoho Park*, 1925, 107.3 × 122.3 cm, oil on canvas, Art Gallery of Ontario. Photo: © AGO.

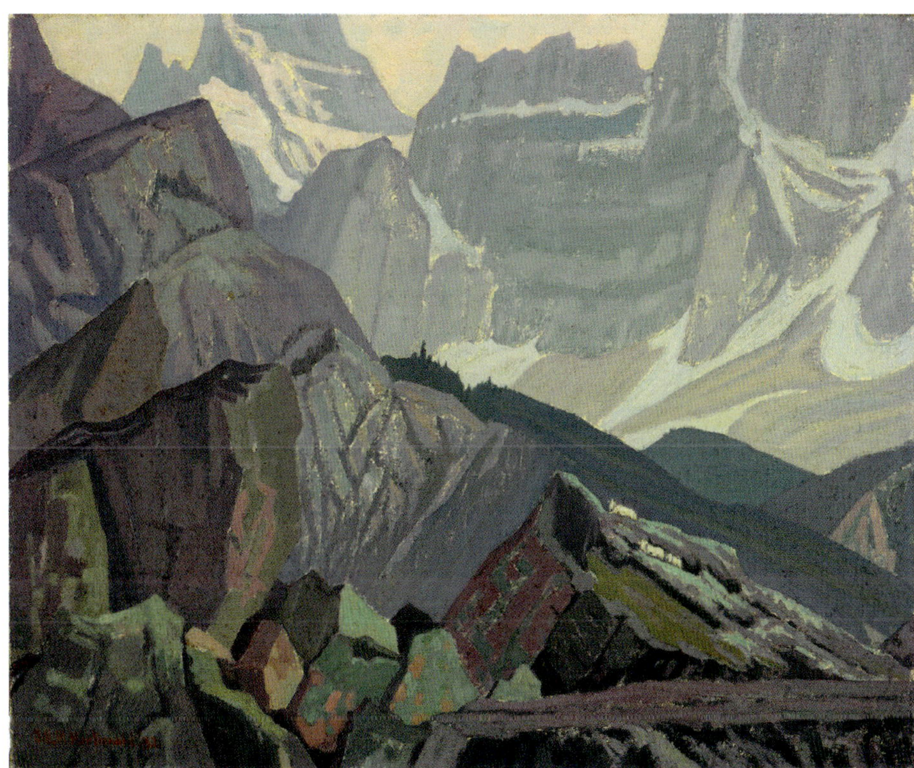

Fig. 1.22: *Goat Range, Rocky Mountains*, 1932, 53.8 × 66.2 cm, oil on canvas, McMichael Canadian Art Collection, 1979.35. Photo: McMichael.

recorded the date that he made this sketch on the spot, by incising "Aug 24, '31" into the wet paint in the bottom right corner of the composition.

In November 1931, shortly after his trip to Georgian Bay, MacDonald suffered a mild stroke and was confined to bed for several weeks. From January until April of 1932, he took leave from his position at the OCA, and he and his wife travelled to Barbados, hoping that rest and the warm climate would help him recover.[96] As usual, he made good use of his time: he kept a diary,[97] observed details of his surroundings, and sketched as much as he could. Near the end of the trip, MacDonald wrote to Eric Brown, director of the NGC: "I have made some 50 or 60 sketches, mostly sea-shore studies, rather limited in outlook as my walking powers are not as free as they used to be."[98] One of these sketches, illustrated in Fig. 1.24, shows how he responded to the new landscape with lighter colour tones in order to render what he described in his letter to Brown as "a combination of English delicacy and Rocky Mountain clearness in the atmosphere."

After his return to Toronto in the spring of 1932, MacDonald felt well enough to work on several canvases inspired by his sketches of the Rocky Mountains. Setting up a studio in his woodshed at Thornhill,[99] he completed the last paintings of his career that summer, including *Goat Range, Rocky Mountains* (Fig. 1.22) and another important work, *Mountain Snowfall, Lake Oesa*. MacDonald appeared to be in good health throughout the summer, but soon after returning to the OCA for the school

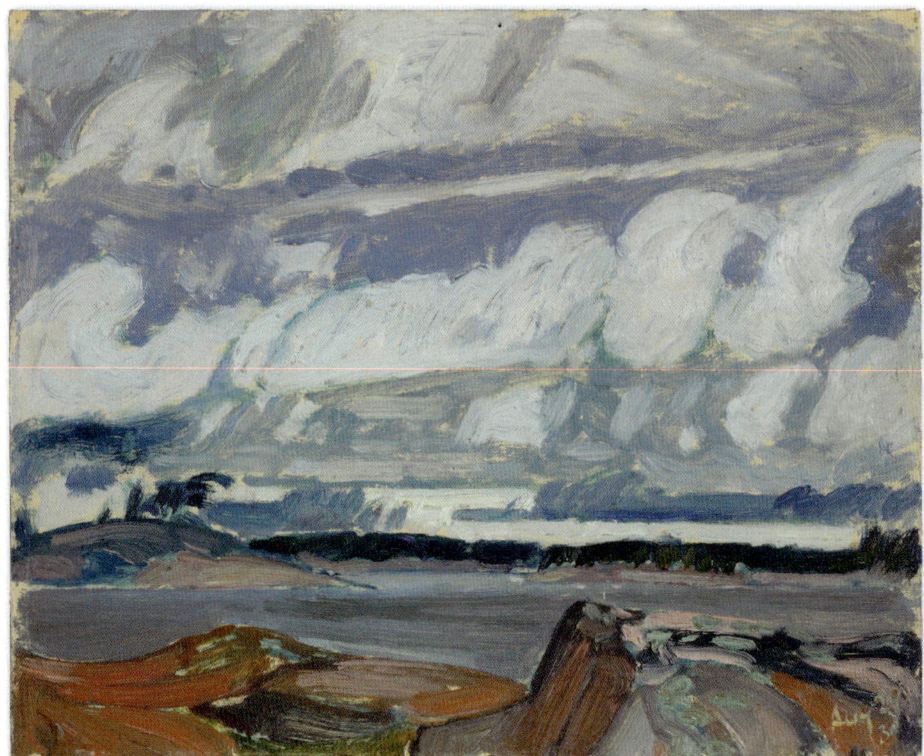

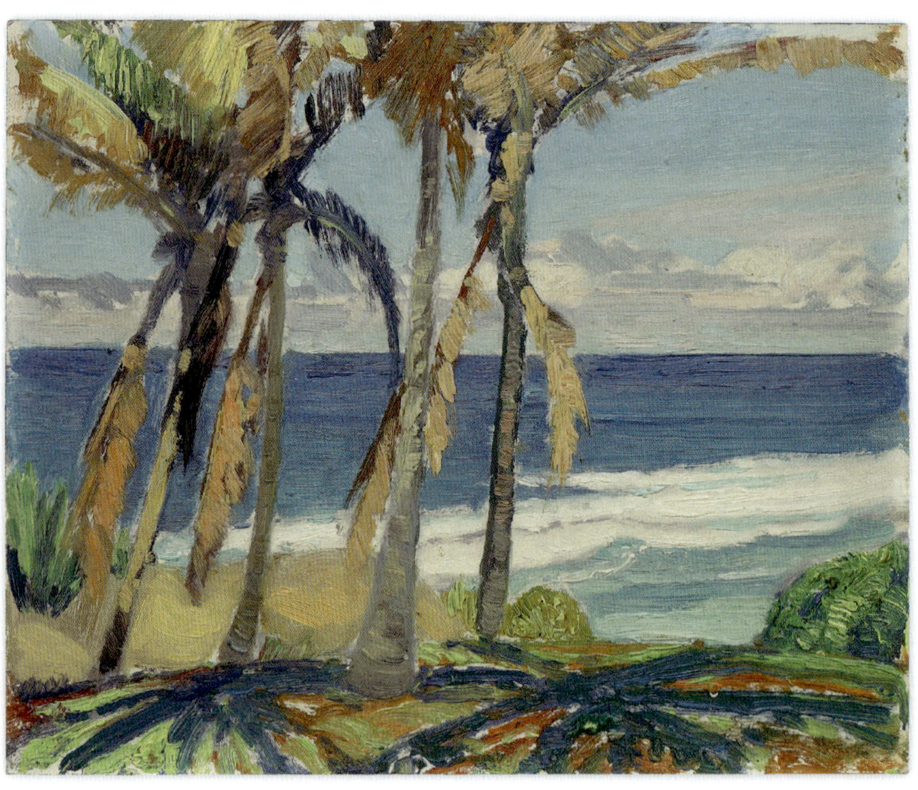

(top to bottom)
Fig. 1.23: *Windy Sky near Pointe au Baril*, 1931, 21.5 × 26.6 cm, oil on paperboard, National Gallery of Canada, Ottawa. Photo: NGC.

Fig. 1.24: *Palms, Barbados*, 1932, 21.6 × 26.7 cm, oil on paperboard, Art Gallery of Ontario. Photo: © AGO.

year, he suffered a serious stroke and died just a few days later, on November 26, 1932, at the age of 59.

J.E.H. MacDonald is remembered as a distinguished Canadian artist of the early twentieth century and a founding member of the Group of Seven. He approached all his endeavours, whether commercial design, teaching, writing, or painting, with the same serious dedication. However, it was plein-air sketching that brought him the most peace and satisfaction, and he often wished that he could spend more time painting, "free from the rush and motives of ordinary business."[100] MacDonald's own description of an artist sketching outdoors, then, seems an appropriate place to leave him:

> He goes forth to look at sky and mountains and tree, and sitting quietly in wood or field he sees intimately the life of animal and bird. He needs no sport to amuse him outdoors. He has the one great sport, and in pursuit of it he can enjoy swimming or paddling or tramping or climbing with always the rare quietude of the sketch thrown in for full measure."[101]

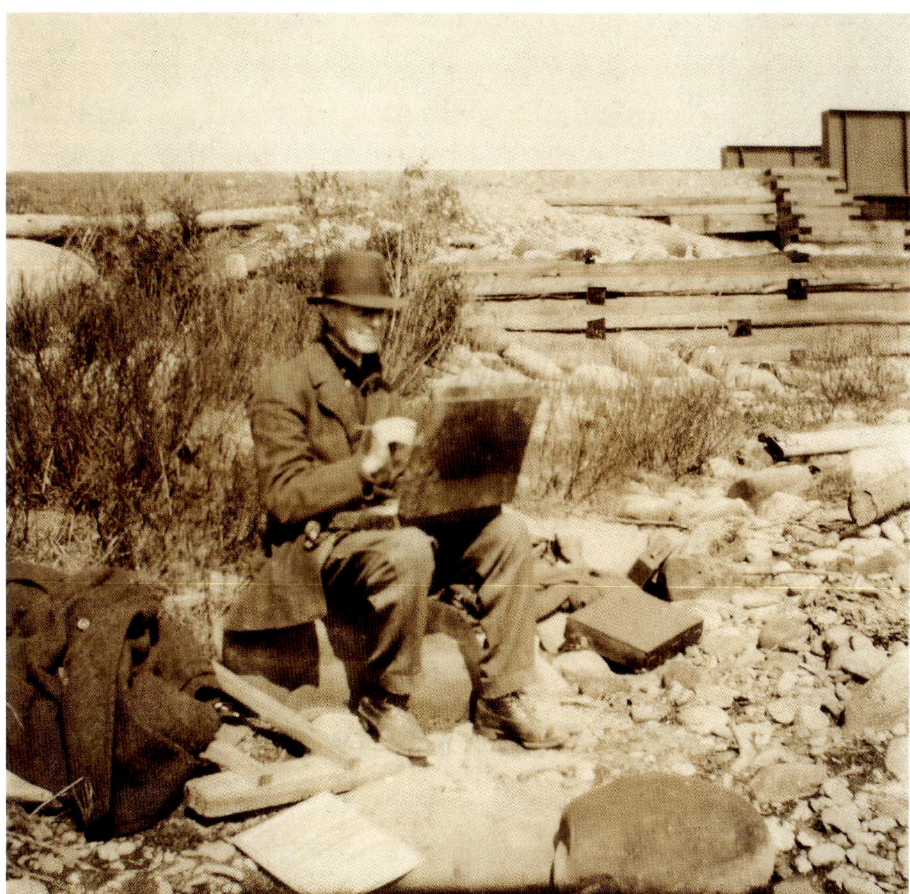

Fig. 1.25: J.E.H. MacDonald painting in Algoma, circa 1918–1919. A.Y. Jackson Scrapbook, National Gallery of Canada Library and Archives, Ottawa. Photo: NGC.

Equipment: a few tools, some enthusiasm and an open mind.
– J.E.H. MacDonald, Lecture Notes, Untitled, General Art, n.d. [circa 1925].

Jackson uses small panels of birch in sketching the 8 ½ × 10 ½ [inch] size. He paints directly on the unprimed wood, letting the clear wood show through a great deal to make a unifying tone. I have worked for the same size on bookbinder's mill-board of fairly heavy quality. A light-colored board shellaced [sic] with orange shellac makes a fine surface of good color to work on. Some of us use beaver-board shellaced with orange shellac. Frank Carmichael uses mill-board a good deal, priming it with a warm pink or buff or golden-yellow coat of oil paint. We don't use canvas for small sizes.
– J.E.H. MacDonald, Letter to W.J. Wood, March 15, 1920.

2. SUPPORTS AND PREPARATION

Both the support – that is, the substrate on which a work is painted – and the way it has been prepared are key to the overall appearance of MacDonald's oil sketches and paintings. The excerpt opposite, from a letter to fellow artist W.J. Wood, shows that MacDonald considered his options carefully. The data in this chapter, based on close visual examination of 160 of MacDonald's sketches and 14 of his studio paintings, reveals his preferences for specific support materials and preparation methods. A detailed description for each of the examined works is available elsewhere[1], and a summary is given here. Throughout the chapter, documentary evidence is provided as context for the results of the visual survey.

The Sketches

Overview and Terminology

MacDonald carried his oil painting supplies to many regions of Canada and, on occasion, abroad, often sketching with artist friends on his longer expeditions. He and his travelling companions painted their outdoor sketches on small, lightweight supports that were easy to transport. Previous research on the supports used by some of these artists, for example, Tom Thomson and A.Y. Jackson, has shown that they favoured specific sizes and types at different times during their careers.[2] MacDonald's oil sketches are a key part of his oeuvre, and a similar in-depth examination of their characteristics is long overdue.

Our survey of MacDonald's oil sketches, summarized in the following sections, revealed a consistent, chronological pattern to the type and dimensions of his sketching supports.[3] As illustrated in the examples presented in the final chapter of the book, this new information not only gives insight into the progression of MacDonald's technique, but it can also be used as one aspect of authentication and dating research.

While MacDonald occasionally painted on small plywood or wood panel supports, most of his sketches are on lightweight, rigid boards, just a few millimetres thick, that are built up from thin layers of paper pulp. The layered appearance, or lamination, of the paper pulp is usually visible at the edges or corners of the boards. Examination of the back of the boards under the microscope shows additional components embedded in the surface of the primary fine matrix of wood pulp fibres, including small woody fragments, bits of recycled paper, and spots of pigmented or resinous material. For two Algoma sketches, analysis of microscopic samples of the board revealed that the main pulp type is unbleached, mechanical softwood pulp.[4] The colours of MacDonald's boards are generally in the grey-brown to light brown range.

The terminology used to denote these rigid sketching boards made from layers of paper pulp is inconsistent. The artists themselves sometimes referred to them as "cardboard" or "millboard."[5] In other sources, both modern and historic, various terms have been used for such boards, including cardboard, card, millboard, bookbinding board, pulp board, wood-pulp board, composite wood-pulp board, or paperboard.[6] The definitions of some of these terms have been interpreted in different ways or have changed over time. Here, we have chosen to refer to this type of sketching support with the general name "paperboard." As defined in the glossary, the term "paperboard" comprises boards made of paper by any means: a single, thick layer of paper pulp; laminated sheets of paper held together with adhesive; or layers of wet paper pulp bonded together using pressure during drying.

MacDonald prepared his sketching supports in several different ways. Early in his career, he usually painted on paperboard that was prepared with an oil ground layer. A traditional oil ground, sometimes called a "priming," is an opaque layer, composed of pigments in a drying oil medium, that covers the support and provides a suitable surface for painting. Although careful observation revealed that MacDonald generally applied these ground layers himself,[7] early on, he sometimes purchased sketching supports with an oil ground already applied by the manufacturer. As described in the glossary, these pre-primed paperboard supports were called "prepared millboards" or "academy boards" in catalogues of artists' materials at the time. In this publication, we refer to pre-prepared paperboard as "academy board," since this term is still in general use.[8]

Later in his career, MacDonald more often prepared his paperboard sketching supports with a transparent, resin-based coating rather than with a traditional pigmented oil ground layer. This type of transparent coating, which we refer to throughout as "varnish," is typically applied to the top surfaces of paintings or furniture to saturate and protect them. MacDonald's application of varnish to his sketching supports to prepare them before painting is an unconventional use of the material.

Documentary Evidence

MacDonald sketched on rigid paperboard much more regularly than either A.Y. Jackson or Tom Thomson, who, under MacDonald's influence, also sometimes painted on this type of support, beginning in about 1914.[9] Paperboard may have appealed to MacDonald in part because it was a more economical choice than the thin wooden panels that Jackson and Thomson often used. Several authors indicate that MacDonald purchased his paperboard from bookbinding firms.[10] A letter, dated March 15, 1920, from MacDonald to fellow artist W.J. Wood, provides direct evidence for this. MacDonald advised Wood about sketching boards and sizes in this letter, writing that he used supports made from "bookbinder's mill-board of fairly heavy quality."[11]

As explained in the glossary, boards used for bookbinding in the first half of the twentieth century were usually dense, laminate paperboard of about 1 mm to 5 mm thick.[12] Brown Brothers and Warwick Bro's & Rutter, two Toronto-based wholesalers and retailers of bookbinding and stationery supplies, have been mentioned as sources for MacDonald's oil sketching supports.[13] The publication *On the Making of Blank Books*, issued by Warwick Bro's & Rutter near the beginning of the twentieth century, specified that various thicknesses of boards were available: "The thickness of the boards depends altogether on the size and weight of the book, and must be of the best quality of millboard, so as not to warp or break."[14]

As well as bookbinding boards, it has been suggested that MacDonald sometimes used cartons or cardboard boxes cut to size.[15] MacDonald may also have purchased paperboard supports from sources other than bookbinding firms during certain periods of his career. Catalogues from three leading Toronto-based artists' supply firms (the Art Metropole,[16] the E. Harris Company,[17] and the Artists' Supply Company[18]) show that a variety of rigid paperboard products were available at the time he was painting. These included academy boards, pre-prepared with a ground layer for oil painting. Paperboard intended for other uses, such as for cards, posters, mounting, or matting, was also available. These unprepared boards could be purchased in various standard sizes, colours, and thicknesses.[19]

Our research to date has uncovered some limited documentary evidence about the way MacDonald prepared his sketching supports for painting. While we came across no written descriptions about the traditional oil ground layers that MacDonald favoured early in his career, some information about his later practices was available. Paul Duval, through interviews with MacDonald's son, Thoreau, determined that during the period when Thoreau assisted his father, from about 1918 onwards, MacDonald regularly painted on boards coated with shellac rather than a ground layer. Duval reported that MacDonald "painted mostly on millboard panels, a bookbinder's board from Brown Brothers in Toronto. His son prepared these for him with a coat of shellac."[20]

Other evidence is found in MacDonald's 1920 letter to Wood, where he described coating his bookbinding board with shellac before painting, writing that "a light-colored board shellaced [sic] with orange shellac makes a fine surface of good color to work on."[21] Shellac is a natural resin varnish from an insect source. As described in the glossary, unbleached shellac, also referred to as orange shellac, produces a varnish with a slight yellow-orange tone, while bleached shellac is essentially colourless.

There is also a cryptic note in MacDonald's 1925 diary from the Rockies, where he described his evening activities: "Lit fire this evg. Shaved and washed socks and got panels ready for mng."[22] MacDonald provided no further description about what he meant by "got panels ready." While this could simply mean that he packed up a set of boards for the following day, it is also possible that he was referring to coating the boards with varnish in advance of sketching. Unlike a traditional oil ground layer, a solvent-based varnish like shellac would dry quickly and could possibly have been applied the night before a sketching excursion. When MacDonald used traditional ground layers, on the other hand, they would most likely have been applied further in advance. An oil-based ground should be left for at least several days, and ideally longer, to ensure that it is dry enough to paint on.

Results of the Survey

Sketches from 1909 and 1910. We examined four of MacDonald's early sketches. While they have variable dimensions, all are quite small in scale. The smallest, *Snow, High Park*, measures only 12.5 × 17.6 cm (about 5 × 7 in.).[23]

Three of these early sketches are painted on thick, grey-brown, laminate paperboard. The supports vary from about 4 mm to 6 mm thick, significantly heavier than the paperboard MacDonald used later in his career, and at the upper limit of thickness typically used for bookbinding.[24] Under magnification, the backs of the boards show small woody fragments, thin dark fibres, and tiny brown and black specks embedded in the wood pulp matrix (Fig. 2.1a). All three were prepared for painting with a thin, grey ground layer that has sometimes extended onto the unevenly cut edges of the support (Fig. 2.1b). MacDonald appears to have cut the boards to size and applied the grey ground layers himself.

Snow, High Park (illustrated in chapter 1, Fig. 1.1), from 1909, differs from the three other early sketches. It is painted on thinner paperboard that has been coated with an even, white ground layer that stops cleanly at the top and left borders. This indicates a commercial ground application, which, as described in the glossary, is consistent with academy board. The other two edges are crooked and exhibit chipping and loss of both ground and paint, revealing that MacDonald cut the sketch down from what was originally a larger work.[25] The composition of the commercial ground layer on this academy board support is detailed in chapter 4, which focuses on the chemical analysis of MacDonald's materials.

Details of *Oaks, October Morning*, 1909, McMichael Canadian Art Collection, 1966.15.15. Photos: McMichael.

(top to bottom)
Fig. 2.1a: A 5 cm × 5 cm area of the back of the board.

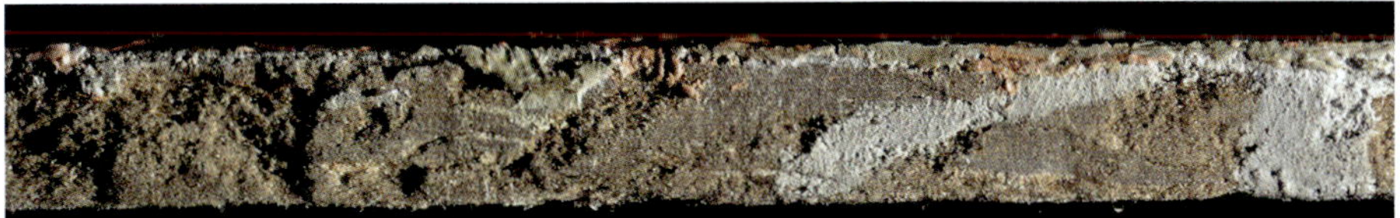

Fig. 2.1b: An edge of the board with its rough profile and strokes of the grey ground extending over the edge. The board is 5.8 mm thick.

Sketches from 1911 to 1913. Seventeen of MacDonald's oil sketches dating from 1911 to 1913 were examined. The group includes sketches from his trips to Burk's Falls and the Magnetawan River in the spring of 1912, to the MacCallum cottage during the summer of 1912, to the Laurentians with Lawren Harris in 1913, as well as sketches painted closer to home.

Like the earliest works, some sketches from this period are very small. *Laurentian Storm*, painted in 1913, measures only 10.1 × 10.1 cm (about 4 × 4 in.). While MacDonald's sketch sizes varied during the 1911 to 1913 period, there are dimensions that he favoured. Most of the sketches examined are on supports that are either approximately 17.8 × 22.7 cm (close to 7 × 9 in.) or 20.2 × 25.3 cm (close to 8 × 10 in.).

These sketches are painted on laminate paperboard supports of two distinct types. While most are on paperboard that MacDonald prepared himself with an oil ground layer, six works are on pre-prepared academy boards. The six academy boards have a light-coloured priming applied to one side and a dark-coloured priming on the other. MacDonald chose to paint on either the light-coloured or the dark-coloured ground, depending on what suited his composition.

The academy board used for *View from Split Rock*, a sketch painted at Dr. MacCallum's cottage in 1912, has a paper label on the back showing that it was

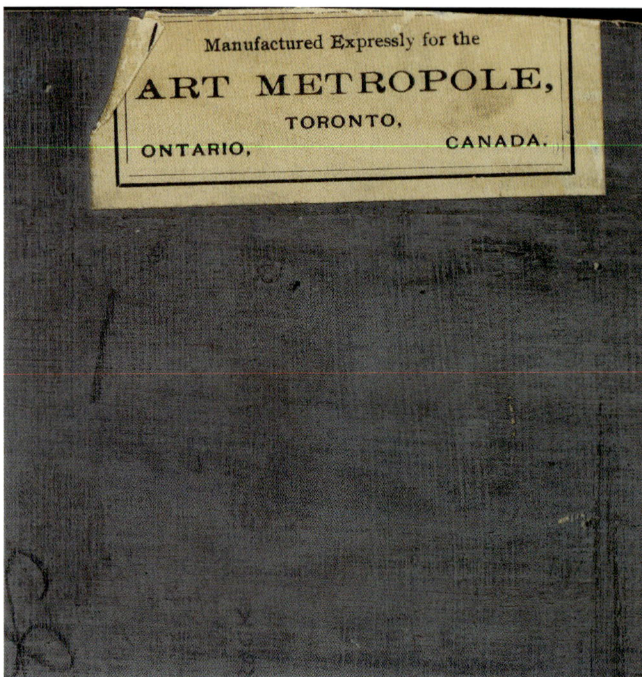

Fig. 2.2: A 10 cm × 10 cm area of the back of the support for *View from Split Rock*, 1912, National Gallery of Canada, Ottawa, with its dark grey commercial ground and label from the Art Metropole. Photo: © Government of Canada.

manufactured for the Art Metropole (Fig. 2.2). As described earlier, the Art Metropole was an important supplier of artists' materials in Toronto during the early twentieth century,[26] and this label provides evidence that MacDonald purchased materials there. Three other Georgian Bay sketches from 1912 were painted on academy boards with a very similar appearance to the one used for *View from Split Rock*, with a light grey ground on one side and a darker, charcoal grey ground on the other. In all cases, MacDonald painted on the light grey commercial ground; its composition is described in chapter 4.

All six sketches on academy board have at least one uneven, presumably hand-cut edge, indicating that MacDonald purchased larger-sized boards and cut them to the desired dimensions before painting. The fact that we did not identify academy board as the support for any sketches painted after 1912 suggests that MacDonald stopped using these pre-primed artist's boards early in his career.

MacDonald painted the remaining 11 sketches from this period on laminate paperboard that he prepared with a traditional ground layer, applied relatively thickly by brush. The ground often runs over the edges of the board and sometimes onto the back. Apart from one sketch, *Storm Clouds*, circa 1913, which has a pale pink ground, he used a warm, off-white ground layer.

The paperboard supports for these sketches vary in colour from grey to dark grey-brown. The backs of the boards typically show scattered woody fragments, dark fibres, and specks within the wood pulp matrix (Fig. 2.3a). Their surfaces are slightly rough and often show a faint textured pattern, most visible in raking light. Varying from about 2 mm to 3 mm thick, these boards are thinner than MacDonald's earliest

Details of *Oakwood*, 1913, McMichael Canadian Art Collection, 1972.5.3. Photos: McMichael.

(top to bottom)
Fig. 2.3a: A 5 cm × 5 cm area of the back of the board.

Fig. 2.3b: An edge of the board with its rough profile. The board is 2.3 mm thick.

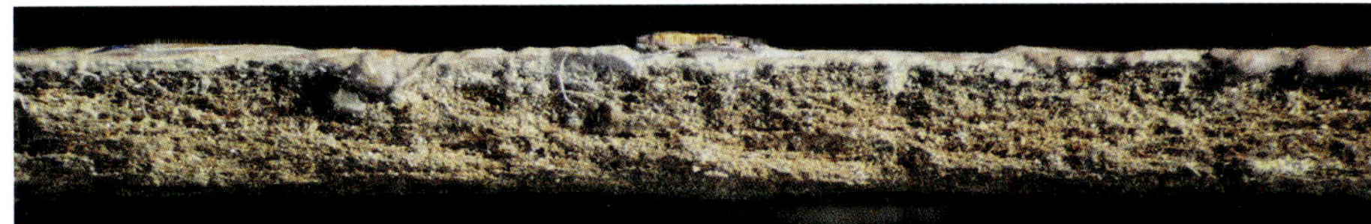

paperboard supports. Although the cut edges of the boards are all quite straight, by looking through a microscope, we can see that the cutting method produced a rough edge profile (Fig. 2.3b). This rough profile means that the laminate structure of the board is generally only visible at the corners, where slight splaying and separation of the thin pulp layers often occur.

Sketches from 1914 to 1917. We documented the characteristics of 15 of MacDonald's sketches dating from 1914 to 1917. Eleven are on paperboard, one is on wood panel, and three are on plywood.[27] MacDonald painted these sketches in various locations, including Algonquin Park; the Gatineau region of Quebec; Minden, Ontario; the MacCallum cottage in Georgian Bay; and in the garden of his Thornhill home. The last sketch from this period is a view of Canoe Lake, Algonquin Park, thought to be from MacDonald's October 1917 trip with J.W. Beatty to install the memorial cairn for Tom Thomson (Fig. 1.9).

By 1914, MacDonald appears to have begun using 8 × 10-inch sketching supports as his preferred size. All examined sketches, regardless of support type, from the 1914 to 1917 period measure about 20.2 × 25.3 cm (approximately 8 × 10 in.). Their dimensions are regular, varying by only a few millimetres from sketch to sketch. For the works on paperboard, MacDonald may have been purchasing them pre-cut to a standard format. However, he was a skilled craftsman, and it is also possible that he used equipment in his studio to cut the boards accurately to size.

Although MacDonald sketched primarily on paperboard during this period, he also sometimes used other support types. One of the sketches examined, thought to have been painted around 1913–14, is on a thin wood panel support. This appears to be an uncommon support type for MacDonald. Of the 160 sketches examined, wooden supports were only observed in two other cases, both painted during the summer of 1918.

MacDonald also occasionally used plywood supports; the study group included three sketches on plywood, all dating between 1914 and 1917. He used 3-ply plywood with an average thickness of 4.6 mm (close to 3/16 in.) for these sketches. Two of the three plywood panels include either a bevel or a channel on the left and right to allow them to slide into a slotted paintbox lid or carrying case.

Snow, Algonquin Park, from MacDonald's 1914 sketching trip with A.Y. Jackson and J.W. Beatty, is the earliest work painted on plywood in the study group. During this trip, both Jackson and Beatty used small paintboxes that accommodated 8½ × 10½-inch wooden panels.[28] Unlike his painting colleagues, MacDonald did not adopt the use of 8½ × 10½-inch supports during this period. However, his use of wood and plywood supports beginning around this time is thought to have been due to Jackson's influence.[29]

Except for the few works on wood or plywood, the sketches of 1914 to 1917 are on grey to grey-brown laminate paperboard supports of about 2 mm to 3 mm in thickness. They are of a similar colour and weight to the boards that MacDonald used in the 1911 to 1913 period. Like the earlier sketches, the backs of the boards show scattered specks and woody fragments, have a slightly rough appearance, and often show a faint textured pattern. The boards were also cut in a similar manner: the edges are straight, but the cutting tool produced a rough profile, so that lamination is usually only visible at the corners. Figure 2.4 illustrates details of the back and an edge of the support for *Near Minden* (Fig. 1.7), painted in 1916 or 1917.

Apart from two of the sketches on plywood that MacDonald painted directly on the support, all the examined works from this period include an artist-applied ground layer. MacDonald sometimes used an off-white or light grey ground as he had done earlier, but more often, he preferred to use warmly coloured grounds, usually in mid to light shades of warm pink through red and yellow-orange. These grounds are generally quite thick, and many show distinct brushstroke texture. The coloured grounds for several sketches were analyzed, and their chemical compositions are reported in chapter 4. The colours that MacDonald used for his grounds in this period are similar to those observed on Tom Thomson's sketches on paperboard from 1914 and 1915.[30]

Several sketches from this period include two superposed ground layers. In an unusual combination, *Near Minden* and *Georgian Bay* both show a green ground

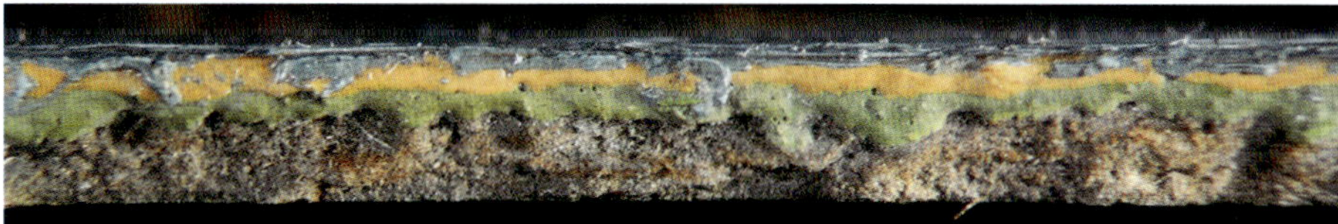

Details of *Near Minden*, 1916 or 1917, McMichael Canadian Art Collection, 1966.15.12. Photos: McMichael.

(top to bottom)
Fig. 2.4a: A 5 cm × 5 cm area of the back of the board.

Fig. 2.4b: An edge of the board with its rough profile and two layers of artist applied ground. The board is 2.8 mm thick.

followed by a light yellow-orange ground (Fig. 2.4b). In both cases, the yellow-orange preparation completely covers the green below, so that the lower ground has little to no effect on the final colour. This could indicate that MacDonald changed his mind about the colour choice.[31]

Sketches from 1918 to 1923. MacDonald's November 1917 illness left him unable to paint for several months. His return to sketching in the spring of 1918 marked a transition away from the 8 × 10-inch support size that he favoured in the preceding years to a slightly larger dimension, measuring approximately 8½ × 10½ in. Two sketches on thin wood panel from the summer of 1918 are the earliest works of this size in the study group.[32] Based on our survey, it appears that once MacDonald switched to this larger support dimension in 1918, he used it consistently for the remainder of his career.

When MacDonald left for his first boxcar trip to Algoma in September 1918, the sketching supports he brought in his supply kit were laminate paperboard of this new dimension. With the notable exception of *Poplar and Pine*, an atypical sketch discussed in more detail in the final chapter of the book, the average measurements of the 49 Algoma sketches that we examined are 21.4 × 26.4 cm, which is just slightly smaller than 8½ × 10½ in.

There are several possible reasons that could explain the change in MacDonald's sketching format in 1918. For example, it seems plausible that he could have acquired a new sketch box of the type used by A.Y. Jackson, Tom Thomson, and J.W. Beatty, which allowed 8½ × 10½-inch boards to be held in slots at the left and right edges of the lid.[33] However, examination of two of MacDonald's paintboxes[34] showed no evidence that his choice of sketching format was related to the size of his paintbox. In addition, we noted that his paint almost always extends completely to the left and right edges of the support, which would have been difficult to achieve with the paperboard held within slots in the lid.[35] A number of MacDonald's sketches have pin or finishing nail holes, which could suggest that he sometimes attached his paperboard to a secondary support while painting, rather than holding it in place using slots in his paintbox lid.

Perhaps a more likely reason for the change in MacDonald's sketch format was to match the support size of some of his painting colleagues who had been using 8½ × 10½-inch boards for several years. Correspondence between MacDonald and W.J. Wood from March 1920[36] suggests that the Group of Seven painters shared exhibition frames for their oil sketches; consequently, it would have been practical for them to paint on supports of the same dimension. In his letter to Wood from March 15, 1920, MacDonald offered to lend him a few frames for exhibition, specifying that "if you cut your painting bds. [boards] to 8½ × 10½ they will fit the frame back and front. The opening, or 'space of exposure,' is 8¼ × 10¼, the rebate of the frame covering ⅛ of an inch all round."[37]

As well as changing his support dimension, MacDonald also appears to have begun using a new type of paperboard in 1918. The supports for his Algoma sketches differ from the earlier ones in aspects other than their new, slightly larger size. Overall, compared to his earlier paperboard, the Algoma supports are somewhat thinner and appear denser, with more heavily compressed pulp layers. The majority are also paler and browner in colour than the earlier supports. The backs of the boards have a pressed or flattened appearance, often with a subtle texture of vertical or horizontal lines, which is distinct from the earlier boards with their slightly rough texture.

While MacDonald's Algoma supports have certain similarities overall that distinguish them from earlier ones, we noted three distinct paperboard types within the group of 49 Algoma sketches, which we have designated as Algoma Type A, Type B, and Type C.

An example of an Algoma Type A support is shown in Figs. 2.5a and 2.5b. These supports are grey-brown, laminate paperboards with an average thickness of 2.0 mm. The backs have a characteristic pattern of round, brown-black, resinous spots of various sizes, measuring from about 0.5 mm to 4 mm in diameter, that gives them a blotchy or freckled appearance. These round spots appear unintentional and are

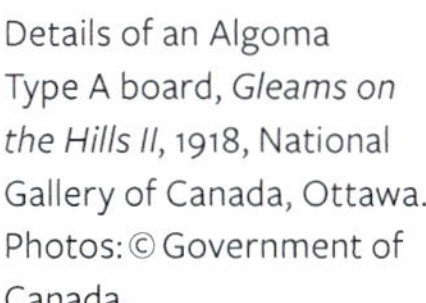

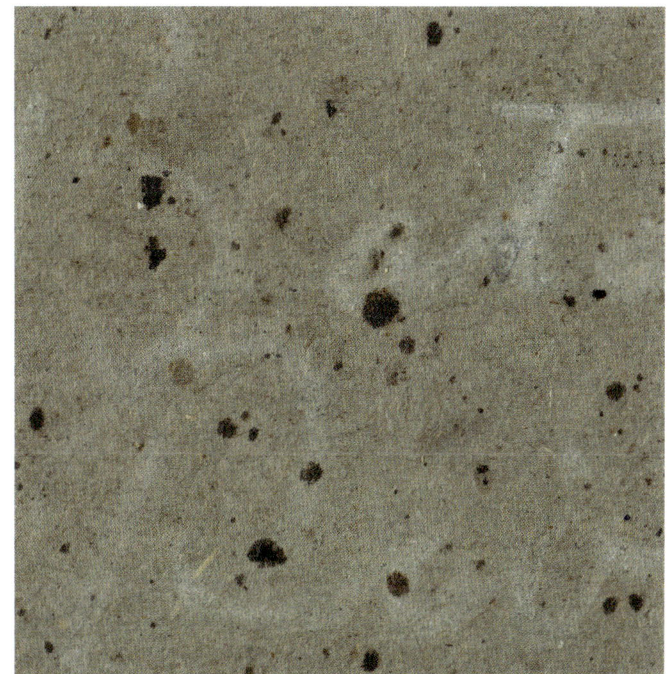

Details of an Algoma Type A board, *Gleams on the Hills II*, 1918, National Gallery of Canada, Ottawa. Photos: © Government of Canada.

(top to bottom)
Fig. 2.5a: A 5 cm × 5 cm area of the back of the board with its round, brown-black resinous spots.

Fig. 2.5b: An edge of the board with its smooth profile, diagonal cut marks, and uniform layers of pulp. The board is 1.8 mm thick.

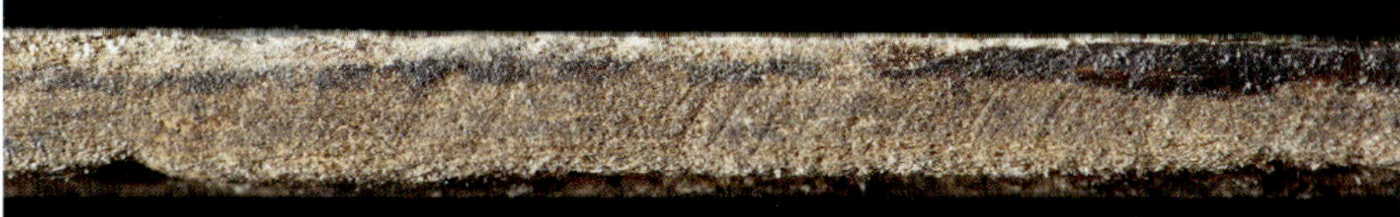

perhaps the result of a manufacturing defect. The backs of the boards also include small woody fragments and fine, dark fibres. As shown in Fig. 2.5b, unlike his earlier sketching boards, the edges of the Algoma Type A boards have a smooth profile with fine, diagonal lines from the instrument used to cut them.[38] The laminate structure is ususally visible along the edge profile, and the pulp appears uniform throughout its thickness. Seven of the Algoma sketches that we examined are on this type of support.

An example of an Algoma Type B support is shown in Figs. 2.6a and 2.6b. The survey revealed that the Algoma Type B paperboards were the most common; just over half of the Algoma sketching supports examined are of this type. They are pale brown, laminate paperboards with an average thickness of 1.8 mm. As shown in Fig. 2.6a, the backs of the boards include dark specks and fine, dark fibres along with small woody fibres and fragments embedded within the primary wood pulp matrix. There are also often bits of recycled, coloured paper, and pigmented or resinous spots or flecks. These materials give a heterogeneous appearance to the backs of the boards; however, they do not have the characteristic freckled appearance of the Algoma Type A supports and are also lighter and browner in colour. Like the Type A boards, the edges are straight and have a smooth profile with fine, diagonal lines from cutting (Fig. 2.6b). Examination of the edges often reveals that the wood

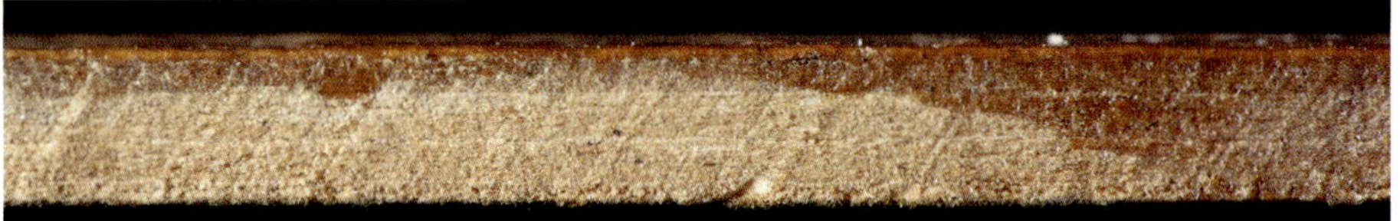

Details of an Algoma Type B board, *Algoma Bush, Autumn*, circa 1919, National Gallery of Canada, Ottawa. Photos: © Government of Canada.

(top to bottom)
Fig. 2.6a: A 5 cm × 5 cm area of the back of the board with its heterogeneous appearance.

Fig. 2.6b: An edge of the board with its smooth profile, three plies, and diagonal cut marks. The board is 1.8 mm thick.

pulp core is segmented into three or four distinct plies, each made up of multiple thin layers of pulp. There is sometimes a thin, lighter layer of pulp or a slight layer separation at the boundaries between the plies.

An example of an Algoma Type C support is shown in Figs. 2.7a to 2.7c. This paperboard type is visually similar to Algoma Type B, both in colour and in the range of embedded materials on the back. They are marginally thicker than the Algoma Type B boards, measuring on average 2.2 mm thick. The Algoma Type C boards are distinguishable from the other types based on their unique edge profiles. They have two parallel edges (most often the left and right) that are smooth, that show fine, diagonal cut marks, and that have visible lamination, often with plies. The opposite edges (most often the top and bottom), on the other hand, were cut using a different method, which produced a rough profile. Figure 2.7b shows the rough top edge of an Algoma Type C board, while Fig. 2.7c shows the smooth left edge of the same board. There are 14 boards of this type within the Algoma group.

There appears to be a correlation between the Algoma board type and the date of the sketch. The Type A board, with its freckled surface, was most frequent in sketches from MacDonald's first trip to Algoma in 1918. With one exception, the Type C boards, with their combination of rough and smooth edges, were only identified in sketches with estimated dates of 1919 or 1920. The most common,

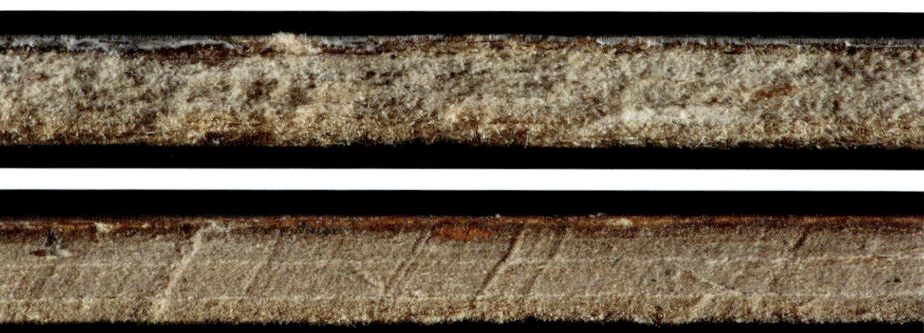

Details of an Algoma Type C board, *Mist Fantasy*, 1920, National Gallery of Canada, Ottawa. Photos: © Government of Canada.

(top to bottom)
Fig. 2.7a: A 5 cm × 5 cm area of the back of the board with its heterogeneous appearance.

Fig. 2.7b: The rough top edge of the board, without visible plies or cutting marks.

Fig. 2.7c: The smooth left edge of the board, with three plies and diagonal cut marks. The board is 2.2 mm thick.

Type B boards, were found in sketches with estimated dates covering all three trips. Determining a link between board type and date is complicated by the fact that many of MacDonald's Algoma sketches have not been conclusively attributed to a particular sketching trip. Future research could lead to a stronger correlation of board type with execution date for the Algoma sketches.

The study group included 12 of MacDonald's sketches from the early 1920s, directly following his last trip to Algoma. Apart from one small sketch that MacDonald cut down from a larger board, these sketches, like the Algoma works, have average dimensions of 21.4 × 26.3 cm (just under 8½ × 10½ in.). They are on laminate paperboard supports, and most have characteristics like MacDonald's Algoma Type B or Type C boards. We noted some subtle variations, including, for example, a more pronounced surface texture on the backs of some of the supports for his sketches made in Nova Scotia.

The switch to a different size and type of paperboard was not the only important change in MacDonald's technique in 1918. Beginning with his first trip to Algoma,

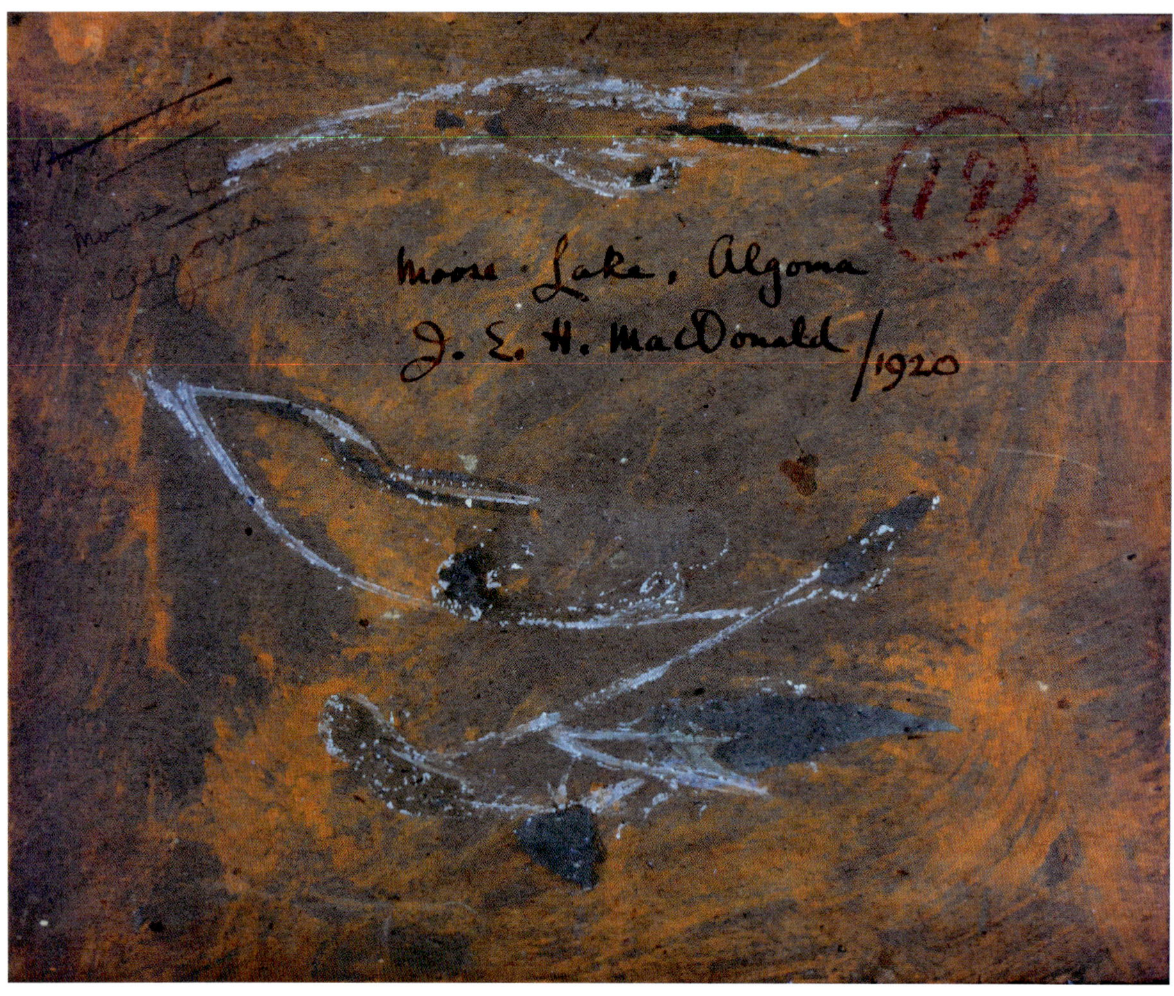

Fig. 2.8: *Moose Lake, Algoma*, 1920, McMichael Canadian Art Collection, 1966.15.4. Back of the board under UV illumination, showing the orange-fluorescing shellac, along with blue-fluorescing, adhesive residue. Photo: McMichael.

MacDonald abandoned the use of a traditional ground layer on his sketches, preferring to paint directly on the support, usually after coating it with varnish, a transparent resinous layer that covered the surface while allowing the paperboard to show through. Except for the atypical sketch *Poplar and Pine*, which is described further in chapter 5, none of the Algoma sketches examined include a traditional ground layer.

We established the presence of a varnish preparatory layer on the front or back of the boards by examining them with ultraviolet (UV) illumination and observing the visible fluorescence, a phenomenon described in the glossary. Many of the boards showed an orange fluorescence, which is characteristic of unbleached shellac, also known as orange shellac. Figure 2.8 is a UV fluorescence image of the back of the support for the 1920 sketch, *Moose Lake, Algoma*, showing the uneven, brush application of orange-fluorescing shellac. As described in chapter 4, shellac was also confirmed through chemical analysis. The use of orange shellac instead of a traditional ground in this period is consistent with the descriptions in MacDonald's correspondence with W.J. Wood and with Thoreau MacDonald's recollections, both described earlier in the chapter.[39] Occasionally, yellow-green fluorescence was observed under UV illumination rather than orange. While this type of fluorescence established that the board was coated with varnish, possibly a natural resin, it was not indicative of a specific resin type.[40]

MacDonald applied varnish to his paperboard supports prior to painting, as least in part, for aesthetic reasons. As described in the following chapter, he often left areas of the paperboard support exposed in his Algoma sketches, and the colour of the support played an important role in the design. The shellac, with its yellow-orange tone, gave a warmer, more saturated colour to the support that MacDonald appreciated. He pointed this out in his 1920 letter to Wood, writing that coating a light-coloured paperboard with orange shellac "makes a fine surface of good color to work on."[41] He may also have been aware of the practical advantage of coating the board with varnish prior to painting; the shellac would prevent the initial paint layers from soaking into the paperboard surface.

For MacDonald's Algoma Type B and Type C boards, we most often observed a shellac coating on the front of the board and no varnish on the back, other than spillover from the front. This is consistent with MacDonald's description of his practice. In a small proportion of the sketches, mostly works dating from the 1920 trip, both front and back were coated with orange-fluorescing shellac. Applying shellac to both sides would help to equalize the moisture absorption from the front and back faces and help to prevent warping of the paperboard. However, since MacDonald only coated both faces in a small number of sketches, this may not have been an intentional choice.

For the seven sketches on the freckled, grey-brown boards designated as Algoma Type A, which MacDonald appears to have used primarily during his 1918 Algoma trip, the preparation of the boards differs from MacDonald's 1920 description. We observed a thin, uneven layer of shellac on the back of about half of the works. In some cases, there was evidence that the front of the board was also coated with varnish prior to painting; however, the yellow-green fluorescence indicated a different type of resin. The use of different coatings on the front and back could indicate that they were applied at different times.

Sketches from 1924 to 1930. MacDonald made seven sketching trips to the Rocky Mountains in British Columbia, one each year from 1924 to 1930. The study group included 41 sketches from these trips, all on paperboard supports. Except for two supports that were cut down from larger boards, MacDonald's mountain sketches have very similar dimensions to his Algoma works, measuring on average 21.4 × 26.5 cm (just under 8½ × 10½ in.). Overall, the backs of these supports have a relatively uniform appearance, with fewer embedded particles and fibres compared to the Algoma supports.

We noted three distinct types of paperboard supports within the group of sketches from the Rocky Mountains: they are designated as Rockies Type A, Type B, and Type C. Like the Algoma sketches, there appears to be a correlation between the sketch date and the type of paperboard support. However, since close to half of the mountain sketches examined have not been definitively dated to a specific trip, any link between board type and date is approximate.

An example of a Rockies Type A board is shown in Figs. 2.9a and 2.9b. The supports designated as Rockies Type A are composed of pale brown to light brown-grey, thin, laminate paperboard. The backs of the boards have a uniform appearance, with few other materials embedded in the primary wood pulp matrix. They are distinguished from other paperboard types because they are only about 1.5 mm thick, which makes them the thinnest supports that MacDonald used over the course of his career. As shown in Fig. 2.9b, their edges have a smooth profile and show fine, diagonal cut marks. Segmentation of the fine pulp layers into plies is usually evident. MacDonald appears to have favoured these supports during his earliest trips to the Rockies. All but one of the nine sketches dated to 1924 or 1925 that we examined are on this type of board. However, there are also occurrences of the Rockies Type A board for sketches attributed to later trips. In total, 15 of the 41 sketches from the Rockies that we examined are on this type of board.

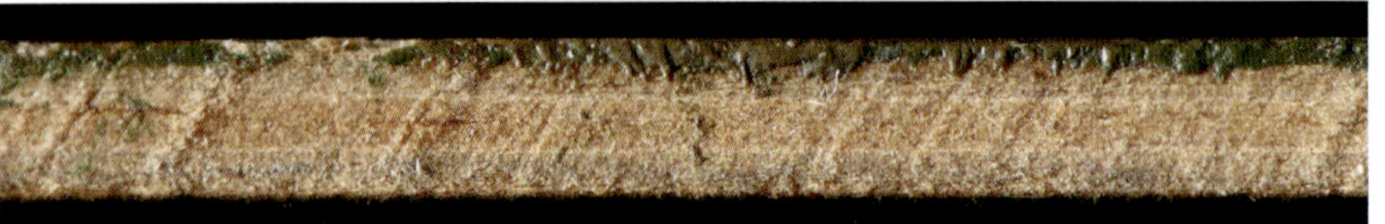

Details of a Rockies Type A board, *Study, Lake McArthur (Grey Weather)*, 1924 to 1930, National Gallery of Canada, Ottawa. Photos: © Government of Canada.

(top to bottom)
Fig. 2.9a: A 5 cm × 5 cm area of the relatively uniform back of the board.

Fig. 2.9b: An edge of the board, with plies and diagonal cut marks. The board is 1.5 mm thick.

An example of a Rockies Type B support is shown in Figs. 2.10a and 2.10b. These boards are pale brown, and the backs are slightly less uniform in appearance than the Type A boards, with more embedded fibres and paper fragments. The Rockies Type B boards are approximately 2.5 mm thick, and unlike the Type A boards, they have edges with a rough profile and no visible marks from cutting. As shown in Fig. 2.10b, these boards are distinguishable by their rough edge profiles and by the characteristic layering of the pulp. Examination of the edges under a microscope shows that there are almost always three distinct layers comprised of a thin, dark brown pulp layer sandwiched between two thicker, paler brown layers.[42] Of the 41 sketches from the Rocky Mountains that we examined, 19 are on this type of support. MacDonald used Type B supports for the majority of the examined sketches dating from 1926 through 1930. This support type, however, was not found for any sketches from his first two trips to the Rockies in 1924 and 1925.

An example of a Rockies Type C board is shown in Figs. 2.11a and 2.11b. MacDonald appears to have used the boards designated as Type C almost exclusively during his last two trips to the Rockies. Apart from one sketch dated circa 1925,[43] these supports were only observed for sketches dating from 1929 or 1930. These Rockies Type C boards are pale brown to pale grey-brown in colour. They are distinguishable by their thickness: they are heavier than the other types, measuring

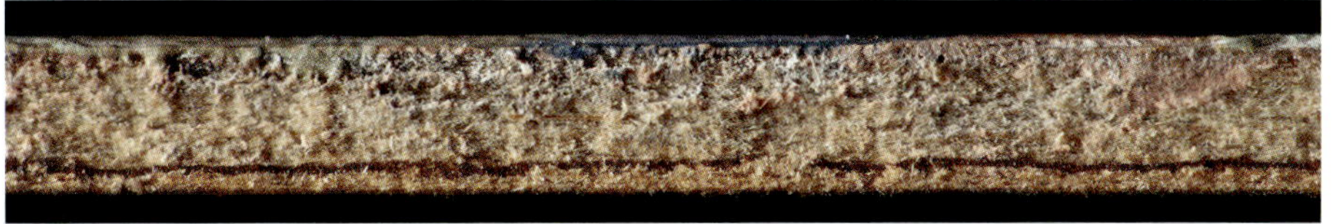

Details of a Rockies Type B board, *Near Lake Oesa, Abbot's Pass*, 1930, National Gallery of Canada, Ottawa. Photos: © Government of Canada.

(top to bottom)
Fig. 2.10a: A 5 cm × 5 cm area of the back of the board. A recycled paper fragment with the letter "B" is circled.

Fig. 2.10b: An edge of the board, with its rough texture and characteristic thin, dark brown pulp layer sandwiched between two thicker, paler brown layers. The board is 2.7 mm thick.

approximately 3.0 mm thick. The backs of the boards are uniform with only a few specks or embedded materials and most also show a distinct horizontal texture, most obvious in raking light.[44] The edges have a smooth profile and show diagonal cut marks. The edges of these boards all show clear plies, usually three or four, and a gradation of colour is usually visible within the pulp layers of each ply. Seven of the sketches from the Rocky Mountains that we examined are on this type of support.

The study group included a small number of sketches painted in locations other than the Rocky Mountains between 1924 and 1930. We examined seven sketches painted in Thornhill, Coboconk, and Georgian Bay during this period. It is interesting to note that the supports for these sketches differ from those for MacDonald's mountain sketches. It seems possible that he may have purchased sketching supports specifically for his trips to British Columbia and kept them primarily for that purpose until after his final trip in 1930.

In most of his sketches from the 1924 to 1930 period, either painted in the Rockies or in other locations, MacDonald continued the practice he established in his Algoma works of forgoing a traditional ground. He generally coated the front of his supports with shellac before painting, and in a few cases, worked directly on the bare paperboard. However, in a smaller number of sketches, MacDonald returned to his earlier method of covering the boards with a traditional ground layer before

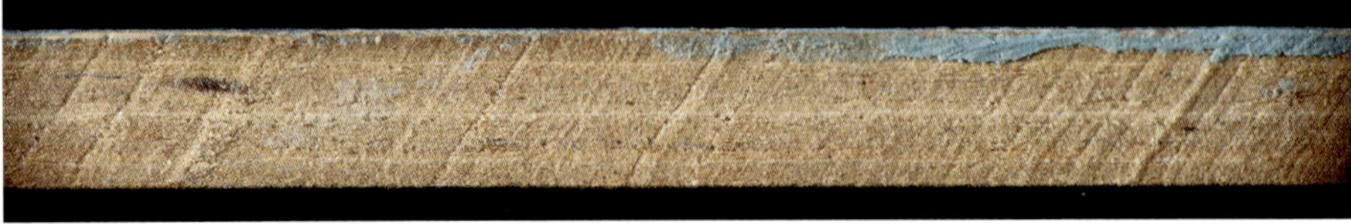

Example of a Rockies Type C board, *Mount Odaray*, 1930, National Gallery of Canada, Ottawa. Photos: © Government of Canada.

(top to bottom)
Fig. 2.11a: A 5 cm × 5 cm detail of the pale grey-brown back with relatively uniform appearance and a slight horizontal texture.

Fig. 2.11b: An edge of the board showing plies and diagonal cut marks. The board is 3.0 mm thick.

painting. Ground layers were most often observed on sketches from the latter part of the period: over half of the mountain sketches from 1930 that we examined included a traditional ground. The colour of the ground layers for these sketches varies from off-white through pale shades of pink or yellow. A few sketches show a more unusual layering that includes a shellac application combined with a thin, translucent underlayer, which was white in one case and green in three others.

Sketches from 1931 to 1932. We examined 11 sketches dating from the final years of MacDonald's life. Three were painted close to his home, and another three during his final sketching trip to Georgian Bay in 1931. The last five sketches in the study were painted during his 1932 trip to Barbados. Except for one double-sided sketch,[45] the supports that MacDonald used for these late sketches are similar to the Rockies Type C paperboard that he favoured during his 1929 and 1930 trips to British Columbia.

During 1931 and 1932, MacDonald appears to have returned more consistently to his earlier practice of coating his supports with a ground prior to painting. All but one of the sketches from this period that we examined include a light-coloured ground layer, with colours ranging from off-white through light yellow to orange or pink. As described in the following chapter, these light-coloured grounds reflect the brighter compositions seen in MacDonald's later interpretations of the atmosphere in the mountains and the southern light in Barbados.

The Studio Paintings

Throughout his career, MacDonald chose specific plein-air oil sketches as the inspiration for larger works that he painted in his studio. Although the supports for his sketches were the focus of our research, we also studied the supports and grounds for a small group of these studio paintings: five on rigid supports and nine on canvas.[46] These works span his career, with the earliest dating from 1912 and the latest from 1932.

Paintings on Rigid Supports

Although MacDonald painted most of his studio works on canvas, he sometimes chose to paint on rigid supports. In early exhibition catalogues and publications, these paintings are usually described simply as "oil on board." Other terms used in the past to describe these supports include pressed board, cardboard, or panel. MacDonald's studio paintings on rigid boards date primarily from the 1915 to 1918 period.[47] Notably, all nine studio paintings that MacDonald showed at the OSA exhibitions for 1916 and 1917 are described in E.R. Hunter's catalogue raisonné as "oil on board."[48]

We examined five studio paintings on rigid board from the years 1915 to 1917. *Belgium*, a mid-sized work produced in 1915, was commissioned for the war effort as either a poster or design for one. *The Tangled Garden* and *The Elements* are both well-known paintings from 1916. *In November* and *Harvest Evening Moon* were painted in 1917.

The supports for these five paintings are similar. They are all laminated, wood pulp-based fibreboards with a thickness of approximately 5 mm. When the faces of the board were accessible, we observed that they were orange-brown and exhibited a pebbled texture (Fig. 2.12). The laminated core of coarse wood pulp had an open, slightly porous appearance and was always paler than the outer faces. In a few cases, plies were visible within the core, while in other cases, there was less structure to the lamination. An example is illustrated in chapter 5 (Fig. 5.7).

Trademark stamps on the backs of two works, *Belgium* and *Harvest Evening Moon*, confirm that they were painted on the Beaver Board brand of fibreboard (Figs. 2.13a and 2.13b). This product was a type of medium-density, wood-pulp based fibreboard produced by the Beaver Manufacturing Company (renamed the Beaver Board Companies in 1914).[49] It was a very popular finishing board for interior walls during the first decades of the twentieth century.[50] In a testament to the success of the company, any fibreboard with characteristics similar to the Beaver Board brand is often referred to as "beaverboard," whether it includes a trademark stamp or not.

While the supports for *Belgium* and *Harvest Evening Moon* were confirmed to be the Beaver Board brand, in the case of the other three works on rigid supports, MacDonald painted the back face of the board and no manufacturer's stamps were

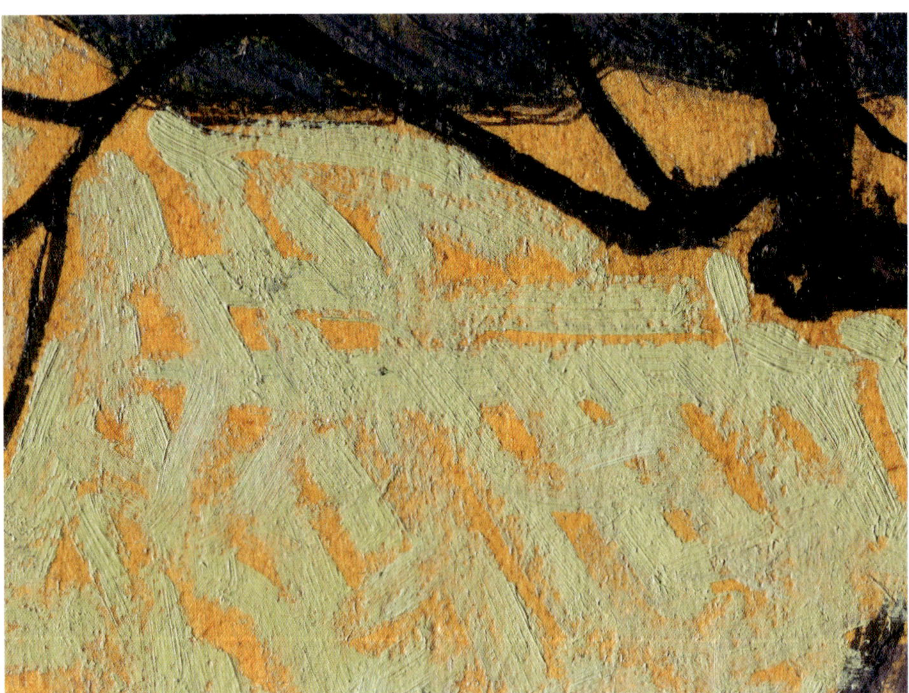

Fig. 2.12: A detail of *Belgium*, 1915, Art Gallery of Ontario, showing the orange-brown colour and pebbled texture of the exposed beaverboard support. Photo: © AGO.

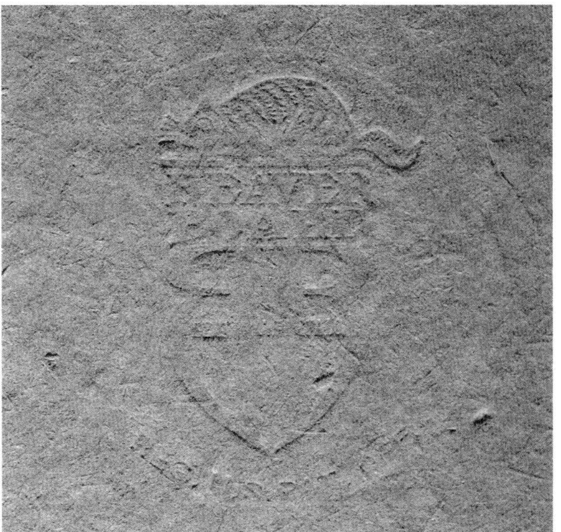

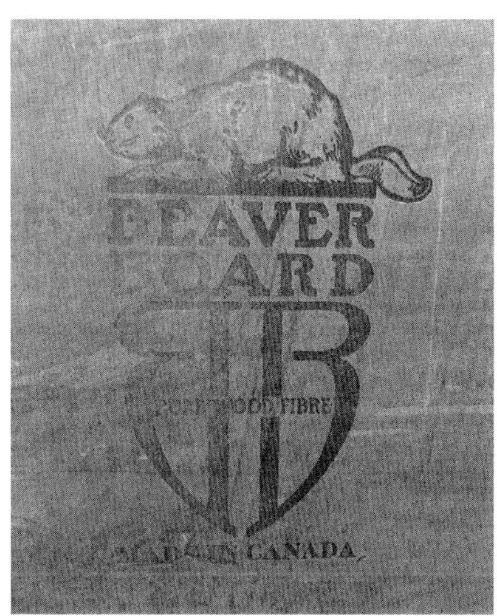

(left to right)
Fig. 2.13a: Impressed Beaver Board trademark, 5.6 cm high, on the back of *Belgium*, 1915, Art Gallery of Ontario. Photo: © AGO.

Fig. 2.13b: Inked Beaver Board trademark, 18.5 cm high, on the back of *Harvest Evening Moon*, 1917, McMichael Canadian Art Collection, 1978.31. Photo: © Government of Canada.

visible. However, the similarity of their characteristics to the stamped boards indicates they were undoubtedly also painted on supports manufactured by the Beaver Board Companies. We refer to all these supports with the generic name "beaverboard." It is notable that the support for *The Tangled Garden* is described as "beaver-board" in early correspondence held in the NGC curatorial files.[51]

A summary of the characteristics of the Beaver Board brand of wallboard, as described in patents and manufacturer's literature from the 1910 to 1920 period, is provided in the glossary. These characteristics match well with those of the supports for the five studio paintings that we examined, including the board thickness, colour, texture, and lamination. There were changes in the Beaver Board product over time.[52] Several examples of supports with a Beaver Board trademark used for paintings from the mid to late 1920s by other Group of Seven artists differ from MacDonald's earlier supports from the same manufacturer.[53]

At the time MacDonald was painting, wallboard from the Beaver Board company could be purchased from lumber dealers in 32- or 48-inch widths and with lengths of up to 9 feet.[54] The five paintings examined have varying dimensions and would have been cut down from larger boards. *The Tangled Garden*, like MacDonald's large-scale Algoma works on canvas, measures 121.3 × 152.3 cm (close to 4 × 5 ft.). In this case, it appears that he used the full 48-inch width of the board.

MacDonald began using beaverboard supports for his studio paintings around the time of his 1915 commission to paint a series of decorative murals for the living room of Dr. MacCallum's Georgian Bay cottage.[55] MacDonald, Arthur Lismer, and Tom Thomson used beaverboard as a painting support for these murals,[56] which is not surprising given its popularity as an interior wallboard. MacDonald would have become familiar with the properties of beaverboard while working on the murals, and he obviously found it suitable as a painting support. He may also have favoured beaverboard as a support during this period because it was inexpensive. MacDonald was never wealthy, and money was particularly short during the war years.

Preparation. None of the paintings on beaverboard that we studied include a traditional ground layer. Examination with UV illumination suggested that, in most cases, MacDonald coated the front of the boards with varnish prior to painting. The yellow-green fluorescence of these varnish layers indicates that they do not correspond to orange shellac.[57] Certain of the paintings on beaverboard have an overall varnish on top of the painted composition. These surface varnishes partially obscured the fluorescence of layers beneath, making it difficult to determine through examination with UV illumination whether MacDonald coated the front of the board with varnish before painting. As described in chapter 4, the presence of a varnish coating on the beaverboard applied prior to painting was confirmed for several of the works through the examination of cross-sections.

For three paintings (*The Tangled Garden*, *The Elements*, and *In November*) MacDonald coated the back of the beaverboard with grey paint. In the case of *The Tangled Garden* and *The Elements*, the UV fluorescence suggested that shellac was applied on top of the grey paint in areas on the back. MacDonald did not paint or varnish the back of the support for *Belgium*. *Harvest Evening Moon*, on the other hand, showed evidence of an uneven varnish layer on the back.

Paintings on Canvas

MacDonald painted most of his studio works on canvas, a traditional painting support made of woven fabric. The characteristics that influence the appearance and properties of canvases for painting include the fibre composition, the weave type, and the thread count (a measure of the fineness of the weave). Canvases were typically tacked or nailed to a wooden framework, called a stretcher, to hold them taut for painting. Technical terms related to canvas and stretcher properties are defined in the glossary.

Sources for canvas. Early-twentieth-century catalogues from Toronto-based artists' supply firms[58] list a variety of canvas types for sale. Linen, cotton, jute, and burlap fabric are all itemized and are sometimes specified as British, French, or American in origin. The glossary provides brief descriptions of these fabric types. Price lists available for consultation indicate that linen was significantly more expensive than cotton or jute.[59] Some canvas types were available in various textures, from coarse to very fine, as well as with different weave types.[60] In the catalogues consulted, while linen and cotton were available in various formats cut to size, jute or burlap canvas could only be purchased by the yard in a limited range of widths. MacDonald would also have had access to canvas from sources other than local artists' supply companies. For example, as described in the previous chapter, Lawren Harris purchased a large roll of jute canvas from New Jersey in around 1913 and shared it with his painting colleagues.[61]

Artists could purchase canvases with a ground layer already applied by the manufacturer or could purchase bare canvas and prepare it themselves. In the period when MacDonald was active, artists' supply firms most often sold canvases for painting that were pre-prepared with a ground layer. In the catalogues consulted, only "prepared canvases" are listed, indicating that they had a ground layer applied by the manufacturer. This was the case whether the fabric was purchased as a roll, by the yard, or already mounted on a stretcher. Both double-primed (with two ground layers) or single-primed canvases were available.[62] Although the catalogues only listed prepared canvases, unprimed canvas may have been available on request.[63] MacDonald may also have purchased fabric from sources other than artists' supply firms.

Prepared canvases were available for purchase, mounted on pre-assembled stretchers in standard sizes. The historic catalogues show that, at this time, artists could also purchase individual stretcher bars cut to various lengths,[64] allowing them to build stretchers with a wide range of dimensions. Only one type of stretcher construction style, referred to as the "Pfleger type," is listed in the catalogues that we consulted. This stretcher construction, described in the glossary, was commonly used throughout the twentieth century.

Canvas supports. Of the nine studio paintings on canvas that we examined, three were on cotton supports, with either a plain or a basket weave.[65] The paintings on cotton fabric include two from MacDonald's Algoma period and an earlier work from 1912. Five of the nine examined paintings are on a plain-woven, coarse, open-weave jute fabric. Works on jute include four representing Algoma subjects and a 1925 view of the Rocky Mountains. Finally, one late painting, *Goat Range, Rocky Mountains*, completed shortly before MacDonald's death, is on a basket-woven, jute and linen fabric (Fig. 2.14).

While jute is a less traditional choice than linen as a painting support, MacDonald used it regularly, as did other painters of the period, including Tom Thomson and Group of Seven colleagues. There is evidence that MacDonald used jute as a painting support as early as 1913.[66] The jute fabric for three of MacDonald's Algoma paintings has a very similar appearance and thread count (approximately 7v × 7h threads per cm), suggesting that they could be from the same bolt.

As described in the following chapter on MacDonald's painting technique, one of the reasons that he chose coarse, open-weave jute as a support was to provide intentional texture to his painted surfaces. The lower cost of jute and its availability in wide rolls may also have been factors. Although these jute canvases had qualities that MacDonald valued, the fabric is less elastic than cotton or linen and becomes even more brittle as it ages. Condition issues related to MacDonald's paintings on jute are discussed further in chapter 5.

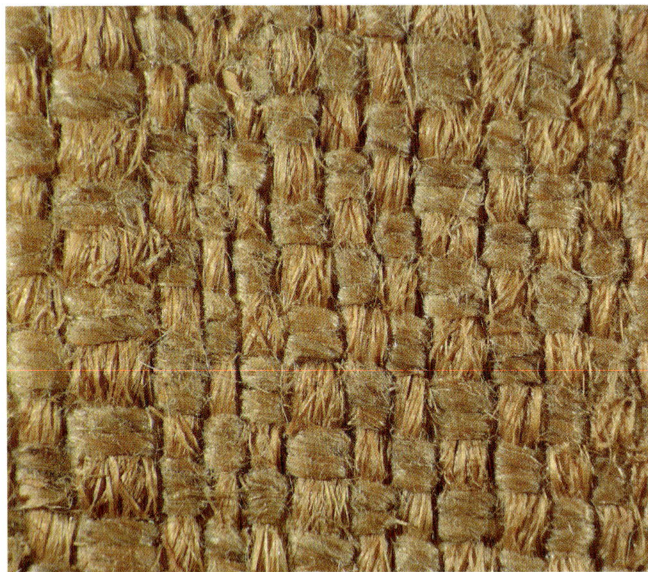

Fig. 2.14: Detail of the back of the canvas support for *Goat Range, Rocky Mountains*, 1932, McMichael Canadian Art Collection, 1979.35, showing double threads of linen fibres (horizontal) and jute fibres (vertical). Photo: McMichael.

The dimensions of MacDonald's oil paintings on canvas are variable; however, there were certain sizes that he favoured.[67] For example, *Leaves in the Brook* and *Goat Range, Rocky Mountains* are of similar dimensions, both measuring approximately 53 × 65 cm (21 × 26 in.), a size that MacDonald also used for a number of other mid-scale oil paintings on canvas. Three of the large-scale paintings in the study group are approximately 122 × 153 cm (4 × 5 ft.). This is a common format for MacDonald's largest paintings and suggests that he may have been using canvas from a 48-inch-wide roll.

While the stretchers for MacDonald's paintings on canvas were often replaced during past restorations, four of the examined works remain on their original stretchers. Three of these have the same corner join construction, described in the glossary, which matches the Pfleger-type stretchers illustrated in the consulted catalogues. The original stretcher for *The Solemn Land*, painted in 1921, on the other hand, has a slightly different construction, with simple mortise-and-tenon slot joins.

The sizes of MacDonald's works on canvas do not generally correspond to the standard pre-assembled stretcher dimensions listed in the artists' supply catalogues. MacDonald may have purchased his stretcher bars by the piece and assembled them to his preferred dimensions. An ink stamp on the stretcher for the 1925 painting *Mount Goodsir, Yoho Park* confirms that this stretcher, either already assembled or by the piece, was purchased from the E. Harris Company. While the stamp shows that MacDonald sometimes purchased commercial stretcher components, it is also possible that he made some of his own stretchers from scratch; he was an experienced woodworker and is known to have built and carved decorative frames for certain paintings.[68]

Preparation. The nine paintings on canvas that we examined were all prepared with a traditional ground, an opaque layer composed of pigments in a drying oil medium. In all cases, the ground layers appear white to off-white. The ground for *Early Evening, Winter* has a slight grey tone, while the Algoma paintings have warmer, off-white grounds, some with a slight orange tint. As is shown in chapter 4, chemical analysis of the ground layers illustrates that there is a wide variation in their compositions.

Even with close examination, we could not always determine with certainty whether the ground layer on a given painting was applied by MacDonald himself or if he used a pre-prepared canvas. This determination was especially difficult for paintings that had undergone previous conservation treatments. Nevertheless, among the nine paintings in our study group, we were able to establish that MacDonald used both canvases with commercially applied grounds as well as canvases that he prepared himself.

The grey-white ground for *Early Evening, Winter* and the warm, off-white ground of *The Solemn Land* are both almost certainly commercially applied. For these two paintings, the ground layer is even and uniform in both thickness and colour. It extends to the tacked edges of the canvas, which remains on its original stretcher. The ground layer for *Goat Range, Rocky Mountains*, on the other hand, appears to be artist-applied. The thick application of white ground has an unusual pebbly texture, and some of the ground has pushed through the open-weave canvas to the back of the painting. The ground is only present on the front surface of the fabric, leaving the canvas edges bare. This indicates that the canvas was on its stretcher when the ground was applied.[69] Research on Tom Thomson's materials showed that he also painted on canvas supports that he prepared himself as well as on commercially prepared canvas.[70]

A good sketch is a strong suggestion of nature, so confident that its simplicity is not perceived.

– J.E.H. MacDonald, Lecture Notes, Untitled, General Art, n.d. [circa 1925]

Design from nature rather than copy her. You will find a general trend in the lines and masses under varying details. Bring that out.

– J.E.H. MacDonald, Lecture Notes, Untitled, General Art, n.d. [circa 1925]

A picture is not the reflection of a thing seen, but a compound of feelings aroused in the artist by the thing seen, resulting, according to his skill, in a more concentrated expression than the natural objects can give.

– J.E.H. MacDonald, Lectures, Painting and Poetry, 1929

3. PAINTING TECHNIQUE

At the height of his career, MacDonald's paintings reveal a mastery of colour mixing, a sureness of brushstroke, and a deep understanding of compositional design that allowed him to capture form, light, and movement. This chapter describes the evolution of MacDonald's painting technique, highlighting some of the key methods that he developed as he matured as an artist. Excerpts from his diaries and lecture notes provide a glimpse into some of his thoughts about painting and give a framework for our observations.

The Sketches

Sketching, the First Outdoor Sport

MacDonald created his small, plein-air oil sketches through direct observation of nature. As he gained experience, he developed a quick and efficient sketching style, finding ways of painting that helped him capture both the essence of the subject and the subtle effects of light and weather. These sketches show a range of completeness; while many are a rapid summary of a view, others are more fully developed and detailed.

When sketching outdoors, it would have taken MacDonald about two to three hours to realize a sketch from start to finish. If all went well, by the end of the day, he would have had three, or possibly even four, completed works. In a letter from A.Y. Jackson to his cousin, written during the second boxcar trip to Algoma in 1919, he wrote, "The other chaps are all out sketching under umbrellas. They are all trying to turn out four a day and can't stop if it rains."[1]

Based on entries from his 1930 diary, MacDonald often completed three sketches a day on his trips to the Rocky Mountains. On September 1, 1930, he wrote that in the morning he "tried a sketch by big cliff once more but got lost in rock drawing.... Cached kit to save bringing up again after lunch." That same afternoon, he "made two sketches, a bit better."[2] The following day, he also described making one sketch in the morning and two in the afternoon. We learned from his diaries that MacDonald did not always finish a sketch in a single sitting. On September 12, 1930, he wrote that he was "up on slopes of Wiwaxy to work on an unfinished sketch."[3]

Although MacDonald would have painted most of his oil sketches outdoors, directly in front of his subject, there is evidence that he also sometimes worked from pencil drawings or from recollections of a view. In a diary entry from 1905, MacDonald's wife described an early instance of him painting from memory, perhaps inspired to work on his oil painting technique after a visit to the Tate Gallery earlier in the day. She wrote that when he returned from the gallery in the afternoon, "he made a sketch at home in oils. Moonlight – elms and water." A note in MacDonald's own diary from his trip to the Rockies in 1930 provides further evidence. During an afternoon of poor weather, he wrote, "Pouring rain. Sat in cabin dozing beside stove and afterwards worked a little at moonlight memory of [O'Hara]."[4] Moreover, the extensive colour notes that he added on certain pencil drawings in his sketchbooks[5] suggests that he considered working them up in paint.

MacDonald usually sketched with a compact wooden paintbox on his lap, with the open lid functioning as an easel (pages 47 and 173). We were able to locate two of his paintboxes for study. One of these, made for MacDonald by his son, is in the McMichael collection, while the other is owned by a private collector. Appendix A provides descriptions and photographs of the two boxes and some of their contents. A note from Thoreau MacDonald on the lid of the McMichael paintbox states that his father used it from 1920 to 1932, including on all his trips to the Rocky Mountains. The privately owned paintbox is commercial, originating from the paint manufacturer Madderton & Company. MacDonald likely used it before 1920, after which he presumably sketched with the box that his son had made for him.[6]

The bottoms of both paintboxes were equipped with dividers to organize brushes and other painting materials. This differs from the type of portable paintbox that A.Y. Jackson designed in 1914, in which the bottom of the box functioned as a palette.[7] MacDonald would have carried a separate palette and, as illustrated in Appendix A, the materials in his Madderton & Company paintbox included one.

While MacDonald regularly used his paintbox lid to support his boards as he sketched, there is evidence that he sometimes carried a portable easel for working outdoors.[8] Moreover, he considered an umbrella to be essential equipment for sketching[9] to protect against both rain and bright sunlight, and he is pictured with one in a number of photographs (page 154 and 173). His friend Tommy Link described him sketching in the Rockies, saying that "he always carried a heavy ulster [overcoat] folded over his arm and a collapsible umbrella, which he stuck into the ground."[10] In addition, his sketching gear would have included a palette, paint tubes, brushes, an oil bottle,[11] and possibly a small carrier to transport completed sketches.[12] A description of MacDonald hiking some of the difficult trails in the Rockies portrays him with "a backpack strapped on aft and a paintbox and portable easel fore."[13]

As well as the difficulties of carrying painting equipment over rough terrain, MacDonald and his painting friends also regularly faced inclement weather when sketching outdoors. In a letter to his son from Coboconk, Ontario, in July 1921, MacDonald wrote that "sketching is not being done by yours truly. Too warm and the landscape not compelling enough to beat the heat."[14] At the other extreme was the often cold weather in the Rockies. For example, in a late August 1925 diary entry he recorded, "Very misty and cold windy weather. Had to find tree or rock shelter to work."[15] In September 1930, he wrote, "Very cold and bleak and got stomach chill, etc."[16] Low temperatures not only made sketching uncomfortable, but they could also affect the materials. For example, in March 1920, Jackson wrote to MacDonald from Georgian Bay, "Still dull and windy, but the cold is no longer making the flake white hard and I have used a considerable quantity of it."[17]

Despite its challenges, outdoor sketching was one of MacDonald's greatest pleasures. In a 1925 book review, MacDonald wrote that a plein-air painter "needs no sport to amuse him outdoors. He has the one great sport."[18] This idea is echoed in a set of MacDonald's fragmentary lecture notes, likely written around the same time, titled "Sketching, the first outdoor sport" at the top of the first page.[19] An intriguing mix of instructional and philosophical information, these unpublished lecture notes provide insight not only into MacDonald's passion for sketching and his ideas about art in general, but also include information about the techniques that he considered important to create a successful oil sketch. Appendix C includes reproductions and transcriptions of the four pages of notes.

The following sections summarize our observations about MacDonald's painting technique, based on examination of 160 sketches. Careful observation revealed that MacDonald put into practice many of the ideas described in his lecture notes. He began to apply these concepts to his oil sketches early in his career and, at the height of his artistic powers during the Algoma period, he used them with great skill. His lecture notes informed our observations about his sketching methods, and we have included excerpts from them throughout.

Early Sketches: 1909 to 1913

The role of the ground. As described in the previous chapter, MacDonald's sketching supports were prepared with a traditional ground layer, usually off-white or grey, in all the early oil sketches that we examined. During this period, MacDonald covered the ground almost completely using a thick, multi-layered paint application. There are occasional thinly applied passages or small areas between brushstrokes where the ground remains visible in these early sketches; however, any exposed ground does not play a significant role in the design, and its colour has a negligible effect on the overall impression of the work.

Underdrawing and underpainting. A common technique to delineate compositional elements before painting is to create a rapid drawing of the general outlines of forms on top of the ground layer. This type of preliminary drawing, or underdrawing, is usually done in a carbon-based medium such as graphite pencil or charcoal. While some members of the Group of Seven used pencil underdrawings to guide their oil sketches,[20] we found no evidence of this on MacDonald's early sketches. To supplement the visual observations, we also undertook infrared (IR) photography of two early sketches.[21] When carbon-based underdrawings are present, they often preferentially absorb IR radiation, rendering them visible using IR photography. No indication of this type of preliminary drawing was visible in the IR photographs of the two early sketches that were examined.

While no pencil underdrawings were observed, our visual examinations did reveal that MacDonald used thin lines of fluid brown paint to delineate outlines of the composition in some of these early works. Figure 3.1 shows a small area of exposed grey ground on a sketch from 1909 where a stroke of this brown underpainting is visible. Unlike MacDonald's later technique, the only role of these preliminary lines is to act as a guide for the painting; they are essentially invisible after the work is complete. Because these preliminary outlines are only visible in very small areas of exposed ground, it is difficult to know the extent to which MacDonald used such underpainting in his early works.

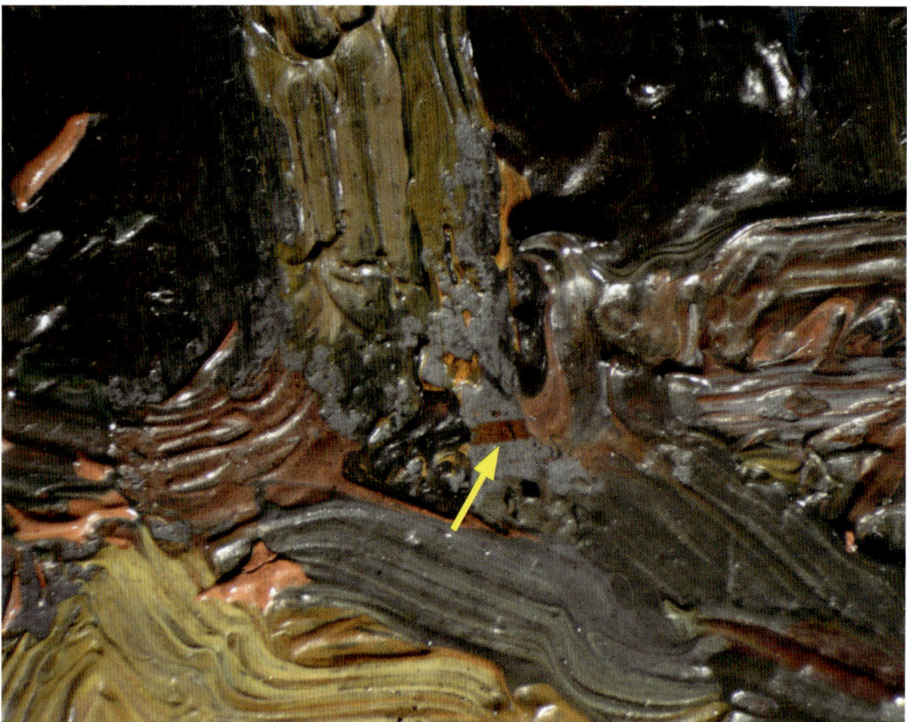

Fig. 3.1: Detail of *Oaks, October Morning*, 1909, McMichael Canadian Art Collection, 1966.15.15. A small area of exposed grey ground, and a thin, horizontal line of dilute brown underpainting (marked with an arrow) are visible. Photo: © McMichael.

Composition and brushwork. *Snow, High Park* (Fig. 1.1), painted in 1909, is typical of MacDonald's earliest sketches. He applied his opaque oil paint vigorously, with fluid strokes. The pronounced brushstrokes produce a low relief or texture on the surface, known as impasto. Paint strokes were brushed one on top of the other, with the upper layer often applied while the lower layer of paint was still wet, called a "wet-in-wet" technique. The way that MacDonald blended and layered the wet paint has led to a subdued, somewhat muddy effect in some areas (Fig. 3.2). Passages of heavily worked paint and muted colours are typical of his earliest sketches. Also typical of this period, and observed in later sketches as well, is the addition of details and highlights with small dabs and strokes of paint, applied after the paint beneath was dry to the touch. Works from 1912 and 1913, from the end of his early period, although still showing areas of wet-in-wet layering and colour blending, often have a cleaner and brighter palette.

MacDonald's early technique is evident in a cross-section sample from *Snow, High Park* (Fig. 3.3). As described in the glossary, a cross-section is a microscopic fragment removed from a painting that is specially prepared to illustrate the layering of the ground and paint. The cross-section in Fig. 3.3 shows multiple, thick applications of variously coloured paint, revealing a high degree of layering and reworking. In fact, close examination of the painting indicated that MacDonald painted the current image over an earlier one that he must have considered unsuccessful.[22]

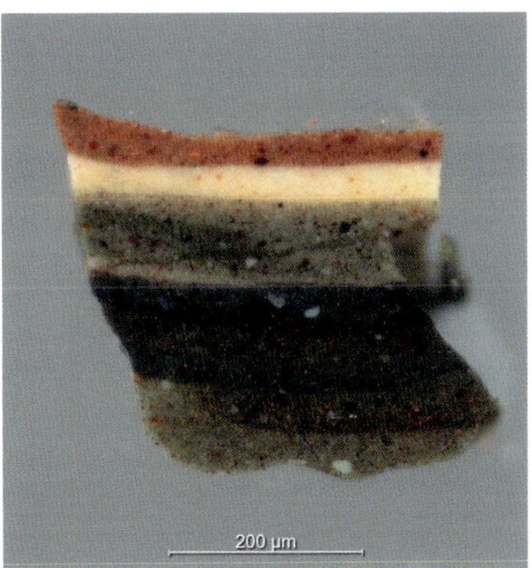

Fig. 3.3: A partial cross-section from the top edge of *Snow, High Park*, 1909, McMichael Canadian Art Collection, 1981.24, with multiple applications of variously coloured paint. The sample is missing the white ground layer at the bottom, and the blue paint of the sky at the top. Photo: © Government of Canada.

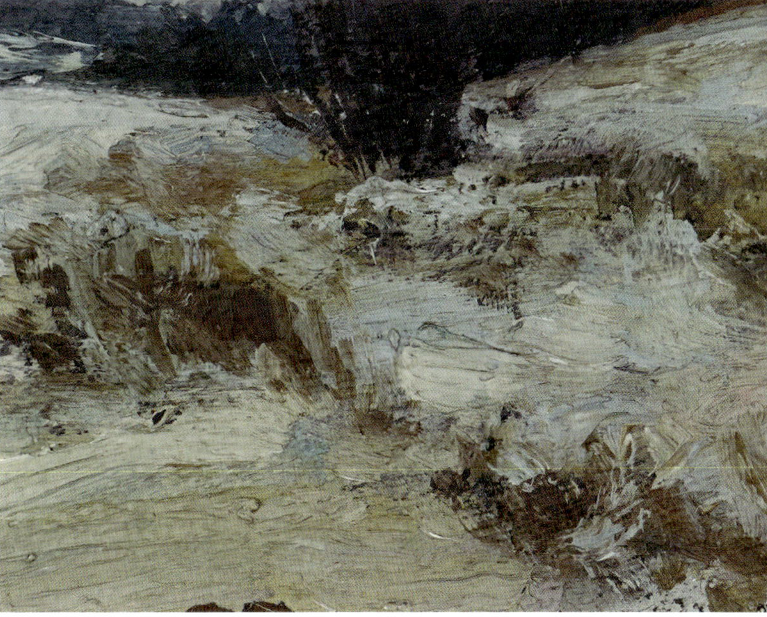

Fig. 3.2: Detail of *Snow, High Park*, 1909, McMichael Canadian Art Collection, 1981.24, showing wet-in-wet paint application. Photo: McMichael. (see p. 20)

Transitional Sketches: 1914 to 1917

The role of the ground. For most of the examined sketches from the 1914 to 1917 period, we observed that MacDonald applied coloured ground layers to his paperboard supports. These coloured grounds were usually in warm tones of pink or red through orange or yellow. As described in the previous chapter, this range of colours is similar to those observed for the grounds of Tom Thomson's sketches on paperboard from 1914 and 1915.[23]

Like Thomson,[24] MacDonald left areas of these grounds deliberately exposed at brushstroke edges so that the bare areas of warmly coloured ground became part of the overall colour and texture of the sketch. Figure 3.4 is a detail of *Near Minden*, painted in 1916 or 1917, showing exposed areas of the yellow-orange ground. This method represents the first step towards the technique that MacDonald used in his Algoma sketches, where unpainted areas of support play an important structural role in the overall design.

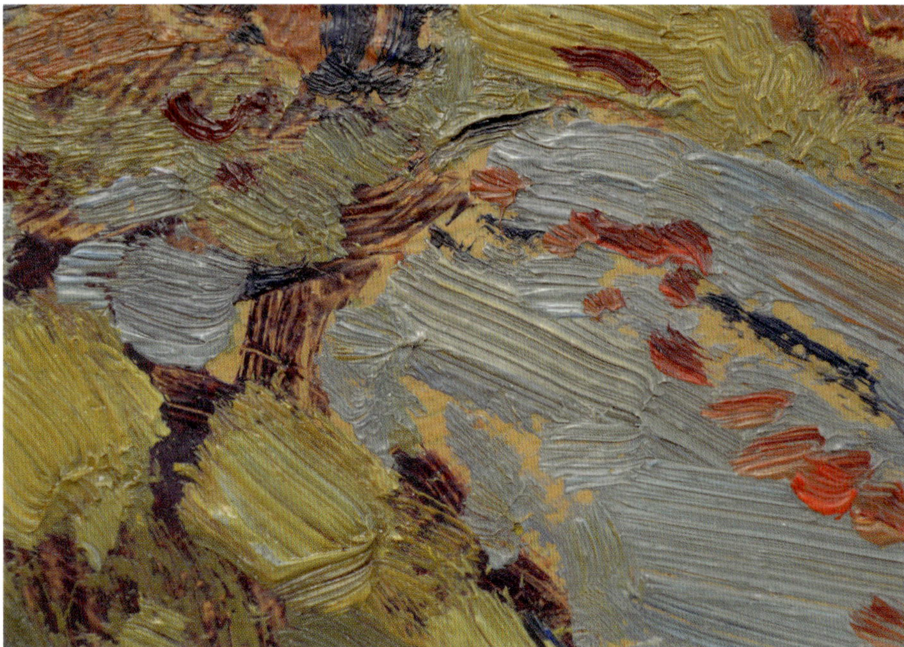

Fig. 3.4: Detail of *Near Minden*, 1916 or 1917, McMichael Canadian Art Collection, 1966.15.12, showing areas of exposed yellow-orange ground at brushstroke edges. Sketchy, purple underpainting is also visible at centre left. Photo: McMichael. (see p. 26)

Underdrawing and underpainting. None of the examined sketches from this period showed visual evidence of carbon-based underdrawing. However, IR photography of two sketches revealed that one of them, *Sunflower Study, Tangled Garden Sketch*, included a few compositional drawing lines under the paint, likely in graphite pencil. Although MacDonald used some limited underdrawing in this sketch, he created more extensive preliminary outlines with dilute red-orange and deep pink oil paint (Fig. 3.5). This outlining in paint – a sketch before the sketch, so to speak – was used to delineate basic compositional elements for many of his works during this period.

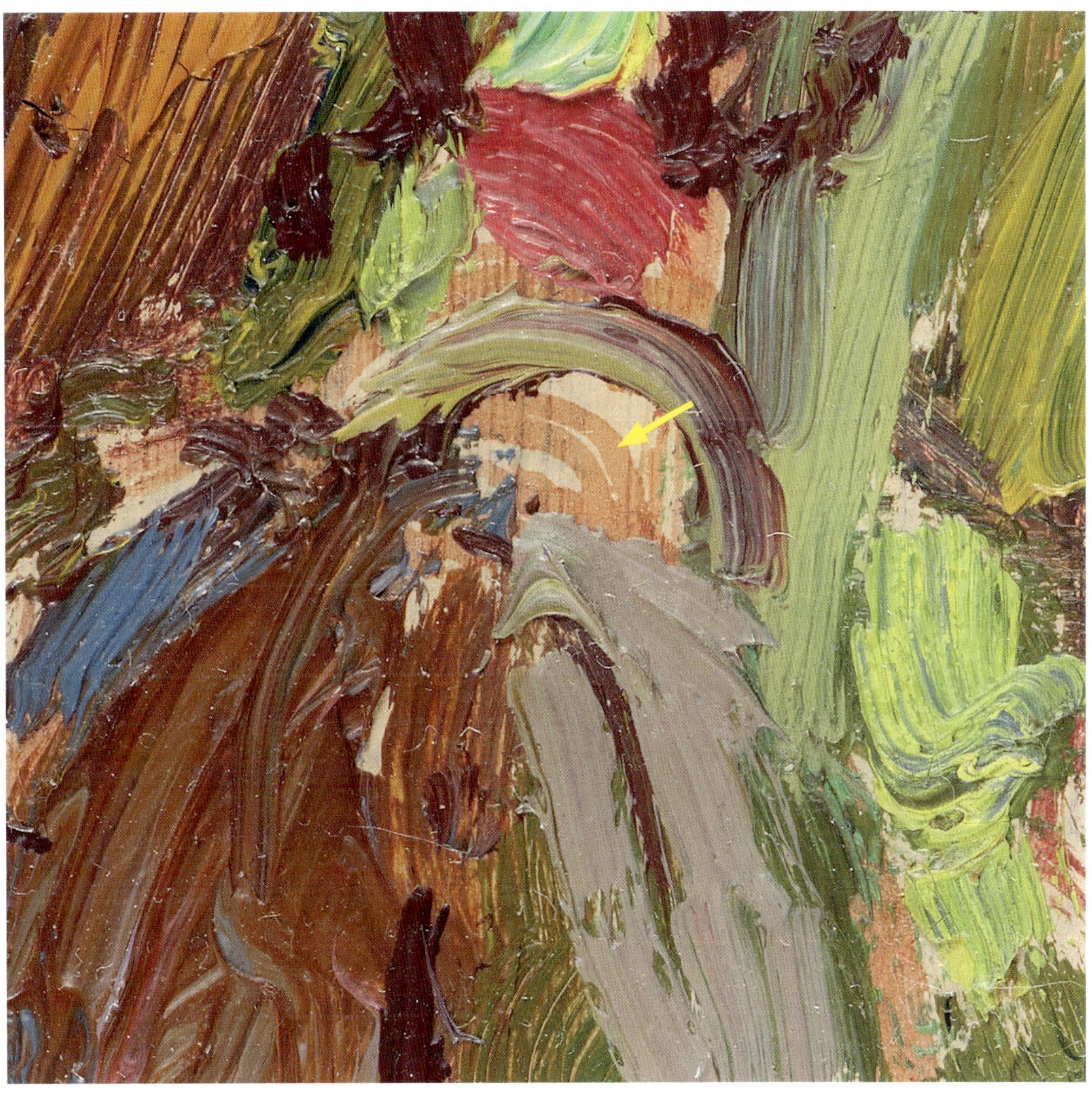

Fig. 3.5: Detail of *Sunflower Study, Tangled Garden Sketch*, circa 1915, McMichael Canadian Art Collection, 1966.16.38. Curved lines of dilute orange-brown underpainting are visible at centre right (shown with an arrow). Exposed pale pink ground can be seen between the strokes of underpainting. Photo: © Government of Canada.

Because MacDonald left areas of the ground bare in these sketches, the underpainting is usually visible in multiple areas.

MacDonald's use of thinned underpainting to outline the composition is consistent with his notes on sketching. His instructions on "drawing for the oil sketch" include an abbreviated explanation of his method: "Brush outline, thin wash in, highlights strong."[25] The paint that MacDonald used for his preliminary underpainting lines often appears to have been diluted, likely with either turpentine or oil. Oil paint thinned with turpentine would have dried quickly, allowing him to progress rapidly to the application of the opaque oil paint of his image layers. In this period, these preliminary outlines are most often in hues of dark red, red-brown, purple, or blue.

Composition and brushwork. MacDonald's sketches from 1914 to 1917 show a more confident handling of paint than in his earlier works. The 1914 sketch *Logs on the Gatineau River* (Fig. 1.4) exemplifies how MacDonald was developing new ways of painting while still maintaining earlier methods.

In *Logs on the Gatineau River*, as in other sketches from this period, he continued to apply his paint in opaque, vigorous strokes, using passages of wet-in-wet technique with highlights and details added with dabs or short strokes of colour. However, he also began to apply more directional, adjacent paint strokes of individual hues. He placed some of these brushstrokes side-by-side, separated by areas of exposed ground. Other brushstrokes overlap. In these overlapping strokes, MacDonald skillfully applied the upper paint so that it picked up some wet paint beneath, creating streaks of colour without marring the individual tones, allowing him to achieve more vibrant hues (Fig. 3.6). He also began to favour complementary colour combinations, such as the strong blue and orange hues used in *Logs on the Gatineau River*.

Many sketches from this period give the impression that MacDonald painted them rapidly, compared to some of his earlier, more highly worked compositions. MacDonald definitely understood that sketching quickly was an asset. In his unpublished notes, he wrote that "Speed helps in sketching just as in sprinting. Try to grasp the idea of your subject quickly. Then put it down before you can form any doubts about it. Get the effect, it goes quickest, the objects remain and can be studied at leisure if need be."[26]

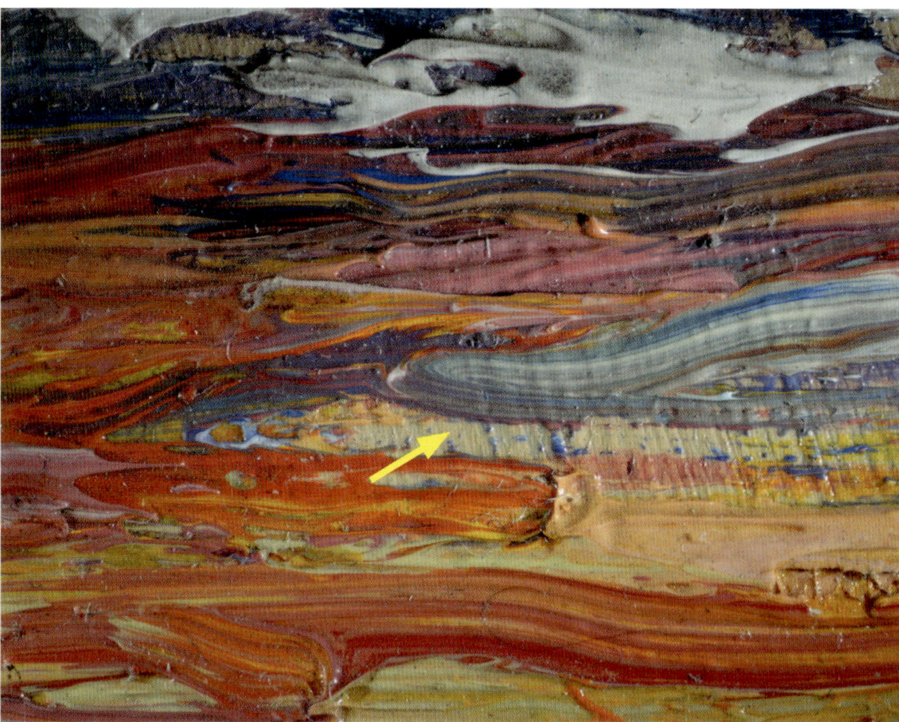

Fig. 3.6: Detail of foreground logs in *Logs on the Gatineau River*, 1914, McMichael Canadian Art Collection, 1981.85.5, showing overlapping brushstrokes with streaks of colour. Areas of the pale orange ground (shown with an arrow) are visible between some of the strokes. Photo: McMichael. (see p. 23)

Algoma: 1918 to 1923

The role of the support. As described in the previous chapter, MacDonald stopped using traditional ground layers at the time of his first trip to Algoma in 1918, preferring to paint directly on his thin paperboard supports, usually after sealing them with shellac. He regularly left areas of the support unpainted so that the pale brown to grey-brown paperboard, often saturated and warmed with a shellac coating, became an integral part of the finished sketch. This technique parallels and builds upon his earlier method of leaving areas of his coloured grounds visible between brushstrokes and forms.

The colour of MacDonald's paperboard supports is a unifying component in the design of his Algoma sketches. The exposed board between areas of paint acts to structure and contain the vigorous strokes of colour. A striking example is the representation of the shadowed, rocky hillside in *Solemn Land, Algoma* (Fig. 3.7). Sometimes, patterns of exposed support serve to draw the eye along compositional elements like trees, water, and horizon lines. In *Moose Lake, Algoma* (Fig. 1.12), the linear, diagonal dashes of exposed brown paperboard in the water help to lead the viewer's eye across the waves to the island shore, then the visible board between sky and clouds creates a slanted path across the sky in the opposite direction.

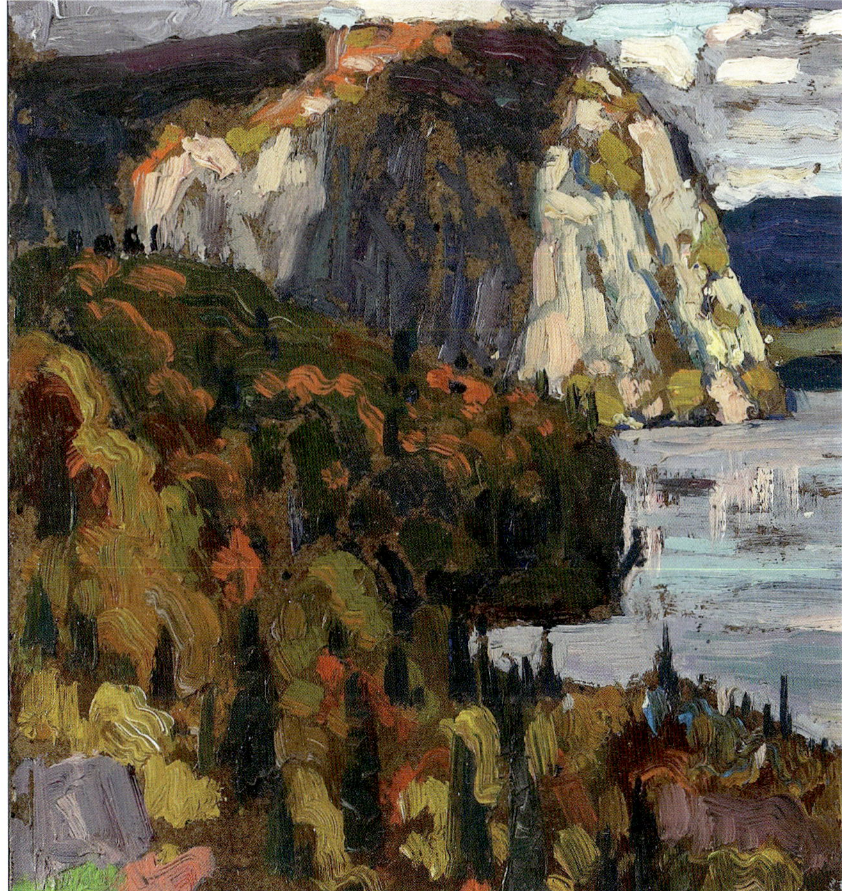

Fig. 3.7: Detail of *Solemn Land, Algoma*, circa 1919, Art Gallery of Ontario, showing areas of exposed, grey-brown paperboard that give structure to the shadowed, rocky shoreline. Photo: © AGO. (see p. 36)

Other future members of the Group of Seven, as well as Tom Thomson, used this same device. Harold Town described the method as "invisible drawing" because the bare board or panel created a path for the eye between colour areas.[27] MacDonald himself mentioned A.Y. Jackson's use of this technique in a 1920 letter to W.J. Wood: "Jackson uses small panels of birch in sketching the 8 ½ × 10 ½ size. He paints directly on the unprimed wood, letting the clear wood show through a great deal to make a unifying tone."[28]

These artists regularly exchanged ideas and learned by studying each other's sketches. For example, describing one of the Algoma trips, MacDonald wrote that "after dishwashing, the sketches are taken out of the painting boxes and each sketcher is required to show his productions."[29] Their mutual influence is clear in many aspects of their technique, including the rigorous and deliberate use of the support as a design element.

Underdrawing and underpainting. While we noted no indication of pencil underdrawing, the delineation of forms with lines of translucent, thinned oil paint became a staple of MacDonald's practice in his Algoma sketches. The most common colours for these compositional designs were dark blue, purple, or shades of red, from deep crimson through red-brown (Fig. 3.8). He occasionally used tints that appear close to black or dark green, created through mixing multiple paint colours, and he sometimes used more than one colour for underpainting on a single sketch. Thoreau MacDonald described his father laying in these preliminary painted outlines, writing that "in the open he was a fast, expert worker, and it was a pleasure to watch him at it. He swiftly drew in his layout or design, usually with permanent blue, then with nervous energy put down the complete drawing."[30]

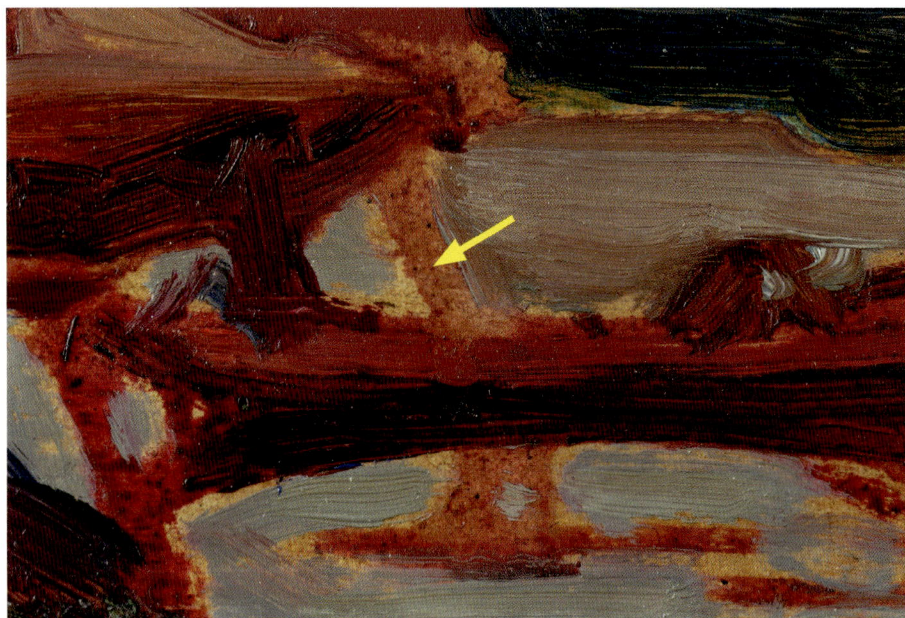

Fig. 3.8: Detail of *Mist Fantasy*, 1920, National Gallery of Canada, Ottawa. Slightly grainy, dilute red underpainting (one stroke shown with an arrow) is visible between the grey strokes of paint near the centre of the image. Photo © Government of Canada.

MacDonald covered, or partially covered, his underpainting in the completed sketch. However, he regularly left areas of these compositional outlines visible, so that they became part of the finished work. For example, he often created tree trunk forms with these underpainting lines. Figure 3.9 shows a detail from *Moose Lake, Algoma* where the lively, red-brown underpainting creates the foreground tree trunks and branches.

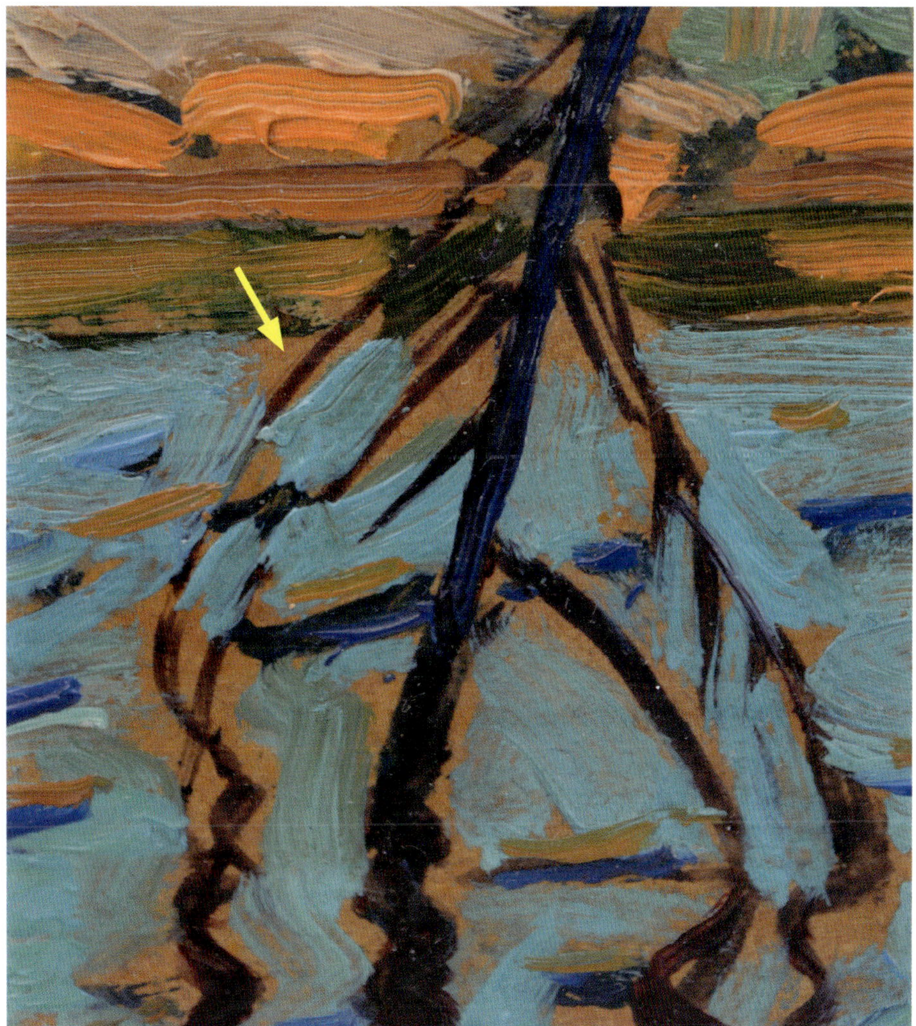

Fig. 3.9: Detail of *Moose Lake, Algoma*, 1920, McMichael Canadian Art Collection, 1966.15.4, showing red-brown underpainting used to create the tree trunk and branches. Areas of the shellac-coated paperboard are exposed between the branches and the blue paint of the water (shown with an arrow). Photo: McMichael. (see p. 33)

Composition and brushwork. MacDonald shows an artistic maturity in his Algoma sketches, manifested by the virtuosity of his colour mixing, the confidence of his brushstrokes, and his skill in compositional design.

His lecture notes on sketching speak to the value of observing rhythms in the profiles and masses of forms as part of compositional design. He wrote, for example, "A profile is the limit of a solid mass. Even though that solidity has the different qualities of cloud and rock," and went on to add that "the eye tends to travel along the edges of masses – make their direction rhythmical." He described the overall composition, stating that "the foreground should be in the front of the sketch and the background in the rear. Things should move inwards on the earth and outwards in the sky."[31] In another set of notes, for a lecture entitled "The Decorative Element in Art," MacDonald defined rhythm as "joint action or movement, a relation or connection of parts that leads the eye pleasantly through all the details of a design."[32]

These thoughts on rhythm and design are reflected in some earlier sketches, like *Logs on the Gatineau River* (Fig. 1.4), where the diagonal brushstrokes of the logs in the foreground lead the viewer to the mid-ground shore and background hills. By the Algoma period, MacDonald executed these concepts with exceptional skill.

In *Algoma Hills* (Fig. 1.11), the eye travels along the upwardly curving profile of the rocks to the mid-ground and finally outwards with the open, fanning brushstrokes of the sky. MacDonald's expert grasp of design is also embodied in his sketch for *Leaves in the Brook* (Fig. 1.13), where the large rock in the foreground leads the viewer into the composition, then along the diagonal brushstrokes of the stream upwards to the dark shadows under the foliage.

These Algoma sketches also exemplify how MacDonald used brushwork to create a sense of solidity, or what he called "values of mass."[33] He built up individual elements, such as a rock or a flowing brook, by applying directional, rhythmical brushstrokes that follow the form. He then created contrast as well as a sense of depth by adding perpendicular, juxtaposed strokes in adjacent areas or forms.

MacDonald's Algoma sketches typically show a fluid application of paint with an oil-rich, thick texture.[34] MacDonald applied the paint assuredly and deliberately, using pronounced brushstrokes to create low impasto. He sometimes laid down his colours side-by-side with bare support in the areas between, and in other passages, he confidently layered wet-in-wet paint to achieve a controlled partial blending of hues (Fig. 3.10).

His palette is bright, sometimes with dramatic complementary colour combinations, but remains naturalistic, with foliage reflecting the brilliant autumn colours in Ontario. MacDonald created the values and hues in his sketches with a masterful mixing of colour. As described in the following chapter, which provides an in-depth discussion of the composition of his paints, MacDonald achieved his mixed colours with combinations from a relatively restrained palette of about eight pigments, along with black and white.

Based on our examination of his brushstrokes, in some cases, MacDonald appears to have used a single brush of about a centimetre in width to create an entire sketch, brushing in longer strokes as well as in short dab-like applications. He also sometimes chose a larger brush, producing strokes just under two centimetres in width. For selected areas of the foreground, defined leaves, and bright highlights of reflected light, he chose smaller brushes of approximately 3 mm in width (Fig. 3.10). As

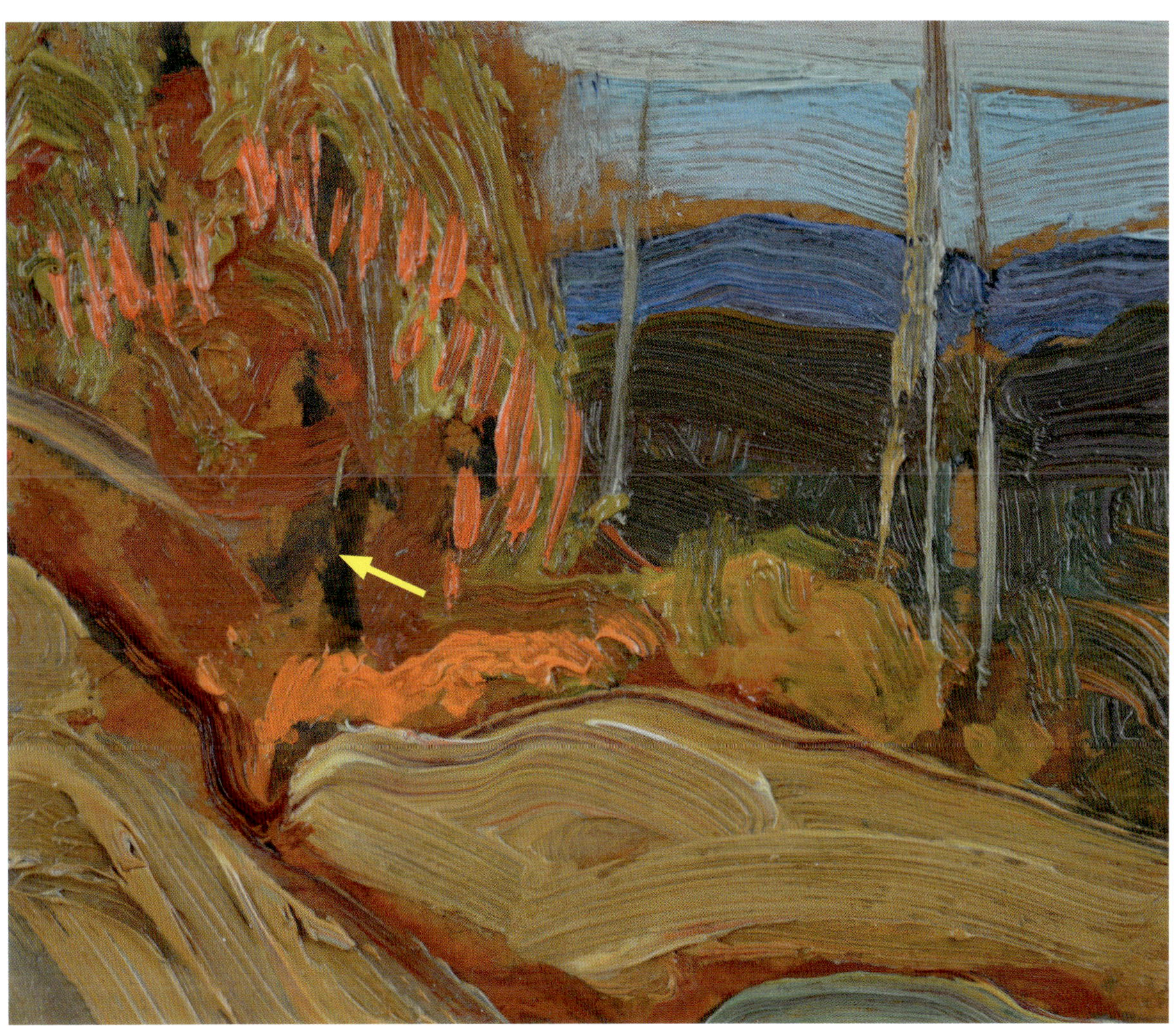

Fig. 3.10: Detail of *Algoma Hills*, 1920, McMichael Canadian Art Collection, 1966.15.6. At upper right are side-by-side blue paint strokes with exposed support between them. At upper left is partially blended yellow and red-brown paint with smaller orange strokes added on top. Dilute, dark blue underpainting is marked with an arrow. Photo: McMichael. (see p. 32)

described in Appendix A, well-worn brushes of these approximate dimensions found among MacDonald's materials corroborate these observations. While there was also a palette knife among his painting materials, there is no indication that he made use of it in his small sketches.

We noted that some Algoma sketches, most often from 1918 or circa 1919, include more passages of concentrated, short strokes and dabs of paint applied with a small brush. Many of these same sketches are on a paperboard support (Algoma Type A as described in chapter 2) that is slightly darker and greyer than most of the Algoma supports. The tighter brushwork, combined with this particular paperboard type adds a darker, denser appearance to the sketches. An example is *Autumn Leaves, Batchewana, Algoma*, illustrated in chapter 1 (Fig. 1.10).

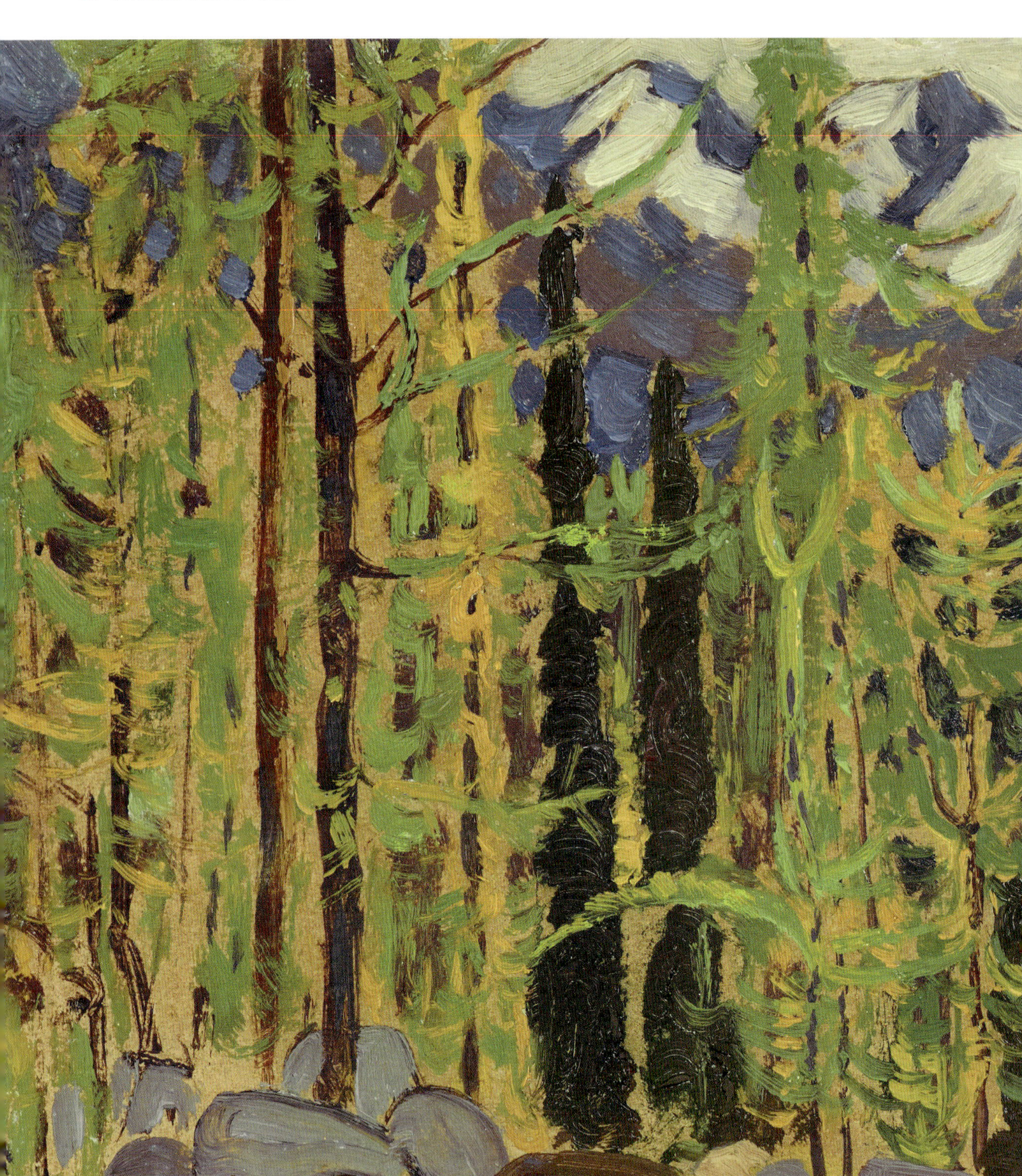

(opposite)
Fig. 3.11: Detail of *Tamarack, Lake O'Hara*, circa 1929, McMichael Canadian Art Collection, 1969.14.2, showing exposed light brown board between trees and thin sketchy lines of purple underpainting. Photo: McMichael.

The Rockies: 1924 to 1932

The role of the support. MacDonald continued to paint directly on paperboard supports sealed with shellac for most of the sketches made during his 1924 to 1930 trips to the Rocky Mountains. As in his Algoma sketches, he used exposed areas of the support as a compositional device. For example, the vertical bands of exposed paperboard between the trees in *Tamarack, Lake O'Hara* enrich the linear pattern of the trunks (Fig. 3.11). In some of the snowy sketches, areas of unpainted board separate mounds of snow in the foreground, emphasizing the rhythm of their forms. MacDonald often applied his paint very thinly in this period. For this reason, the brown paperboard support shows through the bristle texture of individual brushstrokes, adding warmth to the colours (Figs. 3.12a and 3.12b).

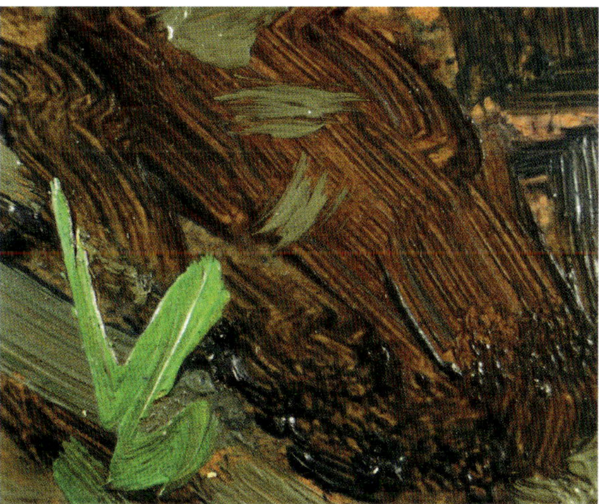

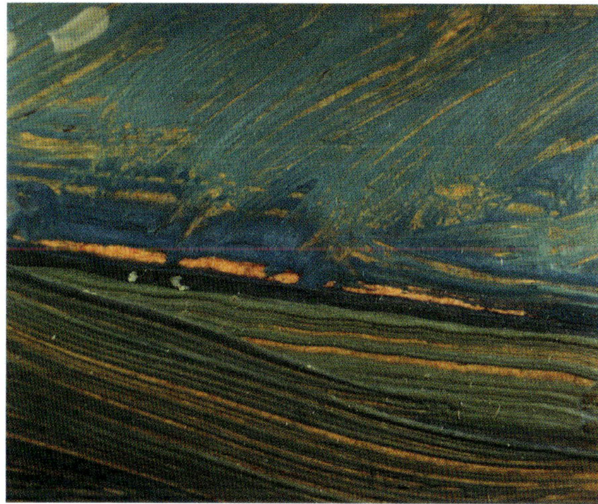

(left to right)
Figs. 3.12a and 3.12b: Details of *Cathedral Peak and Lake O'Hara*, 1927, McMichael Canadian Art Collection, 1966.15.9, showing thinly applied paint over the varnished paperboard support. The brown paperboard shows through the bristle texture of brushstrokes. Photos: McMichael.
(see p. 42)

The role of the ground. For a smaller number of mountain sketches, primarily from his last two trips to the Rockies in 1929 and 1930, MacDonald returned to his earlier method of applying a traditional ground layer before painting. This is also the case for many sketches from 1931 and 1932. The colour of the ground layers for MacDonald's late career sketches varies from off-white through pale hues of pink, orange, or yellow. He left areas of these grounds unpainted at the edges of forms to allow their colour to contribute to the final image. In passages of thinly applied paint, the ground also sometimes shines through individual brushstrokes.

MacDonald may have begun experimenting with light-coloured grounds in response to the bright and changeable light in the Rockies. He often described the mountain light in his diaries and expressed his frustration with transient light effects in several entries. For example, on August 31, 1930, he wrote that he "made another attempt at sketching, snow and reflections were beautiful, but transient effects and other difficulties were beyond [him]," and about a week later, he wrote that he "troubled much with detail and changing lights and labored along from 11 to about 1:45."[35]

Using exposed areas of pale-coloured grounds seems to have provided him with a successful way to render light in some of these mountain sketches. For example, the exposed areas of pale pink ground on *Lake Oesa, Abbot's Pass* give a sense of reflected light from the rocks in the foreground (Fig. 3.13). MacDonald used exposed areas of bright, off-white ground to similar effect in the sunny, southern views of his 1932 sketches made during his trip to Barbados.

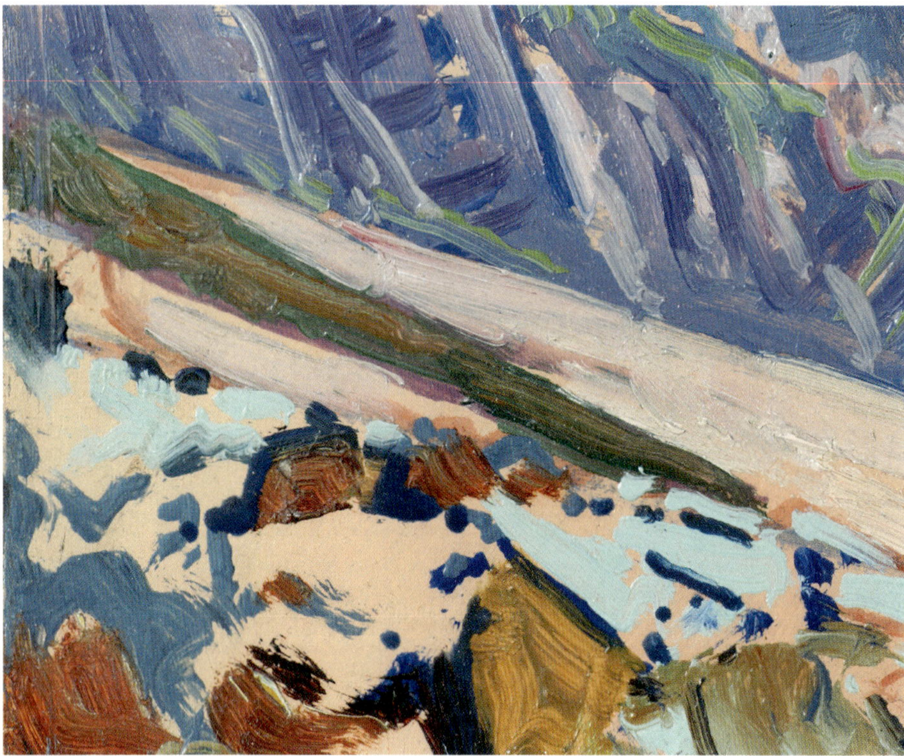

Fig. 3.13: Detail of *Near Lake Oesa, Abbot's Pass*, 1930, National Gallery of Canada, Ottawa, showing exposed pink ground in foreground rocks. Photo: © Government of Canada. (see p. 42)

Underdrawing and underpainting. MacDonald continued to use preliminary outlines in oil paint to lay in the composition in his mountain sketches. The underpainting often has a rougher, drier appearance than seen in the Algoma works, suggesting application of a drier paint with a lightly loaded brush. The underpainting colours are most often blue or purple, consistent with the cooler palette of many of his works from the Rockies. Figure 3.11 shows several sketchy, purple underpainting lines of tree trunks that have become part of the final composition in *Tamarack, Lake O'Hara*.

Composition and brushwork. MacDonald exhibited a notable adaptability in his sketches from the Rockies, altering his style, colour palette, and compositional plan, depending on the view and the effect he was trying to create. His early biographer E.R. Hunter described the sketches of this period: "While one will be filled to overflowing with colour, design, dark forms and movement, another will be an idyllic mountain peak shown against a clear blue sky, the sun shining on it and lighting up its smallest detail."[36]

The sketches of the Rockies that are most distinct from his Algoma works focus on the geology and underlying structure of mountain and rock. MacDonald was attracted by these natural forms, which he referred to as "mountain architecture" in his diary.[37] In the sketches of this style, the design includes large, flat planes of rock, water, and sky to achieve a sense of solidity and stillness. MacDonald emphasized geometric forms in the landscape: tumbled rocks become squares or rectangles with jagged fissures; mountain faces are flattened, angular expanses (Fig. 3.14).

It is clear from his writings that the colours in the mountains and the quality of light fascinated MacDonald.[38] In his higher-key sketches from alpine vantage points, he captured this by adding white to many of his hues; a rocky palette of pale blues, greens, and greys is dominant. For contrast and drama, he added bold splashes of colour to the rocky tones: the bright yellow of the larch or the vibrant colour he dubbed "rainbow-green" of an alpine lake.[39]

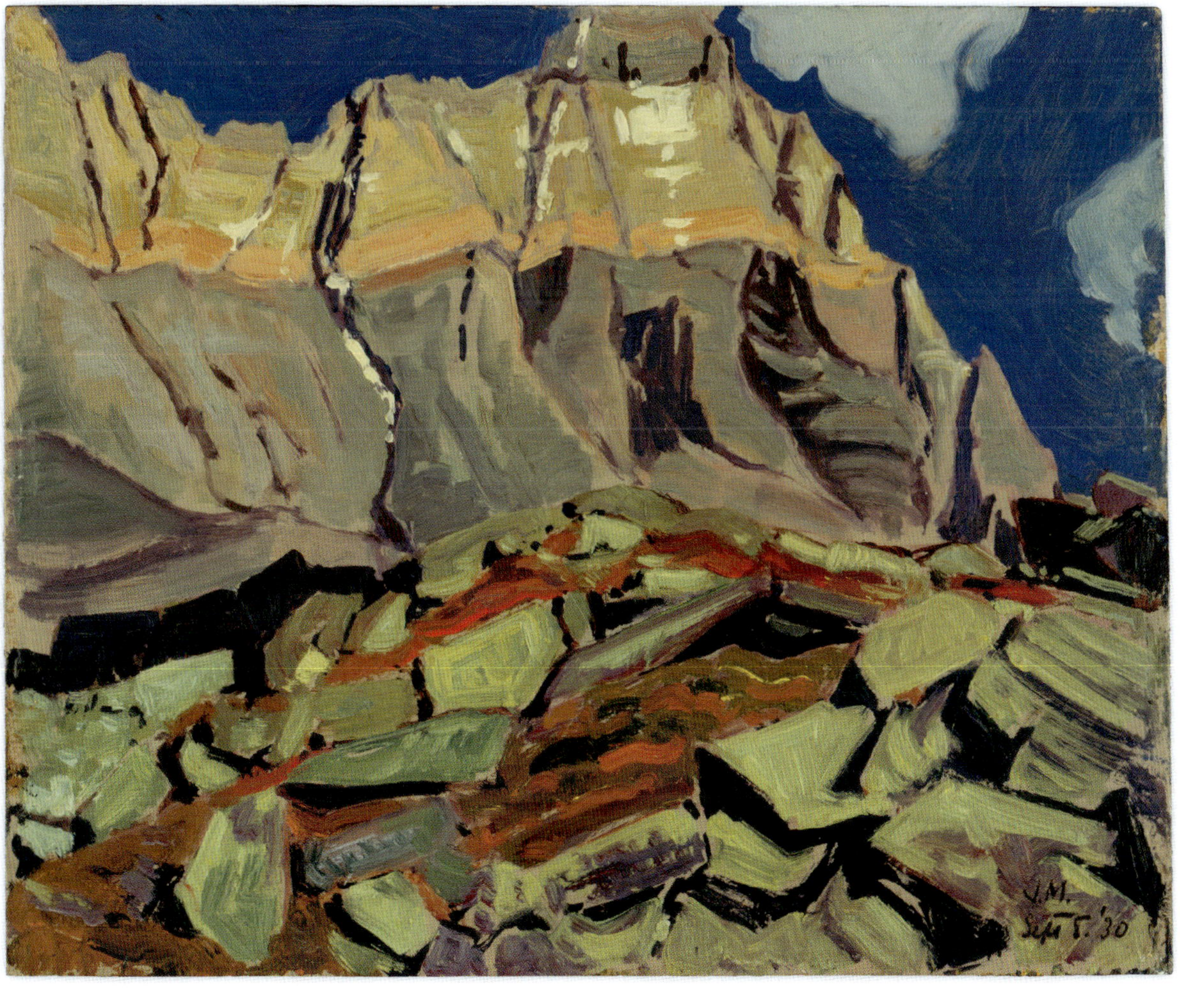

Fig. 3.14: *Lichen-Covered Shale Slabs*, 1930, 21.4 × 26.6, oil on paperboard, McMichael Canadian Art Collection, 1969.7.3. Photo: McMichael.

We observed limited layering of colour in the sketches from the Rocky Mountains, regardless of compositional style and colour palette. While he still applied his paint strokes vigorously, the paint is markedly thinner than in earlier works. While MacDonald sometimes made use of low impasto, particularly for highlights and tree foliage, he applied much of his paint in flat, thin strokes that appear diluted with oil or turpentine. We know that MacDonald carried a bottle of oil along with his tube paints in his portable sketching kit. In an entry in his 1925 diary, he wrote, "Found my oil bottle left there last year. It seems incredible that it should have stayed in the same place through winter snows.... The bottle was glued to the ground."[40]

In areas of these thinly painted works, individual paint strokes expose the support – or ground, when there is one – between bristles that have splayed under the pressure of the artist's brush (Figs. 3.12a and 3.12b). MacDonald created this bristle texture by dragging a thin layer of paint over the support with a lightly loaded brush. The use of hard, worn paintbrushes could also be a factor in producing this effect. Notably, one of MacDonald's sketching companions in the Rockies described him as using "stubby, worn brushes that he brushed against a tree instead of a rag."[41]

The Studio Paintings

MacDonald's studio paintings vary from mid-scale to large-scale, with the largest being about 122 × 153 cm (4 ft. × 5 ft.). He painted these works mostly on canvas but also sometimes used rigid fibreboard supports. Compared to his rapid, on-the-spot sketches, MacDonald's studio works were created over a longer time frame, and this is evident in his painting technique.

The group of studio paintings that we studied comprised nine works painted on canvas supports and five on fibreboard. While this represents only a small selection of MacDonald's overall oeuvre, their examination provided a snapshot of his studio painting technique at different points in his long and varied career.

MacDonald's small oil sketches served as the inspiration for most of his studio paintings. At times, he made more than one sketch of the same subject in preparation for a larger-scale painting. For example, as described in chapter 1, he produced several studies for both *The Tangled Garden* and *The Solemn Land*. MacDonald also occasionally combined elements of sketches from distinct locations to create a new composition. His 1916 painting *The Elements*, for example, is based on sketches from Georgian Bay with an earlier sketch from the Laurentians providing the inspiration for the sky.[42]

Paintings on Rigid Supports

The five paintings on fibreboard that we examined date between 1915 and 1917, a period during which MacDonald regularly painted on this type of support. As described in the previous chapter, two of these boards have stamps confirming that they are the Beaver Board brand, an early type of fibreboard popular for interior wall finishing. The other three works were painted on a very similar type of fibreboard. We refer to all these supports as "beaverboard," a term that encompasses any medium-density fibreboard with these characteristics, whether they include a trademark stamp or not.

MacDonald's studio works on beaverboard from 1915 to 1917 show certain technical features that we also observed in his plein-air sketches from Algoma. Since beaverboard bears a resemblance to the laminated paperboard MacDonald used for oil sketching, he may have translated methods from these studio paintings to his oil sketches, starting in around 1918.

The role of the support. The beaverboard support was not prepared with a traditional ground layer in any of the five examined works. As in MacDonald's Algoma sketches, he intentionally left the support unpainted at the edges of brushstrokes and forms: the exposed areas of the pebbled, orange-brown beaverboard become part of the design, rhythm, and texture of the finished work (Fig. 3.15). MacDonald appears to have developed this technique around the time of his 1915 commission, undertaken with Arthur Lismer and Tom Thomson, to paint a series of decorative murals on beaverboard for Dr. MacCallum's Georgian Bay cottage.[43] Like the studio paintings, these murals were painted directly on the beaverboard, after sealing it with shellac, and the artists, particularly MacDonald, left areas of the support exposed.[44]

Underpainting. Our examination revealed that MacDonald used dilute underpainting to lay out the composition of his studio works on beaverboard. This underpainting, visible in areas of exposed support (Fig. 3.15), varied in colour. We observed both red and green underpainting on *The Tangled Garden*. Dilute, dark red underpainting was noted on both *The Elements* and *In November*, and pale orange-red underpainting was observed in areas of *Harvest Evening Moon*.[45]

Composition and brushwork. As described in the discussion on his sketching technique, MacDonald's unpublished lecture notes include instructions about observing patterns in the profiles and masses of forms when designing a composition.[46] He was clearly putting these ideas into practice at the time he painted the studio works on beaverboard that we examined.

In *The Elements* (illustrated in chapter 1, Fig. 1.6), for example, MacDonald used bold, diagonal brushstrokes in the rocks of the foreground, the mid-ground trees, and in the sky to create the impression of shoreline wind and changing light under the shadows of the moving, heavy clouds. In *The Tangled Garden* (Fig. 1.5), the vertical tree trunks and sunflower stems contrast with the horizontal rhythmic brushstrokes of the wooden siding of the building behind. These leaning vertical

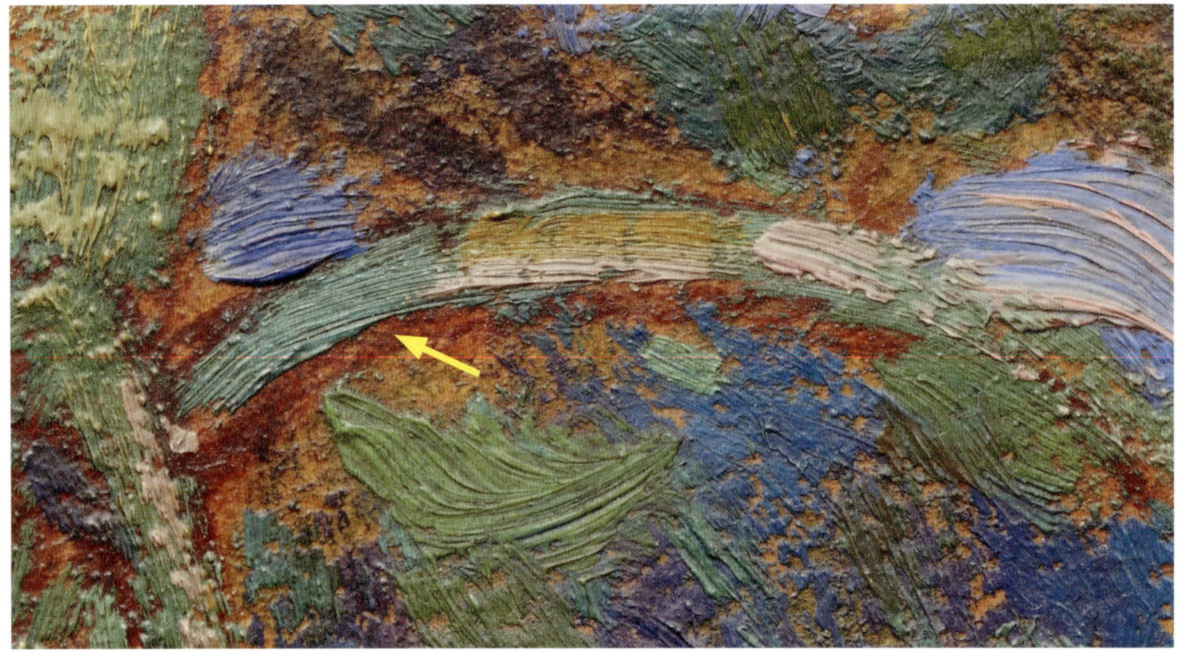

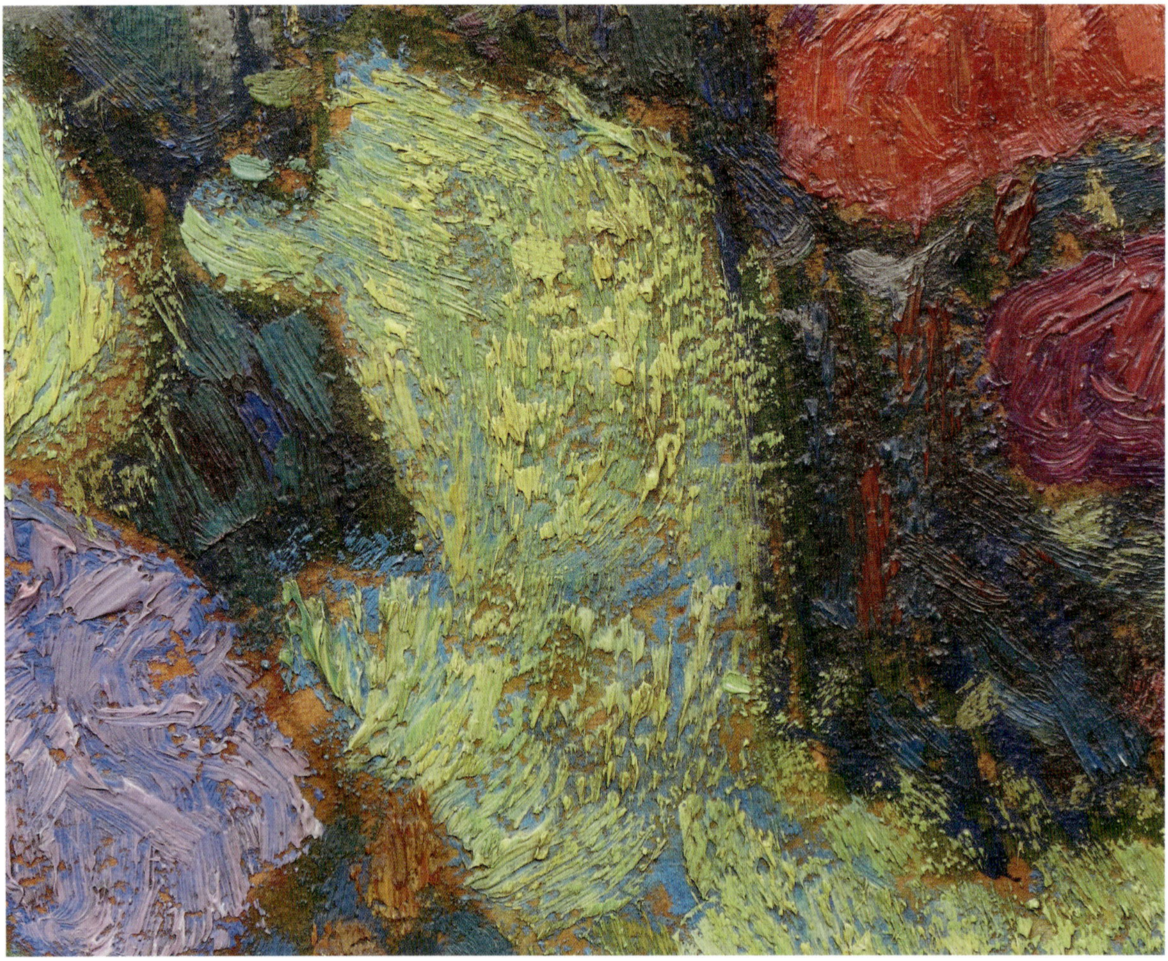

elements also frame the tapestry of bright flowers that form a triangular focal point in the painting. In both works, opposing directional brushstrokes in adjacent forms create movement and contrast, a technique also noted in MacDonald's Algoma sketches. MacDonald's palette varies in this period, depending on his subject. For example, brilliant, contrasting colours dominate in *The Tangled Garden*, while the late autumn light of *In November* is reflected in the darker landscape and cloud hues.

(opposite, top to bottom) Fig. 3.15: Detail of *The Tangled Garden*, 1916, National Gallery of Canada, Ottawa, showing exposed orange-brown beaverboard at brushstroke edges. Dark red underpainting (shown with an arrow) extends past the stroke of mid-green paint applied on top. Photo: © Government of Canada. (see p. 24)

Fig. 3.16: Detail of *The Tangled Garden*, 1916, National Gallery of Canada, Ottawa, showing paler colours, applied with a dry-brush method, layered over darker hues. Photo: © Government of Canada. (see p. 24)

These paintings were created more slowly than his on-the-spot sketches, and this is evident in the paint application. He produced forms and masses with areas of side-by-side brushstrokes, combined with passages where he built up the paint in multiple, overlapping layers. In multi-layered areas, the underlayer was usually touch dry before the next layer was applied. MacDonald produced impasto in these works with repeating dabs and long parallel brushstrokes. He also appears to have applied paint with a palette knife to produce texture in some passages. As described in Appendix A, a palette knife is among the materials in MacDonald's Madderton & Company paintbox.

MacDonald sometimes used a dry-brush technique, also called scumbling, in his studio works. As described in the glossary, for this method, a brush lightly loaded with paint is dragged over an underlying textured layer to create a thin application of surface paint. He may have rendered his paint drier and stiffer for dry-brushing, either by partially drying it on the palette or by leaching out some of the oil onto an absorbent material.

In both *The Elements* and *The Tangled Garden*, the most extensive layering of colours is found in the central areas of major forms. The flowers and leaves of *The Tangled Garden* are built up from dry-brushing lighter hues over the already dry darker paint beneath, using a wide brush. The upper layers of paint catch the high points of the paint texture below, creating depth and pattern (Fig. 3.16).

Paintings on Canvas

We examined MacDonald's painting technique for nine works on canvas. They include an early painting from 1912, six Algoma works painted between 1919 and 1921, and two depictions of the Rocky Mountains.

The role of the support and ground. The support for five of the nine works on canvas that were examined is a coarse jute-based fabric. The coarse fabric produces a noticeable rough texture at the surface of these paintings. This is most pronounced in thinly painted areas of *The Solemn Land*, *Gleams in the Hills*, and *Mount Goodsir, Yoho Park*. The surface variation and softening of paint edges created by the rough consistency of the jute was undoubtedly an intentional effect.[47] One piece of documentary evidence showing that MacDonald thought about the influence of canvas texture is a note he made on a 1924 exhibition catalogue of American art. In this catalogue, among other interesting marginalia, MacDonald made special mention that one of the works was painted on a very rough canvas.[48]

All the examined studio works on canvas were prepared with white to off-white grounds. In *Early Evening, Winter*, from 1912, the paint of the image layers covers the ground layer completely. In some of the Algoma and Rocky Mountains studio paintings, there are small areas of exposed ground at brushstroke edges or in passages of thinned brushwork. In a few paintings, particularly the works from the Rocky Mountains, the ground layer plays a minor role in lightening the overall tonality of the painting. In contrast to his paintings on beaverboard, however, the areas of exposed ground do not add to the overall design or structure of the work.

In most cases, we observed that the ground layer was applied relatively smoothly. An exception is the overall pebbled surface texture on *Goat Range, Rocky Mountains* that appears to originate in the ground layer (Fig. 3.17). As described in chapter 4, this uneven, lumpy appearance may not have been purposeful.

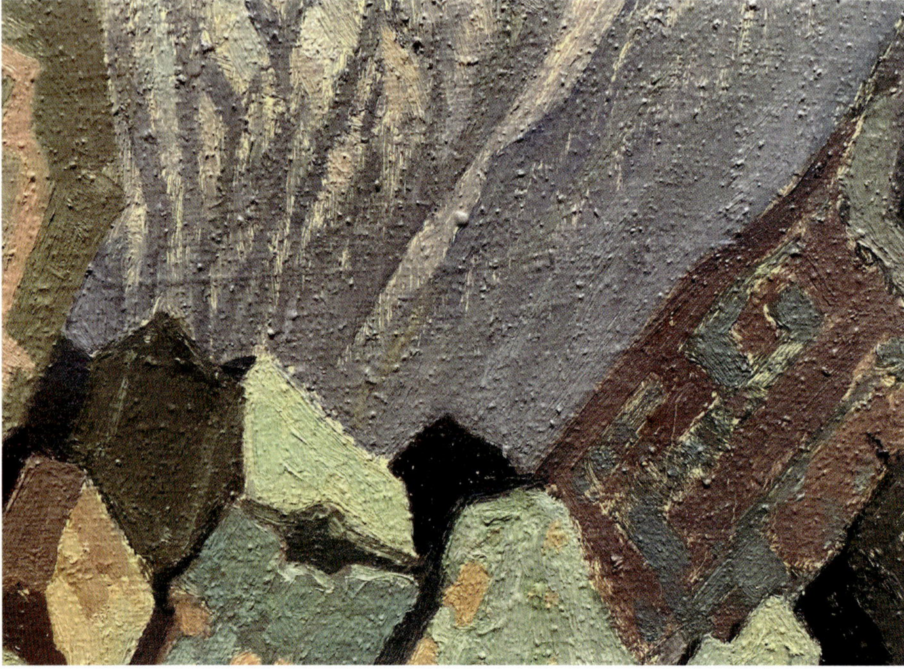

Fig. 3.17: Detail of *Goat Range, Rocky Mountains*, 1932, McMichael Canadian Art Collection, 1979.35, showing the lumpy texture produced by the ground layer. Photo: McMichael. (see p. 45)

Toning layers. We found evidence that MacDonald sometimes applied an overall or selective paint layer, referred to as a "toning layer" or an "imprimatura," to modify the off-white ground of his works on canvas prior to painting. For several of MacDonald's Algoma paintings, close visual examination suggested that he applied selective yellow-beige to pale brown toning layers over the ground (Fig. 3.18). Cross-sections confirmed the use of toning layers on *Leaves in the Brook* and *Forest Wilderness* (Fig. 3.19). MacDonald may have been emulating the warm brown tone of the paperboard support of the preparatory studies he made for these large-scale oil paintings on canvas.

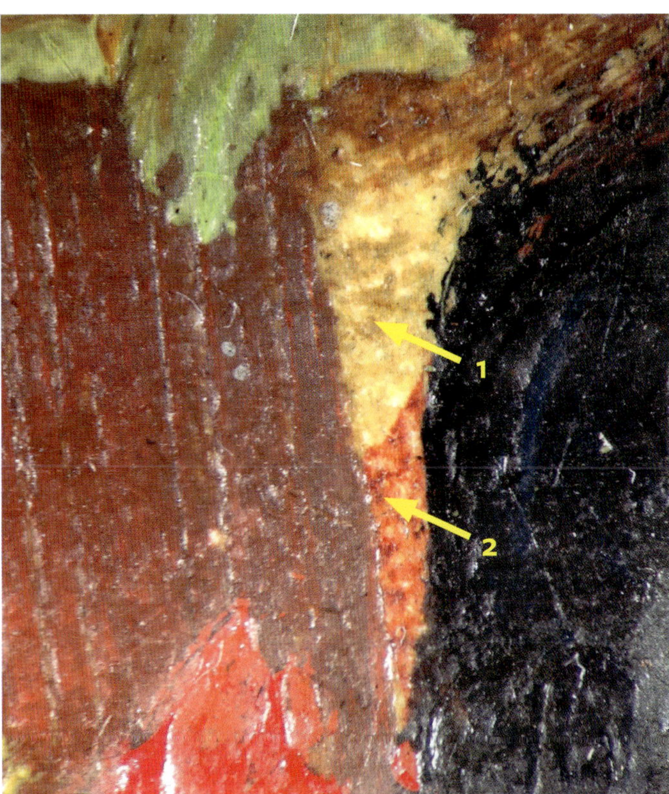

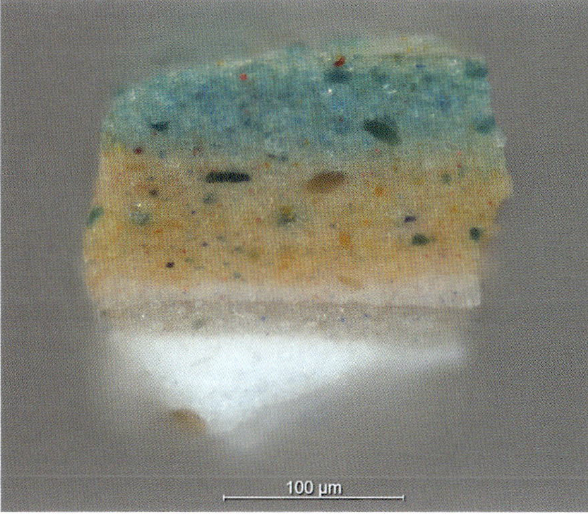

Fig. 3.19: Cross-section from *Forest Wilderness*, 1921, McMichael Canadian Art Collection, 1968.7.1, incident light. Layers from bottom to top: off-white ground; two beige toning layers; thick yellow and green paint of the image layers. Photo: © Government of Canada.

Fig. 3.18: Detail of *Forest Wilderness*, 1921, McMichael Canadian Art Collection, 1968.7.1, showing the possible toning layer over the ground (1) and an area of thin, red underpainting (2). Photo: McMichael. (see p. 38)

Underdrawing and underpainting. There was no visual evidence of compositional underdrawings in pencil or other carbon-based media on these studio paintings. However, IR photography was undertaken on two of the Algoma paintings on canvas, and one of them, *Leaves in the Brook*, 1919, revealed faint, straight vertical and horizontal lines, likely applied in pencil, underneath the paint layers. This grid would have helped him enlarge his preliminary sketch to the scale of the canvas painting. IR photography of a larger group of paintings could determine whether this was a technique that MacDonald commonly used. It is interesting to note that A.Y. Jackson used a different type of grid technique: he sometimes attached a framework of horizontal and vertical white threads to his sketches to block the composition into squares as an aid during enlargement.[49]

As in his sketches, MacDonald used strokes of dilute oil paint to outline compositional elements on his oil paintings on canvas. On the Algoma paintings that were examined, this underpainting was most often dark red (Fig. 3.18), although other colours in addition to red were also noted in a few cases. Underpainting was also visible in the two studio paintings depicting the Rocky Mountains. Mauve and grey underpainting was observed in the foreground of *Goat Range, Rocky Mountains*, while thin, dark red outlining was noted at the edges of the composition of *Mount Goodsir, Yoho Park*. A cross-section from this painting illustrates the very thin, dark red underpaint applied to the white ground layer (Fig. 3.20).

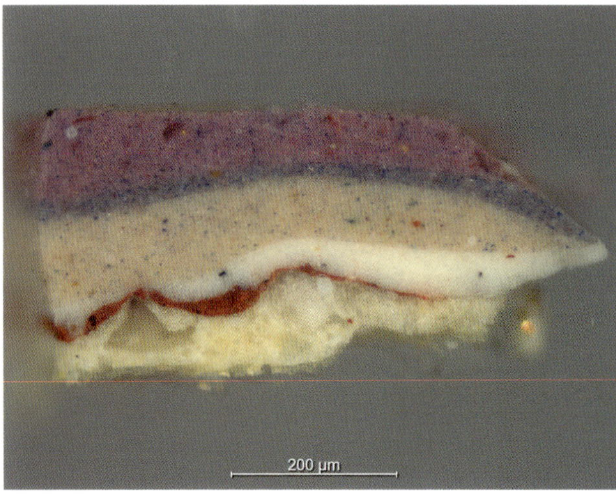

Fig. 3.20: Cross-section from *Mount Goodsir, Yoho Park*, 1925, Art Gallery of Ontario, 79/228, incident light. Layers from bottom to top: off-white ground; thin, dark red underpainting; white underlayer; beige, blue, and purple paint of the image layers. Photo: © Government of Canada.

Composition and brushwork. In the earliest studio painting on canvas that we examined, *Early Evening, Winter*, 1912, MacDonald used tight brushwork with short dabs and multidirectional strokes of colour (Fig. 3.21). The short strokes of muted pinks, greens, and yellows are reminiscent of French Impressionist technique. The paint has been built up in layers, with some wet-in-wet blending. There are areas of low impasto, particularly in the moon and reflected light on the snow. There is also an underlying rough texture unrelated to the composition, possibly created with a palette knife. Nancy Robertson described this effect in several of MacDonald's early works, including this one.[50]

By the Algoma period, MacDonald's palette had brightened considerably. The six Algoma paintings on canvas that we examined were characterized by layered,

Fig. 3.21: Detail of *Early Evening, Winter*, 1912, Art Gallery of Ontario, illustrating dab-like brushwork and muted colours. Photo: © AGO. (see p. 21)

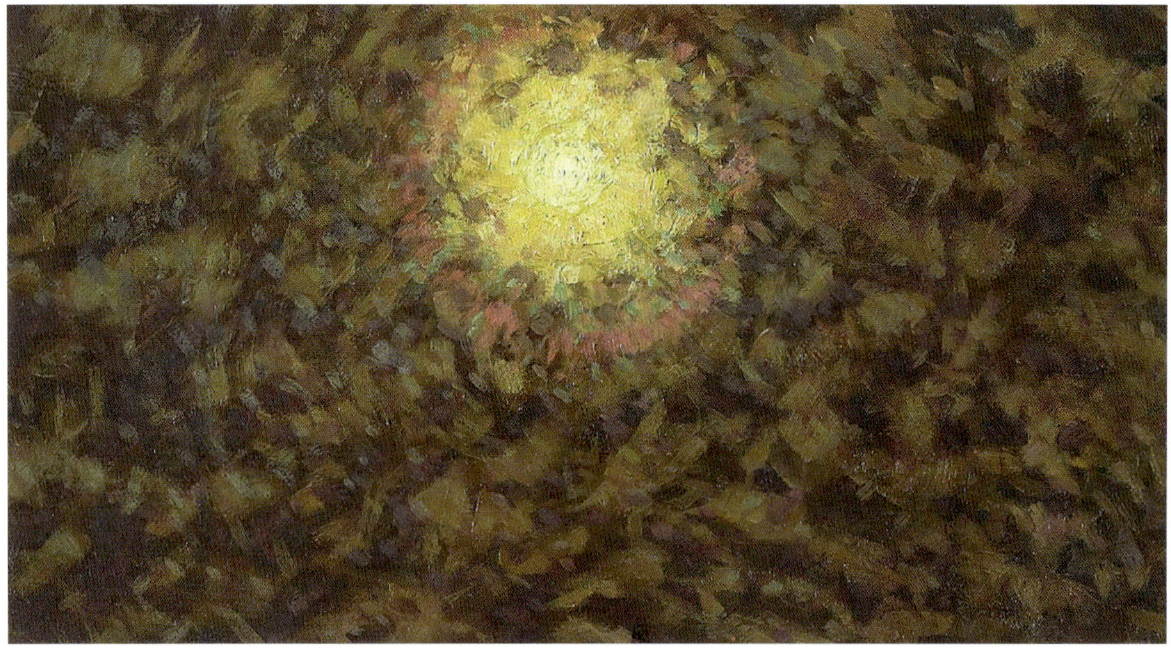

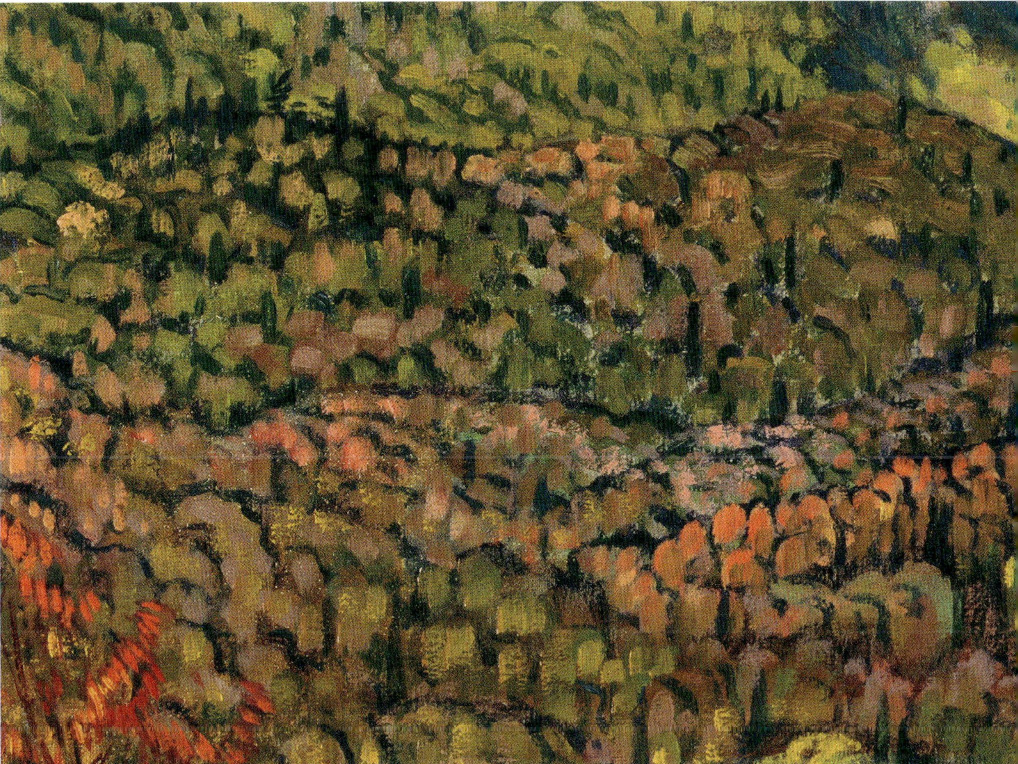

(right)
Fig. 3.22: Detail of *Forest Wilderness*, 1921, McMichael Canadian Art Collection, 1968.7.1, showing patterned strokes of individual bright colours. Photo: McMichael. (see p. 38)

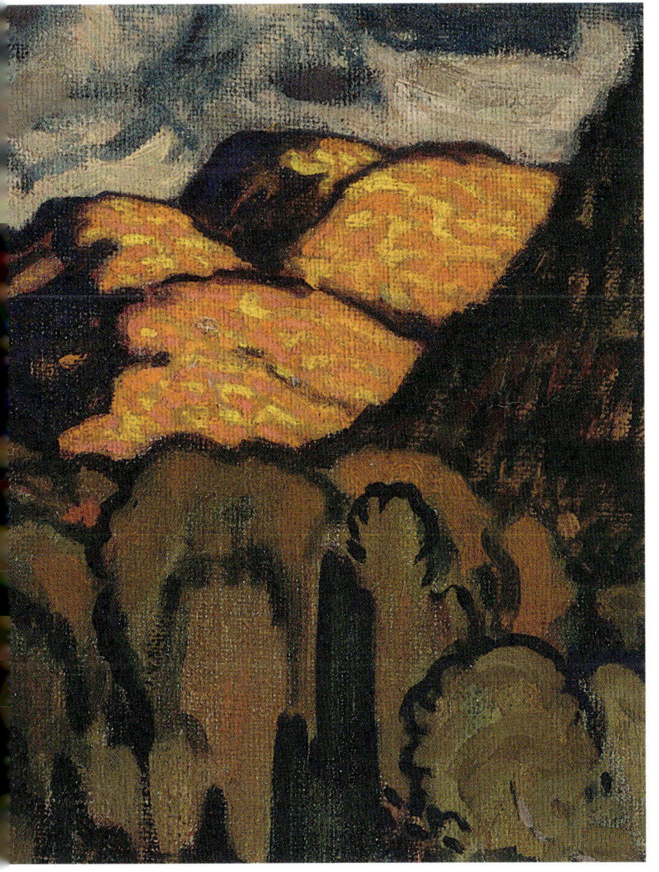

(below)
Fig. 3.23: Detail of *Gleams on the Hills*, 1921, National Gallery of Canada, Ottawa, showing dark outlining of forms and texture of the jute support. Photo: NGC.

fluid brushstrokes applied with repeating dabs and strokes of alternating vivid colours, creating a decorative, patterned effect (Fig. 3.22). The individual brushstrokes remain bright due to the upper layers being applied after the lower layer was dry to the touch.

As described earlier, MacDonald used exposed areas of support as a unifying component in the design of his Algoma sketches, the so-called invisible line.[51] In his Algoma oil paintings on canvas, this is replaced by dark, painted outlines that create structure and contain the bright colour and patterning within forms (Fig. 3.23). The result is that these paintings exhibit a structured, still weightiness that contrasts with the more spontaneous effect of his preliminary sketches.

Since the designs of MacDonald's Algoma paintings are based to a large extent on his sketches, similar rhythms in the profiles of the compositional elements create a sense of movement. As in the sketches, he also used brushwork to create solidity and contrast by applying juxtaposed perpendicular brushstrokes to differentiate adjacent forms.

The paint texture of the Algoma studio paintings appears somewhat drier than the medium-rich paint used for his sketches of the period. This could be due to some absorption of paint medium by the ground layer on the canvas. The crisper texture of the paint may also be a result of the way that MacDonald applied it – in short, firm strokes of alternating colour, sometimes with a dry-brush technique. For example, in the patterned treatment of the background foliage in *Forest Wilderness*, MacDonald layered short strokes of dry-brushed light and high-key colours over darker paints of a similar hue. As described in the previous section, this is also a method that he used in certain paintings on beaverboard, like *The Tangled Garden*.

There is also evidence that MacDonald sometimes thinned his paints at this time. A.Y. Jackson described the paint in *The Solemn Land* as having been thinned with turpentine and, in fact, as described further in chapter 5, he considered it to have been overdiluted.[52]

Several authors have pointed out the marked differences between MacDonald's Algoma paintings compared to his works depicting the Rocky Mountains. Paul Duval, for example, noted that "the rich textures and compositional movement of Algoma are replaced by a generally smooth, almost flat paint surface." He attributed this not only to the change in location and subject matter, but also to a "fresh approach to picture-making for MacDonald" and possibly a reflection of the fact that he was working on several architectural design projects at the time.[53] We examined two studio paintings based on sketches from MacDonald's trips to the Rocky Mountains: *Mount Goodsir, Yoho Park* from 1925, and *Goat Range, Rocky Mountains*, completed in 1932.

Mount Goodsir, Yoho Park was painted with a flat, simplified design, composed of hard-edged planes of relatively saturated colours (illustrated in chapter 1, Fig. 1.21). MacDonald's early mountain paintings of this type have been described as having a "poster-like quality," lacking the light and atmosphere of his on-the-spot sketches from the Rockies.[54] In *Mount Goodsir, Yoho Park*, MacDonald applied the paint smoothly and evenly with little blending or shading. A cross-section from the painting (Fig. 3.20) illustrates how he applied the flat paint layers one on top of the other: the interface between colours is clean, with no evidence of intermixing.

In *Goat Range, Rocky Mountains*, one of MacDonald's final paintings (Fig. 1.22), he returned to a more naturalistic colour scheme, using muted tones of green, grey, and blue. He mixed most hues with white to create a sense of the bright light in the mountains. Like *Mount Goodsir, Yoho Park*, this painting emphasizes geometric areas of paint and angular brushstrokes, producing a somewhat static but grounded composition. However, in this later painting, the edges of forms are less severe, and the overall impression is softer and more natural.

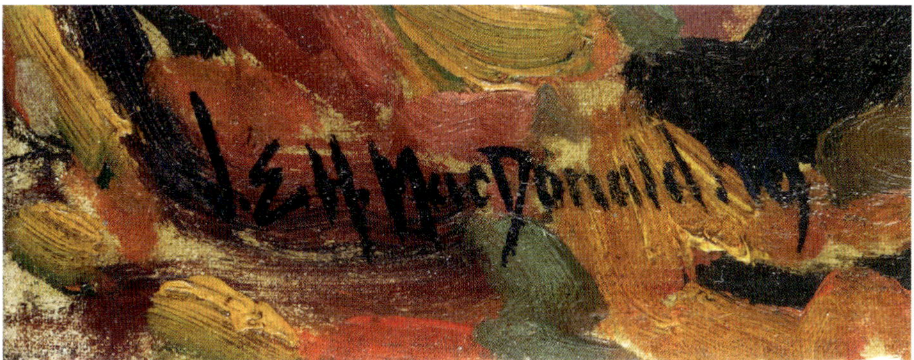

Figs. 3.24: Detail of signature on *Leaves in the Brook*, 1919, McMichael Canadian Art Collection, 1966.16.32. Photo: © Government of Canada.

Signatures, Inscriptions, and Stamps

We recorded basic information about signatures on the front of all the oil sketches and studio paintings examined. For the sketches, we also collected information about inscriptions and stamps on the backs. While forensic handwriting examination of the signatures and inscriptions was beyond the scope of our project, the following summarizes some general observations.

Signatures

The studio paintings. MacDonald signed the front of all 14 of the studio paintings that we examined. On these works, he applied his signature after the underlying paint of the composition was mostly dry. He used paint, usually red, brown, or black in colour, for these signatures. On all but one painting, he printed his name in full, followed by an abbreviated two-digit date (Fig. 3.24). *Belgium*, a 1915 painting on beaverboard, was an exception. On this work, he signed only with the initials "J.M." This type of abbreviated signature was more commonly used for his small oil sketches.

The sketches. MacDonald signed the front of his oil sketches less often than his studio paintings, albeit still with some regularity; about half of the 160 sketches that we examined bear a signature. He most frequently signed his sketches with the simple initials "J.M." This was often followed by an abbreviated two-digit date. He also sometimes signed with his full name as "J.E.H. MacDonald" or with a more abbreviated "J.E.H. MacD." or "J. MacD."[55]

MacDonald habitually used printing, not cursive, to sign his sketches, although some of his early signatures are written on a slight diagonal with a curvilinear quality to the letters. In certain sketches, primarily early works, we observed that he signed before the paint was dry, so that the signature blends in with the paint of the composition, a wet-in-wet technique. However, for the most part, MacDonald signed his sketches sometime after they had dried completely. He most often added his signature over the dry paint in finely written letters using a somewhat dilute black or dark brown medium with the appearance of ink. Some of these ink signatures have faded or become worn over time. We also noted occasional signatures on the sketches that he applied with paint rather than ink. In several late sketches from the 1929 to 1932 period, MacDonald incised the date into the wet paint, either with a graphite pencil or with a pointed instrument such as the butt end of a paintbrush. Figures 3.25a to 3.25g illustrate a selection of observed signature types.

MacDonald appears to have signed the front of his sketches more regularly during certain periods of his career. For example, almost all the examined sketches painted before 1914 include both a signature and date on the front, while in contrast, only a few sketches from the 1914 to 1917 period bear a signature. For the sketches from the Algoma period, 17 of the 49 examined sketches are signed on the front.

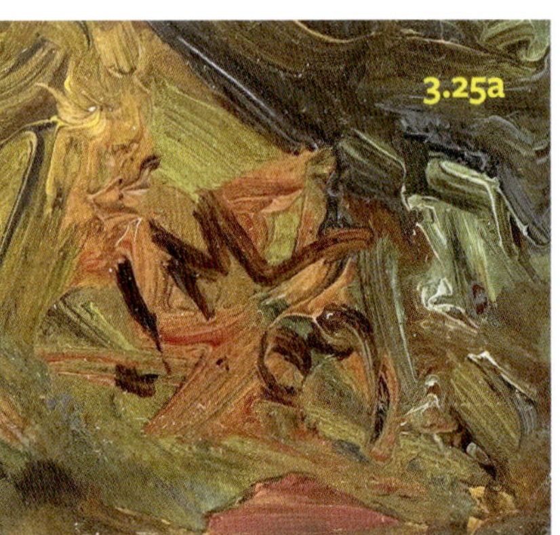

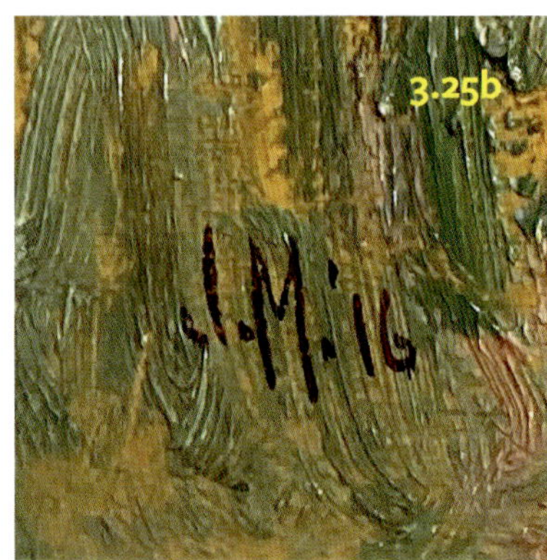

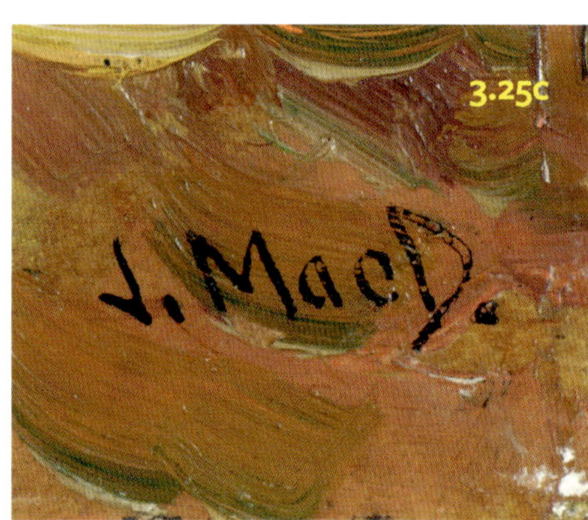

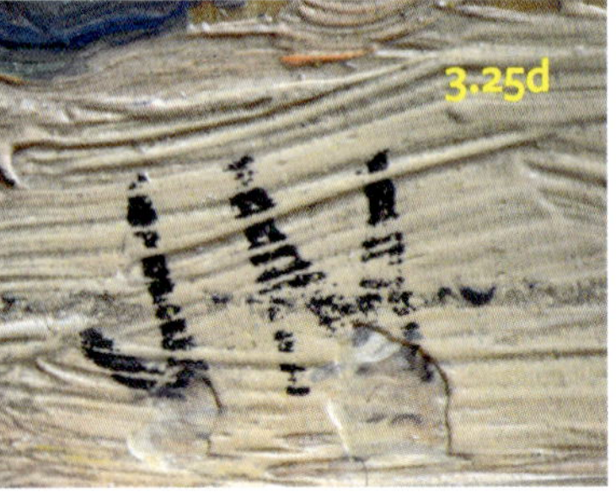

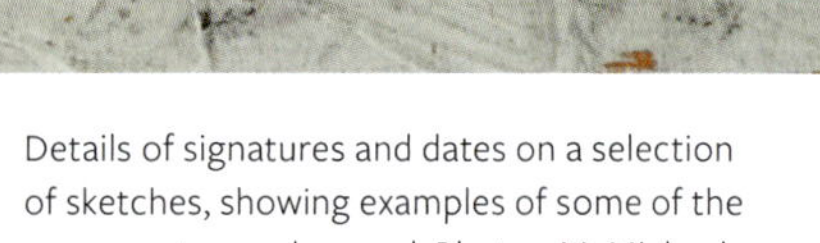

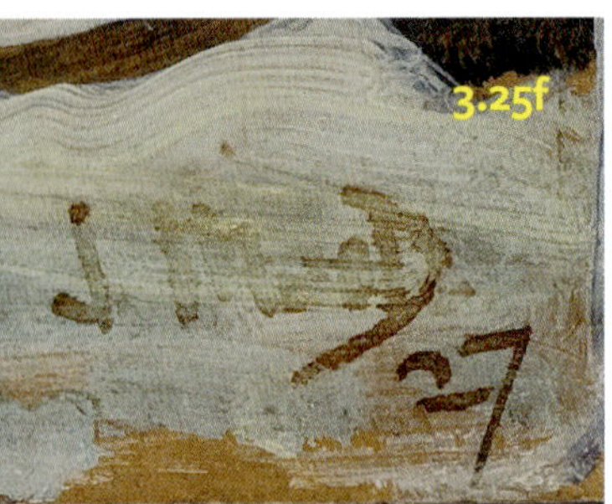

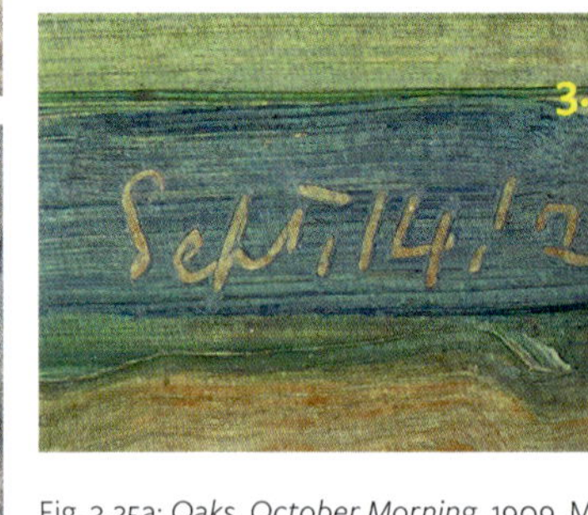

Details of signatures and dates on a selection of sketches, showing examples of some of the common types observed. Photos: McMichael unless otherwise indicated.

Fig. 3.25a: *Oaks, October Morning*, 1909, McMichael Canadian Art Collection, 1966.15.15.
Fig. 3.25b: *Thornhill Garden, No.2*, 1916, Art Gallery of Ontario.
Fig. 3.25c: *Algoma Bush, Autumn*, circa 1919, National Gallery of Canada, Ottawa.
Fig. 3.25d: *Nova Scotia Barn*, circa 1922, McMichael Canadian Art Collection, 1966.16.53.
Fig. 3.25e: *Wiwaxy Peaks, Lake O'Hara*, 1926, McMichael Canadian Art Collection, 1968.25.15.
Fig. 3.25f: *Snow, Lake O'Hara*, 1927, McMichael Canadian Art Collection, 1966.15.10.
Fig. 3.25g: *O'Hara Shores Stormy Weather*, 1929, McMichael Canadian Art Collection, 1969.23.4.
Fig. 3.25b and 3.25c photos: © Government of Canada.

Inscriptions

MacDonald regularly signed, dated, or titled his oil sketches on the backs of the boards. When he gave sketches to friends and colleagues, he sometimes also added personalized inscriptions.

While he occasionally used pencil, MacDonald more often inscribed the back of his sketches in brown or black ink that now has a slightly faded appearance. He generally used cursive handwriting but also printed his inscriptions from time to time. Figures 3.26a to 3.26e illustrate examples of inscriptions of various dates with handwriting that we have attributed to MacDonald with a good degree of confidence. In some other cases, we were not certain whether an inscription was written by MacDonald or by someone else. Definitive determination would require expertise in forensic handwriting examination combined with an in-depth study of a large group of known samples of MacDonald's writing in different media.[56]

Many sketches include inscriptions on the back written in hands other than MacDonald's, for example, from gallerists, previous owners, Group of Seven colleagues, or family members. While not written by MacDonald, these inscriptions are still very useful in provenance and authentication research.

MacDonald's son, Thoreau, added titles, dates, and locations to the backs of a number of sketches. He also sometimes noted when a work was not for sale ("NFS") or confirmed the authorship of a particular sketch or inscription. At times, Thoreau's cursive handwriting appears similar to his father's, and although he often included his initials ("TM"), this is not always the case. Figures 3.27a to 3.27d show a few examples of inscriptions by Thoreau MacDonald, A.Y. Jackson, and A.J. Casson on the backs of MacDonald's sketches.

Estate Stamp

Soon after MacDonald's death in 1932, his son designed a stamp as a means of identifying the authorship of unsigned works. The original stamp included MacDonald's initials and the year of his death. Sometime after it was made, the "1932" section of the stamp was damaged and removed; from that point on, the stamp only included initials.[57] A number of the examined sketches have Thoreau's identification stamp on the back, either incised or inked (Figs. 3.28a and 3.28b). The back of one sketch in the McMichael collection, entitled *Prairie Sunrise*, was first incised with the earlier version, including the 1932 date, and subsequently marked in a second location with the inked stamp including initials only.

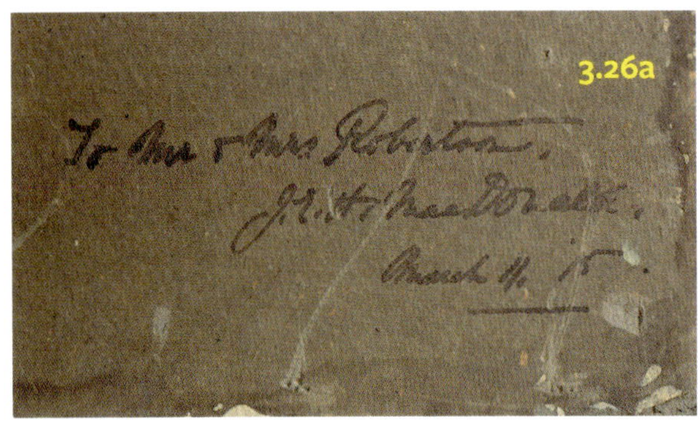

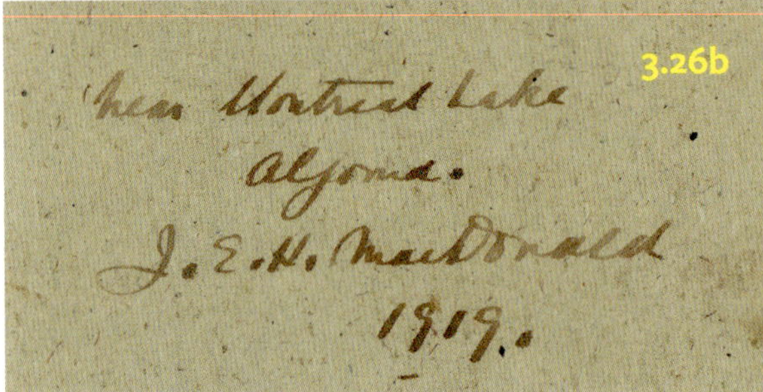

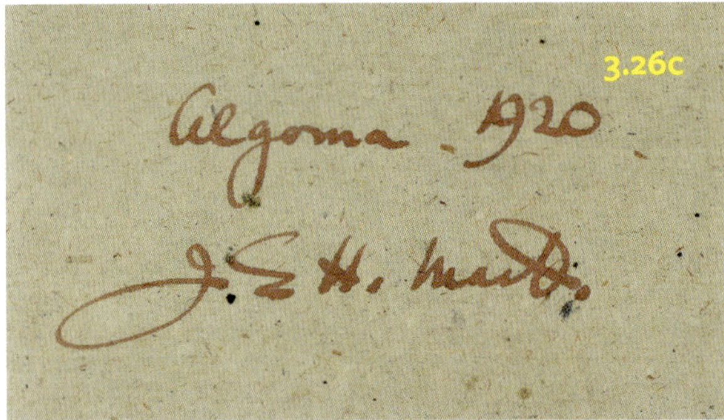

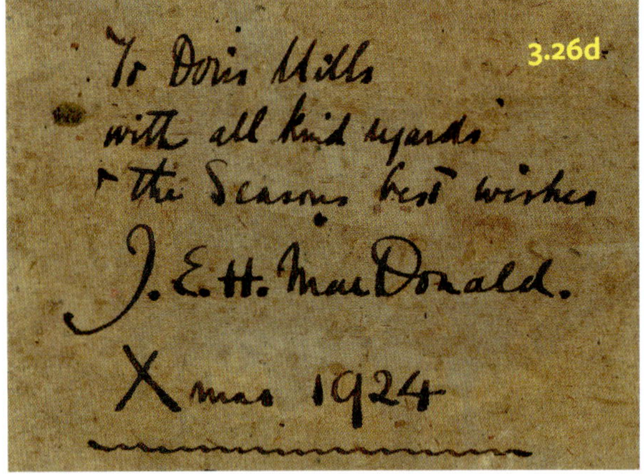

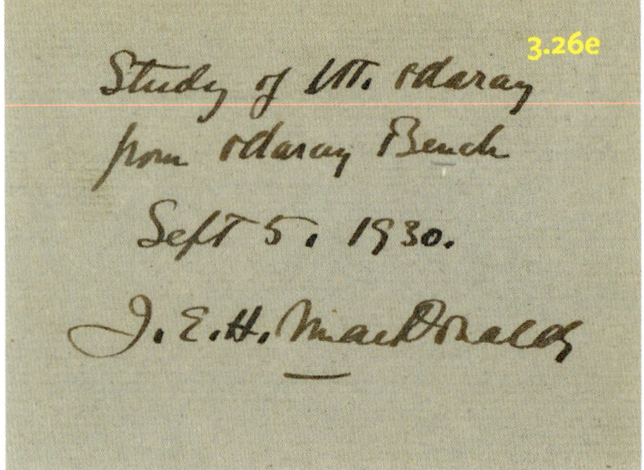

Examples of inscriptions in MacDonald's hand on the back of five sketches. Photos: © Government of Canada unless otherwise indicated.

Fig. 3.26a: *Oakwood*, 1913, McMichael Canadian Art Collection, 1972.5.3. Photo: McMichael.
Fig. 3.26b: *Near Montreal Lake, Algoma*, 1919, National Gallery of Canada, Ottawa.
Fig. 3.26c: *Mongoose Lake, Algoma*, 1920, National Gallery of Canada, Ottawa.
Fig. 3.26d: *Windy Day, Little Turtle Lake*, 1922, National Gallery of Canada, Ottawa.
Fig. 3.26e: *Mount Odaray*, 1930, National Gallery of Canada, Ottawa.

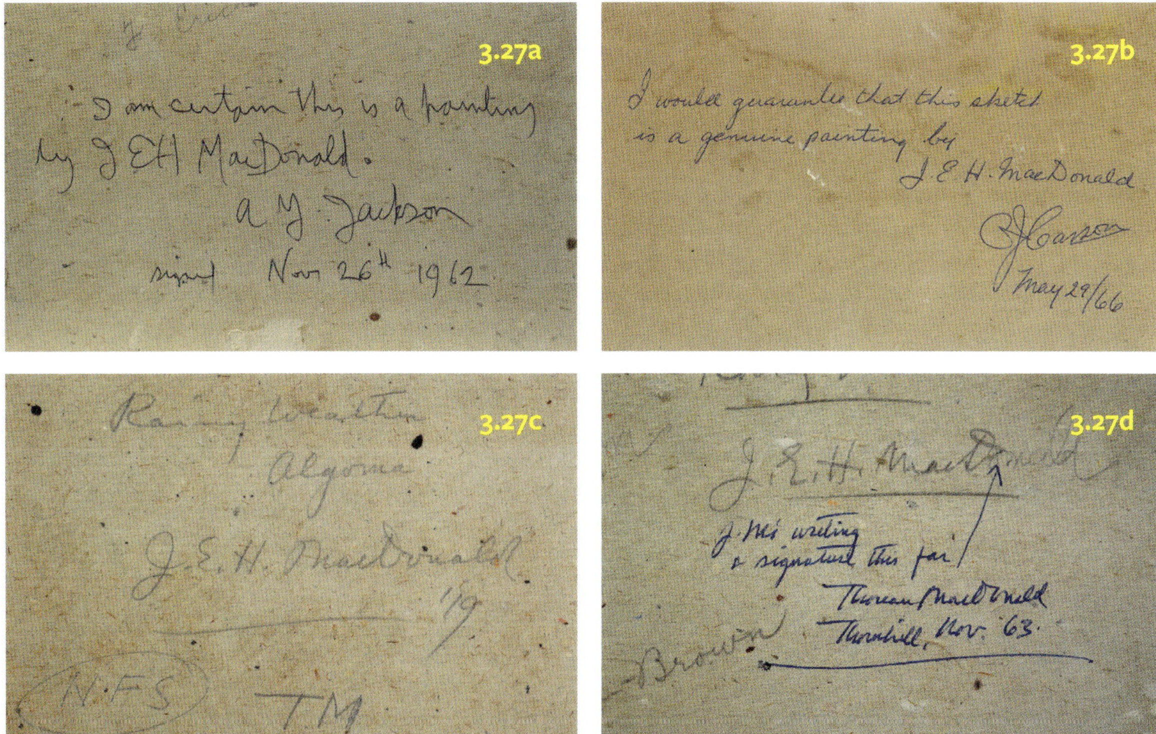

Examples of inscriptions on the backs of three sketches in the McMichael Canadian Art Collection. Photos: McMichael.

Fig. 3.27a Inscription by A.Y. Jackson on *Rocky Stream, Algoma*, c. 1918, 1966.16.45
Fig. 3.27b Inscription by A.J. Casson on *Tamarack, Lake O'Hara*, 1969.14.2
Fig. 3.27c Inscription by Thoreau MacDonald on *Rainy Weather, Algoma*, 1919, 1966.16.34
Fig. 3.27a Inscription byThoreau MacDonald (in blue pen) on *Rocky Stream, Algoma*, circa 1918, 1966.16.45

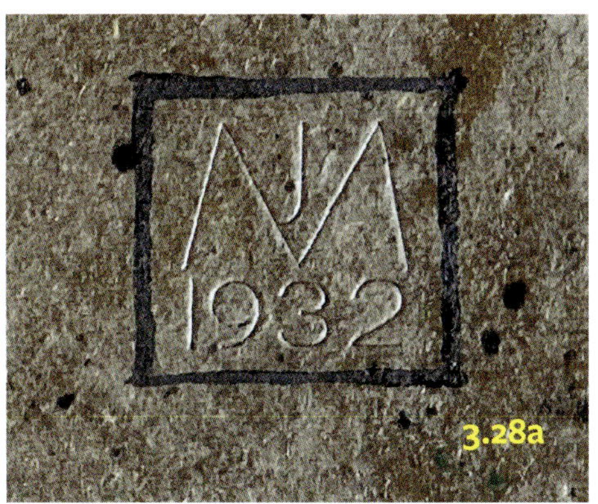

Two versions of the identification stamp applied by Thoreau MacDonald to the back of some of MacDonald's sketches.

Fig. 3.28a: Incised version of the stamp on *Solemn Land, Algoma*, circa 1919, Art Gallery of Ontario; the ink outline is not part of the stamp. Photo: © Government of Canada.
Fig. 3.28b: Inked version of the stamp without the year on *O'Hara Shores Stormy Weather*, 1929, McMichael Canadian Art Collection, 1969.23.4. Photo: McMichael.

Art is the ordering of the material in harmony with the spirit.
– J.E.H. MacDonald, Miscellaneous notes, Endeavors After Art, 1930.

Too many colours spoil the sketch.
– J.E.H. MacDonald, Lecture Notes, Untitled, General Art, n.d. [circa 1925].

A limited number of colors were used, and combined or reduced, they gave a great variety.
– J.E.H. MacDonald, "Interior Decorations of St. Anne's Church, Toronto," 1925.

4. PAINTING MATERIALS

MacDonald was an expert colourist, and the scientific investigation of his paints is a rich area for study. While previous chapters describe close visual examination for a large collection of MacDonald's oil sketches and paintings, this chapter focuses on the detailed scientific analysis of a smaller group of works. Documentary information about the painting materials available at the time MacDonald was active, primarily from catalogues and advertisements from artists' oil paint suppliers in Toronto, is included as background for the analysis results. The glossary provides definitions of technical terms used.

Methodology

We removed small samples for chemical analysis from the oil sketches and paintings listed in Table 4.1. Although limited in number, these 32 works were chosen as representative of MacDonald's oeuvre, spanning his active years from 1909 to 1932 and including oil sketches and paintings on a variety of support types.

To ensure that samples were obtained safely and unobtrusively, we worked through a microscope and used surgical tools to remove tiny amounts of material.[1] Typical samples were composed of a few microscopic fragments, barely visible without magnification. Some samples were in the form of cross-sections. These multi-layer fragments illustrate how MacDonald built up the layers of ground and paint.

In total, over 400 samples were analyzed at the Canadian Conservation Institute (CCI), allowing the production of an extensive database of MacDonald's oil painting materials. The samples included the main paint colours in each work, and the preparation layers, when possible. Preparation layers analyzed included traditional grounds, made of pigments and fillers in an oil binding medium, as well as varnish layers that MacDonald often used to prepare his paperboard and beaverboard supports before painting.

A team of CCI conservation scientists analyzed the samples, using a combination of instrumental methods. The various analysis techniques provided complementary information, which allowed the chemical constituents of the samples to be determined with a high degree of certainty. Pigments, fillers, and accessory minerals in the samples were identified, using at least three, and often four or five, of the following techniques: Fourier transform infrared (FTIR) spectroscopy; X-ray diffraction (XRD); scanning electron microscopy with energy dispersive X-ray spectrometry (SEM/EDX); Raman spectroscopy; and polarized light microscopy (PLM).

For binding media and varnishes, results of FTIR spectroscopy allowed identification of the general class of material. Analysis with pyrolysis-gas chromatography-mass spectrometry (Py-GC-MS) provided more detailed characterization of selected varnishes. Appendix B describes the choice of instrumental methods, the order in which they were applied, and details about each of the instruments.

Chemical Analysis: Preparation

The Sketches

The chemical analysis of the preparation layers reported here complements the visual observations in chapter 2. Preparation layers that were analyzed included examples of each of the types observed on MacDonald's sketches: commercial grounds on academy boards, ground layers that MacDonald applied himself, and varnish preparation layers. A summary of the major findings is presented here, with detailed results provided in Appendix D.

Commercial grounds. As described in chapter 2, visual examination of 21 of MacDonald's sketches from the 1909 to 1913 period showed that they were all prepared with a traditional ground layer. While many of these grounds were artist-applied, in this early period, MacDonald sometimes sketched on academy boards with commercial grounds. We chose two of these sketches on academy board for analysis: *Snow, High Park* from 1909 and *View from Split Rock* from 1912.

Figure 4.1 illustrates a cross-section from the sky of Snow, High Park. The thick, white layer (labelled 1 on the image) is a commercial white ground. It is composed of lead white, calcium carbonate, and barium sulfate in a drying oil binding medium. Lead white pigment produces an opaque ground layer for oil painting. Calcium carbonate and barium sulfate, on the other hand, are lower-cost fillers that are relatively transparent in oil. As described in the glossary, fillers are added to paints and grounds to reduce costs and, in some cases, to adjust their properties. Barium sulfate and calcium carbonate are both known to have been used in ground formulations in the early twentieth century. They functioned, in part, to optimize the properties of the ground as a base layer for painting by increasing absorbency and

Table 4.1: Paintings and sketches chosen for scientific analysis

Title	Type	Date	Dimensions h × w (cm)*	Collection	Figure Number
Snow, High Park	sketch	1909	12.5 × 17.6	McMichael	Fig. 1.1, p. 20
View from Split Rock	sketch	1912	18.0 × 22.8	NGC	Fig. 1.2, p. 20
Early Evening, Winter	painting	1912	84.0 × 71.5	AGO	Fig. 1.3, p. 21
Logs on the Gatineau River	sketch	1914	20.2 × 25.3	McMichael	Fig. 1.4, p. 23
Thornhill Garden, No.1	sketch	c. 1916	25.3 × 20.3	AGO	—
The Tangled Garden	painting	1916	121.3 × 152.3	NGC	Fig. 1.5, p. 24
The Elements	painting	1916	71.4 × 92.0	AGO	Fig. 1.6, p. 25
Near Minden	sketch	1916 or 1917	20.2 × 25.3	McMichael	Fig. 1.7, p. 26
Canoe Lake	sketch	c. 1917	20.2 × 25.3	McMichael	Fig. 1.9, p. 27
Leaves in the Brook	sketch	c. 1918	21.4 × 26.6	McMichael	Fig. 1.13, p. 34
Leaves in the Brook	painting	1919	52.7 × 65.0	McMichael	Fig. 1.14, p. 35
Solemn Land, Algoma	sketch	c. 1919	21.5 × 26.6	AGO	Fig. 1.15, p. 36
Autumn Leaves, Batchewana, Algoma	sketch	c. 1919	21.5 × 26.6	AGO	Fig. 1.10, p. 30
Algoma Hills	sketch	1920	21.3 × 26.4	McMichael	Fig. 1.11, p. 32
Moose Lake, Algoma	sketch	1920	21.4 × 26.5	McMichael	Fig. 1.12, p 33
Algoma Waterfall	painting	1920	76.3 × 88.5	McMichael	—
Falls, Montreal River	painting	1920	122.8 × 153.2	AGO	—
The Solemn Land	painting	1921	122.6 × 153.2	NGC	Fig. 1.16, p. 37
Forest Wilderness	painting	1921	122.0 × 152.0	McMichael	Fig. 1.17, p. 38
Gleams on the Hills	painting	1921	82.0 × 87.2	NGC	—
Old Dock, Petite Rivière, Nova Scotia	sketch	1922	21.4 × 26.4	NGC	Fig. 1.18, p. 40
Petite Rivière, Nova Scotia	sketch	1922	21.4 × 26.3	AGO	—
Lake McArthur, Yoho Park	sketch	1924	21.3 × 26.5	NGC	—
Mount Goodsir, Yoho Park	painting	1925	107.3 × 122.3	AGO	Fig. 1.21, p. 44
Cathedral Peak and Lake O'Hara	sketch	1927	21.3 × 26.5	McMichael	Fig. 1.19, p. 42
Jack Pine	sketch	1929	21.5 × 26.5	AGO	—
Near Lake Oesa, Abbot's Pass	sketch	1930	21.4 × 26.5	NGC	Fig. 1.20, p. 42
Ottertail Valley	sketch	1930	21.3 × 26.5	NGC	—
Windy Sky near Pointe au Baril	sketch	1931	21.5 × 26.6	NGC	Fig. 1.23, p. 46
Goat Range, Rocky Mountains	painting	1932	53.7 × 66.1	McMichael	Fig. 1.22, p. 45
Palms, Barbados	sketch	1932	21.4 × 26.6	AGO	Fig. 1.24, p. 46
Barbados	sketch	1932	21.5 × 26.7	AGO	—

*The measurements are from our examination of the works and may differ slightly from dimensions given on the institutional websites.

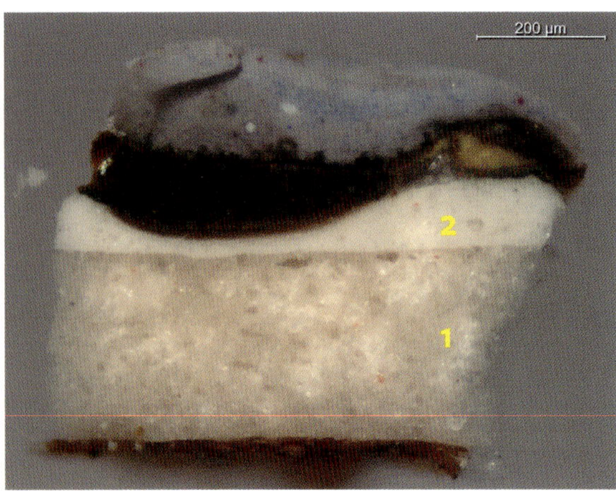

Fig. 4.1: Cross-section from the sky of *Snow, High Park*, 1909, McMichael Canadian Art Collection, 1981.24, incident light. Layers from bottom to top: thin layer of brown paperboard; thick, white commercial ground (labelled 1); thinner lead white layer (labelled 2); brown and blue paint of the composition. Photo: © Government of Canada.

providing the ground with more texture or "tooth."[2] The cross-section in Fig. 4.1 also revealed a thinner white layer (labelled 2 on the image) on top of the ground. This layer is composed of lead white in drying oil. It could have been added by MacDonald or could correspond to a second ground applied by the manufacturer.[3]

The preparation for a second sketch with a commercial ground, *View from Split Rock*, has a different composition. This sketch is one of several that MacDonald painted on academy board supports during a trip to Dr. MacCallum's cottage in 1912. These boards were commercially prepared on both faces, with a light grey ground on one side and dark grey on the other. In *View from Split Rock*, MacDonald painted on the lighter side. A cross-section sample showed that the light grey ground was applied as a single layer. It is composed of lead white in a drying oil medium. It has no added fillers but includes a small amount of carbon black to create the grey tone.

Artist-applied ground layers (1914 to 1917). Visual examination of 11 of MacDonald's sketches on paperboard from the 1914 to 1917 period revealed that they all had an artist-applied ground. MacDonald often used warmly coloured grounds to prepare his boards during this period, and in some cases, applied two layers of ground with different colours. We analyzed the ground layers for two sketches on paperboard from this period: *Logs on the Gatineau River* and *Near Minden*. Since MacDonald created his outdoor sketches rapidly, he most likely applied these ground layers in advance of a sketching trip to ensure that they were dry enough to paint on.[4] MacDonald coated the support for *Logs on the Gatineau River* with a single layer of light yellow-orange ground. *Near Minden* includes two ground layers: green followed by light yellow-orange (Fig. 4.2).[5]

In both sketches, the ground layers are based on a mixture of lead white and zinc white in drying oil. The yellow-orange layers are tinted with iron oxide pigments; Prussian blue was added to the mix for the green layer. These grounds also include calcium carbonate, barium sulfate, and kaolin. Although kaolin is sometimes added to paint or ground formulations as a filler, it is also commonly present as a naturally

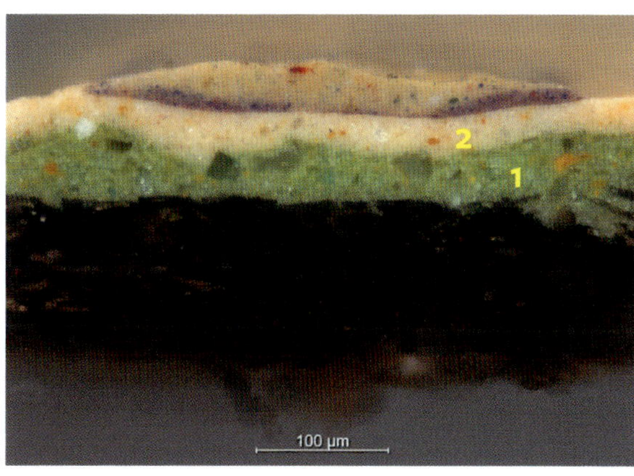

Fig. 4.2: Cross-section sample from *Near Minden*, 1916 or 1917, McMichael Canadian Art Collection, 1966.15.12, incident light. Layers from bottom to top: brown paperboard support; green ground (labelled 1); light yellow-orange ground (labelled 2); thin purple paint, possibly underpainting as seen in Fig. 3.4; beige paint of the composition. Photo: © Government of Canada.

occurring mineral in iron oxide pigments.[6] As described later, we identified kaolin in some of the paint samples, usually associated with iron oxide pigments. Calcium carbonate and barium sulfate fillers, on the other hand, were rarely identified in MacDonald's paint. Their presence in the grounds suggests that MacDonald deliberately chose a ground formulation that differed from the paint above, either because it was less expensive or because it had properties that made it a suitable surface to apply the oil paint of the image layers.

We also examined three sketches on plywood from this period. Two of these (*Thornhill Garden, No.1* and *Snow, Algonquin Park*) appear to have been painted directly on the plywood support. *Canoe Lake*, a circa 1917 sketch on plywood, on the other hand, includes a traditional ground layer. Cross-section samples show that MacDonald applied two ground layers, pale grey-blue followed by off-white, to the plywood before painting. These ground layers do not contain fillers: they are composed of pigments that MacDonald commonly used in his paint. Unlike his works on paperboard, then, there is no indication that he chose a specific ground formulation to prepare this plywood support.[7]

Varnish preparation layers. In 1918, MacDonald stopped using traditional ground layers for his sketches; instead, he painted directly on the paperboard support, usually after coating it with varnish. We established the presence of varnish coatings by examining the sketches front and back with ultraviolet (UV) illumination and observing the visible fluorescence. The characteristic orange fluorescence observed regularly on his sketching boards indicates the presence of unbleached shellac. The documentary evidence presented in chapter 2 also supports the use of this material.

For several sketches, these varnish preparation layers were documented with cross-sections. In most cases, the cross-sections showed a clear boundary between the paint and the varnish used to coat the board, which indicates that the varnish was dry when the paint was applied. An exception was the sketch for *Leaves in the Brook*, for which the cross-section showed intermixing of paint and varnish, suggesting that MacDonald applied the preparatory varnish at the time of painting.

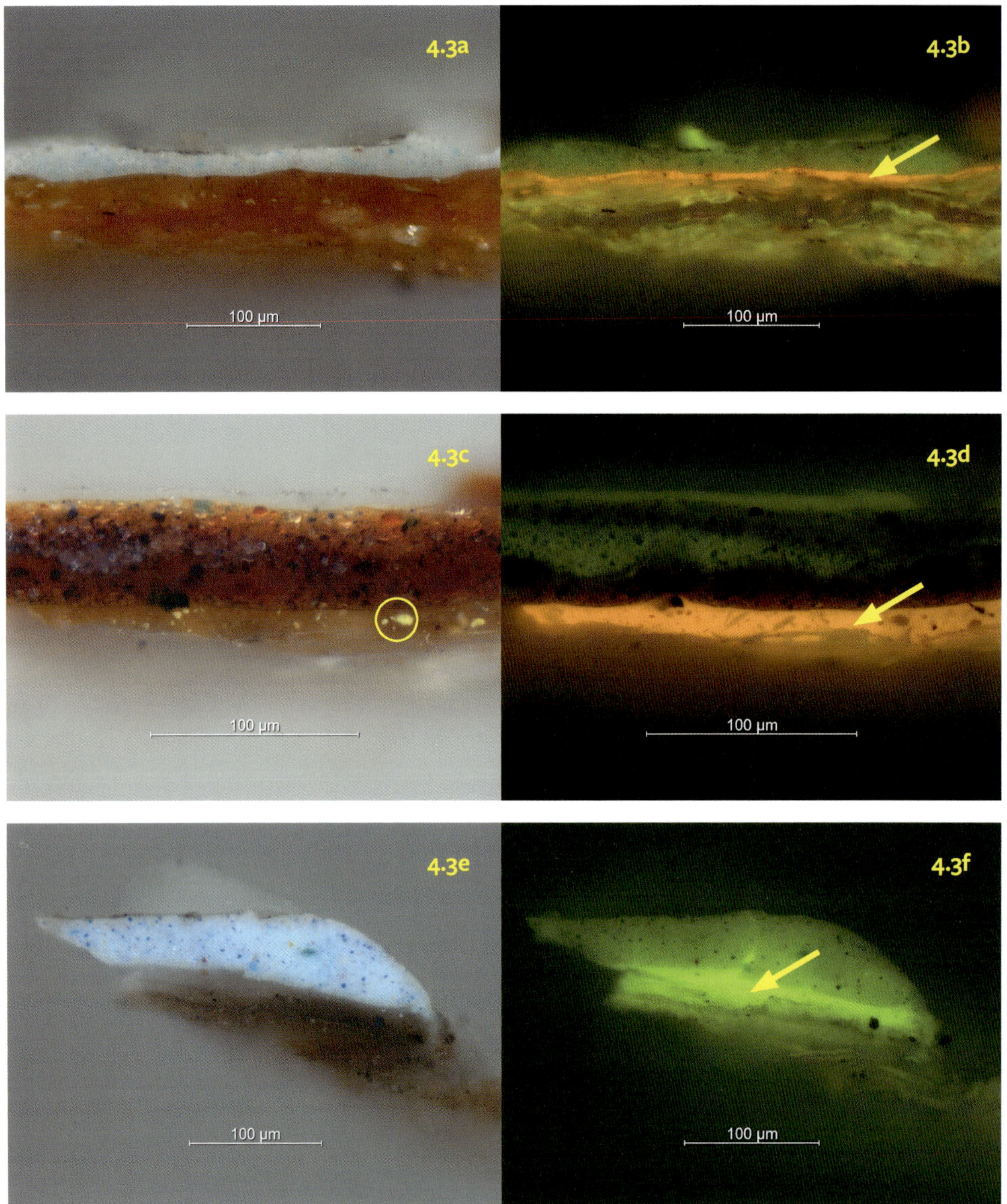

Cross-sections from three sketches showing the varnish used to coat the support before painting (marked with arrows); incident light at left, fluorescence at right. Photos: © Government of Canada.
Figs. 4.3a and 4.3b: *Algoma Hills*, 1920, McMichael Canadian Art Collection, 1966.15.6.
Figs. 4.3c and 4.3d: *Old Dock, Petite Rivière, Nova Scotia*, 1922, National Gallery of Canada, Ottawa.
Figs. 4.3e and 4.3f: *Solemn Land, Algoma*, circa 1919, Art Gallery of Ontario.

Figures 4.3a to 4.3f illustrate cross-sections from three sketches. Normal (incident) light images are on the left and fluorescence images, using a blue excitation filter, are on the right. The varnish preparation layers applied to the paperboard prior to painting are marked on the fluorescence images with arrows. In the cross-section from *Algoma Hills* (Figs. 4.3a and 4.3b), the thin, transparent layer between the brown paperboard support and the pale blue paint has the typical orange fluorescence of unbleached shellac. Figures 4.3c and 4.3d illustrate a similar shellac varnish beneath the brown paint layers on *Old Dock, Petite Rivière, Nova Scotia*. Figures 4.3e and 4.3f, from *Solemn Land, Algoma*, on the other hand, show that the varnish layer between the brown paperboard and the blue paint has a yellow-green fluorescence. While the fluorescence of this layer indicates that the board was sealed with varnish, possibly a natural resin, it is not indicative of a specific resin type. This sample was too small to allow chemical analysis of the varnish.

For six sketches, analysis confirmed that the varnish used to prepare the boards was based on shellac. As listed in Appendix D, smaller amounts of other organic components (conifer tree resin, drying oil, and wax) were also identified in a few of the samples.[8] These components could be part of MacDonald's varnish formulation; however, because the varnish samples were mixed with paperboard fibres, the tree resin, oil, and wax could possibly also correspond to additives in the paperboard.

Analysis showed that the shellac layers contain orpiment, an opaque, bright yellow pigment composed of arsenic sulfide. The particles of orpiment are easily visible in the cross-section from *Old Dock, Petite Rivière, Nova Scotia* in Figs. 4.3c and 4.3d. One of the larger orpiment particles is circled on the normal light image at the left. The orpiment was undoubtedly included during the manufacture of the shellac. While not a pigment that MacDonald used in his paintings, orpiment was a common additive during traditional shellac processing to give a yellow tone and a slight opacity to the varnish.[9]

Artist-applied ground layers (1930 to 1932). MacDonald returned to the practice of applying a ground layer to his sketching supports late in his career, particularly during the last two years of his life. We analyzed the ground layers for four sketches on paperboard from this period: *Near Lake Oesa, Abbot's Pass* from his last trip to the Rockies; *Windy Sky near Pointe au Baril* from a 1931 visit to Georgian Bay; and finally, two sketches from his recuperative visit to Barbados in 1932.

The grounds for all four of these sketches are similar: they are based on lead white, zinc white, and barium sulfate in a drying oil medium and have been lightly tinted with small amounts of coloured pigments. The ground for the 1931 Georgian Bay sketch, *Windy Sky near Pointe au Baril*, also contains talc, an uncommon filler in MacDonald's works.

As in the earlier sketches, MacDonald generally chose a ground formulation that differed from the paint of the image layers. An exception is *Palms, Barbados*, where the white pigments and fillers used to paint the sketch (lead white, zinc white, and barium sulfate) are the same as those found in the ground. This is the only sketch examined where barium sulfate was identified in the paint layers. It is possible that MacDonald ran out of his preferred white paint during this trip and resorted to using the white formulation he usually reserved for his grounds.

The Studio Paintings

Paintings on rigid supports. MacDonald regularly painted on beaverboard, an early type of medium-density fibreboard, during the period from about 1915 to 1918. As in the case of the sketches, we established the presence of varnish coatings on the boards by illuminating them with UV radiation and observing the visible fluorescence. In several cases, the green-yellow fluorescence suggested that MacDonald sealed the beaverboard support with varnish before painting. However, this was sometimes difficult to confirm when a final surface varnish partially obscured the fluorescence of layers beneath.

Analysis of samples from *The Elements* and *The Tangled Garden* confirmed that the beaverboard supports for these two works were, indeed, prepared with varnish. In both cases, cross-sections showed that MacDonald first brushed on some of the thin lines of underpainting to sketch out the composition and, subsequently, coated the board with a varnish layer before painting the composition.[10]

The thin, dark red layer, labelled 1, at the bottom of the cross-section from *The Elements* (Fig. 4.4a) corresponds to MacDonald's underpainting. As shown in Appendix D, analysis revealed that it is pigmented with alizarin lake and ultramarine. The varnish layer with green-yellow fluorescence, labelled 2, covers the underpainting. While its fluorescence suggests a natural resin, it is not indicative of a specific resin type. The multiple tones of dull to bright red paint above the varnish correspond to the image layers. The intermixing between the varnish and the paint layer above suggests that MacDonald painted parts of his composition before the varnish beneath was completely dry.

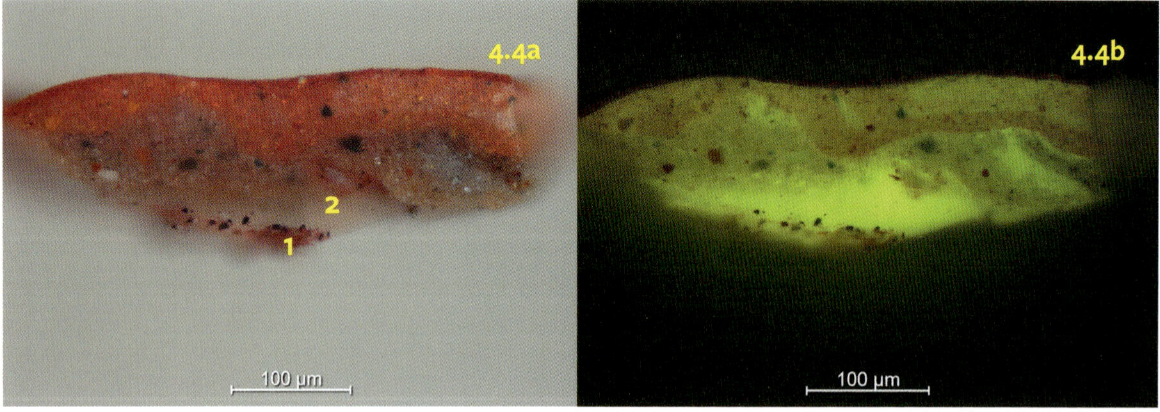

Cross-section from *The Elements*, 1916, Art Gallery of Ontario; incident light (Fig. 4.4a) and fluorescence (Fig. 4.4b). Photos: © Government of Canada.

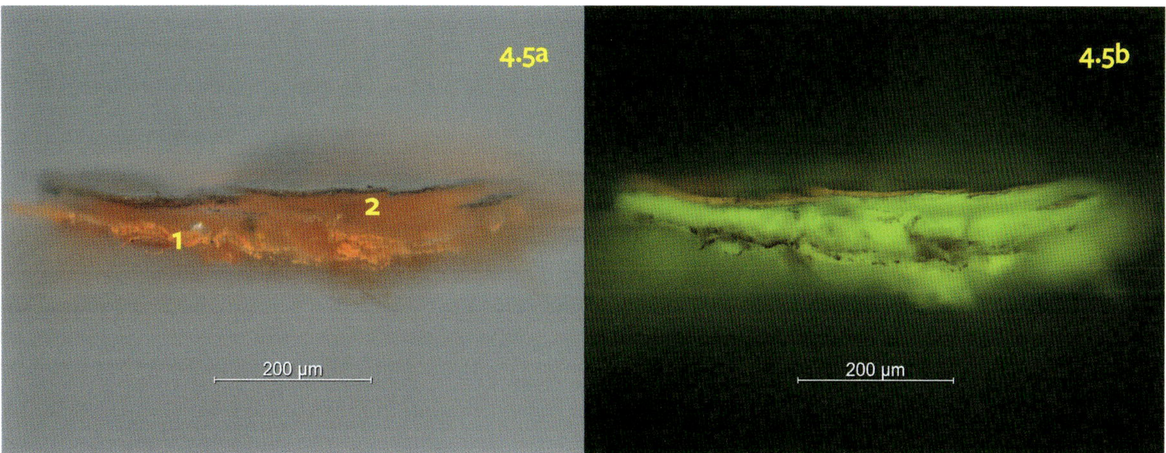

Cross-section from *The Tangled Garden*, 1916, National Gallery of Canada, Ottawa; incident light (Fig. 4.5a) and fluorescence (Fig. 4.5b). Photos: © Government of Canada.

A cross-section sample from *The Tangled Garden* (Fig. 4.5a) similarly shows red underpainting, labelled 1, embedded in the beaverboard support. It is followed by a varnish layer with green-yellow fluorescence, labelled 2. In this case, the orange-red underpainting was coloured primarily with vermilion. Analysis of the varnish above showed that it contains predominantly heated pine resin,[11] consistent with the observed fluorescence. The thin, dark green layer on top of the varnish corresponds to the painted image. A small amount of another varnish, its orange fluorescence indicating shellac, is visible at the surface. Since this sample is from an edge, this varnish layer may correspond to spillover of the shellac that was applied to the back of the board.

Paintings on canvas. The ground layers appear white to off-white for all nine of MacDonald's studio paintings on canvas supports. In some cases, the grounds have a slightly grey tone and in other cases exhibit a warmer, slightly orange hue. As tabulated in Appendix D, it was not always possible to determine whether the ground layer was commercially applied or if MacDonald applied the ground layer to the canvas himself. Nevertheless, among the nine paintings in the study group, visual examination allowed us to establish that MacDonald used both types.

The commercial ground on the 1912 painting *Early Evening, Winter* has a simple composition. It is composed of a single layer of lead white in a drying oil medium with a small amount of carbon black to give a pale grey colour. The chemical analysis of the grounds for the eight later paintings revealed that they are more complex: they are based on various combinations of lead white, zinc-containing pigments, barium sulfate, and calcium carbonate in a drying oil medium, with small amounts of tinting pigments added to adjust the colour. This type of composition is typical of the period. As described in the previous section on grounds for the sketches, fillers like calcium carbonate and barium sulfate were added to ground formulations to decrease the cost, and in some cases, to adjust the working properties.[12]

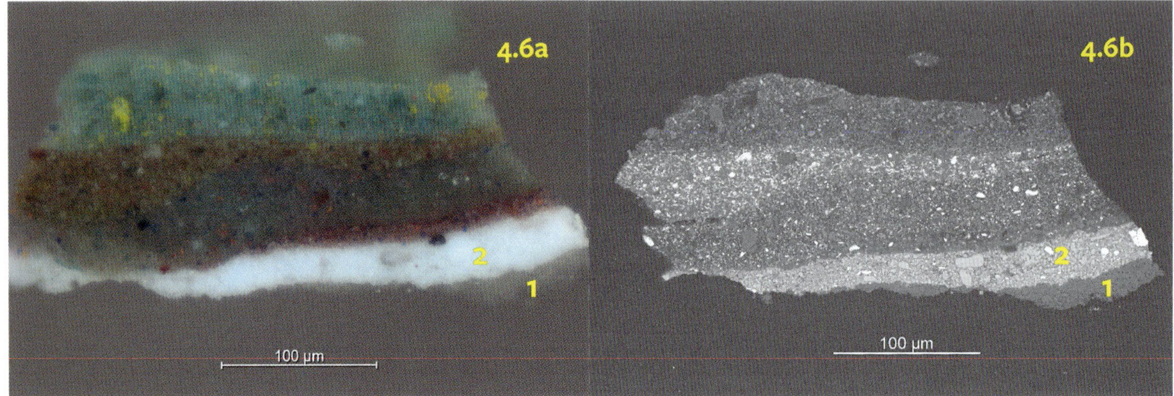

Cross-section from *Algoma Waterfall*, 1920, McMichael Canadian Art Collection, 1968.7.2, incident light (Fig. 4.6a) and backscattered electron image (Fig. 4.6b). The translucent, calcium carbonate ground (labelled 1) at the lower right side of the cross-section is most evident in the backscattered electron image. It followed by an opaque white ground (labelled 2). The thin, purple-red layer above the ground may correspond to underpainting. The green and brown layers above correspond to the paint of the composition. Photos: © Government of Canada.

Of the six Algoma paintings analyzed, three were prepared in a like manner: the grounds for *Leaves in the Brook*; *Falls, Montreal River*; and *The Solemn Land* are all based on a mixture of lead white and calcium carbonate, very lightly tinted with yellow or orange iron oxides.[13]

The grounds for *Gleams on the Hills* and *Forest Wilderness* contained these same components along with additional white pigments and fillers. *Algoma Waterfall* was the only painting for which two ground layers were observed. A cross-section from this painting (Fig. 4.6a) showed a translucent, white ground layer, based on calcium carbonate (labelled 1), followed by an opaque white ground containing barium sulfate, lead white, and a zinc-based pigment (labelled 2). This layering suggests that *Algoma Waterfall* may have been painted on a "double-primed" commercial canvas.

Mount Goodsir, Yoho Park, from 1925, is an early studio painting on canvas depicting the Rocky Mountains. A cross-section from this painting, illustrated in the previous chapter (Fig. 3.20) shows the off-white ground layer followed by a thin layer of red underpainting. Like several of the Algoma paintings on canvas, the ground for *Mount Goodsir, Yoho Park* is based on a mixture of lead white and calcium carbonate; however, in this case, it is tinted with chrome yellow rather than iron oxides. The underpainting is pigmented with red iron oxide.

Goat Range, Rocky Mountains is one of MacDonald's last paintings. He completed it in 1932, working in a makeshift studio in the woodshed of his Thornhill home.[14] The ground, which MacDonald applied himself, differs from the other ground layers that were analyzed: it is composed of a mixture of barium sulfate and zinc sulfide, known as lithopone, along with a small amount of talc. This painting has an unusual bumpy texture that originates in the ground (Fig. 3.17). Analysis of ground samples, including cross-sections through several of the bumpy areas, indicates that these small lumps have the same composition as the rest of the ground. The bumpy texture appears to be related to the way MacDonald applied the ground layer. Some of the lumps have formed through a buildup of thicker ground around protruding jute fibres from the underlying canvas, while others may be fragments of partially dried ground material that MacDonald accidentally incorporated into the liquid formulation during mixing.

Chemical Analysis: Paint

Sources for Oil Paint

Although Toronto-based artists' supply firms stocked all manner of materials at the beginning of the twentieth century, they did not make their own oil paints; rather, they imported them from paint manufacturers known as artists' colourmen. These Toronto establishments appear to have sold paints primarily from British or European colourmen; no American brands were listed in the consulted documents.[15] By this time, oil paints were sold in collapsible metal tubes, which were very convenient for outdoor oil sketching. Turpentine, drying oils, and varnishes were available in bottles and allowed for thinning and modifying the paint.

A previous publication compiled information from catalogues and advertisements about artists' oil paints in Toronto in the early twentieth century, focusing on three major agents: the E. Harris Company, the Art Metropole, and the Artists' Supply Company.[16] Since the oil paints offered by these Toronto firms represent many of the brands that MacDonald would have used, this information provides useful context for the results of the scientific analysis of his paints.[17] The findings of the previous research are summarized here, along with new information linking MacDonald to these Toronto establishments.

The E. Harris Company. The E. Harris Company was established in Toronto in 1850 and was located on King Street East.[18] Their primary oil paint brand in the 1900 to 1932 period appears to have been Winsor & Newton.[19] One of the foremost British colourmen of the time, Winsor & Newton produced a wide range of oil paints. In an E. Harris Company catalogue from 1900, well over a hundred Winsor & Newton oil colours are listed for sale. Oil paints from Rowney, another well-known British firm, are also mentioned, albeit very briefly.[20] Later advertisements indicate that in the 1927 to 1932 period the company had added oil paints from both Reeves and Schmincke to their product line.[21] There is evidence that MacDonald purchased materials from the E. Harris Company: as described in chapter 2, a supplier's stamp from the company was found on the original stretcher for a 1925 painting. It is also notable that MacDonald designed an advertisement for the company that appeared in the Arts & Letters Club publication *The Lamps* in 1919.[22]

The Art Metropole. The Art Metropole, founded in 1888, was situated on Yonge Street.[23] At the turn of the twentieth century, their major oil paint brand was Winsor & Newton. A 1906 catalogue describes Winsor & Newton paints as the Art Metropole's recommended choice for professional artists. Heyl's oil colours from Germany are also listed, although they note that this brand was not of equivalent quality.[24] Specific paint brands were rarely mentioned in advertisements for the Art Metropole from 1906 to 1932,[25] although they presumably continued to sell primarily Winsor & Newton paints, likely along with other brands. A commercial label on the back of a 1912 oil sketch (illustrated in chapter 2, Fig. 2.2) shows that MacDonald purchased materials from the Art Metropole early in his career. Another link between MacDonald and this company is the fact that the Art Metropole manager, Alex G. Cumming, rented space in the Studio Building in the 1916 to 1918 period and is known to have supplied the painters with materials.[26]

The Artists' Supply Company. The Artists' Supply Company was created in about 1905 as a branch of the Toronto dry goods wholesaler George Ridout & Co. to handle their artists' materials sales.[27] At the time MacDonald was painting, the company was located on York Street.[28] It acted as a Toronto agent for two main paint manufacturers: the Dutch firm Talens & Zoon and the British manufacturer Madderton & Company. The Artists' Supply Company imported and sold the Rembrandt line of oil paint from Talens & Zoon throughout the first decades of the twentieth century.[29] The brand that they advertised more prominently, however, was the Cambridge Colours line of oil paints from Madderton.[30]

Madderton & Company, founded by chemist and art scientist A.P. Laurie, operated out of Loughton, Essex, and produced the Cambridge Colours from 1891 until 1939.[31] Although not as well known today as brands like Winsor & Newton, the Cambridge Colours were highly regarded artists' oil paints at the time. They were endorsed, for example, by a number of late-nineteenth-century and early-twentieth-century British artists, with Holman Hunt and other pre-Raphaelites among their numbers.[32] Advertisements and catalogues for the Cambridge Colours emphasized the purity and stability of their paints. The company provided a carefully chosen colour palette, excluding pigments that they believed to be unstable like chrome yellow and emerald green.[33]

From 1906 onwards, the Artists' Supply Company appears to have been the sole Toronto agent for the Cambridge Colours, selling the brand to both retailers and individuals. Cambridge Colours were advertised by the Artists' Supply Company in Canadian National Exhibition (CNE) catalogues beginning in 1906 and in publications of the Central Ontario School of Art and Design (COSAD) from 1908.[34] Order forms indicate that the company also sold their products beyond the

Toronto market; shipping prices were given for Quebec and Ontario as well as for locations west of Ontario.[35]

One of MacDonald's existing paintboxes provides a key piece of evidence that he knew of, and undoubtedly used, the Cambridge Colours brand. As shown in Appendix A, this paintbox, supplied by Madderton, is labelled "The Cambridge Colours Materials." MacDonald may have first learned about this paint brand in the 1904 to 1907 period when he was living in Loughton, Essex, the same small town where Madderton's factory was located. However, he may also have purchased this box from the Artists' Supply Company after his return to Toronto in 1908. Although we have not located any of MacDonald's extant paint tubes or purchase receipts to date, our research has uncovered archival evidence to indicate that A.Y. Jackson[36] and, later, MacDonald's student and assistant, Carl Schaefer,[37] both used Cambridge Colours purchased from the Artists' Supply Company.[38]

Results of the Analysis

Binding medium. As expected, analysis revealed that the binding medium in all paint samples is a drying oil. More detailed characterization to determine the type of drying oil would be an area for future research.[39] The consulted catalogues indicate that linseed, walnut, and poppyseed oil were all available at the time MacDonald was painting.[40] When zinc white was present in the paint, zinc fatty acid salts (known as zinc soaps) were routinely identified using Fourier transform infrared (FTIR) spectroscopy. These commonly identified compounds are formed by a reaction between components of the oil medium and the zinc oxide in the pigment.[41]

Overall palette. Table 4.2 is a list of the pigments identified in the 32 paintings that were analyzed. It groups the pigments into categories based on the frequency with which they were found. The numbers in parentheses indicate in how many paintings we identified the pigment. For simplicity, fillers and accessory minerals have been omitted from the table but are provided in Appendix D.

A comparison of the data to previous research on Tom Thomson's materials[42] shows that there are many similarities in the palettes of the two painters. However, there are also a few notable differences. Based on the works analyzed, MacDonald appears to have included Prussian blue and chrome yellow in his palette more regularly than Thomson. Conversely, although Thomson often chose to paint with cobalt yellow and cobalt blue, they are not among MacDonald's common pigments.

Table 4.2: MacDonald's palette, based on an analysis of 32 works

Colour	**Principal pigments** (identified in over 20 paintings)	**Regularly used** (identified in more than 5 but fewer than 20 paintings)	**Occasionally used** (Identified in 5 paintings or fewer)
○	Cambridge White (25)*	lead white (9)	zinc white (4)
●	yellow iron oxide (29) cadmium yellow (25)	barium yellow (12) chrome yellow (7)	
●	ultramarine (31) cerulean blue (23)	Prussian blue (15)	cobalt blue (2)
●	viridian (32)		green earth (3)
●	alizarin lake or red lake (31) red to orange iron oxide (29) vermilion (23)		chrome orange/red (5) toluidine red (2)
●	carbon-based black (27), but only in small amounts		bone black (1) brown iron oxide/umber (2)

*This pigment is a commercial mixture of lead sulfate and zinc oxide (zinc white) in specific proportions. We have chosen the name Cambridge White because, as described in the following section, this name best represents its source.

While Table 4.2 provides a simple overview of MacDonald's pigments throughout his career, it does not include the finer details about their use, such as how he mixed them to create various colour hues on his paintings and whether his choice of pigments changed over time. To this end, more detailed results about the pigments, fillers, and accessory minerals found in each painting are presented in Appendix D. This appendix also includes the chemical formulae corresponding to the pigment names and a list of the methods used to identify them.

The data in Appendix D shows that MacDonald preferred to limit his pigments to an essential palette: most of the examined paintings included between seven and nine coloured pigments, plus black and white. This is consistent with MacDonald's unpublished lecture notes on outdoor sketching, where he lists "colors, about 8" as part of the required equipment for sketching and later adds that "too many colors spoil the sketch."[43] MacDonald created his compositions by mixing various combinations of these individual colours. Key results about the pigments that MacDonald used are discussed below, followed by a summary of some of his characteristic mixtures.

White pigments. Three white pigments were identified in MacDonald's sketches and paintings: lead white, zinc white, and the pigment we refer to as "Cambridge White," which is composed of a commercial mixture of lead sulfate and zinc white, combined in specific proportions. We have chosen the name Cambridge White for this pigment, since, as outlined below, this name best describes its source.

Lead white and zinc white were both common pigments of the time and were available from numerous artists' colourmen. The white pigment we refer to as

Cambridge white, produced from a commercial mixture of lead sulfate and zinc white, on the other hand, appears to have been less widely distributed. Major manufacturers like Winsor & Newton, Lefranc, and Talens did not sell this pigment.[44]

Madderton & Company, however, did include this characteristic white pigment as part of their Cambridge Colours line. They described it as consisting of "lead sulfate and zinc oxide [i.e., zinc white], prepared by a patented process."[45] They recommended this white pigment over traditional lead white because they considered it to be more stable and less toxic.[46] They named the pigment "New Flake White" to emphasize that it was a substitute for traditional lead white, commonly called "Flake White."[47] The Cambridge Colours, including this new white pigment, were available in Toronto as early as 1906.

A group of historic Cambridge Colours oil paint tubes found in the paintbox of Canadian artist Kathleen Munn, a contemporary of MacDonald's who was active as a painter from about 1909 to 1940, provides valuable reference material for comparison with MacDonald's paint.[48] Several Cambridge Colours paint tubes labelled "New Flake White" were found in the Munn paintbox (p. 178). Analysis of their contents showed that this white pigment is indeed composed of a lead sulfate–zinc white mixture, as described by Madderton. The proportions of the two components in the New Flake White paint tubes are similar to those in samples of MacDonald's paint,[49] indicating that this was undoubtedly the source of his lead sulfate–zinc white pigment.

While Madderton labelled this pigment New Flake White in their catalogues, advertisements, and on paint tubes, it has been given various other names in historic sources, including Cambridge White and Freeman's White.[50] We have chosen to refer to this pigment as Cambridge White, since this name has the advantage of indicating the source of the pigment and avoids confusion between the terms "New Flake White" and "Flake White."

Since MacDonald owned a Cambridge Colours Materials paintbox, it is not surprising to find that he used this brand. The Artists' Supply Company appears to have been the sole Toronto agent for these paints, so this establishment would have been MacDonald's source for Cambridge White after he returned to Canada in 1908.

Table 4.2 illustrates that MacDonald used Cambridge White more extensively than either zinc white or lead white: it was identified in 25 of the 32 works that we studied, representing 80% of his sketches and over 70% of his paintings. MacDonald made use of this pigment throughout his career. It was found in the earliest sketch analyzed, dated 1909, as well as in works painted during the last year of his life. Lead white was identified in nine of the works examined, and zinc white in only four. MacDonald occasionally used more than one white pigment on the same painting.

Figure 4.7 shows excerpts from a 1908 Madderton catalogue, *Permanent Colours for Artists*, which includes the composition and prices of the white pigments they offered. They noted in their catalogue that Cambridge White – or New Flake White,

COMPOSITION

OF THE

CAMBRIDGE ARTISTS' COLOURS.

WHITE PIGMENTS.

CHINESE WHITE - - (*Permanent*)	This is prepared from pure Oxide of Zinc, and is absolutely permanent. Supplied for Water Colour only.
FLAKE WHITE - -	This pigment consists of Carbonate and Hydrate of lead. It is permanent in sunlight, but in common with the Flake Whites of other makers blackens if exposed to the impure air of our large cities. (*See* page 8.)
FOUNDATION WHITE -	Similar to Flake White but less carefully prepared and ground.
NEW FLAKE WHITE -	It is a substitute for Flake White, consisting of Lead Sulphate and Zinc Oxide, prepared by a patented process. This will be found to resist the darkening effect of impure air. It has furthermore the advantage of being practically non-poisonous, the ordinary Flake White being poisonous. (*See* page 8.)
ZINC WHITE - - -	Pure Oxide of Zinc. This pigment is perfectly permanent. After carefully experimenting during the last twelve years we have decided to include it in the Cambridge Palette, although we are aware that some artists believe it has a tendency to crack. On the other hand we are assured by many artists that they have long used it successfully.

PRICES OF THE

FINEST CAMBRIDGE ARTISTS'

OIL AND WATER COLOURS.

ALL PRICES SUBJECT TO THE USUAL CASH DISCOUNT TO THE PROFESSION.

(For Order Forms see accompanying circulars Nos. 1 and 2.)

OIL COLOURS.

WHITES.

Sizes of Tubes—ins.	Single 4" each	Small Studio 2×1 each	Studio 3×1 each	Large Studio 4×1 each	½-lb. each	1-lb each
NEW FLAKE WHITE— (No. 0 Consistency) *EXTRA STIFF* (No. 1 Consistency) *STIFF* (No. 2 Consistency) *MEDIUM* (No. 3 Consistency) *THIN* It is a substitute for Flake White, consisting of Lead Sulphate and Zinc Oxide, prepared by a patented process. This will be found to resist the darkening effect of impure air. It has furthermore the advantage of being practically non-poisonous, the ordinary Flake White being poisonous. FLAKE WHITE (No. 1 Consistency) *STIFF* " " (No. 2 Consistency) *MEDIUM* " " (No. 3 Consistency) *THIN*	-/4	-/8	-/10	1/2	1/3	2/6
ZINC WHITE	-/4	-/8	-/10	1/2	1/6	3/-
FOUNDATION WHITE	—	-/4	-/6	-/7	-/8	1/4

Fig. 4.7: Description of white pigments in a 1908 Madderton & Company catalogue. At left, page 10 of the catalogue. At right, page 21 of the catalogue. Photos: © Government of Canada.

as they called it – had advantages over traditional lead white: it darkened less when exposed to "impure air" and was less toxic.[51] Because of this, they went so far as to admit that "as we are purists on the question of colours, we have sometimes seriously considered whether we were justified in still retaining Flake White [i.e., lead white] in the Cambridge palette."[52] And, in fact, available Canadian price lists for the Cambridge Colours published by the Artists' Supply Company in 1926 and 1934 no longer included lead white.[53]

MacDonald's choice to use Cambridge White may have been related to Madderton's warnings about the darkening and toxicity of lead white and the tendency of zinc white to crack (Fig. 4.7). He was not alone in his preference for the pigment. Previous research has shown that, like MacDonald, Thomson used Cambridge White extensively.[54] There is also evidence that other members of the Group of Seven, as well as some of their contemporaries, made use of this white pigment during the first half of the twentieth century.[55]

Fillers and accessory minerals. As described in the glossary, fillers are added to paints to reduce costs or adjust properties. Some pigments from a mineral source have naturally occurring transparent constituents, like clays and silicates, that we refer to as accessory minerals. Fillers and accessory minerals do not generally play an important role in the colour of the paints that include them.

MacDonald's paints often contain kaolin or other silicates. These compounds are frequently present as accessory minerals in natural iron oxide pigments like ochres and siennas,[56] and when we identified them, they were usually associated with such pigments. Barium sulfate, calcium carbonate, and gypsum fillers were each found in only one or two of the paintings studied. It is notable that while barium sulfate and calcium carbonate are rare in MacDonald's paints, these fillers were frequently identified in his ground formulations.

The filler of most interest in MacDonald's paints is hydromagnesite, a magnesium carbonate hydroxide. This filler was widely used by Winsor & Newton in the first part of the twentieth century and is characteristic of their oil paints.[57] We identified hydromagnesite in six of MacDonald's paintings, all dating between 1916 and 1920. Much of this period overlaps with the First World War, when certain materials and supplies were difficult to obtain. It is possible that MacDonald used the Winsor & Newton brand during the war years because it was more easily available. Alex G. Cumming, manager of the Art Metropole, lived in the Studio Building from 1916 to 1918, and it is also possible that he supplied MacDonald with Winsor & Newton paints, the Art Metropole's main brand.

Yellow pigments. Based on the results from the 32 paintings in the study group, MacDonald relied on four different yellow pigments. Yellow iron oxide and cadmium yellow are among MacDonald's principal pigments, while he appears to have used barium yellow and chrome yellow less often.

MacDonald included yellow iron oxide pigments in almost all the paintings studied. In many cases, yellow iron oxide was present in minor amounts in mixed colours; however, we also occasionally identified it as the primary pigment in some warm, golden-ochre tones.

For his bright, opaque yellows, MacDonald most often used cadmium yellow: this pigment was identified in 25 of the 32 paintings studied. In the early twentieth century, various recipes were used to prepare cadmium yellow, leading to different pigment compositions.[58] There are four main types of this pigment: two crystalline forms of cadmium sulfide (α-CdS and β-CdS), an amorphous form of cadmium sulfide, and a lighter yellow composed of cadmium zinc sulfide. Cadmium yellow pigments were sometimes mixed with barium sulfate or other compounds to lighten the colour or reduce the cost. Small amounts of unreacted starting materials may also be present.[59]

In most of the paintings analyzed, the cadmium yellow is the crystalline α-CdS variety. In a few cases, β-CdS or amorphous cadmium sulfide was found.[60] The cadmium zinc sulfide form of the pigment was identified in only two cases. Both sketches date from MacDonald's 1932 trip to Barbados.

At the time MacDonald was painting, cadmium yellows were considered more durable than chrome yellows, which were based on lead chromate and thought to darken over time due to their lead content. In a 1906 catalogue, Winsor & Newton listed cadmium yellows as permanent, while chrome yellows were only "moderately permanent" in oil.[61] Madderton went further, offering a full range of cadmium yellow pigments, but choosing not to supply chrome yellows. They wrote in their 1908 catalogue, "We do not supply these colours, owing to their tendency to blacken in impure air. We beg to refer artists to our cadmium yellows (daffodil yellows), which are permanent."[62]

While described as permanent by these two colourmen, cadmium yellows of this period are sometimes prone to powdering, cracking, and surface crusts. This type of damage is caused by chemical reactions producing cadmium sulfates, oxalates, and carbonates.[63] The stability of the pigments depended on how they were prepared. As described in chapter 5, while most of MacDonald's cadmium yellow paints remain intact, we observed powdering and cracking in a few cases. Overall analysis of the samples did not reveal a difference in composition in the cadmium yellows that showed cracking compared to those that were intact. However, factors other than the composition of the pigment can also affect its stability (for example, environmental conditions, the thickness of the application, the other pigments mixed with the cadmium yellow, and the layering of the paint and ground).

MacDonald also frequently used barium yellow, a pigment composed of barium chromate that produced a light, lemon-coloured shade. Although Madderton did not supply the lead chromates, they did offer barium chromate under the name "lemon yellow" and considered it to be permanent.[64] In the works that we examined, MacDonald used barium yellow almost exclusively in mixed colours, particularly in various green and turquoise shades. He also added small amounts of barium yellow to some of his whites to produce a warmer tone.

Chrome yellow was found on seven of the paintings studied, and in five of them, Cambridge White was also used. Since Madderton was the source of Cambridge White but did not supply chrome yellow, the presence of both pigments indicates that MacDonald used more than one paint brand in these works.

Blue pigments. MacDonald regularly used three blue pigments: ultramarine, cerulean blue, and Prussian blue. Unlike Thomson,[65] MacDonald does not appear to have used cobalt blue to a great extent: it was identified in only a few of the paintings that were analyzed.

Ultramarine was MacDonald's principal blue pigment, and we identified it in all but one of the paintings studied. MacDonald used ultramarine as the main colourant in many of his blue shades as well as a component in mixed colours such as purples and greens. The size and shape of the particles indicate that the ultramarine was synthetic, rather than the natural mineral lapis lazuli. The synthetic form, the usual variety at that time, was often referred to as French ultramarine or permanent blue.[66] Natural ultramarine, although less commonly used, was still available from Winsor & Newton in the early part of the twentieth century.[67]

MacDonald also frequently made use of cerulean blue, a cobalt tin oxide that produced a paler, more turquoise tint than ultramarine. This pigment was regularly identified in mixed colours, based on its characteristic microscopic properties, although it was often used quite sparingly. Analysis showed that magnesium was often associated with the cerulean blue. The magnesium could originate from an additive or residual starting material in the pigment. However, it is also possible that the cerulean blue was made with partial substitution of magnesium for cobalt in the crystal structure.[68] Similar quantities of magnesium have also been found in both Winsor & Newton and Cambridge Colours paint tubes of cerulean blue from the first half of the twentieth century.[69]

Based on our research, MacDonald appears to have used Prussian blue somewhat less often than ultramarine or cerulean blue. While Prussian blue was identified relatively frequently in paintings from the study group dating prior to 1922, it was found much less often in works dating from the last decade of his life.

Green pigments. Viridian, composed of hydrated chromium oxide, was MacDonald's preferred green pigment. It was identified in all the paintings that were analyzed. In three paint samples, green earth, which is a naturally occurring mineral pigment, was found along with viridian as a component in mixed shades.[70] As discussed more fully in the following section on MacDonald's common pigment mixtures, while most green hues on MacDonald's paintings include viridian, he created some of his green colours by mixing yellow and blue.

Red and orange pigments. MacDonald used a deep crimson-red lake on almost all his paintings. In most cases, it was identified as alizarin lake, precipitated on an aluminum phosphate base.[71] We often found alizarin lake mixed with blue, and sometimes other red pigments, to create purple tones. For opaque reds, MacDonald's principal pigments were vermilion and, in some brick-red shades, red iron oxide. Red to orange iron oxide pigments were often also used in mixed colours; however, in these paints, they were present only in small amounts.

Chrome orange, which can vary in colour from orange to red depending on particle size and composition, is composed of basic lead chromate.[72] Chrome orange appeared more rarely on MacDonald's palette; it was identified on only five paintings. With one exception, these are paintings where MacDonald also used the related pigment chrome yellow. Like the chrome yellows, Winsor & Newton offered chrome orange pigments, while Madderton considered them to be unstable and did not include them in their colour line.

MacDonald appears to have painted with toluidine red, an organic pigment invented in 1904,[73] only occasionally: it was identified in two works from the study group, *Near Minden* and *The Tangled Garden*, both dating from 1916.[74] It is notable that Thomson also used this pigment occasionally. Previous research on his materials revealed toluidine red in a single painting that dated from circa 1915–1916.[75]

Black and brown pigments. Finely divided, carbon-based black was identified in most of MacDonald's paintings. However, he generally used it in only small amounts in mixed colours. Passages that appear black on MacDonald's paintings are usually very dark blue or purple shades. A second black pigment, bone black, was found in a single painting. This pigment, produced from carbonizing bones, was the main colourant in a black area on one of MacDonald's Nova Scotia sketches. MacDonald seldom used brown pigments; instead, he produced brown shades of paint with complex pigment mixtures. On his sketches, he also frequently used the brown tone of the support as part of the composition. Brown iron oxides were observed in only two paintings. In one case the brown pigment was further characterized as umber, based on the presence of significant manganese.[76]

Pigment mixtures: combining and reducing. MacDonald valued the use of an essential palette of colours, which could be carefully mixed to produce a wide range of hues and values. This is clear in his 1931 lecture on Scandinavian art, where he described his admiration for how Anders Zorn created light and shade on objects by "using few colours but mixing and placing them carefully."[77] In an article about his commission for the interior decoration of St. Anne's Church, MacDonald described his method in this way: "A limited number of colors were used, and combined or reduced, they gave a great variety."[78] In MacDonald's vocabulary, "combining" signifies mixing pigments to create a different hue, while "reducing" a colour means to decrease the saturation, presumably by mixing with white, black, or a complementary colour.

Some pigment blends observed on MacDonald's works may have been provided premixed in the tube. For example, Winsor & Newton's "Payne's grey" and "Neutral tint" oil colours were both based on various proportions of carbon black, ochre, and French ultramarine.[79] However, MacDonald would invariably have produced many of his own mixed colours through various combinations of the pigments listed in Table 4.2.

Even MacDonald's bright and saturated colours often contain mixtures of multiple pigments. Most of the hues on his paintings are made from two or three main pigments that were reduced with white and modified with small amounts of other coloured pigments. In the more highly mixed colours, we regularly identified up to seven or eight pigments in a single paint sample.

An example of MacDonald's colour mixing is illustrated in Fig. 4.8. The image is a microscopic sample of mid-blue paint from the sketch *Solemn Land, Algoma*. The variously coloured pigments in the blue paint have been dispersed in a transparent medium to allow observation of their characteristics under different types of lighting. This technique, called polarized light microscopy (PLM), is described in detail in Appendix B. Using PLM, even very small quantities of pigments in a mixture can be identified, based on the colour, size, shape, and optical properties of the particles. These pigment dispersions provide a rare close-up view of MacDonald's painting process.

Figure 4.8 shows that along with very finely divided white pigment, which appears grey in the image, the principal pigments in this sample from the sketch

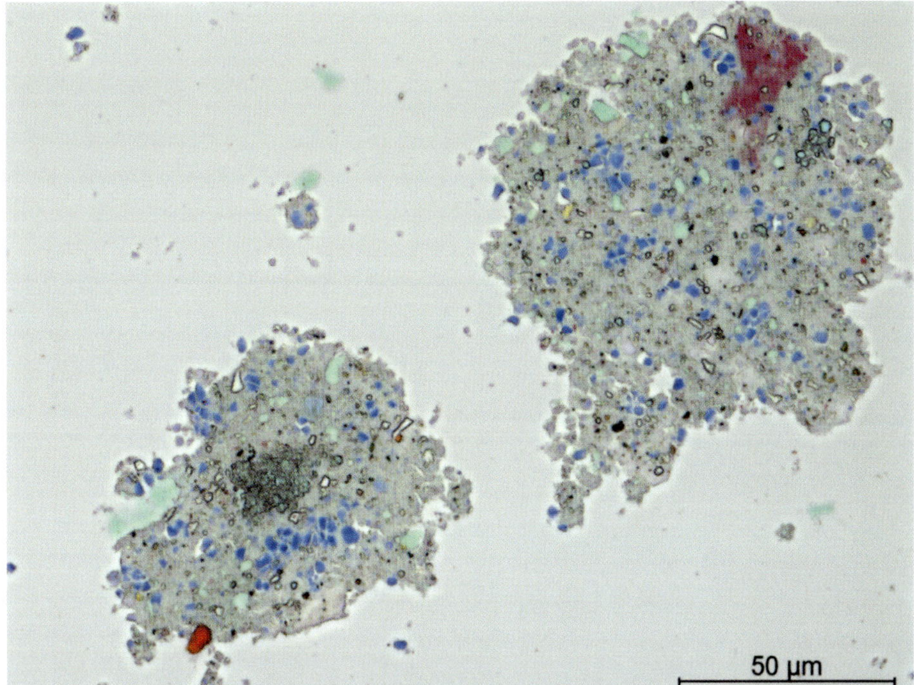

(right)
Fig. 4.8: Microscopic dispersion of mid-blue paint from *Solemn Land, Algoma*, circa 1919, Art Gallery of Ontario, showing a complex mixture of pigments. Transmitted light; partially crossed polarizers. Photo: © Government of Canada.

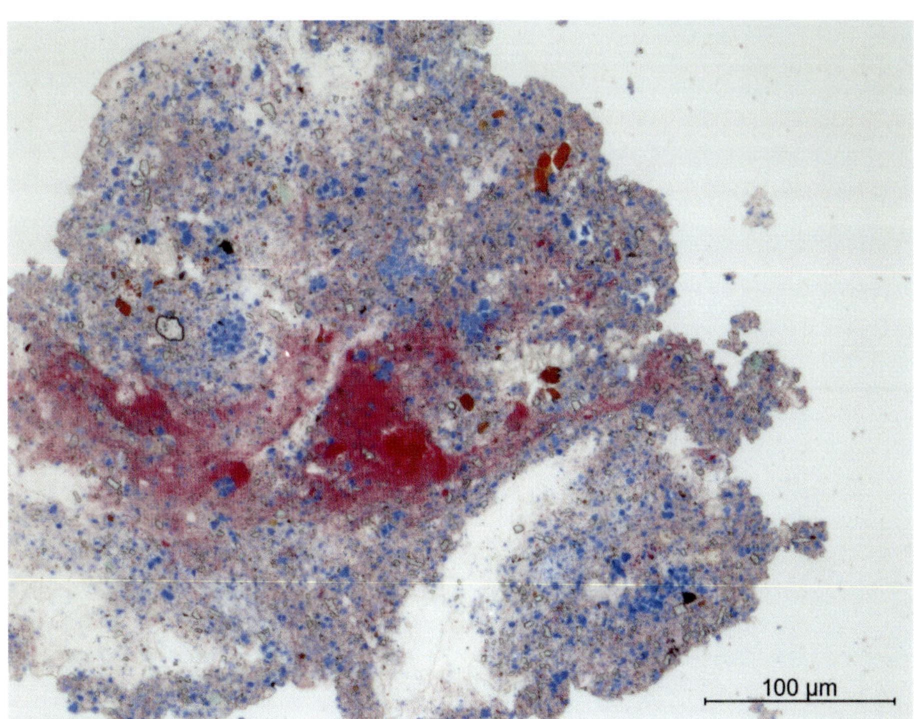

(above) Fig. 4.9: Microscopic dispersion of purple paint from *Old Dock, Petite Rivière, Nova Scotia*, 1922, National Gallery of Canada, Ottawa, showing that the purple colour was produced with a mixture of red and blue pigments. Transmitted light; partially crossed polarizers. Photo: © Government of Canada.

Solemn Land, Algoma are blue and green in colour; based on their microscopical properties, they were identified as ultramarine and viridian. The paint dispersion also shows small amounts of other pigments, identified as orange iron oxide, red lake, cerulean blue, and carbon black. While much of MacDonald's pigment mixing was intentional, some pigments present in trace amounts may have been incorporated accidentally, through carry over from a dirty brush or inadvertent mixing on his palette.

Based on the group of 32 paintings analyzed, MacDonald appears to have created his purple hues exclusively from mixtures of blue and red, even though purple pigments like cobalt violet and manganese violet would have been available to him.[80] Figure 4.9 shows a microscopic dispersion of purple paint from *Old Dock, Petite Rivière, Nova Scotia* made from a mixture of red and blue pigments. Analysis of the sample showed that the paint is composed primarily of bright blue ultramarine mixed with the vivid crimson of alizarin lake, a combination that MacDonald used extensively.

Although MacDonald's principal green was viridian, he created some of the green hues on his paintings by mixing yellow and blue. For example, the dark green shade in the top left corner of MacDonald's 1914 sketch *Logs on the Gatineau River* contains primarily ultramarine and yellow iron oxide with some added Cambridge White. As visible in the microscopic dispersion in Fig. 4.10, this mixed green is quite complex: along with the main blue, yellow, and white pigments, it also includes traces of viridian, vermilion, red lake, black, and cadmium yellow. A bright green paint from *Near Minden*, on the other hand, is an unmixed green, pigmented primarily with viridian along with small amounts of other pigments (Fig. 4.11).

MacDonald often produced shades of turquoise by mixing blue pigments with green viridian along with small amounts of other colourants. In *Thornhill Garden, No.1*, for example, while the pale blue is a pure cerulean blue reduced with white, the turquoise has a more complex composition. It contains ultramarine, viridian, and cerulean blue, which have been toned down with small amounts of complementary colours: orange iron oxide, red lake, and chrome yellow.

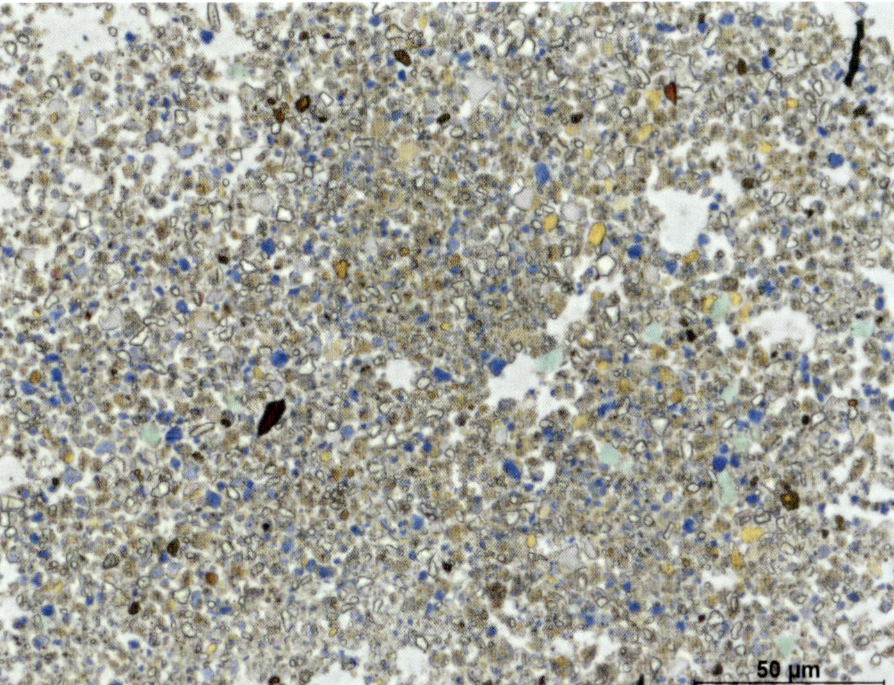

(right)
Fig. 4.10: Microscopic dispersion of green paint from *Logs on the Gatineau River*, 1914, McMichael Canadian Art Collection, 1981.85.5, produced from a mixture of blue and yellow pigments. Transmitted light; partially crossed polarizers. Photo: © Government of Canada.

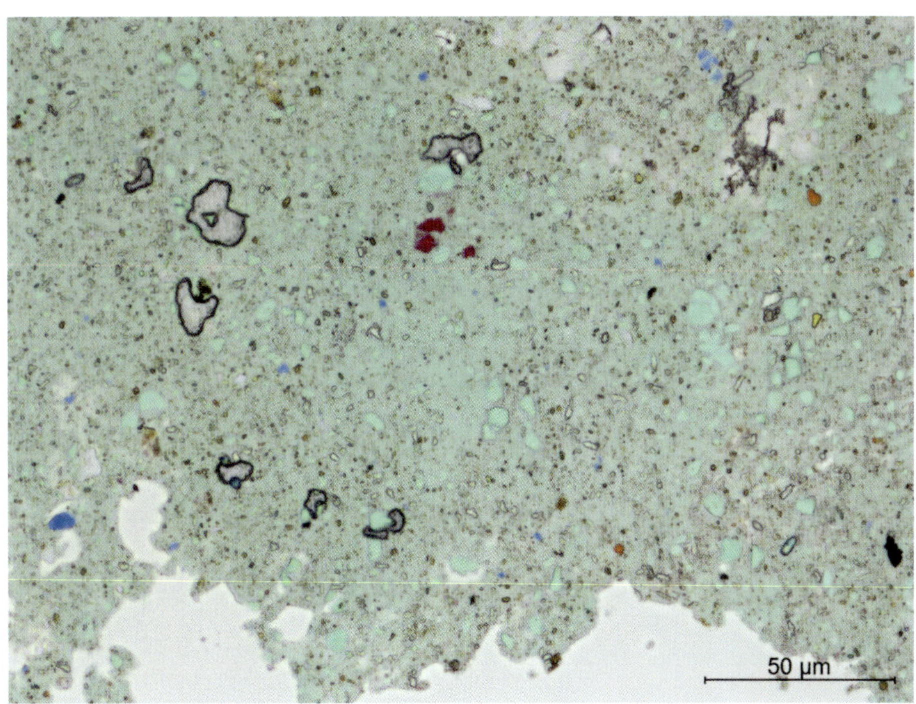

(above) Fig. 4.11: Microscopic dispersion of green paint from *Near Minden*, 1916 or 1917, McMichael Canadian Art Collection, 1966.15.12, produced from the green pigment viridian with small amounts of other pigments added. Transmitted light; partially crossed polarizers. Photo: © Government of Canada.

Trees grow and clouds float but art has a world of her own where science is not so absolute.

– J.E.H. MacDonald, Lecture Notes, Untitled, General Art, n.d. [circa 1925].

I recently borrowed one of MacDonald's paintings, "The Lonely North" from its owner.... In returning it I suggested relining, as it is painted on that poisonous jute so much favoured by our old masters.

– E.R. Hunter, Letter to H.O. McCurry, 1938.

5. APPLYING THE RESEARCH

Our study of MacDonald's materials has produced an extensive database of technical information about his oil sketches and paintings. The following examples illustrate how this material evidence can add to authentication research, to dating of his works, and to understanding condition issues observed on some of his paintings.

Authentication

Authentication of a work of art has traditionally been divided into three aspects: connoisseurship, based on an expert evaluation of form and ways of making; provenance and historical documentation; and finally, scientific examination and analysis.[1] Current research challenges the established boundaries between these fields of study and highlights the advantages of an interdisciplinary approach.[2]

The catalogue of an exhibition that took place in 2021 and 2022, entitled "Tom Thomson? The Art of Authentication," is an interesting exploration of avenues for authentication research in relation to his paintings. It includes discussion of subject matter, style, signatures and inscriptions, provenance, and, finally, the materiality of the works as determined through scientific examination.[3] The authentication of paintings by Thomson and the Group of Seven artists are most often based solely on a secure provenance combined with aspects such as style, form, and subject matter. However, in cases where the provenance is incomplete or there are conflicting opinions among experts about the authorship of a work, scientific research can play an important role.

Possible Outcomes of Scientific Examination

Now that we have amassed a large body of information about MacDonald's materials and methods, it can be used as comparative data when studying an unknown artwork or one with a questioned attribution. The results can fall into three categories:

1. the materials and methods are consistent with the study group of MacDonald's paintings;
2. the work contains uncharacteristic materials and techniques; or
3. the work contains anachronistic materials, that is, those not available during MacDonald's lifetime.

If the materials and techniques of a painting are consistent with those in the study group of authentic works, this adds weight to an attribution. Of course, since many painters had access to these same materials, the results of scientific analysis alone are never enough to authenticate a work. However, if all the paints are typical mixtures of MacDonald's commonly used pigments, described in chapter 4, this would be an encouraging result. In particular, the use of Cambridge White, which is specific to the first part of the twentieth century and was used extensively by MacDonald, would be considered a positive outcome.

If uncharacteristic materials or methods are observed, interpretation is more nuanced. As described in the previous chapters, the study group of MacDonald's paintings showed many commonalities and regular patterns in his material choices. However, artists are never completely consistent in their practice, and MacDonald is no exception. For example, although we observed a chronological pattern to the dimensions of MacDonald's sketching supports, there were occasional outliers, such as when he cut down standard boards to a smaller size. In terms of his paint materials, while we identified a consistent group of pigments that he used very regularly, there were infrequently used pigments, such as toluidine red and bone black, that were only identified in one or two paintings in the study. The possibility remains open, then, that there are pigments occasionally used by MacDonald that did not appear in the group of 32 works chosen for scientific analysis.

Uncharacteristic materials and techniques are important to note and, especially if there are multiple atypical aspects in a work, may be an indication for further research. However, variations in MacDonald's artistic practice, combined with the fact that the study group is small compared to his overall oeuvre, means that the presence of unexpected materials or methods does not conclusively disprove an attribution.

In the case where scientific analysis reveals anachronistic compounds in the original materials of an artwork, a more definite conclusion can be reached. Certain pigments have well-defined, specific dates of use, and this can be very helpful in authentication research. For example, the rutile form of titanium white pigment was not commercially introduced until 1938.[4] Original white passages containing rutile titanium white, then, could not have been painted by MacDonald since this pigment was not available during his lifetime. When drawing conclusions about authenticity based on the presence of an anachronistic component, it is imperative to ensure that it corresponds to an original material applied by the artist and not a restorer's later intervention.

An Example in Practice: "Sketch after The Tangled Garden"

In 2014, the Vancouver Art Gallery (VAG) acquired a group of 10 previously unknown oil sketches attributed to J.E.H. MacDonald. Following the announcement of the donation,[5] several Group of Seven experts put forth varying opinions about the authenticity of the works.[6] In response to this, the VAG initiated diverse avenues of research to learn as much as possible about the sketches. As part of this effort, the 10 sketches were sent to the Canadian Conservation Institute (CCI), and scientific examination was undertaken to document their materials and techniques. Here, we use the example of one of these works to illustrate how scientific examination can play an important role in authentication research.[7]

The VAG sketch, shown front and back in Figs. 5.1a and 5.1b, represents a portion of the full composition of *The Tangled Garden*, MacDonald's studio painting on beaverboard that remains one of his best-known works (chapter 1, Fig. 1.5). At the time of the donation, the VAG work was thought to be a newly discovered preliminary oil sketch for the studio painting. MacDonald painted several preparatory sketches for *The Tangled Garden*. There are two known oil sketches of the full composition, one in the collection of the National Gallery of Canada (NGC) and another in a private collection, as well as a sketch of a single sunflower in the McMichael Canadian Art Collection that may have preceded them.[8] These preparatory works are dated to circa 1915, and they would have been painted in late summer, in advance of the large-scale painting that MacDonald first exhibited in the spring of 1916.

For comparison with the VAG sketch, MacDonald's compositional study for *The Tangled Garden* in the NGC collection is shown in Fig. 5.2a and the final large-scale studio painting is illustrated in Fig. 5.2b. To allow easy comparison among the works, both images have been cropped (at the right, top, and bottom) to show the portion of the composition that is represented in the VAG sketch, and all three works are reproduced at the same scale.

The VAG sketch of *The Tangled Garden* was examined visually and was documented using several photographic techniques. This was followed by the analysis of microscopic paint samples with the same methods used for the study group of authentic MacDonald works described in Appendix B.

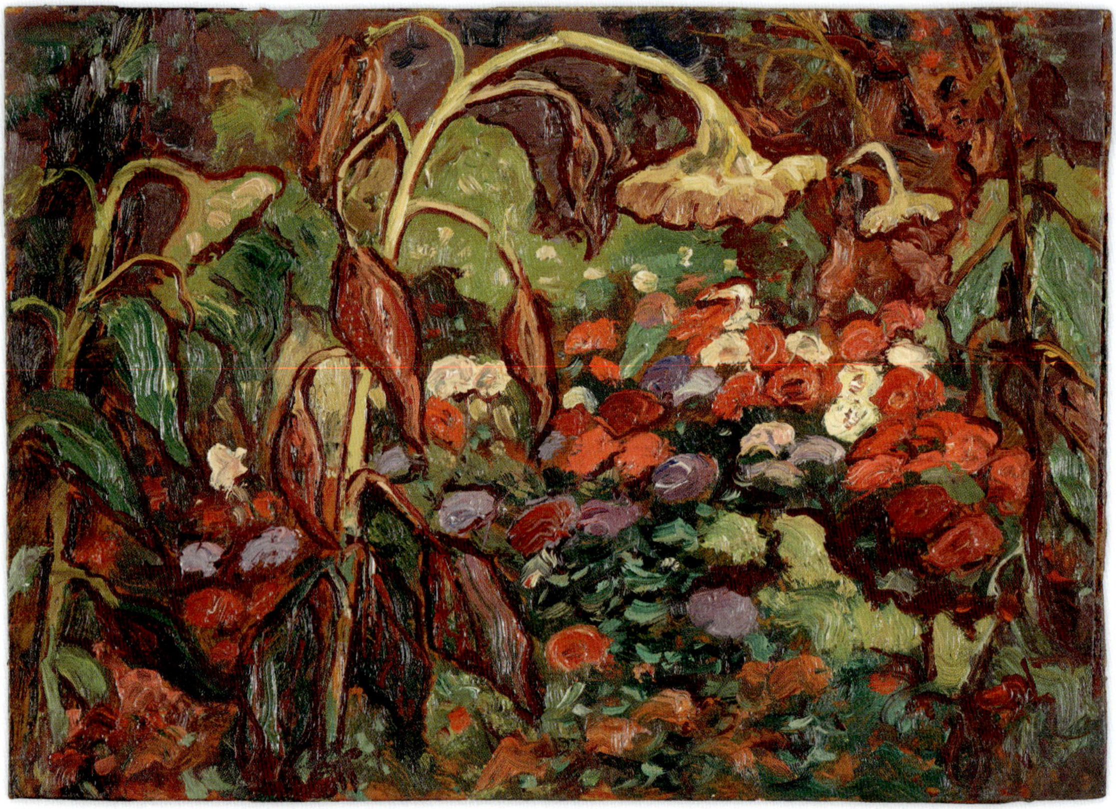

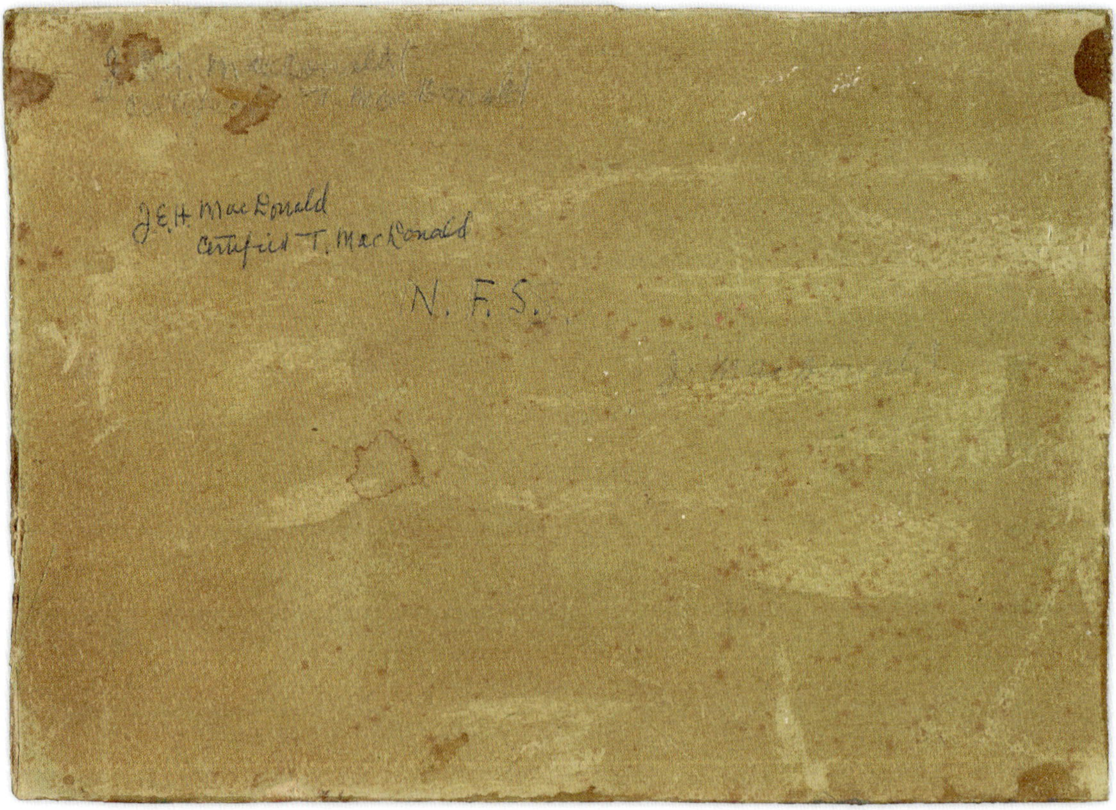

J.E.H. MacDonald
Certified T. MacDonald
N.F.S.

Support and dimensions. The VAG sketch is on a pale yellow-brown, laminated paperboard support with a thickness of 4.5 mm. The top and right sides are uneven and clearly hand-cut. While the use of a paperboard sketching support is characteristic of MacDonald's practice, this board is thicker than those he generally employed. Furthermore, it is not typical of his sketching supports from the 1914 to 1917 period that we examined, which are all on grey to grey-brown boards of about 2 mm to 3 mm in thickness, with evenly cut edges.

(opposite, top to bottom) Figs. 5.1a and 5.1b: Front and back of *Sketch after The Tangled Garden*, 14.6 × 21.1 cm, oil on paperboard, Vancouver Art Gallery. Photos: © Government of Canada.

Based on our study group, the dimensions of the sketch, which measures 14.6 × 21.1 cm, are also unusual for a work from 1915. During the 1914 to 1917 period, MacDonald usually painted on supports that measured about 20.2 × 25.3 cm (approximately 8 × 10 in.). However, while MacDonald favoured specific sizes at different periods of his career, he did occasionally use supports with other dimensions.

Inscriptions. As shown in Fig. 5.1b, there is a graphite pencil inscription, which appears to have been traced over a second time in graphite pencil, in the upper left corner on the back of the support that reads "J.E.H. MacDonald certified T. MacDonald." There is a second inscription in blue ink beneath that also reads "J.E.H. MacDonald certified T. MacDonald." Finally, there is also a faint pencil inscription in the centre that reads "NFS J. MacDonald," with the pencil letters "NFS" traced over in blue ink. As illustrated in chapter 3, these types of inscriptions were noted on the backs of numerous sketches in the study group. Detailed forensic comparison of the inscriptions with known specimens of Thoreau MacDonald's writing was beyond the scope of our scientific examination.

Preparation. The support for the VAG sketch was not prepared with a traditional ground layer, but it appears to have been coated with varnish, likely shellac, before painting.[9] The technique of coating the paperboard with varnish and forgoing a ground layer is typical of MacDonald's practice from 1918 onwards. However, this method would be unusual for a sketch from 1915, given that all 32 of the pre-1918 sketches on paperboard that we examined included a traditional ground layer.

Technique. In terms of painting technique, we noted that, typical of MacDonald's method, small areas of the support were left bare. A wash of thin red paint and lines of compositional underdrawing, likely in graphite pencil, were visible in some of these unpainted areas. In the image layers, the paint was thickly applied and certain elements (for example, the stem and leaves of the central sunflower) have been outlined with brown paint. While we observed this technique on some of MacDonald's studio paintings, it is not characteristic of his plein-air sketches. Overall, the VAG sketch appears more highly finished than the NGC sketch, with a less spontaneous paint application.

Overall visual observations. Although the dimensions, support type, and preparation of the VAG sketch of *The Tangled Garden* are uncharacteristic of the MacDonald sketches from 1914 to 1917 that we examined, taken alone, this is not sufficient evidence to rule out an attribution to him. For example, it is not impossible that MacDonald made a sketch-sized version of his well-known painting later in his career. Or perhaps he occasionally experimented with painting directly on paperboard supports prior to adopting this method consistently in 1918.

(opposite, top to bottom) (Fig. 5.2a) Detail of the central left section of *Study for "The Tangled Garden,"* 20.2 × 25.4 cm, oil on paperboard, National Gallery of Canada, Ottawa

(Fig. 5.2b) Detail of the central left section of *The Tangled Garden,* 121.4 × 152.4 cm, oil on beaverboard, National Gallery of Canada, Ottawa. Photos: NGC.

Painting materials. Chemical analysis of eight paint samples, representing most of the colours in the composition, provided information about the pigments used for the sketch. Table 5.1 lists the overall palette of pigments, along with the methods used for their identification.

Table 5.1: Pigments and fillers identified in the VAG *Sketch after The Tangled Garden*

Colour	Pigments and fillers	Methods of identification*
White and fillers	Titanium white (rutile) Zinc white Hydromagnesite Barium sulfate	XRD, Raman, SEM/EDX XRD, SEM/EDX FTIR, SEM/EDX XRD, FTIR, Raman, SEM/EDX
Blue	Ultramarine	FTIR, SEM/EDX
Green	Phthalocyanine green (Pigment Green 7)	FTIR, Raman, SEM/EDX
Red	Alizarin lake Napthol AS pigment (likely Pigment Red 2)	FTIR, SEM/EDX FTIR, Raman, SEM/EDX
Yellow	Cadmium yellow Zinc yellow	Raman, SEM/EDX FTIR, Raman, SEM/EDX

*The methods are described in Appendix B.

Several of the pigments found on the VAG sketch were also identified in the study group of MacDonald's paintings presented in the previous chapters. This includes certain of his very frequently used pigments like ultramarine, alizarin lake, and cadmium yellow. Hydromagnesite, a filler commonly found in Winsor & Newton oil paints, was identified in some of MacDonald's sketches from the 1916 to 1920 period in our study group.

On the other hand, four of the pigments used to create this sketch were not identified in any of the 32 authentic sketches and paintings by MacDonald that we analyzed. These uncharacteristic pigments are zinc yellow, titanium white (rutile form), phthalocyanine green (Pigment Green 7), and a Napthol AS red pigment. As described earlier, the presence of uncharacteristic materials does not necessarily disprove an attribution. However, in this case, a more definitive conclusion was reached because two of these four pigments were not available during MacDonald's lifetime.

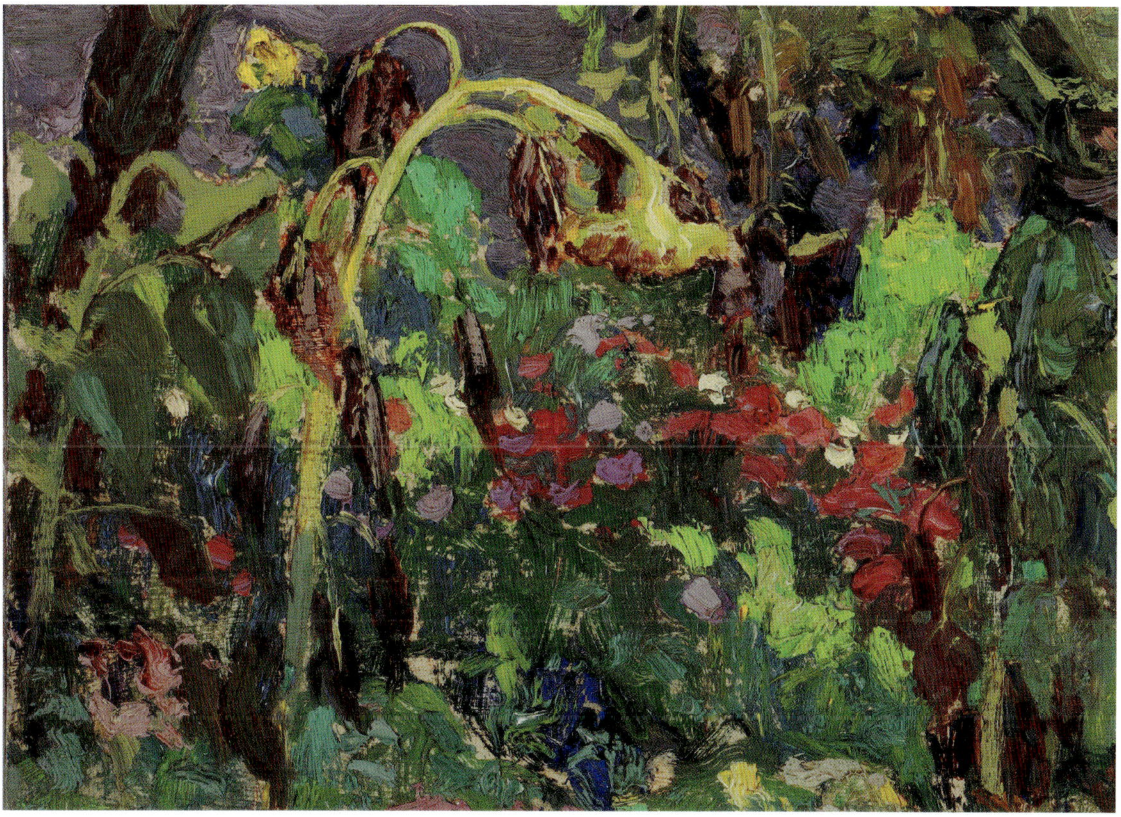

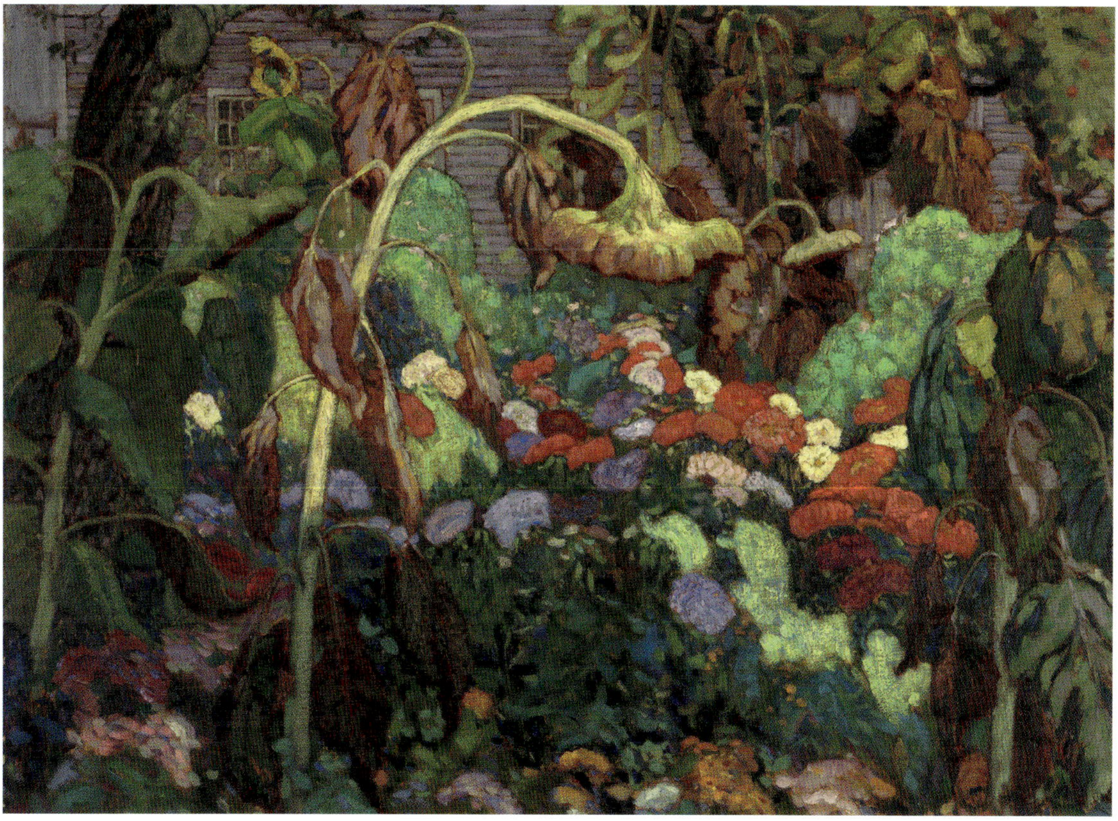

Phthalocyanine green (Pigment Green 7) was discovered in 1935, and pigment production began in 1936,[10] four years after MacDonald's death. The rutile form of titanium white was commercially introduced as a white pigment in Germany in 1938 and in the United States in 1942.[11] Phthalocyanine green and rutile titanium white were found in multiple samples from the sketch. Analysis using both FTIR and Raman spectroscopy showed that phthalocyanine green was the principal pigment in two different green shades on the sketch. Using Raman spectroscopy, a small amount of this pigment was also found in a yellow sample. Rutile titanium white was used in large amounts in the white paint and was also mixed into paint in several of the coloured areas. Its presence was confirmed with both XRD and Raman spectroscopy. Close visual examination combined with ultraviolet-induced (UV-induced) fluorescence photography[12] showed that these paints correspond to original material applied by the artist and not a later intervention.

Conclusion. In the case of the VAG sketch of *The Tangled Garden*, scientific examination provided a clear outcome. The use of multiple anachronistic pigments in various parts of the composition showed that J.E.H. MacDonald did not paint this sketch. The uncharacteristic aspects of the visual examination provide a secondary piece of supporting evidence.

Dating

Our study revealed a consistent chronological pattern of use for certain of MacDonald's materials and techniques. The composition of his paint provides limited information in this regard since he appears to have favoured the same group of principal pigments throughout his career. However, as described in chapter 2, the type and dimensions of MacDonald's paperboard supports for his outdoor sketches, as well as the way he prepared them prior to painting, do follow a chronological progression.

The example presented here illustrates how an examination of the support and preparation can provide useful information about sketches that have a secure attribution to MacDonald but for which the date of execution is unknown. Of course, this material evidence is only one aspect of an overall investigation into the probable date for a sketch, which would also include documentary research and close study of the subject matter and style.

An Example in Practice: "Poplar and Pine"

Poplar and Pine, illustrated front and back in Figs. 5.3a and 5.3b, is an oil sketch by MacDonald in the collection of the NGC that we examined as part of our study of 160 of his sketching supports. Its provenance and attribution are secure; however, there is little documentary information available about its date. Furthermore, the sketch is not signed or dated on the front, and there are no inscriptions that include a date on the back.

A 1997 memorandum in the NGC curatorial file for this sketch postulates a date of circa 1919 based on stylistic grounds and because it may be an Algoma subject. The entry reads, "J.E.H. MacDonald: *Poplar and Pine* (6462). This one is very difficult. It might be an Algoma subject. Stylistically, I would date it to that period. I would suggest circa 1919 without a great deal of conviction."[13]

Although this sketch is tentatively attributed to MacDonald's Algoma period, the results of our examination suggest that it fits more closely with sketches painted prior to his first trip to Algoma in 1918.

Dimensions. *Poplar and Pine* measures 20.3 × 25.3 cm (approximately 8 × 10 in.). As described in chapter 2, MacDonald sometimes used sketching supports of this size beginning in 1912. From 1914 until he temporarily stopped painting near the end of 1917 due to illness, MacDonald appears to have used this 8 × 10-inch format almost exclusively. Once he was well enough to begin sketching again in the summer of 1918, he made a transition to 8½ × 10½-inch supports. Apart from *Poplar and Pine*, all 49 of the examined sketches that are dated to his Algoma trips are on paperboard supports of this slightly larger dimension. There is no evidence that MacDonald returned to the use of 8 × 10-inch boards later in his career. In total, we examined over 120 sketches from the 1918 to 1932 period, and, apart from *Poplar and Pine*, none were painted on 8 × 10-inch supports.

Support. As shown in Fig. 5.3b, the support for *Poplar and Pine* is a grey-brown paperboard. It has a thickness of 2.8 mm. The edges of the board are relatively straight but have been cut with a tool that produced a rough edge profile with no visible cut marks. These features are all characteristic of the supports that MacDonald commonly used during the 1911 to 1917 period. The paperboard that MacDonald chose for his Algoma sketches differs from these earlier boards: his Algoma supports are thinner and denser, with more heavily compressed pulp layers. The majority are also paler and browner in colour than his earlier paperboard. Although three different Algoma paperboard support types were observed, unlike *Poplar and Pine*, they all have at least two edges with a smooth profile showing diagonal marks from the tool used to cut them.

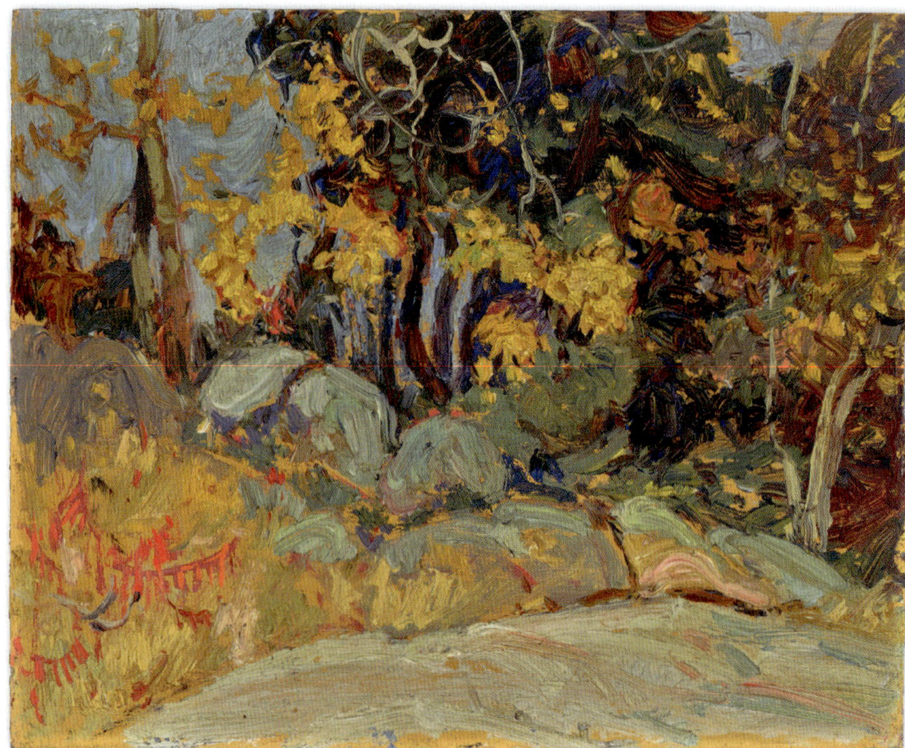

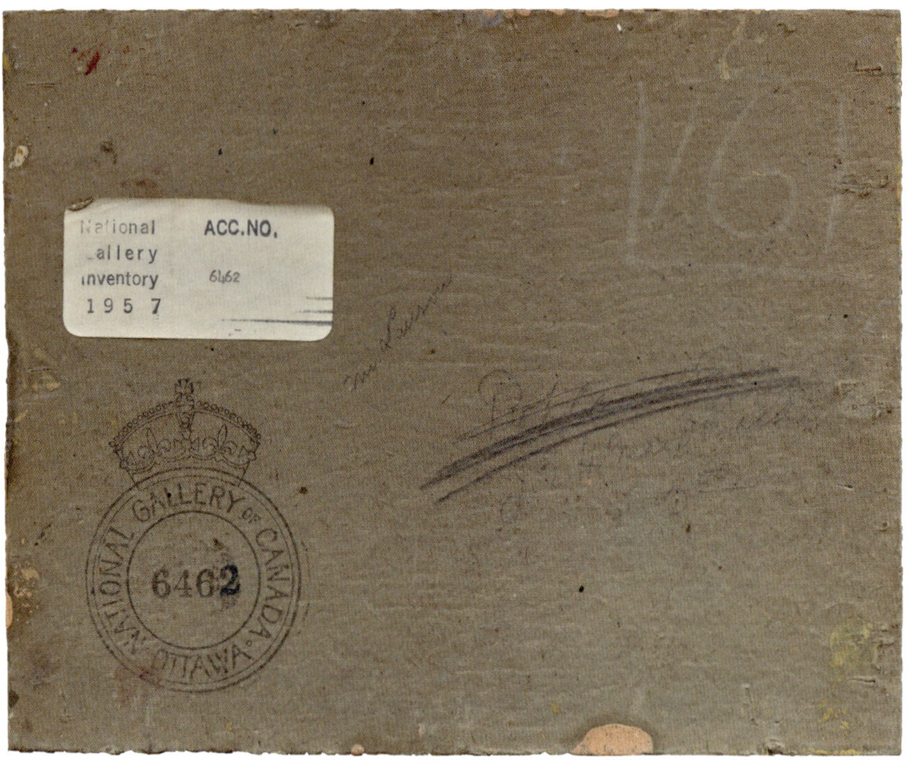

(top to bottom)
Figs. 5.3a and 5.3b: Front and back of *Poplar and Pine*, circa 1919, 20.3 × 25.3 cm, oil on paperboard, National Gallery of Canada, Ottawa. Photos: NGC.

Preparation. MacDonald prepared the paperboard support of *Poplar and Pine* with a traditional ground layer. We observed that the board included two superposed applications: a warm pink ground followed by a yellow-orange ground. Warmly coloured grounds in these shades are typical of MacDonald's sketches dating from 1914 to 1917. He also sometimes superposed two ground layers of different colours in this period. *Thornhill Garden, No.2*, dated circa 1916, has a similar layering to that seen on *Poplar and Pine*: it includes a pink ground followed by a yellow-orange ground. Other examples include *Near Minden*, from 1916 or 1917, and *Georgian Bay, Wild Ducks*, from 1917, which both show a green ground followed by a yellow-orange ground (illustrated in chapter 2, Fig. 2.4 for *Near Minden*). Apart from *Poplar and Pine*, none of the 49 examined sketches dated to the Algoma period include a traditional ground layer. Instead, MacDonald painted directly on the paperboard support, usually after sealing it with varnish.

Conclusion. Overall, the dimensions, the support type, and the preparation for *Poplar and Pine* are not typical of sketches from MacDonald's Algoma period. However, these aspects of his technique match very well to the methods he used from 1914 to 1917. Taken alone, this evidence is not enough to completely rule out the possibility that MacDonald painted this sketch during one of his Algoma trips. For example, perhaps he had a prepared support left over from an earlier sketching trip and brought it with him to Algoma along with his supply of new boards. However, since the curatorial opinion attributing this sketch to MacDonald's Algoma period is considered tentative, the material evidence suggests that further research into the date of this sketch would be warranted.

Condition Issues

Although MacDonald's sketches and paintings are generally in good condition, we observed certain types of deterioration related to his choice of materials. Most of these condition issues are relatively minor or were present only on a few works. However, two of MacDonald's materials are of more significant concern for the long-term preservation of his paintings: jute canvas and, to a lesser extent, beaverboard. This section begins with a discussion of jute and beaverboard and the associated challenges with the conservation of paintings on these problematic supports. This is followed by shorter explanations of some of the other, more minor, condition issues that were noted.

Jute Canvas

MacDonald painted on jute supports as early as 1913[14] and, based on our research, he used this type of canvas regularly throughout his career. Some of MacDonald's contemporaries, including Lawren Harris, A.Y. Jackson, and Tom Thomson, also painted on jute.[15] As described previously, Harris purchased a large roll of jute from New Jersey sometime around 1913 and shared it with his fellow painters.[16] It is possible that this roll of jute was the source of the fabric used for some of MacDonald's paintings.[17]

Jute was considered to be a problematic support early on. In a 1938 letter, MacDonald's biographer E.R. Hunter wrote about *The Lonely North*, a painting that MacDonald completed in 1913, saying that "it is painted on that poisonous jute so much favored by our old masters."[18] In another letter, dating from around the same time, he wrote that "a number of Canadian artists at this time, and subsequently, used jute instead of canvas, and this material dries out in time, turning to powder. Nor has it the elasticity of canvas (or duck), so that when it stretches (e.g., due to wet weather) it has not the power to 'come back.' Hence the longitudinal cracks in this painting."[19]

The deterioration of fabrics made from jute that Hunter describes is caused by the specific physical and chemical properties of the jute fibres. As explained in the glossary, plant fibres are composed of cellulose, along with lignin and other components. Jute fibres contain significantly more lignin than fibres like cotton or linen, and for this reason, fabric made from jute has an inherent lack of elasticity.[20] Lignin and other contributing components in the fibres discolour and degrade through the action of light and air, leading to further embrittlement and damage over time.[21] Fibre degradation is also caused by shrinking and swelling with changes in humidity. Jute fibres absorb moisture at a greater rate than other common canvas fibre types and so are more susceptible to damage from this process as well.[22]

Deterioration of the jute fibres leads to an overall loss of fabric strength, cohesion, and elasticity. Oil paintings on jute can show several types of visible degradation: broken fibres at the edges where the canvas folds over the stretcher (Fig. 5.4), overall sagging and movement of the canvas under the weight of the paint layers, and cracking in the paint along threads as the fibres shrink and swell in response to changes in humidity.

Fig. 5.4: Detail of *Falls, Montreal River*, 1920, Art Gallery of Ontario, showing torn, broken jute yarns at the turnover edge. Photo: McMichael.

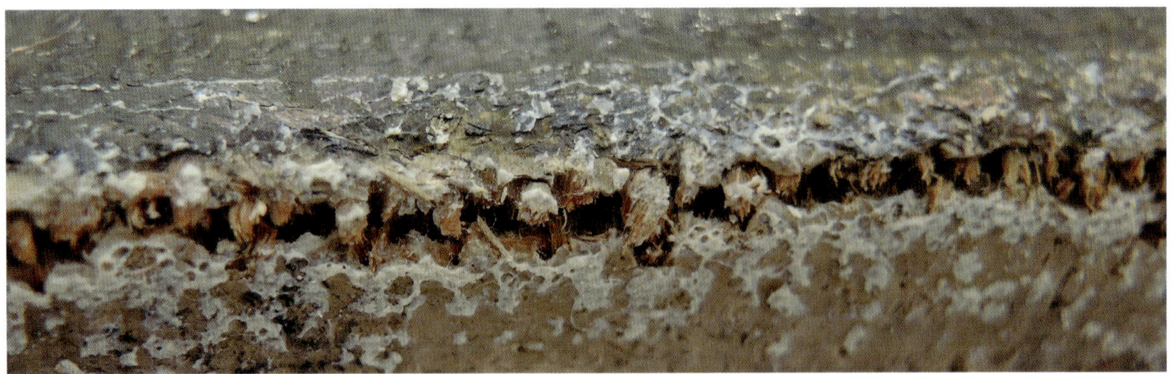

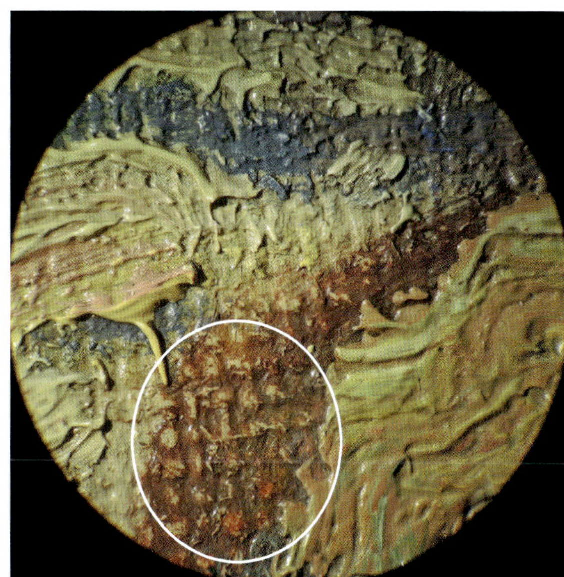

Fig. 5.5: Detail of *Falls, Montreal River*, 1920, Art Gallery of Ontario, showing abrasion and loss of the thinly applied dark brown paint (circled on the image) due to wax-resin lining. Photo: McMichael.

Figure 2.14 in chapter 2 shows a detail of the back of the canvas support for *Goat Range, Rocky Mountains*, which is a mixed linen and jute canvas. The contrast between the brittle, broken vertical jute yarns with the paler, intact linen used for the horizontal yarns is striking.

Bess Harris, Lawren Harris's wife, remarked in a 1962 letter that in using jute supports early in his career, her husband "was not thinking of the future – if Lawren had been, he would not have painted on jute – a material that the National Gallery has since rebacked for him many times."[23] By "rebacking," she is referring to the conservation treatment called "lining," where the original canvas for a painting is adhered overall to another fabric. Of the five studio paintings on jute by MacDonald that we examined, four of them have been lined.

Forest Wilderness and *Falls, Montreal River* are large-scale oil paintings on jute supports that MacDonald painted in 1920. Both paintings were lined onto a secondary canvas and infused with a wax-resin adhesive, using heat and pressure, during conservation treatments in the 1970s. The wax-resin linings were undertaken with the goal of reinforcing the original jute canvas and, at the same time, consolidating the ground and paint layers.[24] Although this type of treatment is no longer commonly used, at the time it was deemed necessary for these paintings, which showed significant cracking and damage. While it improved the stability of the paintings, wax-resin lining has certain disadvantages. The treatment cannot be completely reversed; moreover, the wax-resin mixture can saturate the ground and canvas, leading to overall darkening. In some cases, the heat and pressure of the lining process can make the canvas texture more prominent. The process can also sometimes result in flattening of impasto or abrasion of thinly-applied paint at the high points of the canvas weave (Fig. 5.5).[25]

The Solemn Land, another large-scale studio work painted on jute, has a different conservation history. The NGC purchased this painting in 1921, the same year that MacDonald completed it. It has never been lined and remains on its original stretcher. In a 1935 report on the painting's condition, George Harbour, the first conservator at the NGC,[26] stated that "this picture is painted on a prepared piece of burlap which does not at present show any signs of disintegrating, such as would make it necessary to reline."[27]

The painting was examined regularly during the following decades, and by the early 1980s, conservation assessments indicated that the jute had become brittle and fragile and showed tears along the margins where the fabric was pulled over the edges of the stretcher.[28] In the late 1980s, the fabric was also noted to be slack on its stretcher. At this point, wooden cross-members and a backing board were added to better support the canvas, and the torn margins of the jute fabric were reinforced.[29]

This valuable, long-term record of the painting's condition in the NGC conservation files shows that even within a controlled museum environment, the jute support for *The Solemn Land* degraded significantly over a 50-year period (Fig. 5.6). Due to its current fragility, travel for this painting is restricted to avoid the shock and vibration associated with transportation.

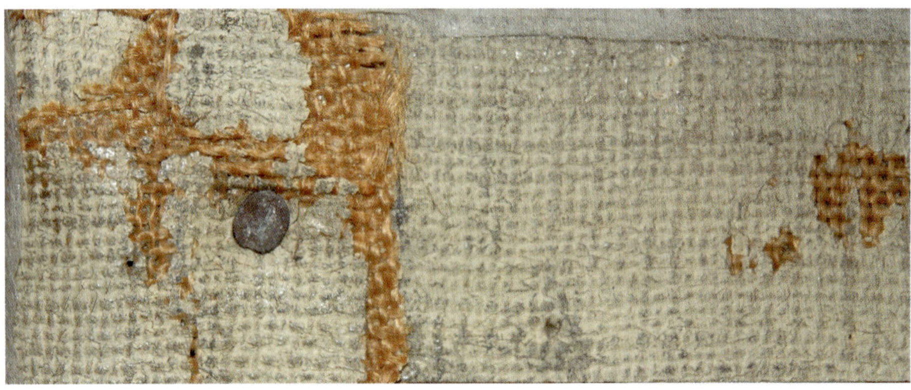

Fig. 5.6: Detail of *The Solemn Land*, 1921, National Gallery of Canada, Ottawa. A corner of the back showing damage to the jute and to the commercial ground layer where it is folded over the stretcher. Photo: McMichael.

Beaverboard

As described in chapter 2, MacDonald regularly used fibreboard supports for his studio paintings in the 1915–1918 period. Of the five paintings on this type of support that we examined, two have trademark stamps on the back confirming that they are the Beaver Board brand. The others have very similar characteristics and are undoubtedly from the same manufacturer. We refer to all these supports as "beaverboard," a term that encompasses any medium-density fibreboard with these characteristics, whether they include a trademark stamp or not. Although perhaps not as problematic as jute, especially if properly prepared and supported, there are potential conservation issues related to the use of beaverboard as a substrate for large-scale paintings.

As described in the glossary, the Beaver Board brand was a commercial, medium-density, wood-pulp based fibreboard. Invented in 1903, it was very popular as a finishing board for interior walls during the first decades of the twentieth century.[30] During the period when MacDonald used it as a painting support, the panels were approximately 5 mm thick and had a mechanically processed wood pulp core.[31] The patent literature indicates that the front and back surfaces of the mechanical wood pulp core were covered with layers of darker, more resistant wood pulp that had been treated with steam and pressure prior to processing, and as a final step, a wax-resin coating could also be applied.[32] These surface layers were intended to make the boards more resistant to moisture. Despite this, it was recognized that they would still expand and contract with changes in humidity.[33]

Loosely matted, relatively low-density mechanical wood pulp was used for the core of boards because of its sound and insulating properties, not for its strength or longevity.[34] Mechanical wood pulp, while economical to produce, retains a high lignin content. This interferes with bonding between the fibres, which decreases the overall strength of the material as compared to purified pulp.[35] The patent literature indicates that the inventors of the Beaver Board brand were aware of this. One of the patents on the product specifies that, although the surface treatments would make the exterior of the board more resistant, the "core is not, however, highly resistant to moisture, nor is it relatively strong, either in tension or to resist puncture."[36]

The lack of mechanical rigidity is an important drawback to the use of beaverboard as a support for large-scale paintings. Beaverboard panels were designed to be nailed to interior walls, held in place with battens, and coated with relatively thin layers of paint. While the board was sufficiently strong for its intended purpose, it is more problematic as a painting support, especially if an artist painted the composition thickly and did not apply a coating to the reverse of the board.

The cellulose, lignin, and other components in mechanically processed wood pulp will deteriorate over time through chemical reactions with oxygen and atmospheric moisture in the environment.[37] The relatively low density and porous structure of beaverboard's wood pulp core, as compared to MacDonald's denser paperboard

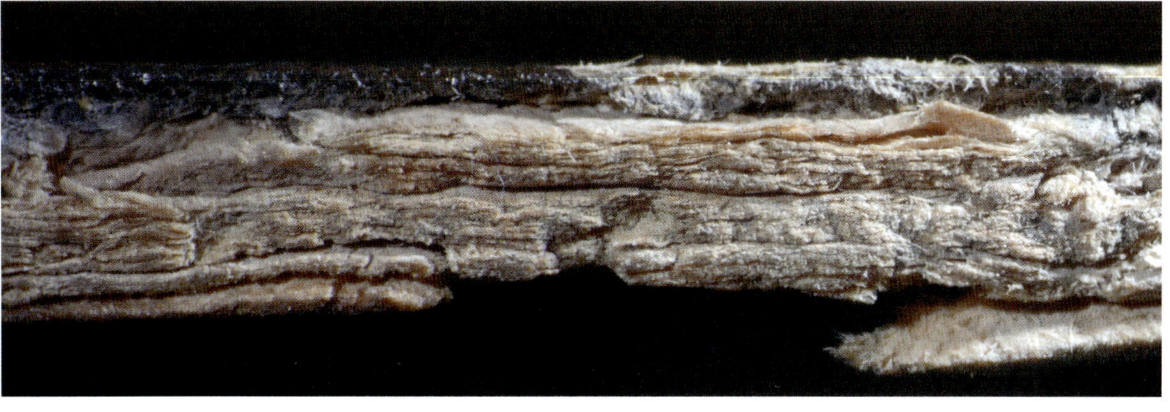

Fig. 5.7: Edge of the beaverboard support for *Harvest Evening Moon*, 1917, McMichael Canadian Art Collection, 1978.31, showing delamination and damage of the relatively low-density wood pulp board. Photo: McMichael.

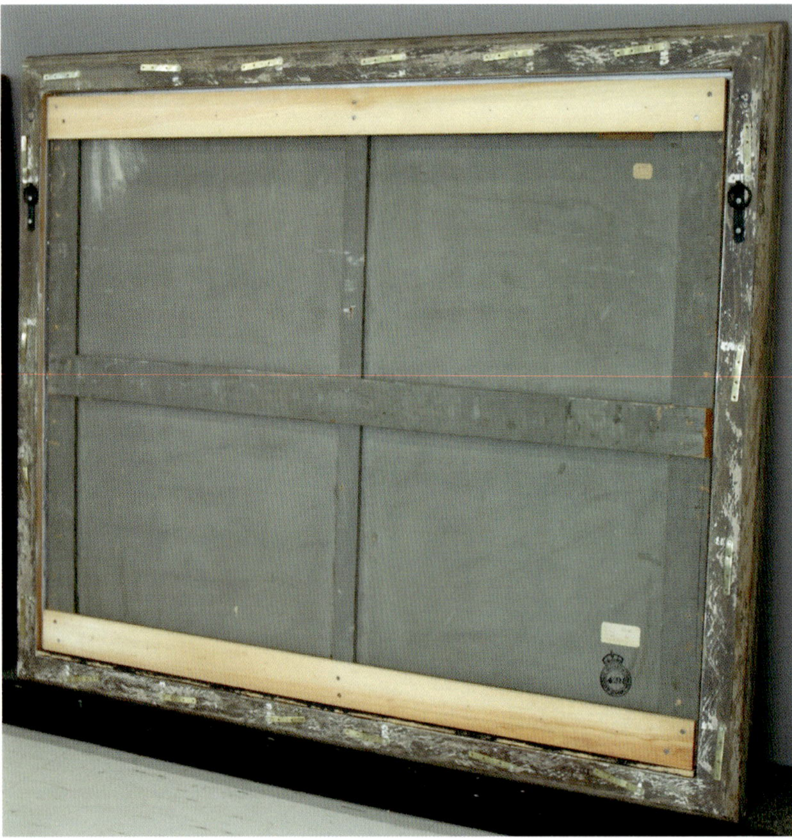

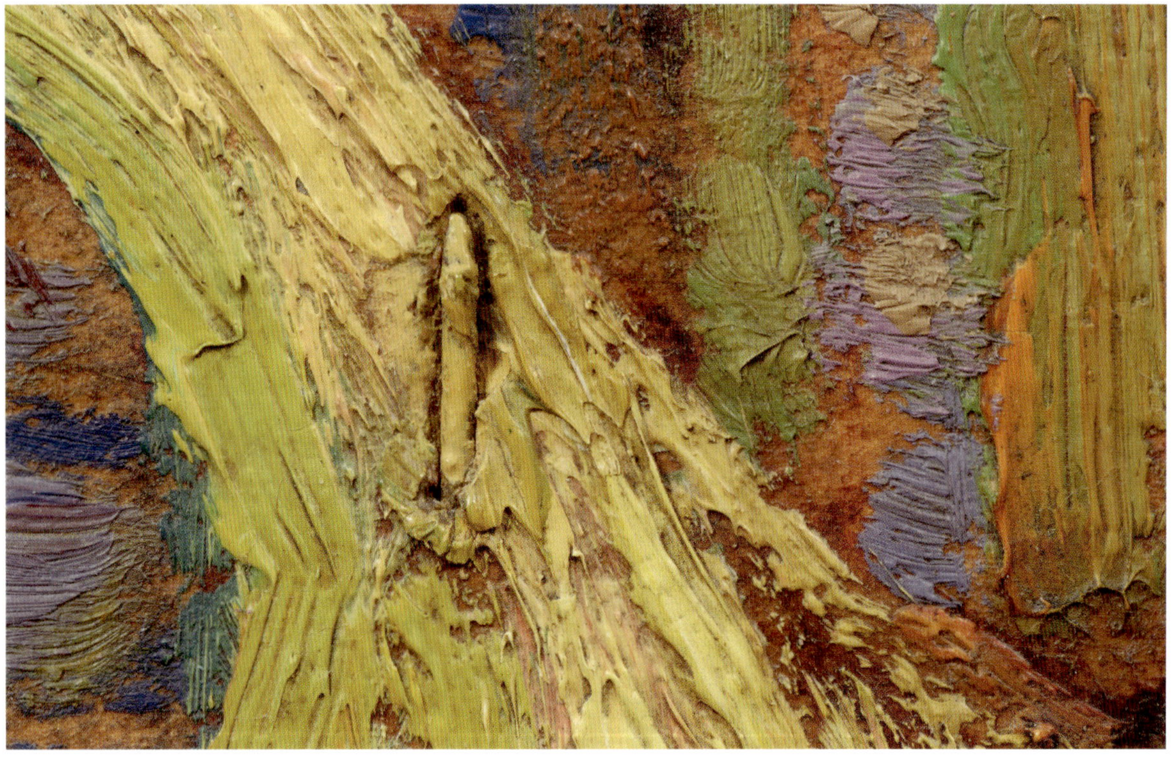

(top to bottom)
Fig. 5.8: Back of *The Tangled Garden*, 1916, National Gallery of Canada, Ottawa, showing the wooden braces and grey oil paint that MacDonald applied to stabilize the support. The unpainted wooden battens were added later by NGC conservators to provide additional support. Photo: McMichael.

Fig. 5.9: Detail of *The Tangled Garden*, 1916, National Gallery of Canada, Ottawa, showing a paint-covered bent nail in the central sunflower. Photo: © Government of Canada.

sketching supports, makes it prone to deterioration since air and moisture can penetrate more easily. As it ages, beaverboard darkens, becomes brittle, and loses strength, usually beginning at the outer edges of the board (Fig. 5.7).

As in the case of jute, concerns about beaverboard as a painting support were expressed early on. For example, in 1939, the artist Wyly Grier wrote to NGC Assistant Director H.O. McCurry about the best way to safeguard a work by Homer Watson painted on beaverboard: "The idea occurred to me to ask you what the National Gallery did with *The Tangled Garden* – loaded, cracked (?) and painted on beaver-board.... I believe that some of the painters back the board with shellac. Did you do that? In fact, what did you do?"[38] McCurry responded that beaverboard is "a perishable support and is certain to go in time. We are still puzzled as to what to do about MacDonald's *Tangled Garden*."[39]

Examination of *The Tangled Garden* showed that MacDonald was aware of some of the potential problems with the use of beaverboard. As described in chapter 2, he sealed the front of the beaverboard with a natural resin and applied a coat of grey oil paint to the back. By coating the back of the board, MacDonald's goal was likely to equalize the moisture absorption from the front and back faces, which would help to prevent warping. He also improved the rigidity of the board by nailing a wooden framework of three vertical braces and one horizontal brace to the back (Fig. 5.8). Several bent nail points that are covered by the paint of the composition confirm that MacDonald attached these wooden supporting components before painting (Fig. 5.9).

Despite MacDonald's careful preparation of the beaverboard, *The Tangled Garden* shows certain condition issues related to the support, including a convex warp, particularly in the lower left. Many areas along the edges of the board show small areas of delamination and loss of the wood pulp layers with associated paint damage.

Sketching Supports

MacDonald's small oil sketches on paperboard supports are in relatively good condition. Although the lignin-containing wood pulp will discolour and weaken over time, the small format and relatively dense lamination of these supports appear to have prevented any major condition issues to date. We observed minor fraying and slight delamination of plies in the corners and edges of some of the boards as well as small areas of associated paint loss. Corner and edge delamination was often more evident on sketches that MacDonald painted prior to 1918 when he was using a less dense variety of paperboard. Some boards show a slight convex warp.

Since MacDonald left areas of the support exposed as a design element in his sketches, his use of shellac or other natural resins to prepare the paperboard prior to painting has certain disadvantages. These varnish preparation layers will darken and yellow over time, leading to a change in contrast between the painted and unpainted areas of a sketch. In addition, for sketches that have been given a protective surface varnish,[40] the common conservation practice of varnish removal may be complicated by the solubility of the varnish preparation layer beneath. If the preparatory varnish layer on the board is partially dissolved during surface varnish removal, the oil paint above could be lifted. This is an important factor for conservators to keep in mind when developing treatment procedures for MacDonald's sketches or for his larger-scale works on beaverboard that have been coated with resin before painting.

Based on our survey of MacDonald's sketching supports, he appears to have painted on plywood only occasionally. The three works on plywood that we examined all showed the same condition issue, namely cracking of the support along the wood grain of the upper veneer layer that has, in turn, caused the paint layers to crack (Fig. 5.10). Robert McMichael, founder of the McMichael collection, commented that although MacDonald, A.Y. Jackson, and Tom Thomson sometimes used plywood supports beginning in 1914, they soon limited their use of this support type due to its tendency to crack along the grain.[41]

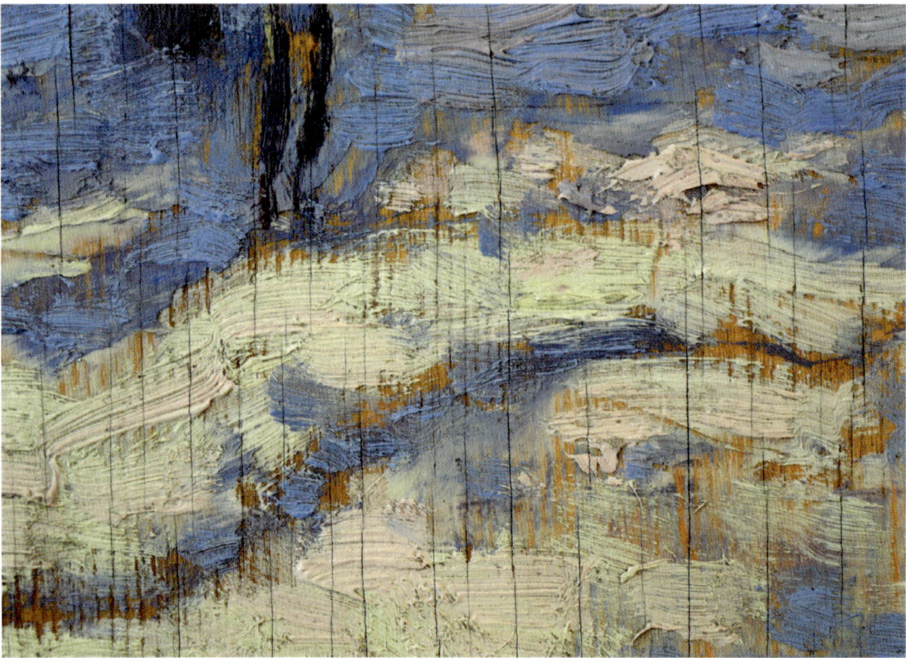

Fig. 5.10: Detail of *Snow, Algonquin Park*, circa 1914, McMichael Canadian Art Collection, 1966.16.43, showing cracking along the grain of the plywood. Photo: McMichael.

Paint Layers

As described in the previous sections, MacDonald's use of problematic supports is the source of most of the observed damage on his works. However, in a few cases, we observed condition issues that were associated with specific pigments or paint application methods.

Cadmium yellow. Cadmium yellow was one of MacDonald's principal pigments. As described in the previous chapter, cadmium yellow oil paints of this period are sometimes prone to powdering, cracking, or surface crusts.[42] While most of

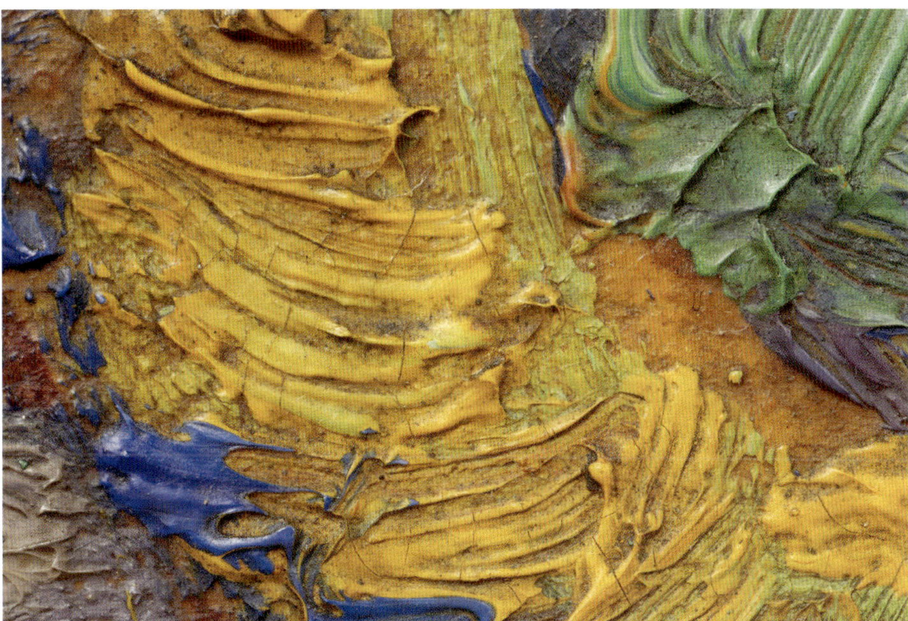

Fig. 5.11: Cracking of cadmium yellow in *The Tangled Garden*, 1916, National Gallery of Canada, Ottawa. Photo: © Government of Canada.

MacDonald's cadmium yellow paints remain intact, we observed cracking in a few cases – for example, in the bright yellow of the small sunflower in the upper left of *The Tangled Garden* (Fig. 5.11). This cracked yellow paint contained almost pure cadmium yellow of the α-CdS type. Two other yellow paints from *The Tangled Garden* that were analyzed contain the same type of cadmium yellow pigment mixed with white paint. These two yellow paints remain in good condition. It is possible that the cadmium yellow was protected from deterioration in these areas because MacDonald diluted it with white.

Zinc white. MacDonald's preferred white paint was Cambridge White, which, as described in the previous chapter, is a manufacturer's mixture of lead sulfate and zinc white. He very occasionally chose a white pigment made solely of zinc white. In the group of 32 paintings that were analyzed, zinc white was identified without lead sulfate in only four works. Furthermore, in two of these four paintings, MacDonald mixed the zinc white with other white pigments. It is notable that the white areas in MacDonald's paintings and sketches that are based on Cambridge White remain in good condition, while the sketch for *Leaves in the Brook*, one of the rare works painted with zinc white, shows mechanical cracking in the thickly painted white passages (Fig. 5.12). It is possible that MacDonald limited his use of this pigment because he knew that zinc white oil paints are brittle and tended to crack, a fact mentioned in artists' materials catalogues in the early part of the twentieth century.[43]

As described in the previous chapter, MacDonald's paints based on zinc white, either alone or in combination with lead sulfate as Cambridge White, contain zinc soaps. Zinc soaps, composed of zinc fatty acid salts, are regularly identified in zinc white oil paints. They are formed by a reaction between components of the oil

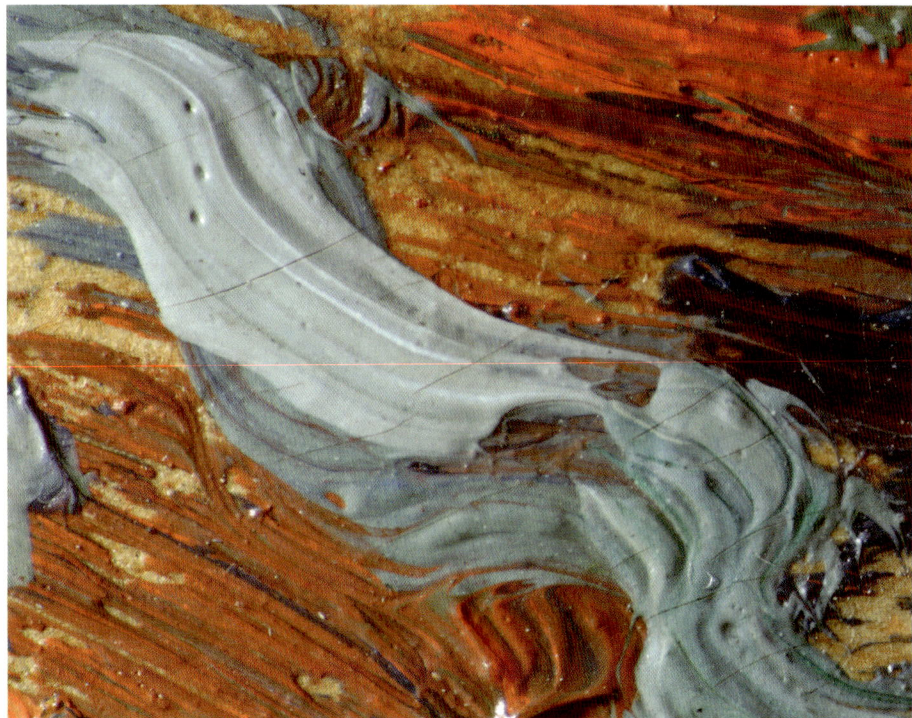

Fig. 5.12: Cracking of zinc white in the sketch for *Leaves in the Brook*, circa 1918, McMichael Canadian Art Collection, 1966.16.35. Photo: McMichael.

medium and the zinc oxide pigment. High concentrations of crystalline zinc soaps have been linked to problematic phenomena on oil paintings such as the formation of protrusions, efflorescence, or the delamination of layers.[44] This type of deterioration was not observed on MacDonald's paintings. The zinc soaps identified on his works are most often in a non-crystalline form, and this stage in their evolution is not usually associated with condition issues.[45]

Solvent-sensitive paints. In what appears to be an isolated case, a 1935 condition report, written by NGC conservator George Harbour, indicated that certain colours in the large-scale canvas painting *The Solemn Land* had become solvent sensitive within fifteen years of its completion. Harbour noted that, while cleaning the painting, some of the colours, primarily blues, greens, and certain red areas, appeared soft and chalky and could be "rubbed off." He described the paint as having been applied "so flat that practically all viscosity had been removed" and judged it to be "not properly bonded together."[46] Visual examination revealed that the paint was applied in very thin, wash-like layers (Fig. 5.13). Combined with Harbour's observations, this suggests that areas in *The Solemn Land* may have been overdiluted with turpentine, leading to paint that lacked sufficient oil binding medium to produce a solid film. This is corroborated in a 1928 letter from A.Y. Jackson to NGC Director Eric Brown in which Jackson describes *The Solemn Land* as "painted very thin, mostly turpentine."[47]

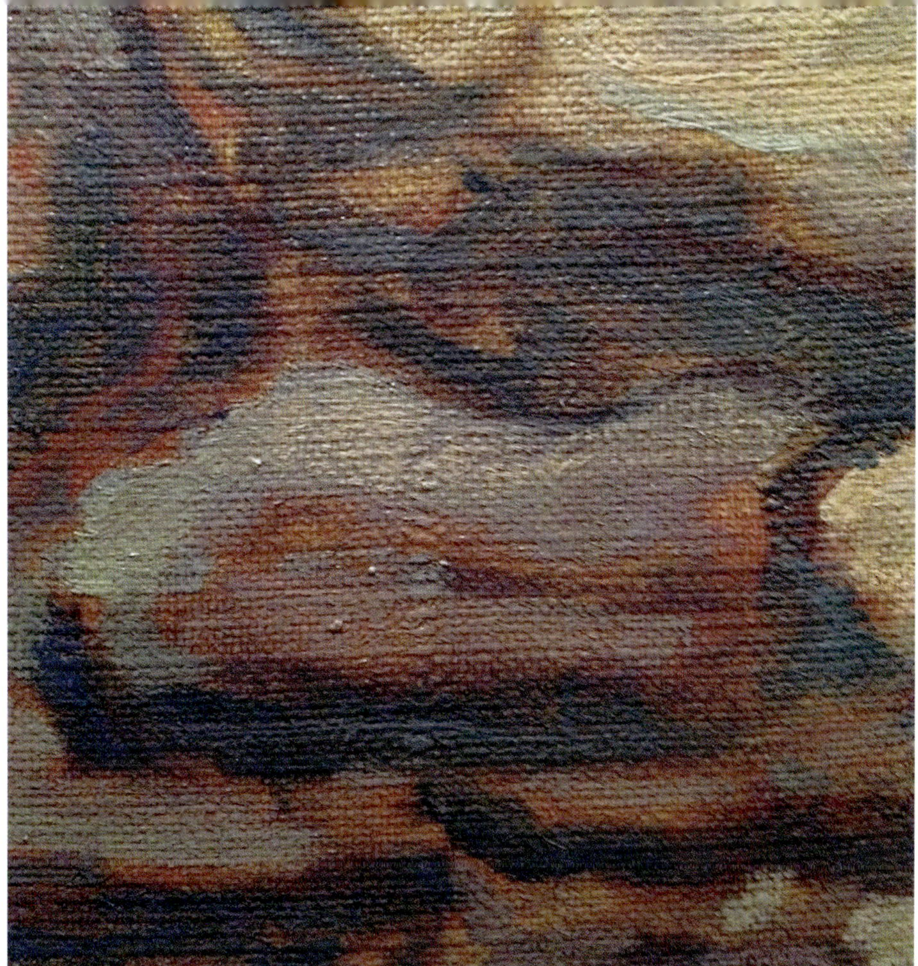

Fig. 5.13: Detail of *The Solemn Land*, 1921, National Gallery of Canada, Ottawa, showing the thinly applied paint and canvas texture. Photo: McMichael.

Harbour undertook a conservation treatment on the chalky, sensitive colour areas on *The Solemn Land*. He kept detailed handwritten notes of this early treatment, leaving a valuable record of his procedure.[48] He treated the problematic areas with a process called "feeding" with linseed oil: he applied a thick linseed oil solution to areas of the painting and allowed it to soak in for several days. According to his notes, the process was successful in stabilizing the paint: "In forty-eight hours the oil left on had become absorbed, and in seventy-two hours the surface had become sufficiently dry to rub lightly with a soft swab. This removed a lot of dirt and old varnish with no trace of colour except from the red in the foreground." Once his treatment was complete, the painting was hung in the galleries for about a year, after which it was stable enough to undergo cleaning and varnish removal. He revarnished the painting with dammar, a natural resin varnish, to protect and saturate the surface.

The method used by Harbour of "feeding" the problematic paints with oil was not uncommon at the time. However, modern art conservators would avoid this type of treatment because it is irreversible: once oil has been added to the paint, it cannot be removed.[49] As well, the added oil may change the appearance of the treated areas over time, leading to shifts in colour balance and saturation on the painting overall.

To the memory of J.E.H. MacDonald, who visualized a Canadian school of painting, and devoted his life to the realization of it.
– A.Y. Jackson, dedication in *A Painter's Country*, 1967.

CONCLUSION

J.E.H. MacDonald's dedication and creative passion allowed him to produce an impressive number of oil sketches and paintings over his lifetime. The striking landscapes and views of nature that we had the privilege to study are an important artistic legacy and confirm his essential place among the Group of Seven painters. Through investigation of both his small outdoor sketches and his larger studio paintings, our research has revealed many details about the materials and methods that MacDonald used to create them.

Some technical preferences that MacDonald developed over the course of his career showed a consistent chronological pattern, such as the format and the type of paperboard that he used for his outdoor oil sketches. Early in his career, he preferred to sketch on supports prepared with a traditional ground layer, while later he painted directly on paperboard that he sealed with a layer of varnish. His painting methods also changed as he matured. While some of his early paintings show an artist still learning and experimenting, by the Algoma period, his works reveal his extensive understanding of colour mixing, his sureness of brushstroke, and his mastery of design that captured form, light, and movement in his compositions.

Although most of MacDonald's studio works were painted on canvas, in the 1915–1918 period, he often painted on beaverboard. He would have become familiar with its properties while working on the MacCallum cottage murals and must have appreciated its qualities as a painting support. He may also have used beaverboard during this period because it was inexpensive; MacDonald was never wealthy, and money was particularly short during the war years.

He used a variety of fabric types for his large-scale paintings on canvas. Jute was a fabric that MacDonald favoured throughout his career. While jute had qualities that he appreciated, its inherent instability means that some of his paintings on this fabric have become fragile over time.

MacDonald preferred an essential palette of pigments, which he expertly mixed to produce an inspiring variety of hues and values on his paintings. Blue and green pigments that are prominent throughout his works include ultramarine, viridian, and cerulean blue. For yellows, oranges, and reds, he preferred cadmium yellow, iron

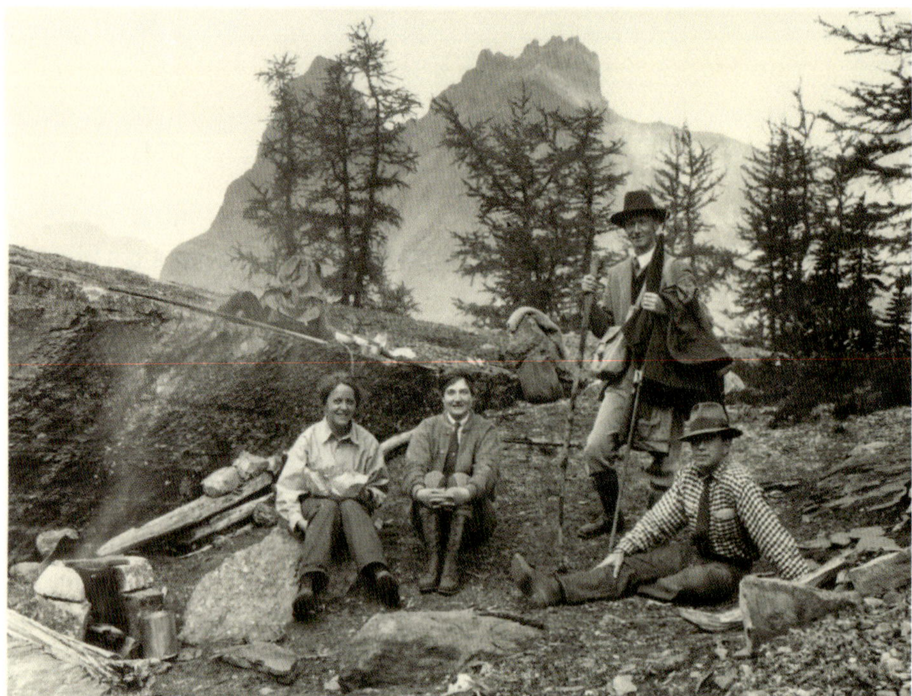

[*Catharine Whyte, Adeline Link, J.E.H. MacDonald, Peter Whyte*], 1930, Whyte Museum of the Canadian Rockies.

oxides, alizarin lake, and vermilion. MacDonald chose to use Cambridge White for most of his paintings and sketches, perhaps valuing its stability compared to other, more common white pigments. This characteristic white pigment is also an important part of Tom Thomson's palette.[1]

Through close looking and modern scientific analysis, we have tried to step back more than 100 years to understand MacDonald's creative process as he painted. The resulting research has produced a considerable body of technical information that will help conservators preserve his paintings and can be used as one aspect of authentication studies. After spending so much time with MacDonald's vivid and evocative paintings, though, we feel compelled to point out that the spirit and the poetry of his art can never be captured through this type of analytical exercise. In his own words, "Trees grow and clouds float but art has a world of her own where science is not so absolute."[2]

ACKNOWLEDGEMENTS

Many colleagues at the Canadian Conservation Institute provided help and advice at different stages of the project. We thank Kamila Bladek, Mylène Choquette, Marie-Claude Corbeil, Renée Dancause, Geneviève Desrochers, Anne-Stéphanie Etienne, Finnbar Healy, Christine McNair, Crystal Maitland, and Maeve Moriarty. We are particularly indebted to Germain Wiseman for his expert photography and to Margaret Gracie for her careful editing. We are also grateful to CCI management, especially Eric J. Henderson, Manager of the Conservation Science Division, who supported the research and the publication of the book.

Special thanks are due to several current and former conservation scientists at CCI for their key contributions to the analysis of samples and the examination of the paintings. This book wouldn't exist without them. We gratefully acknowledge Elizabeth Moffatt, Dominique Duguay, Clémentine Mansas, Stephanie Barnes, and Jennifer Poulin.

We are grateful to the following people from the McMichael Canadian Art Collection: Victoria Dickenson, who initiated the project and encouraged the research; Katerina Atanassova and Sarah Stanners for their curatorial contributions; Ian Dejardin, Sarah Milroy, and Jennifer Withrow for their continued support of the work; and Janine Butler, Linda Morita, Lorena Jurdana, and Marie-Eve Thibeault for providing invaluable assistance at various stages of the research.

We thank Christina McLean, Maria Sullivan, and Sandra Webster-Cook at the Art Gallery of Ontario for providing access and assistance during examination and sampling of MacDonald's works in the AGO collection. Christina McLean also examined some of the works with us and undertook technical photography. We thank Amy Furness and Al Stanton-Hagan for their assistance and advice on archival research.

Thanks are due to Susan Walker, Stephen Gritt, Marie-Catherine Cyr, and Tasia Bulger from the National Gallery of Canada for providing access and assistance during examination and sampling of the NGC works. We are especially grateful to Susan Walker, who examined many of the works with us and provided support and advice throughout the research. We would also like to acknowledge Amy Rose and

Philip Dombowsky for their assistance and guidance on archival research, and Karen Wyatt for her help with the collection database.

We are grateful to the staff at the Vancouver Art Gallery, particularly Richard Hill for his collaboration and for providing access to works in the VAG collection.

We thank Sandra Parcher and Ken Arnott, grandchildren of Mr. Albert William Arnott (1870–1946), long-time manager of the Artists' Supply Company, for providing information about the history of the company. We also thank the late Dennis Reid, and Susan MacDonald, grand-niece of J.E.H. MacDonald, for their advice about the location of archival documents. For their careful and thoughtful input on the manuscript, we thank subject matter experts Charles C. Hill, Crystal Maitland, and Patricia Smithen.

Finally, thank you to the team at Goose Lane Editions for all their help. We are especially grateful to Julie Scriver for her creative and thoughtful design.

Detail of *Autumn Leaves*, Batchewana, Algoma, circa 1919, Art Gallery of Ontario. Photo: © AGO. (see p. 30)

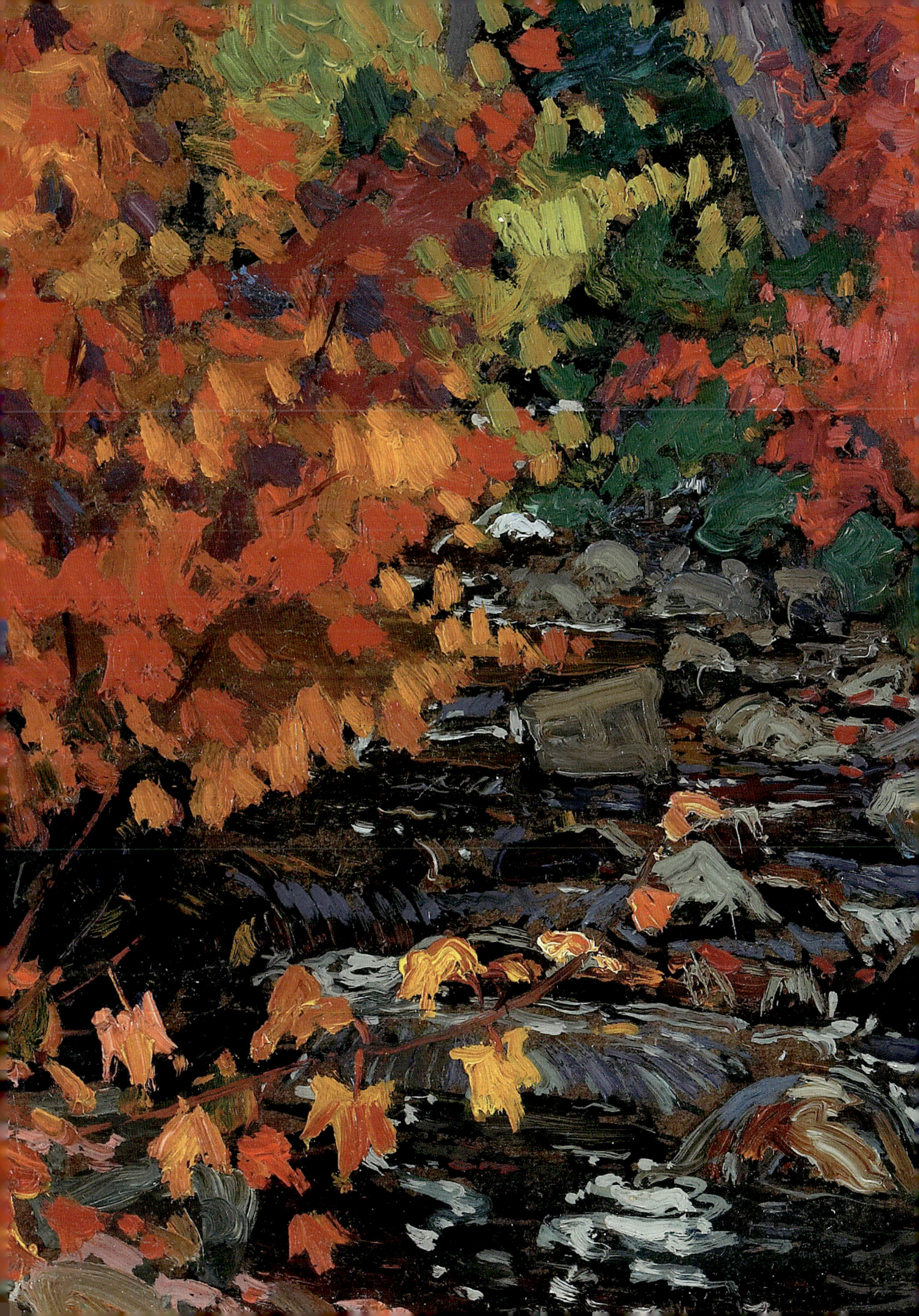

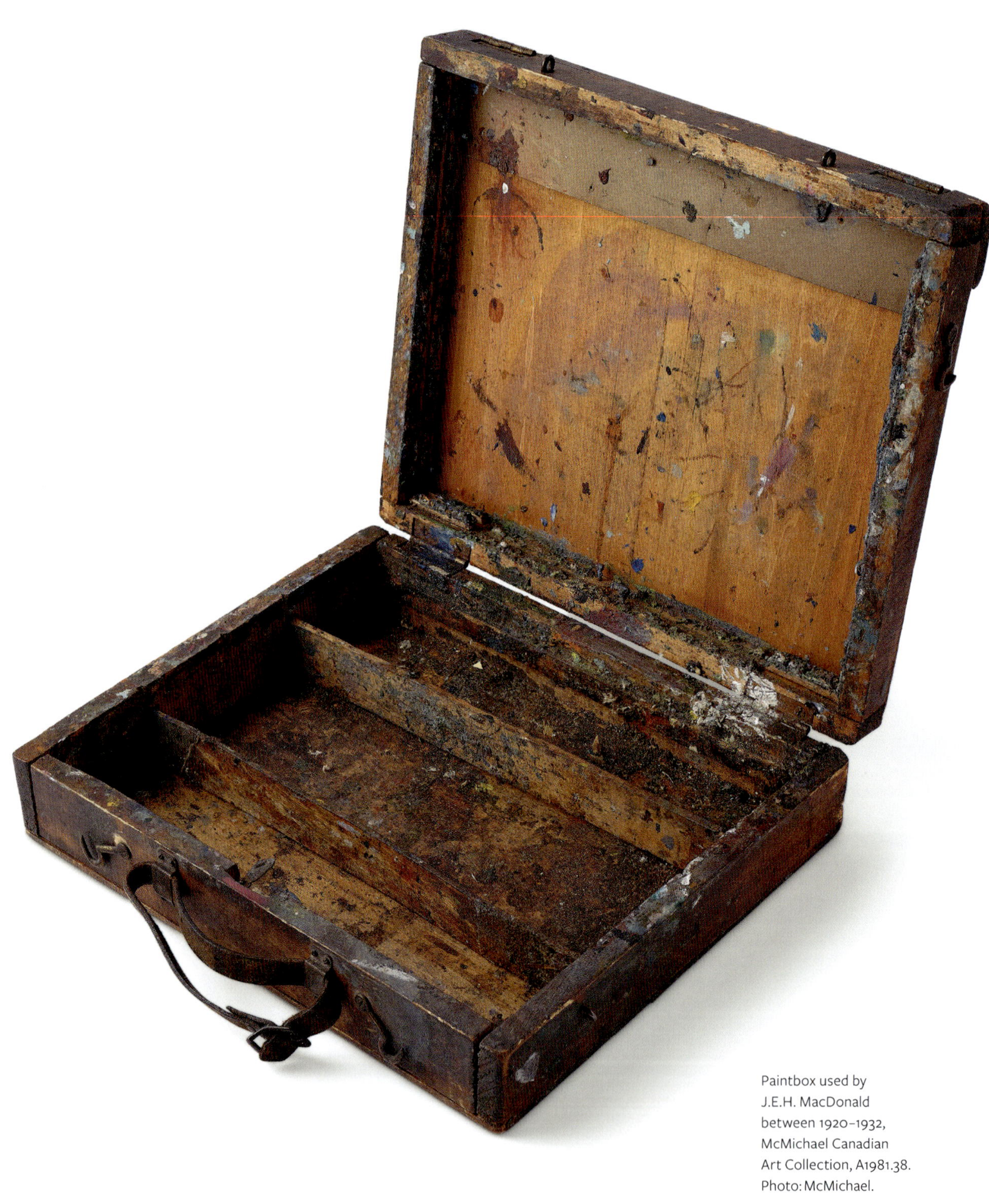

Paintbox used by
J.E.H. MacDonald
between 1920–1932,
McMichael Canadian
Art Collection, A1981.38.
Photo: McMichael.

APPENDIX A

PAINTBOXES

We were able to locate two of MacDonald's paintboxes for study: one in the collection of the McMichael Canadian Art Collection (the McMichael), the other in a private collection. Available archival photographs of MacDonald sketching were not of sufficient quality to determine whether they depict either of the two paintboxes that we examined. It is possible that he also used other portable sketching boxes during his career.

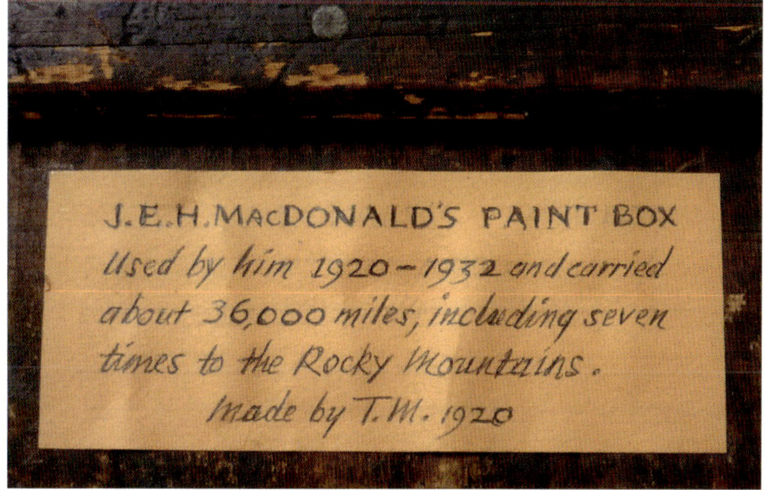

Fig. A.1: Label handwritten by Thoreau MacDonald affixed to the top of the J.E.H. MacDonald paintbox in the McMichael Canadian Art Collection, A1981.38. Photo: McMichael.

The McMichael Paintbox

The J.E.H. MacDonald paintbox in the McMichael collection (opposite) has a note from Thoreau MacDonald adhered to the outer surface of the lid (Fig. A.1), stating that his father used it from 1920 to 1932, including during his seven trips to the Rocky Mountains. The note also specifies that Thoreau made the box for his father.

The outer dimensions of the box are approximately 30 cm wide by 25 cm long by 8 cm deep. Like the boxes that A.Y. Jackson and Tom Thomson began using in 1914, it has a lightweight, compact construction.[1] However, unlike the Jackson-designed boxes, MacDonald's paintbox has a solid lid rather than one composed

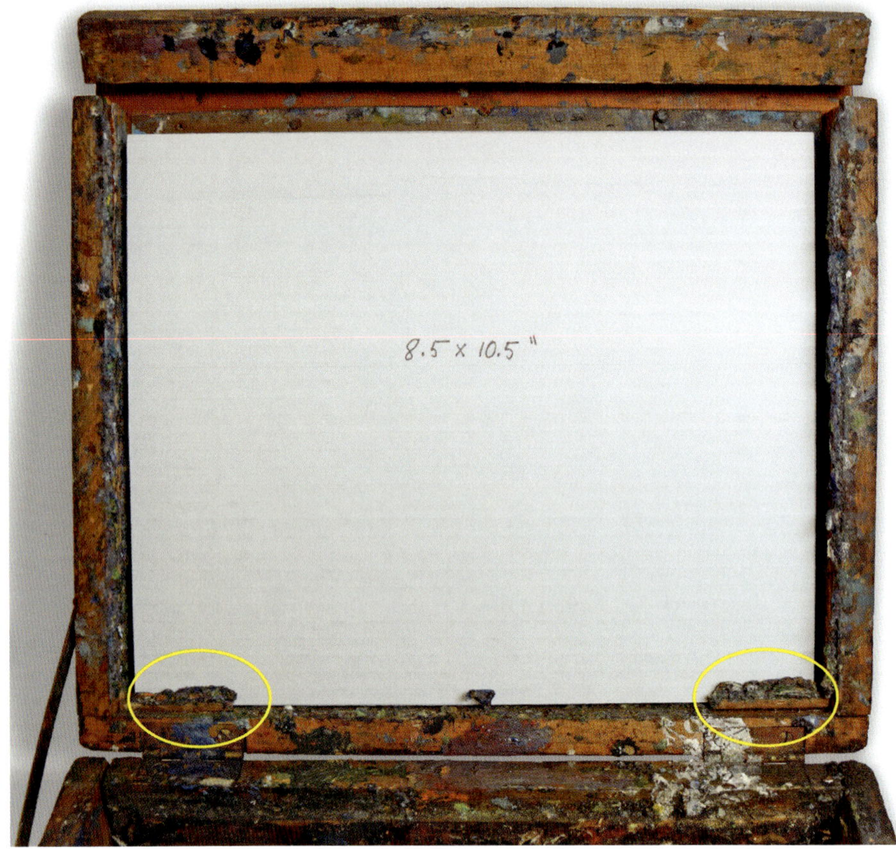

Fig. A.2: Detail of the J.E.H. MacDoanld paintbox in the McMichael Canadian Art Collection, A1981.38, showing an 8½ × 10½-inch test panel inserted in the lid. Wooden blocks to hold a sketching support in place are circled. Photo: McMichael.

of a removable wooden panel that could be used as a sketching support. The solid lid would have been more appropriate for the paperboard sketching supports that MacDonald favoured.

The paintbox does not include a shoulder strap but has a leather handle on top to allow it to be carried like a briefcase. It has a thin sprung brass strip to hold the lid open and includes three sections for brushes and paints in the bottom.[2] There are extensive residues of dried oil paint, particularly along the slots designed to hold a sketching support at the inner left and right sides of the lid.

The hinged front edge of the lid could be opened to slide a sketching support into the slots. However, the inner lid dimensions are just slightly too wide for a standard 8½ × 10½-inch support. Fig. A.2 shows that an 8½ × 10½-inch test board placed in the lid is not supported by the slots at left and right. MacDonald may have sometimes adhered or pinned his paperboard to a secondary support; as described in chapter 3, we observed pin or finishing nail holes on numerous sketches. There are also two small wooden blocks at the lower inner edge of the lid, at the left and right extremities (circled in Fig. A.2) that appear to have been added to hold the bottom edge of the sketching support in place while painting.

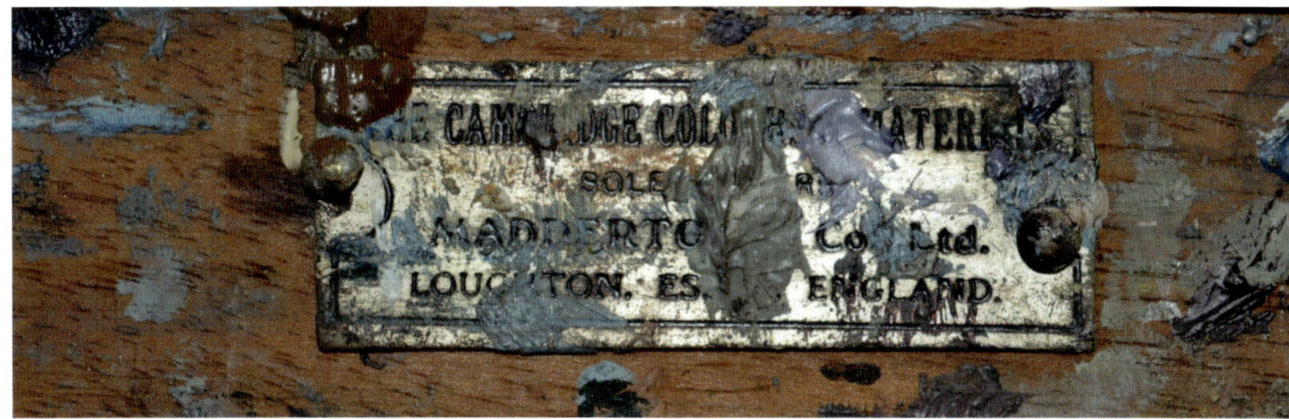

Fig. A.3: Maker's label on the Madderton paintbox, private collection. Photo: McMichael.

The Madderton Paintbox

A second paintbox that belonged to J.E.H. MacDonald was acquired by a private collector from Thoreau MacDonald's estate in 2002.[3] As shown in Fig. A.3, it has a metal maker's label indicating that it is a commercial box from Madderton & Company, labelled "The Cambridge Colours Materials." There is no information about the date that MacDonald would have used this box; however, given that the McMichael box was MacDonald's standard paintbox after 1920, he would have presumably used this Madderton box earlier in his career.

Figure A.4 illustrates the Madderton paintbox with the lid open. The outer dimensions of this commercial box are approximately 40 cm wide by 30 cm long by 8 cm deep. It is significantly larger and made with a heavier wood construction than the box made for MacDonald by his son. Its dimensions are very close to a Cambridge paintbox illustrated in a catalogue from the Artists' Supply Company, the Canadian distributor for the Cambridge Colours oil paint brand.[4] The dimensions of the lid are much too wide to hold an 8½ × 10½-inch support in the slots. However, the left wooden support slides along the brass plate when the release screw (circled in Fig. A.4) is loosened, allowing smaller support sizes to be accommodated. The extensive paint residues along the slots suggest that MacDonald used the box in this way. The bottom of the paintbox is divided into sections to hold brushes and other painting materials (Fig. A.5).

The Madderton box included a wooden palette, numerous paintbrushes, and a palette knife, among other materials. A selection of the brushes is shown in Fig. A.6. They include well-worn paintbrushes of sizes 3, 5, and, what appears to be, 12, with brush widths of 3.2, 4.4 and 9.5 mm, respectively. As described in chapter 3, these sizes correspond well to the brushstroke widths we measured on some of his sketches.

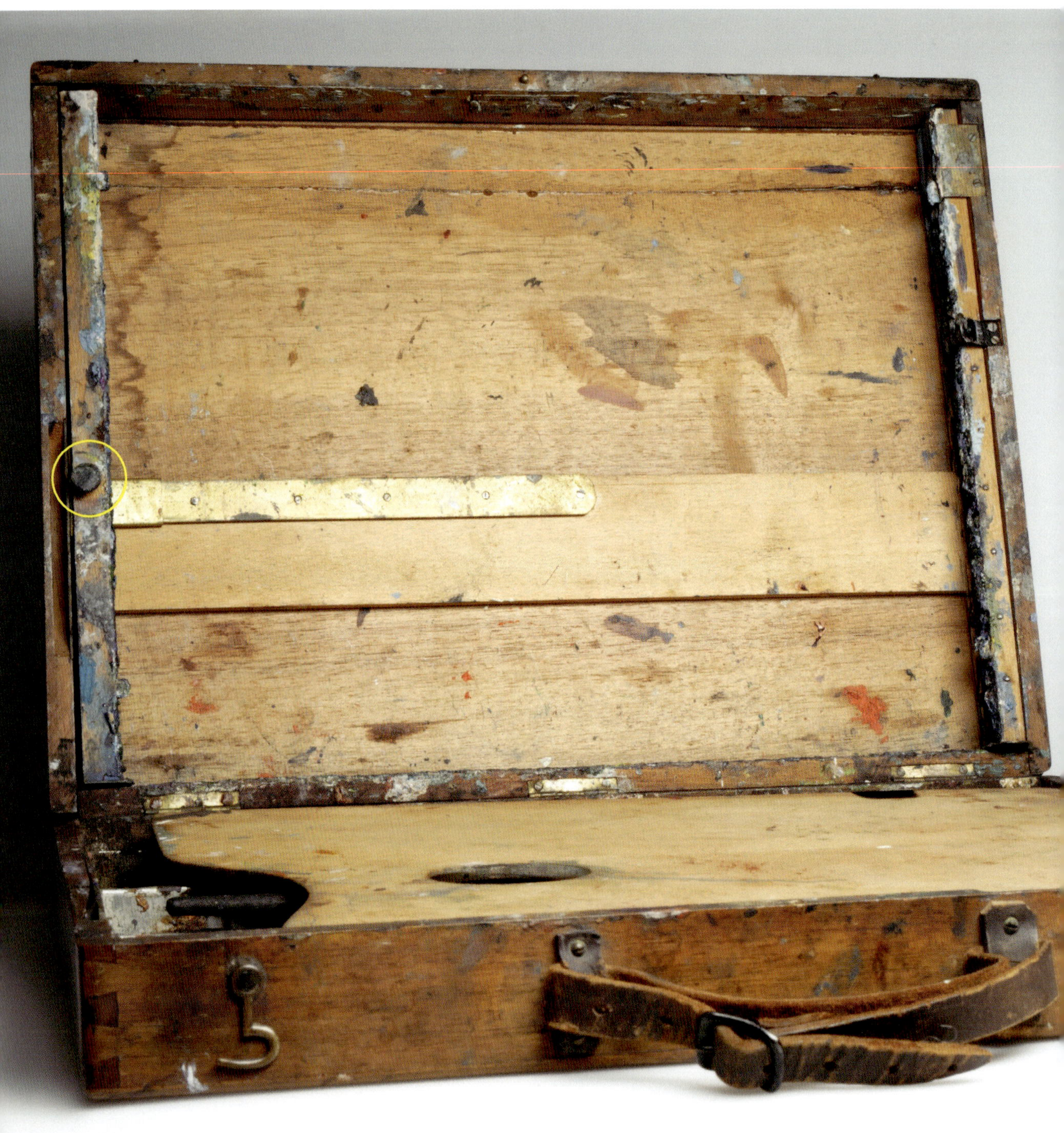

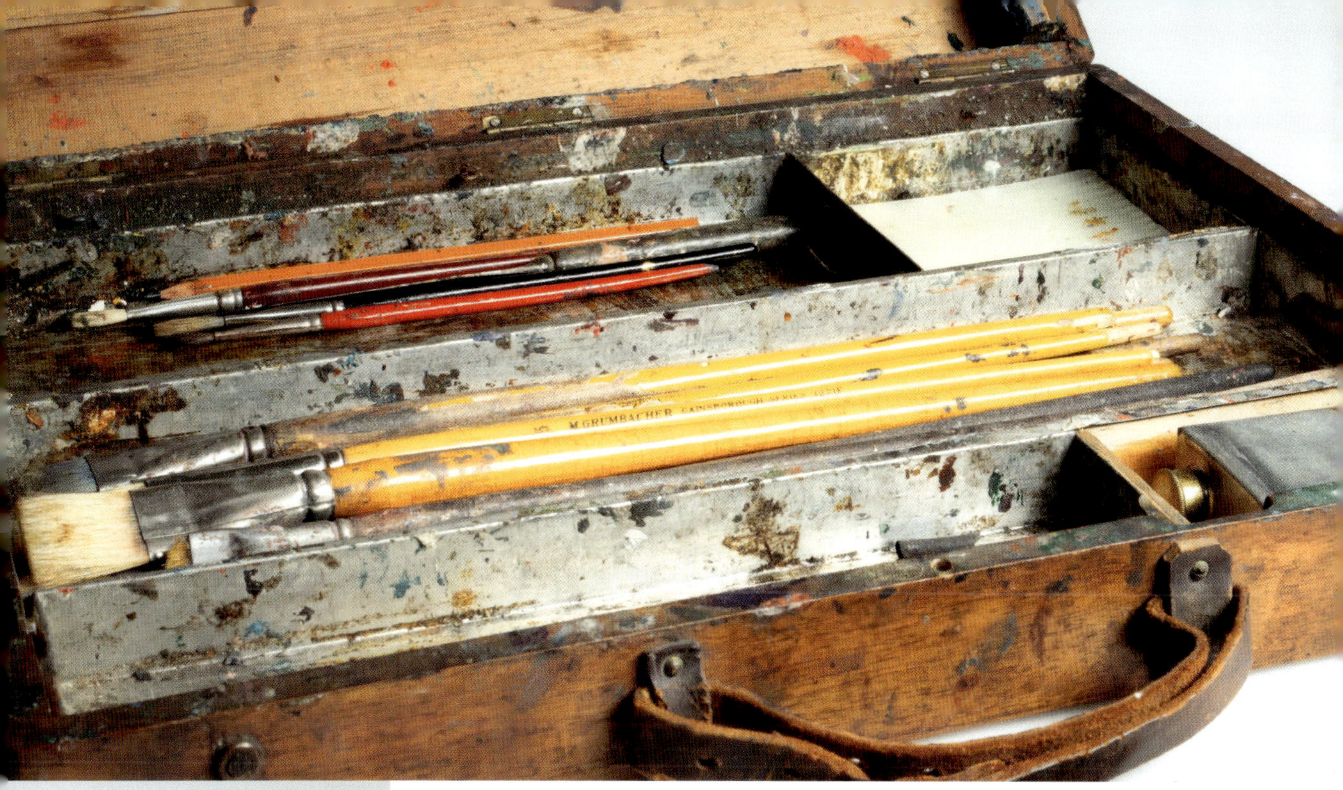

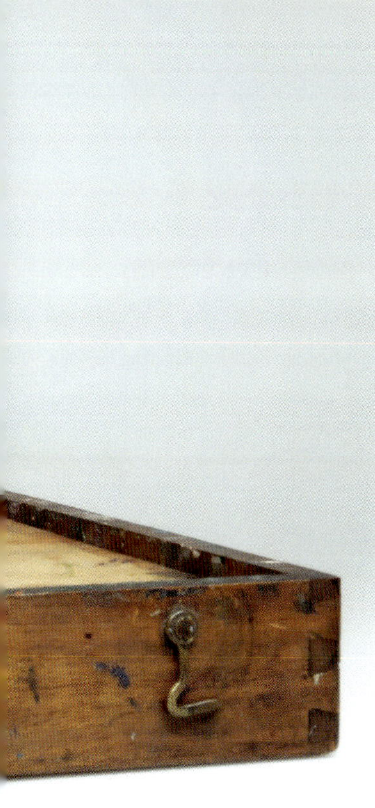

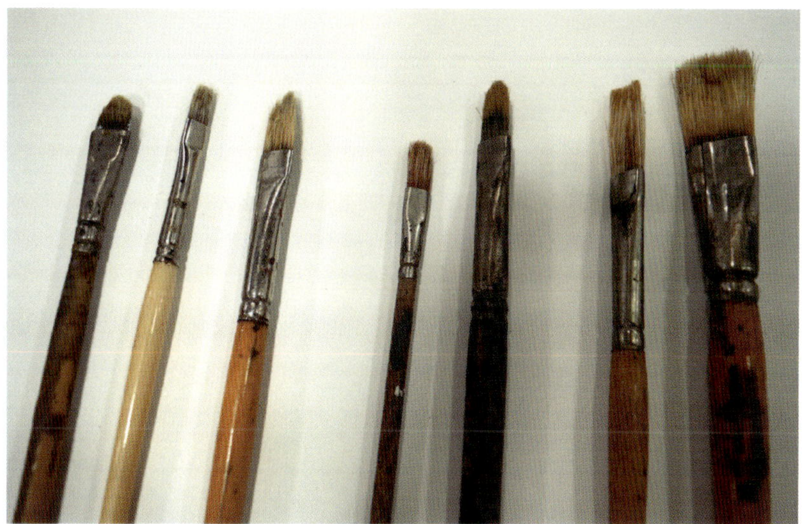

(clockwise from left) The Madderton paintbox and its contents, private collection.

Fig. A.4: The Madderton paintbox with the lid open showing the release screw on the left. Photo: courtesy of the owner.

Fig. A.5: Sections designed to hold brushes and other painting materials. Photo: courtesy of the owner.

Fig. A.6: A selection of brushes found in the Madderton paintbox, private collection. Photo: McMichael.

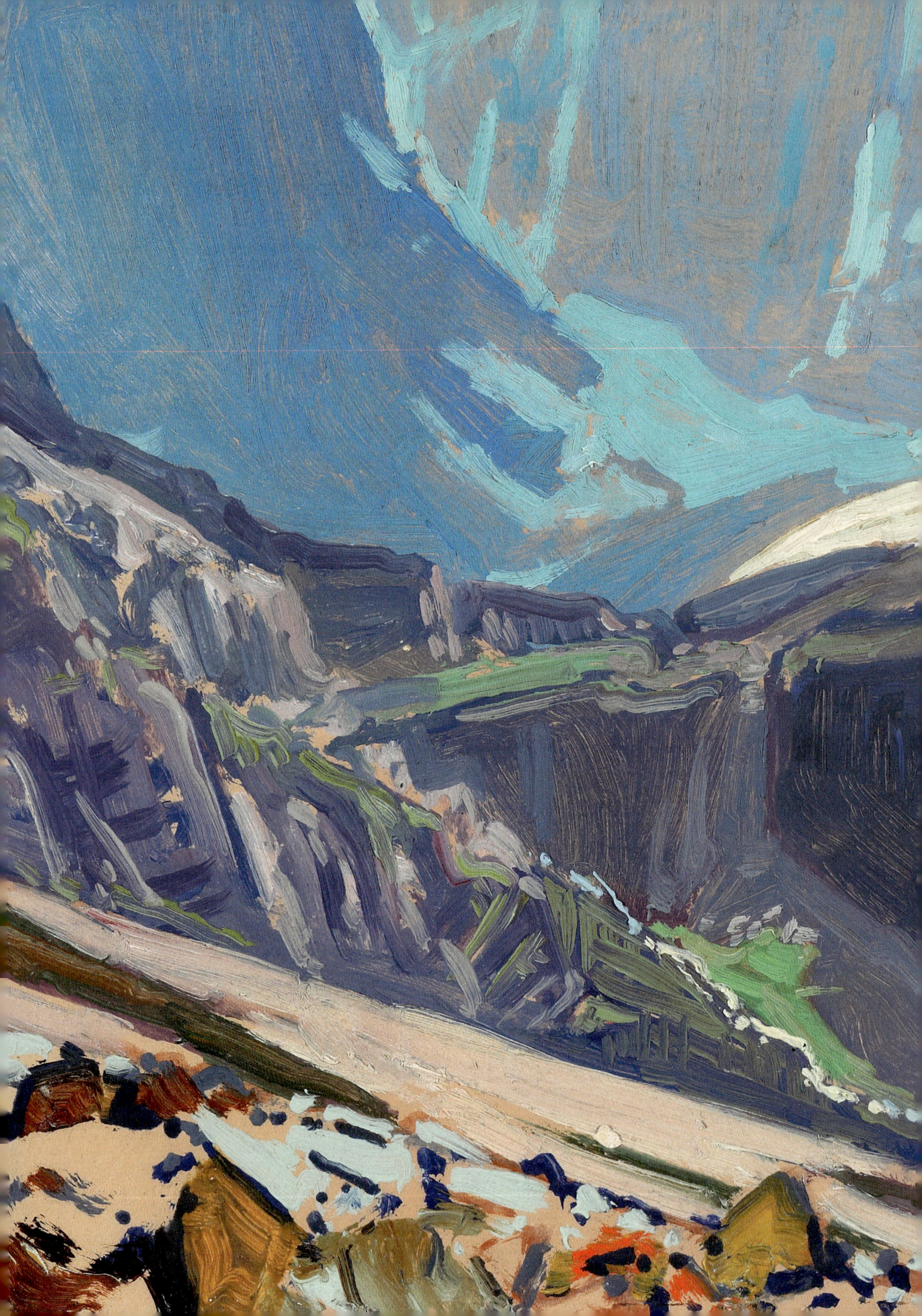

APPENDIX B

ANALYSIS METHODS

The experimental details for each analysis technique are listed below. This is followed by a description of the methodology, which includes the order of application of the techniques and a brief explanation about the choice of methods.

Experimental Details

FTIR spectroscopy. The FTIR system was composed of a Bruker Tensor 27 FTIR spectrometer interfaced to a Bruker Hyperion 2000 microscope. The use of an infrared microscope permitted the analysis of samples in the microgram range. Prior to analysis, scientists compressed a portion of each sample on a Spectra-Tech low-pressure diamond anvil microsample cell, composed of two Type IIA diamonds of 0.6 mm in diameter, to achieve an appropriate thickness for transmission experiments. One half of the diamond cell was mounted on the microscope stage, and spectra were collected in transmission mode using Bruker OPUS 7.5 software. The spectral range was either 4000 to 570 cm^{-1}, using a liquid nitrogen–cooled mid-band mercury cadmium telluride (MCT) D316 detector, or 4000 to 430 cm^{-1}, using a liquid nitrogen–cooled wide-band MCT D315 detector. The infrared spectra were obtained through coaddition of 150 to 200 interferograms. Spectral resolution was 4 cm^{-1}. The area analyzed could be adjusted as required, using variable, transparent, knife-edge apertures on the Hyperion microscope; typical analysis areas were between 400 and 1000 μm^2. Material identification using FTIR spectroscopy was based on comparison to published infrared spectra or to infrared spectra of reference materials held at CCI. Reference data for common pigments, fillers, and minerals is available in published literature, in commercial spectral libraries, and in the Infrared and Raman Users Group (IRUG) database, which is specific to cultural heritage materials.[1]

Detail of *Near Lake Oesa, Abbot's Pass*, 1930, 21.5 × 26.6 cm, oil on paperboard, National Gallery of Canada, Ottawa. Photo: NGC. (see p. 42)

XRD. In most cases, the XRD equipment consisted of a Bruker D8 Discover with GADDS (General Area Detector Diffraction System) equipped with a rotating anode and cobalt target. On this instrument, operating parameters were 40 kV and

85 mA, and the collimator size was 0.5 mm. For a smaller number of samples, the team used a Rigaku Rapid II XRD system equipped with a rotating anode and cobalt target. The operating parameters were 40 kV and 15 mA, and the collimator size was 0.3 mm. The application of search-match software using the PDF databases from the International Center for Diffraction Data (ICDD)[2] to the diffraction patterns allowed for the identification of the crystalline compounds present in the samples.

SEM/EDX. For SEM/EDX, scientists used either a Hitachi SU3500 SEM integrated with an Oxford INCA X-act analytical silicon drift X-ray detector and an AZtec X-ray microanalysis system or with an older Hitachi S-3500N SEM integrated with an Oxford INCA X-act analytical silicon drift X-ray detector and an INCAEnergy+ X-ray microanalysis system. These instrumental configurations permit elemental analysis of volumes down to a few cubic micrometres for elements from boron (B) to uranium (U) in the periodic table at a level of approximately 0.1–1% or greater. For paint and ground samples, small fragments adhered to carbon tape were analyzed, without coating, using an accelerating voltage of 20 kV in high vacuum mode. For cross-sections mounted in polyester resin, a pressure of 60 Pa allowed analysis without the need to coat the samples. The working distance was 10 mm in all cases.

PLM. CCI scientists prepared samples for PLM as dispersions in Cargille Meltmount (optical quality) mounting medium. This mounting medium has a refractive index of 1.662 and becomes fluid at 65°C. Scientists first placed a drop of the heated liquid mounting medium on a glass microscope slide, and then, working through a microscope, placed a small fragment of a sample on top of the cooled mounting medium, before covering it with a cover slip. Subsequently, the slide was heated to approximately 65°C to remelt the mounting medium. Once it had become fluid again, gentle pressure was applied with a pencil eraser to the top of the cover slip to break up and disperse the pigments. Scientists examined the dispersions using a Leica DMRX polarized light microscope with either a 40× dry objective or a 100× oil immersion objective, using several types of illumination: transmitted, plane-polarized, cross-polarized, and, in some cases, reflected illumination. For differentiation of blue pigments, a Chelsea filter was placed in the light path, and the colour of the particles was observed.[3] For microscopy of the paperboard support fibres, pre-treatment with water allowed separation of the fibre fragments. After drying, the fibres were stained with Graff "C" reagent to aid with microscopic identification, using transmitted and cross-polarized illumination. In all cases, identification was based on comparison with dispersions of reference materials held at CCI, supplemented with published articles and atlases.[4]

Raman spectroscopy. CCI scientists obtained Raman spectra of selected samples using a Bruker Senterra dispersive Raman microscope with an excitation wavelength of either 785 nm or 532 nm. The laser power at the sample was less than 1 μW. Objective lenses with 50× and 100× magnification produced analysis areas of approximately 2 or 1 μm in diameter, respectively. The grating and CCD detector combination in the instrument produced a spectral resolution of approximately 3 to 5 cm^{-1}. The choice of collection parameters depended on the sample characteristics: typical settings were a thirty-second integration time with 3 to 5 coadded spectra. With the 785 nm laser, the spectral range was usually 61 to 1512 cm^{-1}. In some cases, for example to identify organic pigments, a wider range of 61 to 2631 cm^{-1} was chosen. For the 532 nm laser, the range was 61 to 1555 cm^{-1}. The high spatial resolution of Raman spectroscopy permitted analysis of individual pigment particles within a paint sample. Pigments were presented to the laser in a variety of ways: within mounted cross-sections, on powder samples adhered to carbon planchets, or through a cover slip on paint samples that had been previously dispersed in Cargille Meltmount for PLM. Scientists identified pigments and fillers by comparison to published Raman spectra or to Raman spectra of reference materials held at CCI.[5]

Py-GC-MS. CCI scientists undertook analysis using Direct Inlet Py-GC-MS[6] for seven varnish preparatory layers. For this method, a few micrograms of each sample were placed in a micro-vial with 2 μL of tetramethylammonium hydroxide (TMAH 2.5% v/v in methanol). The vial was inserted into an Agilent Thermal Separation Probe (TSP) installed in a multimode inlet on an Agilent 7890A GC interfaced to an Agilent 5975C MS. The multimode injector with TSP was operated in splitless mode and ramped from 50°C to 450°C, at a rate of 900°C/minute to perform the pyrolysis. The final temperature was held constant for three minutes and then decreased to 250°C at a rate of 50°C/minute. The GC separation step employed a Phenomenex ZB-SemiVolatiles fused silica column (30 m × 0.25 mm inner diameter, 0.25 μm film thickness) and ultra-high-purity helium carrier gas with a constant flow of 1.2 mL/minute. The oven program extended from 40°C to 200°C at 10°C/minute and 200°C to 300°C at 6°C/minute with a hold time of 20 minutes (run time of 52.67 minutes). The MS was operated with ion-positive electron ionization (EI positive mode) at 70 eV with a transfer line temperature of 280°C; the MS ion source was held at 230°C and the MS quadrupole at 150°C. The MS was run in scan mode from 50 to 550 amu (5 to 25 minutes), 50 to 750 amu (25 to 30 minutes), and 50 to 800 amu (35 to 63 minutes). Data was processed using AMDIS and Agilent ChemStation software.

Key markers for the identification of resins, oils, and waxes include methylated derivatives and pyrolysates of the following compounds:

- specific ratios of azelaic acid, palmitic acid, and stearic acid for drying oils;[7]
- shellolic acid, butolic acid, and aleuitic acid for shellac;[8]
- dehydroabietic acid, 7-hydroxy-tetradehydroabietic acid, and 7-oxodehydroabietic acid for Pinaceae resin, with specific identification of pine resin made by calculating the ratio of pimaric acid to sandaracopimaric acid peaks;[9]
- communic acid and ozic acid for labdane-based resins such as copal, with the addition of sandaracopimaric acid and hydroxysandaracopimaric acid for sandarac resin;[10]
- hydroxy-palmitic acids, long-chain alcohols (C28, C30, C32), and hydrocarbons (C27, C29, C31) for beeswax;[11] and
- long-chain alkane series with distinctly shaped distribution for paraffin wax.[12]

Cross-sections. Scientists prepared cross-sections from selected samples by mounting fragments in Bio-Plastic polyester resin (from Ward's Science) and then grinding and polishing the embedded samples using standard petrographic techniques.[13] For each cross-section, normal (incident) light images, fluorescence images and, in many cases, backscattered electron images were recorded. For incident light and fluorescence microscopy, the equipment consisted of a Leica DMRX microscope interfaced to a Leica DFC500 digital camera. In a few cases, a newer Leica DM4 P microscope interfaced to a Leica DMC6200 camera was used. Leica LAS X software permitted both image capture and image processing. For fluorescence microscopy, scientists observed the visible fluorescence of layers in the cross-sections, induced by either ultraviolet (UV) or blue light. The excitation filter for UV-induced fluorescence had a band pass of 340–380 nm. For blue-induced fluorescence, the band pass was 420–490 nm. Imaging of selected cross-sections was undertaken with a backscattered electron detector in SEM/EDX systems described above. The samples remained uncoated for cross-section imaging. The accelerating voltage was 20 kV, and the chamber pressure was 60 Pa.

Methodology

Step 1. The first techniques applied to the paint and ground samples were FTIR spectroscopy, XRD, and SEM/EDX. Many of the major components were identified using these three methods.

Results of FTIR spectroscopy allowed the identification of the general class of varnish or paint binding medium. In the case of some varnishes, these results were augmented through analysis using Py-GC-MS, a method that allows identification of many types of organic materials, such as resins, oils, and waxes.

FTIR spectroscopy was also a useful method to identify fillers, accessory minerals, and some of the white pigments in the paint and ground samples. The following were regularly identified using FTIR spectroscopy: kaolin, quartz, hydromagnesite, barium sulfate, gypsum, lead sulfate, lead white, and calcium carbonate. These carbonate, sulfate, and silicate compounds produce strong, characteristic bands in the mid-infrared, which makes them easy to identify definitively using this method.

When certain of the coloured pigments were present in high enough concentrations, it was possible to identify them from the overall infrared spectra of the paint. FTIR spectroscopy was particularly useful in identifying barium yellow, ultramarine, Prussian blue, viridian, green earth, alizarin, toluidine red, and bone black. The FTIR spectra also sometimes showed characteristic bands for cerulean blue and yellow iron oxide (goethite form). The infrared absorption bands for pigments based on sulfides, like vermilion and cadmium yellow, are outside the mid-infrared region achievable on the instrumentation available at CCI, which precluded their identification using this technique.

XRD provided complementary results to FTIR spectroscopy, allowing the identification of pigments that are crystalline and present in relatively high concentration. Vermilion and cadmium yellow, pigments that could not be determined with FTIR spectroscopy, were regularly identified using XRD. Other coloured pigments often identified with XRD included ultramarine, cerulean blue, barium yellow, and in a few cases, chrome yellow and chrome orange. For pigments with more than one possible crystal structure, such as cadmium yellow, the diffraction patterns provided structural information. While iron oxide pigments did not usually produce strong diffraction lines, a few samples that included well-crystallized red or yellow iron oxides in high concentration gave patterns for hematite or goethite, respectively.

XRD proved very useful for the identification of white pigments. These included lead white, lead sulfate, zinc white, barium sulfate, and zinc sulfide. These pigments usually produced strong, well-resolved XRD patterns. Certain fillers or accessory minerals readily found using FTIR spectroscopy, such as hydromagnesite and kaolin, were not identified with XRD, due to small particle size, low crystallinity, or low concentration.

Knowledge of the chemical elements, determined using SEM/EDX, was helpful in the interpretation of the results from other techniques. Once analysis using XRD and FTIR spectroscopy was complete, the SEM/EDX results were evaluated to determine if the chemical elements suggested the presence of additional pigments not identified using these two initial methods. Evaluation of the data showed that most samples likely included pigments below the detection limits of FTIR spectroscopy and XRD. For this reason, the majority of samples were further analyzed using PLM and, in some cases, Raman spectroscopy.

Step 2. Results from the first stage of the analysis showed that many of the paints were complex mixtures. In these cases, the CCI team undertook additional analysis using PLM and Raman spectroscopy, two methods that allow identification of low concentration pigments.

PLM is a powerful technique for pigment mixtures. Even when only a few particles are visible in a dispersion, observation of their microscopic characteristics (such as colour, size, shape, birefringence, and refractive index) permits the identification of many common pigments. Pigments frequently identified using PLM included ultramarine, cerulean blue, Prussian blue, viridian, iron oxide pigments, vermilion, bone black, carbon-based black, and chrome yellow. Since the white pigments, fillers, and accessory minerals were well-characterized using FTIR spectroscopy and XRD, they were not a focus for identification using PLM.

Raman spectroscopy was the final step for pigment identification. While this method does not provide an overall determination of the components in a paint, its high spatial resolution allows identification of single pigment particles in a mixture. Raman spectroscopy made it possible to identify specific pigments that were suspected to be present in low concentrations but had not been found by any other method. For example, cadmium yellow is a finely divided pigment that can sometimes be difficult to identify with PLM, and when it is present only in small amounts, it may be below the detection limit for XRD. In these cases, Raman spectroscopy using the 532 nm laser proved to be an effective method for identification. Raman spectroscopy was also useful in identifying iron oxide pigments in some cases: the presence of goethite confirmed yellow iron oxide, while hematite confirmed red iron oxide. Raman spectroscopy allowed differentiation of vermilion from red iron oxide when the results of PLM were inconclusive. The presence of chromate pigments (barium yellow, chrome yellow, and chrome orange) were also confirmed using Raman spectroscopy. This class of pigments produces strong, characteristic Raman spectra using the 785 nm laser.

APPENDIX C

SKETCHING NOTES

Below is a transcription of all four pages of MacDonald's fragmentary lecture notes on outdoor sketching, likely written around 1925.[1] This is followed by images of each of the handwritten pages (Figs. C.2 to C.5), which are preserved in the J.E.H MacDonald fonds, Library and Archives Canada, Ottawa, Ontario. Any errors in transcription are our own.

Sketching
The first outdoor sport
Leisure, Nature study, Enjoyment
Equipment
a few tools, some enthusiasm & an open
mind
Colors about 8
a small box . .
- Morrice & his pocket outfit
Stool or rocks
Umbrella Light in the mountains strong
Snow sketching The mist with [hole?]
Anna Boberg

—

Drawing for the oil sketch
Brush outline, thin wash in
High lights strong

Don't photograph the subject. Give only the characteristic details essential to the composition.

—

Speed helps in sketching just as in sprinting. Try
to grasp the idea of your subject quickly. Then put it down
before you can form any doubts about it.

—

Get the effect, it goes quickest, the objects remain & can be
studied at leisure if need be.

—

Try to have an idea in your sketch as well as a view.
A profile is the limit of a solid mass. Even though that
solidity has the different qualities of cloud & rock.

—

Design from nature rather than copy her. You will find
a general trend in the lines & masses, under
varying details. Bring that out.

—

"The function of painting is to record, to recall
& to instruct" – Albert [Gleizes?]
An ideal work combines all these qualities
but good sketching may have only one.
If your sketch is a good record, only it is worthwhile.

If it is a record of such a nature that it
has a form within it of wide association for
many people, so much the better, if in addition
to this it can instruct through greatness of theme or
treatment it has completed the spelling of the
word ART.

—

We might perhaps take those three letters to mean
Association. Record. Truth.

—

Trees grow & clouds float but art has
a world of her own where science is not
so absolute.

—

If Drawing is the bones of art, painting is the "guts."
Drawing is analytic. Painting synthetic.

—

The sketcher must cultivate a sense of values
values of tones, values of mass, values
of detail.

—

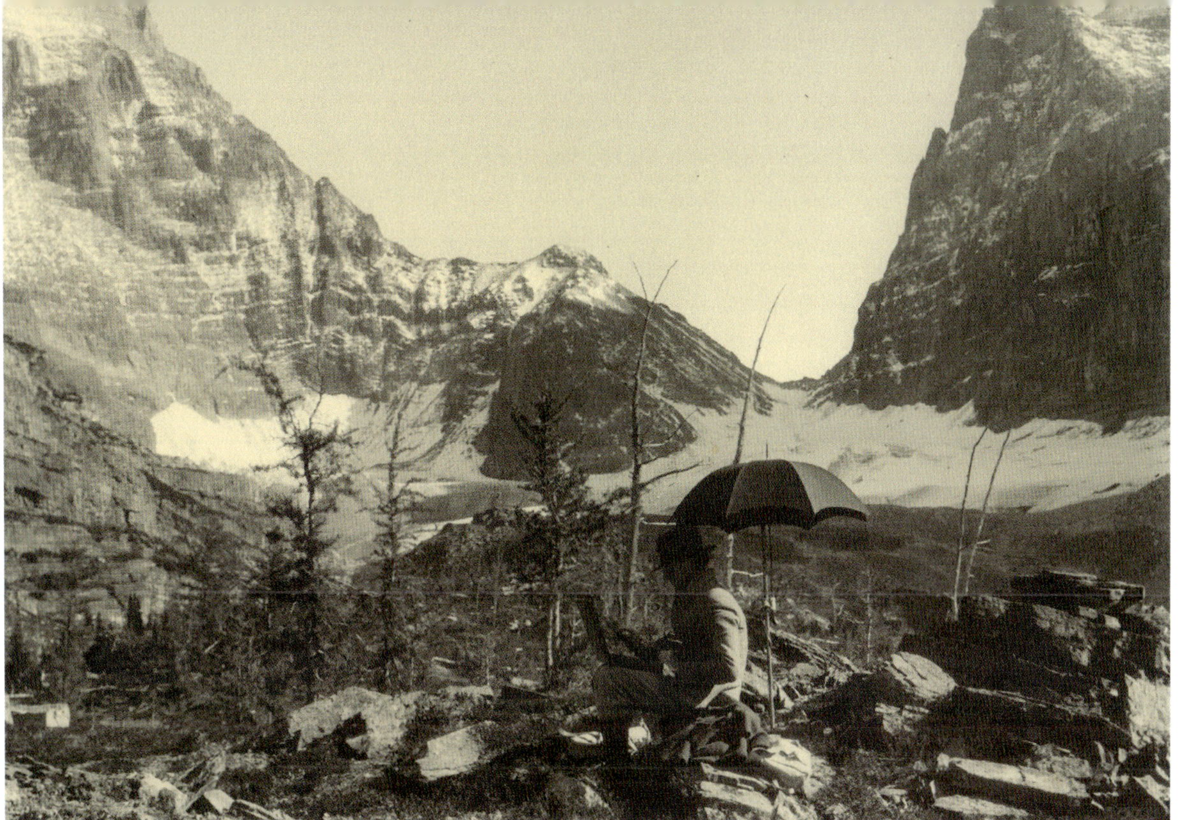

Fig. C.1: *JEH MacDonald Painting on Opabin*, 1929, Whyte Museum of the Canadian Rockies.

The foreground should be in the front of the sketch & the background in the rear. Things should move inwards on the earth & outwards in the sky

—

A good sketch is a strong suggestion of nature, so confident that its simplicity is not perceived.

—

The eye tends to travel along the edges of masses. Make this direction rhythmical.

—

Let there be light. Generally speaking put your sky in first.

—

Too many colors spoil the sketch.

—

The Canadian accent is harsher than that of England but it suits the prairies & the mountains. Let us speak the tongue native to us

—

Art is universal but Canada should contribute.

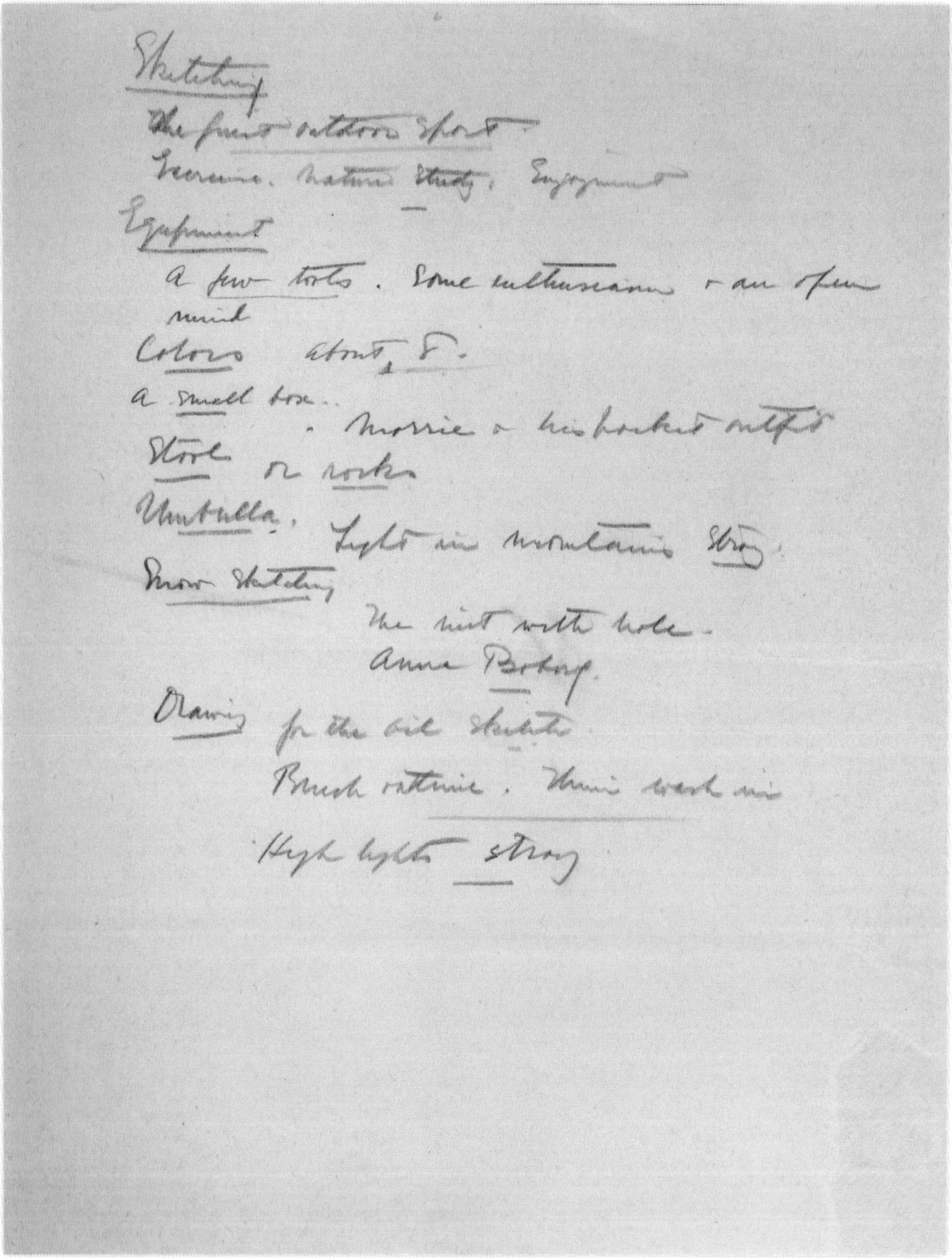

Sketching

The finest outdoor sport

Exercise. Nature Study. Enjoyment

Equipment

A few tools. Some enthusiasm & an open mind

Colors about 8.

A small box..

. Morris & his pocket outfit

Stool or rocks

Umbrella. Light in mountains strong.

Snow Sketching

The hint with hole.

Anne Bishop.

Drawing for the oil sketch.

Brush outline. Thin wash in

High lights strong

Fig. C.2: First page of MacDonald's unpublished lecture notes on outdoor sketching.
Photo: © Government of Canada.

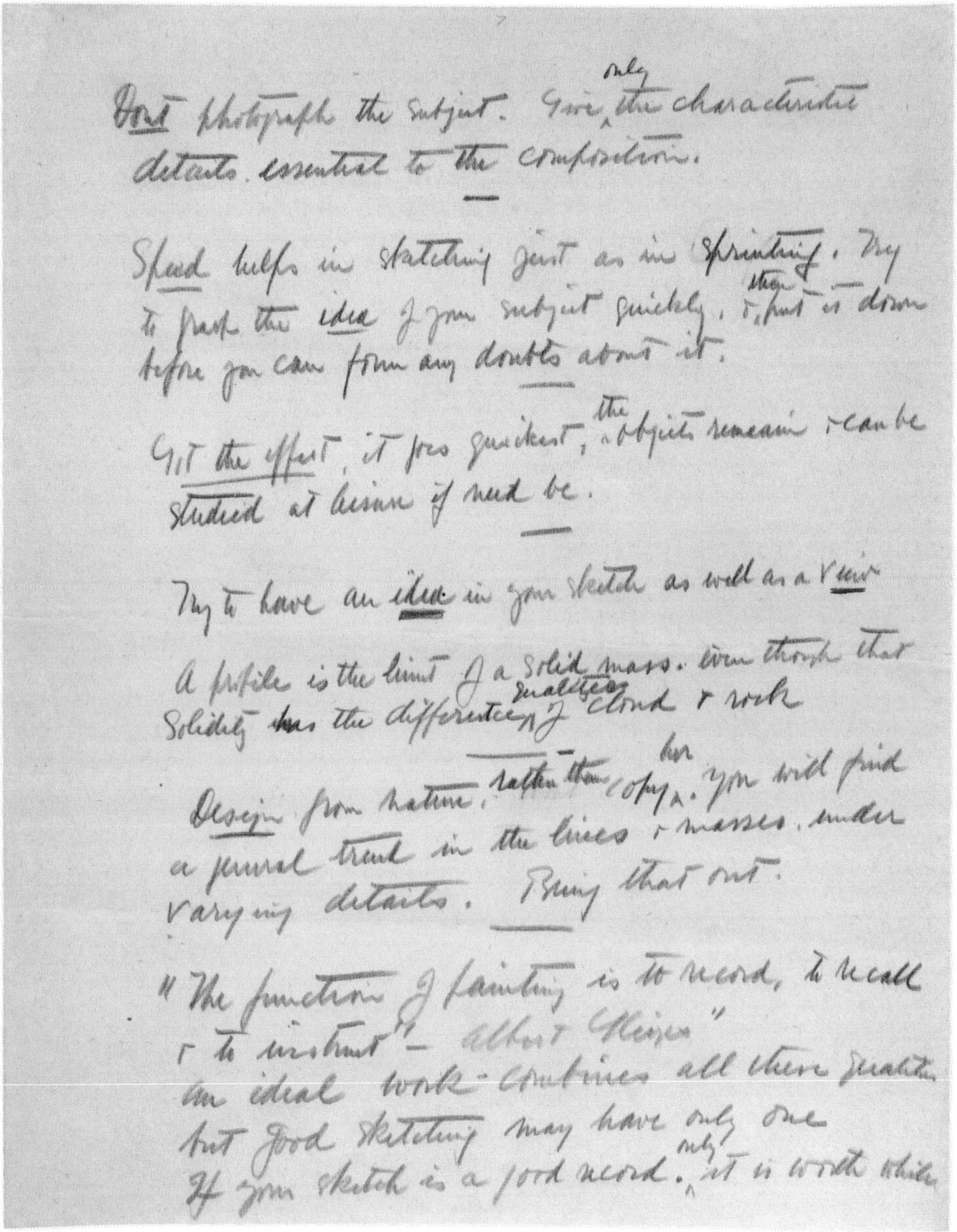

Dont photograph the subject. Give only the characteristic details essential to the composition.

—

Speed helps in sketching just as in sprinting. Try to grasp the idea of your subject quickly, & put it down before you can form any doubts about it.

—

Get the effect, it goes quickest, the objects remain & can be studied at leisure if need be.

—

Try to have an idea in your sketch as well as a view

A profile is the limit of a solid mass. Even though that Solidity has the difference of qualities of cloud & rock

—

Design from nature, rather than copy her. You will find a general trend in the lines & masses, under varying details. Bring that out.

—

"The function of painting is to record, to recall & to instruct" — Albert Gleizes"
An ideal work — combines all these qualities
but good sketching may have only one
If your sketch is a good record only it is worth while

Fig. C.3: Second page of MacDonald's unpublished lecture notes on outdoor sketching.
Photo: © Government of Canada.

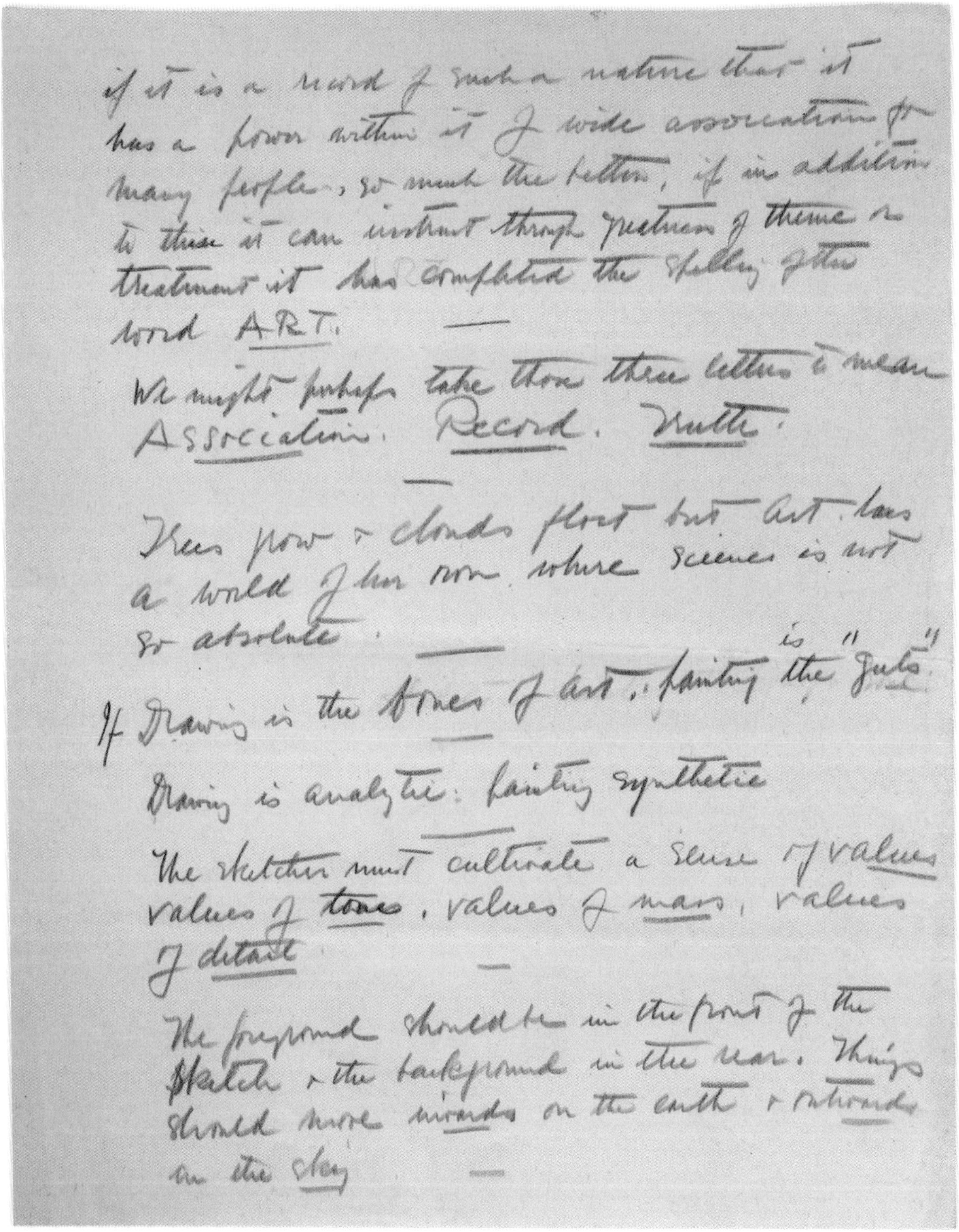

if it is a word of such a nature that it has a power within it of wide association for many people, so much the better, if in addition to this it can without through freshness of theme or treatment it has completed the spelling of the word ART. —

We might perhaps take those three letters to mean Association. Record. Truth.

—

Trees grow & clouds float but Art has a world of her own where science is not so absolute.

—

If Drawing is the bones of art, painting is "the guts"

—

Drawing is analytic: painting synthetic

—

The sketcher must cultivate a sense of values values of tones, values of mass, values of detail

—

The foreground should be in the front of the sketch & the background in the rear. Things should move inwards on the earth & outwards in the sky —

Fig. C.4: Third page of MacDonald's unpublished lecture notes on outdoor sketching.
Photo: © Government of Canada.

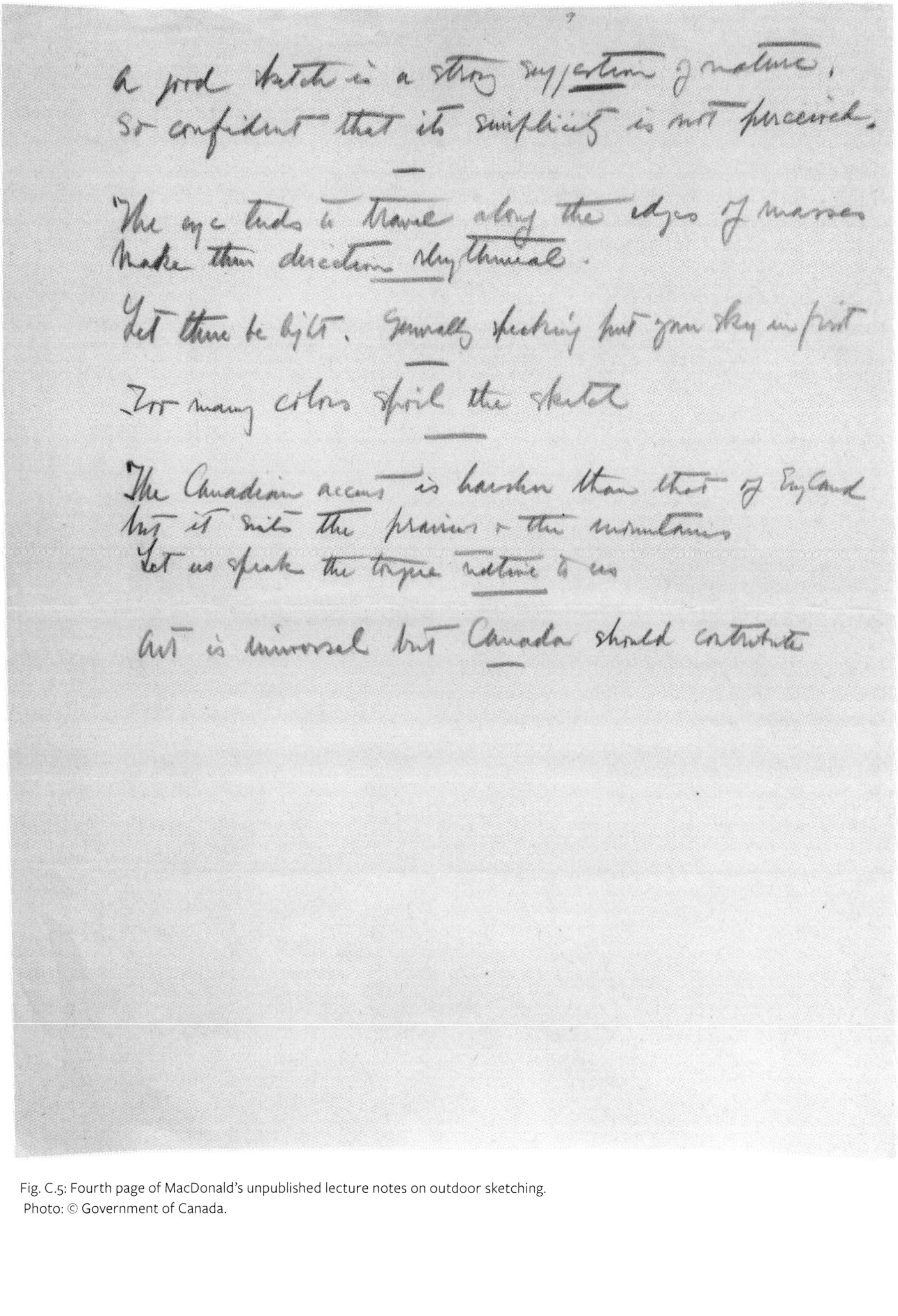

A good sketch is a strong suggestion of nature,
so confident that its simplicity is not perceived.

The eye tends to travel along the edges of masses
make their direction rhythmical.

Let there be light. Generally speaking put your sky in first

Too many colors spoil the sketch

The Canadian accent is harsher than that of England
but it suits the prairies & the mountains
Let us speak the tongue native to us

Art is universal but Canada should contribute

Fig. C.5: Fourth page of MacDonald's unpublished lecture notes on outdoor sketching.
Photo: © Government of Canada.

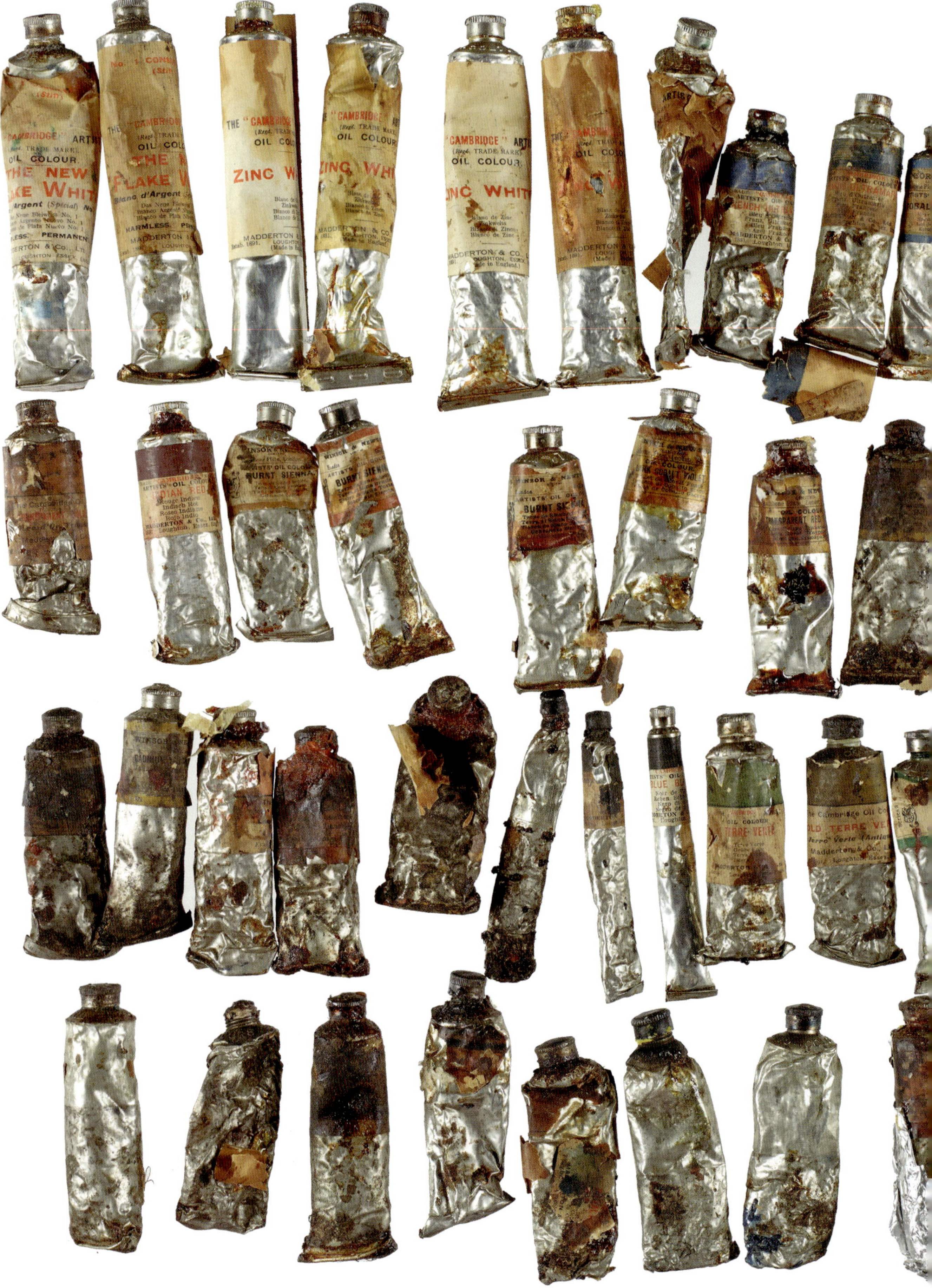

"CAMBRIDGE"
(Regd. TRADE MARK)
OIL COLOUR
Blanc d'Argent
HARMLESS. PERMANENT
(Regd. TRADE MARK)
OIL COLOUR
MADDERTON & CO.
LOUGHTON, ESSEX
(Made in England.)
ARTISTS' OIL COLOUR
BURNT SIENNA
The Cambridge Oil Colour
Madderton & Co.

APPENDIX D

ANALYSIS RESULTS

Oil paint tubes from the paintbox of Kathleen Munn (1887-1974), Kathleen Munn Fonds, Edward P. Taylor Library & Archives, Art Gallery of Ontario. Tubes from both Winsor & Newton and Madderton & Company (Cambridge Colours) are present. Photo: © Government of Canada.

Tables D.1 and D.2 provide the results of chemical analysis of the preparation layers for the sketches and the studio paintings. For sketches or paintings with multiple preparation layers, they are numbered in the tables, with number 1 corresponding to the layer applied first.

The term "preparation" in these tables refers to either a traditional ground layer or a varnish coating applied to the support before painting. Except where noted, the type of varnish was identified using pyrolysis-gas chromatography-mass spectrometry (Py-GC-MS). The chemical markers permitting identification with this method are provided in Appendix B. The orpiment particles in the shellac layers were identified using Raman spectroscopy in all cases. For the traditional ground layers, a combination of scanning electron microscopy/energy dispersive X-ray spectrometry (SEM/EDX), Fourier transform infrared (FTIR) spectroscopy, X-ray diffraction (XRD), Raman spectroscopy, and polarized light microscopy (PLM) allowed the identification of their constituents. Instrument parameters and methodology are described in Appendix B.

Table D.3 (pp. 182–83) provides a summary of the pigments, fillers, and accessory minerals found in the paint layers for each work. The results in this table do not include the components in the preparation layers.

A black dot within the row for a specific painting in Table D.3 indicates that the component in the corresponding column is present. A component reported as present was identified in at least one sample, and usually in multiple samples, from the painting. A white dot indicates that the component is present only in trace amounts or was used very sparingly (for example, in a single sample from the painting). A question mark indicates that a component is tentatively present but was not identified with certainty.

Table D.1: Preparation layers for the sketches

Title and date	Preparation: type and colour*	Composition of preparation layer(s)
Snow, High Park, 1909	2. Second white layer 1. White ground (commercial)	2. Lead white, drying oil 1. Lead white, calcium carbonate, barium sulfate, drying oil
View from Split Rock, 1912	Pale grey ground (commercial)	Lead white, small amount of finely divided carbon black, drying oil
Logs on the Gatineau River, 1914	Pale yellow-orange ground	Lead white, zinc white, small amounts of yellow iron oxide, kaolin, quartz, and barium sulfate, possibly calcium carbonate, drying oil
Near Minden, 1916 or 1917	2. Pale yellow-orange ground 1. Green ground	2. Lead white, zinc white, small amounts of barium sulfate, yellow iron oxide, and kaolin, drying oil 1. Lead white, zinc white, calcium carbonate, barium sulfate, Prussian blue, kaolin, yellow iron oxide, drying oil
Canoe Lake, 1917	2. Off-white ground 1. Pale grey-blue ground	2. Zinc white, lead white, yellow iron oxide, drying oil 1. Cambridge white, ultramarine, probably cerulean blue, drying oil
Leaves in the Brook, c. 1918	Varnish, orange fluorescence	Shellac, pine resin, drying oil, (trace wax and possibly gum), scattered particles of orpiment
Moose Lake, Algoma, 1920	Varnish, orange fluorescence	Shellac, scattered particles of orpiment
Algoma Hills, 1920	Varnish, orange fluorescence	Probably shellac (based on UV fluorescence), scattered particles of orpiment
Old Dock, Petite Rivière, Nova Scotia, 1922	Varnish, orange fluorescence	Shellac, scattered particles of orpiment
Lake McArthur, Yoho Park, 1924	Varnish, orange fluorescence	Shellac, scattered particles of orpiment, traces of Pinaceae resin, drying oil, and beeswax
Cathedral Peak and Lake O'Hara, 1927	Varnish, orange fluorescence	Probably shellac (based on UV fluorescence), scattered particles of orpiment
Jack Pine, 1929	Varnish, orange fluorescence	Shellac
Near Lake Oesa, Abbot's Pass, 1930	Pale pink ground	Lead white, zinc white, barium sulfate, small amounts of red iron oxide, ultramarine, and quartz, drying oil
Ottertail Valley, 1930	Varnish, orange fluorescence	Shellac, labdane resin (probably sandarac), Pinaceae resin, drying oil, trace wax
Windy Sky near Pointe au Baril, 1931	Pale yellow ground	Lead white, zinc white, barium sulfate, kaolin, talc, cadmium yellow, drying oil
Palms, Barbados, 1932	Off-white ground	Zinc white, barium sulfate, lead white, small amounts of yellow iron oxide, kaolin, quartz, drying oil
Barbados, 1932	Off-white ground	Zinc white, barium sulfate, lead white, small amounts of yellow iron oxide, drying oil

*All preparation layers are artist-applied except when otherwise noted.

Table D.2: Preparation layers for the paintings

Title and date	Preparation: type and colour*	Composition of preparation layer(s)
Early Evening, Winter, 1912	Off-white to pale grey ground (commercial)	Lead white, trace carbon-based black, drying oil
The Tangled Garden, 1916	2. Varnish, yellow-green fluorescence 1. Orange-red underpainting (both layers artist-applied)	2. Heated pine resin, smaller amounts of shellac, drying oil, paraffin wax 1. Vermilion (Raman only)
The Elements, 1916	2. Varnish, yellow-green fluorescence 1. Dark red underpainting (both layers artist-applied)	2. Insufficient sample 1. Alizarin lake, ultramarine, sulfate, probably zinc white, drying oil
Leaves in the Brook, 1919	Off-white ground	Lead white, calcium carbonate, trace yellow pigment, drying oil
Algoma Waterfall, 1920	White ground, two layers (probably commercial)	2. Barium sulfate, lead white, and a zinc-based pigment (zinc white or zinc sulfide), drying oil 1. Calcium carbonate, drying oil
Falls, Montreal River, 1920	Off-white to beige ground	Lead white, calcium carbonate, trace of iron oxide, drying oil
The Solemn Land, 1921	Off-white ground (commercial)	Lead white, calcium carbonate, small amount of orange iron oxide, drying oil
Gleams on the Hills, 1921	Off-white to pale orange ground	Lead white, calcium carbonate, zinc-based pigment (probably zinc white), red and yellow iron oxide, drying oil
Forest Wilderness, 1921	Off-white ground	Lead white, calcium carbonate, barium sulfate, and a zinc-based pigment (zinc white or zinc sulfide), drying oil
Mount Goodsir, Yoho Park, 1925	2. Red underpainting 1. Off-white ground	2. Red iron oxide (hematite), lead sulfate, probably zinc white, drying oil 1. Lead white, calcium carbonate, small amount of chrome yellow, drying oil
Goat Range, Rocky Mountains, 1932	Off-white ground (artist-applied)	Barium sulfate, zinc sulfide, small amount of talc, drying oil. (A small amount of lead was identified using SEM/EDX, but no lead-containing compounds were determined through analysis.)

*It was not always possible to determine if the ground was commercial or artist-applied.

Table D.3: Summary of pigments, fillers, and accessory minerals identified in each work

Title	Year	Cambridge White	Lead white	Zinc white	Kaolin, quartz, silicates	Hydromagnesite	Calcium carbonate	Gypsum	Barium sulfate	Yellow iron oxide	Cadmium yellow	Barium yellow	Chrome yellow
Snow, High Park (sketch)	1909	•	•							•			•
View from Split Rock (sketch)	1912	•								•		•	
Early Evening, Winter (studio)	1912	•	•		•					•	o	•	
Logs on the Gatineau River (sketch)	1914	•								•	•		
Thornhill Garden, No.1 (sketch)	c. 1916	•				•							•
The Tangled Garden (studio)	1916	•			•	•				•	•		
The Elements (studio)	1916	•			•					•	•	•	
Near Minden (sketch)	1916–17	•			•	•				•	•		?
Canoe Lake (sketch)	c. 1917		•	?	•			•		•	•		
Leaves in the Brook (sketch)	c. 1918			•		•				•	•		•
Leaves in the Brook (studio)	1919	•			•					•	•		
Solemn Land, Algoma (sketch)	c. 1919	•			•					•	•	•	
Autumn Leaves, Batchewana, Algoma (sketch)	c. 1919	•								•	•	•	
Algoma Hills (sketch)	1920	•			?	•				•			•
Moose Lake, Algoma (sketch)	1920	•			•	•				•			•
Algoma Waterfall (studio)	1920	•	•	•							•	•	
Falls, Montreal River (studio)	1920	?	•	?	•			•		•	•	•	
The Solemn Land (studio)	1921	•					•			•	•	•	
Forest Wilderness (studio)	1921	•								•	•		
Gleams on the Hills (studio)	1921	•			•					•	•		
Old Dock, Petite Rivière, Nova Scotia (sketch)	1922	•								•	•		
Petite Rivière, Nova Scotia (sketch)	1922	•			•					•	•		
Lake McArthur, Yoho Park (sketch)	1924	•								•	•	•	
Mount Goodsir, Yoho Park (studio)	1925	•								•	•	•	•
Cathedral Peak and Lake O'Hara (sketch)	1927		•		•					•	•	•	
Jack Pine (sketch)	1929			•						•			•
Near Lake Oesa, Abbot's Pass (sketch)	1930	•			•					•	•		
Ottertail Valley (sketch)	1930	•								•	•	•	
Windy Sky near Point au Baril (sketch)	1931	•	•							•			
Goat Range, Rocky Mountains (studio)	1932		•							•	•		
Palms, Barbados (sketch)	1932		•	•					•	•	•		
Barbados (sketch)	1932	•									•		

Ultramarine	Cerulean blue	Prussian blue	Cobalt blue	Viridian	Green earth	Alizarin /red lake	Red to orange iron oxide	Vermilion	Chrome orange/red	Toluidine red	Carbon-based black	Bone black	Umber/ brown iron oxide	TABLE KEY: • = present o = trace amounts ? = possibly present
•		•		o		•	•				o		o	*Snow, High Park* (sketch)
•	•	•		•		•	•				•			*View from Split Rock* (sketch)
•	•	•		•		•	•				•			*Early Evening, Winter* (studio)
•				•		•		•			•			*Logs on the Gatineau River* (sketch)
•	•			•		•	•		•		•			*Thornhill Garden, No.1* (sketch)
•	o	•		•		•	•	•		•	o			*The Tangled Garden* (studio)
•	•	•		•	•	•	•	•			o			*The Elements* (studio)
•				•		•	•		•	•	•			*Near Minden* (sketch)
•		•	•	•		•	•	•			o			*Canoe Lake* (sketch)
•		•		•		•	•	•			•			*Leaves in the Brook* (sketch)
•		•		•		•	•	•			•			*Leaves in the Brook* (studio)
•	o			•		•	•	•			•			*Solemn Land, Algoma* (sketch)
•	•	•		•		•	•	•			•			*Autumn Leaves, Batchewana, Algoma* (sketch)
•	•	•		•		•	•	•	•		•			*Algoma Hills* (sketch)
•	•			•		•		•	•					*Moose Lake, Algoma* (sketch)
•	•	•		•	•	•	•	•			•			*Algoma Waterfall* (studio)
•	o			•		•	•	•			o			*Falls, Montreal River* (studio)
•		•		•		•	•	•			o			*The Solemn Land* (studio)
•	•			•		•	•	•			•		•	*Forest Wilderness* (studio)
•	o	•		•		•	•	•			o			*Gleams on the Hills* (studio)
•	o			•	•	•	•	•			•			*Old Dock, Petite Rivière, Nova Scotia* (sketch)
•	•			•			•	•	•			•		*Petite Rivière, Nova Scotia* (sketch)
•	•			•		•	•	•			o			*Lake McArthur, Yoho Park* (sketch)
•	•			•		•	•	•			o			*Mount Goodsir, Yoho Park, 1925* (studio)
•	•			•		•	•	•			•			*Cathedral Peak and Lake O'Hara* (sketch)
•			?	•		•	•							*Jack Pine* (sketch)
•	o			•		•	•	•			o			*Near Lake Oesa, Abbot's Pass* (sketch)
•	o			•		•	•	•			o			*Ottertail Valley* (sketch)
		•	•	•		•	•	•			o			*Windy Sky near Point au Baril* (sketch)
•	•			•		•	•				•			*Goat Range, Rocky Mountains* (studio)
•	•	•		•		•	•							*Palms, Barbados* (sketch)
•	o			•		•								*Barbados* (sketch)

The rows of Table D.3 list the analyzed works in chronological order. The larger scale studio paintings are noted in parentheses (studio) to distinguish them from the oil sketches (sketch). The columns in Table D.3 list the pigments, fillers, and accessory minerals, arranged by colour. The results can be examined in two ways. By looking across a row, the reader will obtain a complete list of the components identified in a specific painting. The table does not, however, provide information about the pigment mixtures that MacDonald used. As described in chapter 4, the hues in each painting were created with various combinations of these pigments. By reading down a column, the chronological distribution of each pigment, filler, or accessory mineral over the course of MacDonald's career is illustrated.

The general chemical formulae and the instrumental methods used to identify each of the components in Table D.3 are given below, arranged by colour. In all cases, SEM/EDX provided supporting evidence for the identifications made with the other techniques. Unless otherwise noted, a 785 nm laser was used for Raman spectroscopy.

Cambridge White, mixture of $PbSO_4$ and ZnO. Cambridge White was identified in 25 of the 32 paintings analyzed. In all cases, XRD patterns showed that lead sulfate and zinc white were present together in specific proportions. Cambridge White also has a distinctive FTIR spectrum: it includes bands for lead sulfate and for zinc soaps, which are formed by the reaction of a zinc-containing pigment with the oil medium. When Cambridge White was present in high concentrations, some FTIR spectra also showed a broad absorption band between 400 and 500 cm^{-1}, which is evidence of the zinc white component.

Lead white, $(PbCO_3)_2{\cdot}Pb(OH)_2$ and $PbCO_3$. Lead white was identified in 9 of the 32 paintings. In each of these nine paintings, analysis results from both FTIR spectroscopy and XRD confirmed its presence.

Zinc white, ZnO. Using XRD, zinc white was identified on its own (not associated with lead sulfate) in four paintings. The presence of zinc soaps, along with a broad absorption band between 400 and 500 cm^{-1} in the FTIR spectra, provided secondary evidence for its presence.

Kaolin, $Al_2Si_2O_5(OH)_4$; quartz, SiO_2; silicates. One or more of these minerals was identified in 13 paintings using FTIR spectroscopy. When the FTIR spectrum included bands that were characteristic of an aluminosilicate component, but the type was not determined, they were reported with the general name "silicates."

Hydromagnesite, $Mg_5(CO_3)_4(OH)_2{\cdot}4H_2O$. Characteristic bands in the FTIR spectra showed the presence of this hydrated magnesium carbonate filler in six paintings.

Calcium carbonate, $CaCO_3$. Calcium carbonate was found in only one painting. Identification was based on FTIR spectroscopy.

Gypsum, $CaSO_4 \cdot 2H_2O$. Results of FTIR spectroscopy showed the presence of gypsum in two paintings.

Barium sulfate, $BaSO_4$. Barium sulfate was found in one painting. It was identified using both FTIR spectroscopy and XRD.

Yellow iron oxide, α-FeOOH. Analysis revealed yellow iron oxides in 29 of the 32 paintings, often in low concentrations in mixed colours but in a few cases as the main colouring pigment. In all cases, the yellow iron oxide was identified with PLM. When present in a relatively high concentration, this pigment was sometimes confirmed using other techniques: iron oxyhydroxide (geothite structure, α-FeOOH) was found in 10 paintings using FTIR spectroscopy, in 9 paintings using Raman spectroscopy, and in 2 paintings using XRD.

Cadmium yellow, CdS or Cd_{1-x} Zn_xS. Cadmium yellow was found in 25 of the 32 paintings. In all cases, results from Raman spectroscopy, using the 532 nm laser, permitted its identification. In 16 paintings, XRD results provided further confirmation. The XRD patterns usually matched the α-CdS variety of cadmium yellow. In one case, β-CdS was identified. Several samples produced no diffraction pattern, even though the samples contained a high concentration of cadmium and sulfur: this indicates an amorphous structure. In two paintings, both from MacDonald's 1932 trip to Barbados, the XRD pattern indicated a zinc-substituted variety of cadmium yellow. In many cases, results of SEM/EDX suggest that additives or residual starting materials containing aluminum, magnesium, and phosphorous are present. No compounds containing these elements were identified by XRD. When cadmium yellow was present in a high concentration, the FTIR spectra showed a possible indication of sulfates (a broad band close to 1100 cm^{-1}) and oxalates (sharp bands at 1320 and 1380 cm^{-1}). On one sketch, *Leaves in the Brook*, cadmium carbonate ($CdCO_3$) was associated with cadmium yellow.[1]

Barium yellow, $BaCrO_4$. Characteristic bands in the FTIR spectra indicated presence of barium yellow in 12 paintings. For seven of these paintings, both XRD and Raman spectroscopy also confirmed its presence.

Chrome yellow, $PbCrO_4$. Raman spectra showed the presence of chrome yellow in 7 of the 32 paintings. In most cases, this pigment was also confirmed using PLM, based on typical rod-shaped chrome yellow particles. In two paintings, chrome yellow was present in sufficient quantity to allow identification with XRD. Samples from several paintings also showed characteristic bands for lead chromate in their FTIR spectra. However, chrome yellow ($PbCrO_4$) could not be distinguished from chrome orange/red ($PbCrO_4 \cdot PbO$) using this method.

Ultramarine, $(Na,Ca)_8(AlSiO_4)_6(SO_4,S,Cl)_2$, variable composition. Ultramarine was found in 31 of the 32 paintings. In all 31 paintings, synthetic ultramarine was identified by PLM. In most cases (24 of the 31 paintings), the ultramarine was present in a high enough concentration to allow confirmation with FTIR spectroscopy. For 17 of the paintings, ultramarine was also identified using XRD.

Cerulean blue, Co_2SnO_4. Analysis revealed cerulean blue in 23 of the 32 paintings, although it was often used quite sparingly. In all cases, identification was based on its characteristic microscopical properties, observed using PLM. In some paintings, cerulean blue was present in a high enough concentration to be identified with other methods: it was identified in 12 paintings using XRD and in 7 paintings with FTIR spectroscopy. Results of SEM/EDX showed that magnesium was usually associated with the cerulean blue; this could suggest some substitution of magnesium for cobalt in the crystal structure. This was not confirmed using XRD, as peak shifts among reference patterns of Mg-substituted and non-substituted varieties were small.

Prussian blue, $Fe_4[Fe(CN)_6]_3 \cdot xH_2O$. Prussian blue was found in 15 of the 32 paintings. In all cases, identification was based on the strong nitrile absorption band at about 2085 cm^{-1} in the FTIR spectrum.[2] Prussian blue was also observed in many of the PLM dispersions. Its presence was also determined in a few samples using Raman spectroscopy.

Cobalt blue, $CoO \cdot Al_2O_3$. Cobalt blue was identified in only two paintings. Identification was based on its microscopic properties, combined with results of SEM/EDX. Cobalt blue always occurred in mixed colours, and due to its low concentration, was not confirmed with other analysis techniques.

Viridian, $Cr_2O_3 \cdot 2H_2O$. PLM revealed the presence of viridian in all 32 paintings. In most cases (28 of the 32 paintings) its presence was also confirmed through FTIR spectroscopy. In many cases, bands from chromium oxide borate, a by-product of the synthesis of the pigment,[3] were present in the infrared spectra.

Green earth, iron-containing clay, variable composition. Green earth was identified in 3 of the 32 paintings, based on characteristic, sharp hydroxyl stretching bands in the 3610 to 3530 cm^{-1} region of the infrared spectrum.[4]

Alizarin lake, $C_{14}H_8O_4$ on an inorganic base. PLM revealed the presence of a red lake pigment in 31 of the 32 paintings. In 24 of these paintings, the red lake was further characterized as alizarin, based on FTIR spectroscopy. In six of the paintings, alizarin was confirmed with Raman spectroscopy. Based on the SEM/EDX results, the substrate for the lake is likely an aluminum phosphate.

Red to orange iron oxide, α-Fe_2O_3. Red to orange iron oxide pigments were identified in 29 of the 32 paintings using PLM. In most samples, PLM revealed the iron oxides to be in the form of translucent, isotropic orange-red globules. In a few cases, the red iron oxide appeared as finely divided, anisotropic red particles, which were difficult to distinguish from finely divided vermilion. In these cases, Raman spectroscopy was used to confirm its presence. The hematite form of red iron oxide was identified in 15 samples using Raman spectroscopy, in 5 samples using XRD, and in a single sample using FTIR spectroscopy.

Vermilion, HgS. Vermilion was identified in 23 of the 32 paintings. This pigment is a strong Raman scatterer and was identified on all 23 paintings using Raman spectroscopy. In 15 cases, the amount of vermilion in the sample was high enough to permit identification with XRD. Observation using PLM indicated that the vermilion was often finely divided, although a coarser variety was also sometimes observed. Finely divided vermilion is difficult to distinguish from finely divided red iron oxide using PLM; for this reason, the presence of vermilion was always confirmed with Raman spectroscopy or XRD.

Chrome orange/red, $PbCrO_4 \cdot PbO$. Chrome orange, composed of lead chromate oxide, was identified in five paintings using Raman spectroscopy. In two cases, it was present in sufficient quantity to allow identification with XRD.

Toluidine red (Pigment Red 3), $C_{17}H_{13}N_3O_3$. Toluidine red was identified in two paintings. In both cases, its presence was confirmed with FTIR and Raman spectroscopy.

Black, carbon-based. Small to trace amounts of finely divided black pigment, presumably a type of carbon-based black, were observed in 27 of the paintings using PLM.

Bone black, carbon with $Ca_5(PO_4)_3(OH)$. Bone black was identified in a single painting. This determination was based on the microscopic properties observed with PLM, combined with characteristic bands for hydroxyl apatite $Ca_5(PO_4)_3(OH)$ in the FTIR spectrum.

Brown iron oxide/umber. Small amounts of brown iron oxide were observed in two paintings using PLM. In one case, the presence of significant manganese with SEM/EDX indicates that it corresponds to umber.

GLOSSARY

accessory minerals: Some pigments from mineral deposits, such as iron earth pigments, have naturally occurring accessory minerals, like kaolin or quartz, associated with them. However, because certain of these minerals are also added as fillers to paints by the manufacturer, it is not always possible to determine if the component is an additive or a naturally occurring accessory mineral. See also entry for **fillers or extenders**.

beaverboard and the Beaver Board brand (type of studio painting support): Beaverboard is a type of fibreboard. Its name is derived from the Beaver Board brand of wallboard, which was invented in 1903 in Beaver Falls, NY. The Beaver Board brand became a very popular finishing board for interior walls during the first decades of the twentieth century.[1] In a testament to the brand's success, similar fibreboards are often referred to as "beaverboard," even if their source is unknown. The Beaver Board brand was made of medium-density, laminated fibreboard.[2] Literature from 1910 to 1920 describes the product as having a core of pale-coloured, mechanically ground wood pulp, called "ground wood," which had either a single ply or multi-ply structure. The front and back faces were coated with layers of cooked wood: darker, more resistant pulp that was steam-heated under pressure before mechanical processing. The front face could be given a final layer of pale-coloured ground wood and could also be given a decorative, pebbled finish.[3] The layers were cemented together using pressure and a sodium silicate adhesive.[4] Front and back could be sized with a wax-resin mixture to provide water resistance.[5] In the 1910 to 1920 period, the boards were approximately 3/16 in. to ¼ in. thick.[6] The back was stamped with the Beaver Board trademark, the appearance of which varied over time.[7]

binding medium: The organic material in paint that suspends the pigment particles and dries to create a solid film. Common traditional paint media include, for example, drying oils in oil paints and plant gums in watercolours.

bookbinding board (type of oil sketching support): A type of rigid paperboard used to produce book covers. Bookbinding board is generally between 1.5 and 5.2 mm thick.[8] It is sometimes referred to as "millboard," although this name has lost much of its specific meaning.[9] In the first half of the twentieth century, bookbinding boards were commonly made in a cylinder machine, also called a board machine, by layering sheets of wet pulp and applying pressure to produce a dense, laminated product (couched-laminate board).[10] MacDonald used bookbinding board as an oil sketching support,[11] although he purchased paperboard from other sources as well.

canvas (type of studio painting support): A traditional support for painting composed of woven fabric. Common fabric types in the early twentieth century included linen, cotton, and jute. Canvases vary in the type of weave used (for example, plain weave or basket weave) as well as in the fineness of the weave. A measure of the fineness of the weave, known as the thread count, is determined by counting the number of threads per centimetre in both the warp and weft directions. Canvases for painting could be purchased with a ground layer already applied by the manufacturer, referred to as "commercially applied," or left bare for the artist to prepare themselves.

canvas board (type of oil sketching support): Prepared canvas adhered to paperboard is called canvas board. This support type was available at the time MacDonald was painting, although it was not found in any of the MacDonald sketches that we examined. Tom Thomson sometimes used canvas board as an oil sketching support.[12]

canvas type: Cotton, flax, and jute are among the main fibre types used in the early twentieth century to create yarns to be woven into fabric for painting supports. These cellulosic fibres originate from different plants. Cotton fibres grow around the seeds of the cotton plant, while flax and jute are both bast fibres. Linen is the name used for fabric made from flax fibres. Jute fibres contain significantly more lignin than cotton or linen, leading to an inherent lack of elasticity, which is exacerbated as the fibres age.[13] Jute fibres absorb moisture at a greater rate than other common canvas fibre types and so are more susceptible to damage from shrinking and swelling with changes in humidity.[14] Burlap fabric, mentioned in catalogues from the first half of the twentieth century, normally refers to a coarse fabric made from low-quality jute; however, it may also refer to coarse fabric made from jute mixed with other bast fibres like hemp and flax.[15]

canvas weave: To create fabric, a series of vertical yarns, called the warp, are held in tension on a frame or loom. The horizontal weft yarns are then drawn through and inserted over and under the warp. The way that the warp and weft yarns are interlaced to form a fabric is called the weave type. The simplest type, known as plain or tabby weave, is produced when each weft yarn alternates going over and under each warp yarn. A basket weave is a variation of plain weave where two or more weft yarns alternate over and under two or more warp yarns. When the number of warp and weft yarns is not the same, the weave is referred to as a modified basket weave. Other common weave types include twill and satin.

cross-section: A tiny, multi-layered core sample, normally less than 1 mm^3, removed from a painting to show the sequence, or stratigraphy, of the ground, paint, and surface coatings. In this study, the cross-section samples were mounted in plastic (a two-part polyester resin) and polished to reveal the layers. Photographs of the cross-sections were taken through a microscope. The length scales on the images are in micrometers (100 micrometers = 0.1 millimeters). A complete cross-section of an oil painting could include the following: the bottom layer corresponding to the support, followed by a size (or sealing layer), the ground layer, the paint layers of the composition, and any varnish or other surface coating that is present.

cusping: Also known as garlanding or scalloping. Cusping is a scalloped pattern of distortions to the canvas edges produced by tension from the nails used to hold it on the stretcher. The distortion of the fabric becomes permanent after application of the ground. Cusping provides evidence that the ground was applied with the painting on its stretcher and indicates the original location of nails.

dry-brush (painting technique): The tip of a dry brush (that is, not wetted with a diluent like turpentine) is lightly loaded with paint and dragged over an underlying layer. This is also called scumbling. MacDonald used this technique in his studio paintings to create depth or highlights by dragging his brush over the dry high points of textured paint below. For dry-brush technique, the paint is sometimes rendered drier and stiffer before application, either by leaching out some of the oil medium or by leaving it on the palette so that it is partially dried.

fibreboard (type of studio painting support): A type of manufactured, rigid construction panel or wallboard. Fibreboard is made of finely divided fibrous material, most often wood pulp. It is distinguished from products made from larger flakes or chips of wood, as found in particleboard, for example. Fibreboard is thicker than most paperboard and is sold in large sheets for the building trade. Some fibreboards are made from a single layer of pulp, while others are laminated. Several commercial brands of fibreboard were available in the first half of the twentieth century. These include high-density fibreboards, or hardboards, such as Masonite, as well as medium-density fibreboards, such as the Upson Board and Beaver Board brands.[16]

fillers or extenders: Fillers, also known as extenders, are inexpensive white pigments with low tinting strength and hiding power. They are typically added to paint formulations to reduce costs and, in some cases, to adjust the properties of the paint. Barium sulfate, calcium carbonate, and magnesium carbonate hydroxide (hydromagnesite) are some of the common fillers that were identified in MacDonald's paints and grounds.

ground: Supports for oil paintings are traditionally prepared with a ground layer. The ground is an opaque application of paint, either white or coloured, composed of pigments and fillers in a binding medium. It is also sometimes called a priming or preparation. The ground layer provides an appropriate surface onto which the artist would apply the oil paint of the composition. While all the MacDonald oil paintings on canvas that we studied included a traditional ground layer, many of his works on rigid supports, both sketches and larger format works, did not.

impasto (painting technique): Texture or relief that is produced through pronounced brushstrokes or thick paint application.

imprimatura (painting technique): Also called a toning layer, this is a layer of paint used to adjust the colour of the ground, either overall or in selected areas.

oil sketches: Small-scale oil paintings, usually created outdoors in front of the subject. Often painted quickly, MacDonald's oil sketches efficiently captured the essence and design of his compositions. They served as the inspiration for most of his larger-scale paintings that he worked up in his studio.

paint: Paint is composed of pigments and fillers that are suspended in a binding medium, sometimes with solvent. Once dry, paint forms a solid film.

paint dispersions: Paint samples are prepared for microscopic examination by placing a tiny fragment in a transparent, fluid medium. The paint fragment is broken up and dispersed so that individual pigment particles can be identified by observing their properties with a polarized light microscope under various types of lighting.

paperboard (type of oil sketching support): A board made of paper by whatever means: a single thick layer of paper pulp (pulp board), laminated sheets of paper held together with adhesive (adhesive-laminate board), or layers of wet pulp applied on top of each other and reinforced by heavy pressing (couched-laminate board).[17] Paperboard is thicker than paper and is generally defined as being at least 0.3 mm thick.[18] It can be produced by hand or by machine, and it is composed from either a single type of pulp or from several different pulp types layered into plies.[19] Common ingredients in paperboard pulp during the first half of the twentieth century included virgin wood pulp, recycled or waste stock, fibre types other than wood, and additional components such as sizing, fillers, and colourants.[20]

Pfleger-type stretcher: A common stretcher construction style during the twentieth century that included mitred double mortise-and-tenon corners.[21] A 1906 catalogue from the Art Metropole includes an illustration of the construction.[22]

pigments: Pigments are finely divided particles that provide the colour to paint. Pigments may be inorganic (for example, zinc white or lead white) or organic (for example, indigo) and may be derived from natural or artificial sources.

preparation: A general term that includes traditional grounds (defined above) or any other layer used to prepare the support before painting, as, for example, the layer of varnish that MacDonald often applied to bare paperboard or beaverboard before painting.

prepared paperboard or academy board (type of oil sketching support): Paperboard prepared with a ground layer for oil painting was known as "prepared millboard" or "academy board" in catalogues of artists' materials in the nineteenth and early part of the twentieth century.[23] Different textures were available; both rough and smooth boards are listed in the catalogues. MacDonald sometimes used this type of commercially prepared paperboard as an oil sketching support early in his career.

stretcher or strainer: The wooden framework, or auxiliary support, over which a painting canvas is stretched. A stretcher has expandable corners, while a strainer has fixed corners. At the time MacDonald was painting, canvas for painting could be purchased either by the yard or already attached to a stretcher or strainer of a standard size.

support: The substrate on which a work is created. MacDonald painted his small outdoor oil paintings (oil sketches) on rigid supports, including paperboard, plywood, and thin wood panel. His larger-scale studio paintings are on canvas or sometimes on fibreboard (confirmed to be the Beaver Board brand in several cases).

underdrawing (painting technique): Outlines of compositional elements drawn on the ground layer prior to painting. Underdrawing is most often in a carbon-based medium like charcoal or graphite pencil. Carbon-based underdrawings often preferentially absorb infrared radiation, rendering them visible using infrared photography.

underpainting (painting technique): A term used to describe MacDonald's method of creating preliminary outlines for his paintings by using strokes of oil paint that had often been thinned down. This outlining in paint delineated basic compositional elements. Because MacDonald often left areas of the ground or support bare in his oil sketches, areas of underpainting usually remain visible.

ultraviolet-induced visible fluorescence: Ultraviolet (UV) radiation has a higher energy (shorter wavelength) than visible light. When a painting is illuminated with UV radiation, many of the constituent organic materials, like oils and varnishes, emit visible light due to a phenomenon called UV-induced visible fluorescence. Some varnishes show a characteristic fluorescence colour when viewed with UV illumination. The bright orange fluorescence observed on some of MacDonald's oil sketches is characteristic of unbleached shellac. Natural tree resins (e.g., pine resin) generally show yellow-green fluorescence.

varnish: A natural or synthetic resin dissolved in a solvent that dries to form a transparent film. Varnishes are traditionally applied to the surface of oil paintings to saturate and protect the paint. While MacDonald did not typically apply varnish to the surface of his oil sketches, he often coated his paperboard support with varnish prior to painting, in place of a traditional ground layer. The varnish he used to coat the boards was often shellac, a natural resin secreted by the female lac bug. Shellac is best known for its use as a varnish for furniture. Orange shellac referred to the unbleached variety and had a warm yellow tone.

wet-in-wet (painting technique): The technique of applying a layer of paint over an earlier paint layer that has not yet dried. This always creates some degree of blending between the layers.

BIBLIOGRAPHY

Ahrens, C. "The New Schools of Art." Interviewed in the *Toronto Daily Star*, March 16, 1916.

Anema, J., K. Helwig, and D. Duguay. "Analysis of Samples from The West Wind, CCI Report 125624" [unpublished]. Ottawa, ON: Canadian Conservation Institute, 2013.

Arnott, K. Personal communication, September 2020.

Art Gallery of Ontario. *Art Gallery of Ontario: The Canadian Collection*. Toronto, ON: McGraw Hill Company of Canada Limited, 1970.

Art Gallery of Toronto. *Catalogue of Three Exhibitions: The Society of Canadian Painter-Etchers – J.E.H. MacDonald, Lawren Harris and Frank H. Johnston; and William Cruickshank* [Catalogue]. Toronto, ON: Art Gallery of Toronto, 1919. Available from: https://archive.org/details/catalogueofthreeooartg/page/n1/mode/2up

Art Metropole. *Catalogue and Price List of Colors and Materials for Artists, Architects, Decorators, Designers, Draughtsmen, Illustrators and Modellers* [Catalogue]. Toronto, ON: The Art Metropole, December 1906. Available from: https://archive.org/details/cataloguepriceliooartm/mode/2up

Artists' Supply Company. *Price lists* [Catalogue]. Toronto, ON: Artists' Supply Company, n.d. [1906–1936]. National Gallery of Canada Library and Archives, Ottawa, Ontario.

Artists' Supply Company. *No. 1111, Catalogue of Artists' Materials and Colors: Inks, Bronze Powder, Pictures, Etc.* [Catalogue]. Toronto, ON: The Artists' Supply Company, n.d. [1906–1936]. York University Library, Scott Special Collections, Toronto, Ontario.

Artists' Supply Company. *Artists' Supply Company, Cardwriter's and Showcard Writer's Supplies* [Catalogue]. Toronto, ON: The Artists' Supply Company, 1920. Toronto Public Library, Special Collections, Toronto, Ontario.

Artists' Supply Company. *1926 Price List of Cambridge and Madderton Oil Colours* [Catalogue]. Toronto, ON: Artists' Supply Company, 1926a. Toronto Public Library, Special Collections, Toronto, Ontario.

Artists' Supply Company. *1926 Price List of Talen's "Rembrandt" Oil Colours* [Catalogue]. Toronto, ON: Artists' Supply Company, 1926b. Toronto Public Library, Special Collections, Toronto, Ontario.

Artists' Supply Company. *1934 Price List of Cambridge and Madderton Oil Colours* [Catalogue]. Toronto, ON: Artists' Supply Company, 1934. Toronto Public Library, Special Collections, Toronto, Ontario.

Atkinson, R.R. *Jute: Fibre to Yarn*. London, UK: Temple Press Books Ltd, 1964.

Banik, G., and I. Brückle. *Paper and Water: A Guide for Conservators*, revised. Munich, Germany: Siegl, 2018.

Barclay, M. Restoration & Conservation Laboratory Inspection Record, 1984. In conservation file for *The Solemn Land*, accession no. 1785, National Gallery of Canada, Ottawa, Ontario.

Barclay, M.H. "George Harbour: The First Resident Museum Conservator in Canada." *Journal of the Canadian Association for Conservation* 34 (2009), pp. 39–53.

Beaver Board Companies. *Beaver Board and its Uses*. Buffalo, NY: The Beaver Board Companies, 1920.

Beerse, M., K. Keune, P. Iedema, S. Woutersen, and J. Hermans. "Evolution of Zinc Carboxylate Species in Oil Paint Ionomers." *ACS Applied Polymer Materials* 2,12 (2020), pp. 5674–5685, Available from: https://doi.org/10.1021/acsapm.0c00979.

Berrie, B. "Prussian Blue." In E.W. Fitzhugh, ed., *Artists' Pigments: A Handbook of Their History and Characteristics*, vol. 3. Washington, D.C., and New York, NY: National Gallery of Art and Oxford University Press, 1997, pp. 191–217. Available from: https://www.nga.gov/content/dam/ngaweb/research/publications/pdfs/artists-pigments-vol3.pdf

Bishop, H. Introduction to *J.E.H. MacDonald: Sketchbook 1915–1922: A Facsimile Edition*. Moonbeam, ON: Penumbra Press, 1979, pp. i–xvi.

Bonaduce, I., and M.P. Colombini. "Characterisation of Beeswax in Works of Art by Gas Chromatography–Mass Spectrometry and Pyrolysis–Gas Chromatography–Mass Spectrometry Procedures." *Journal of Chromatography A* 1028,2 (March 2004), pp. 297–306. Available from: https://doi.org/10.1016/j.chroma.2003.11.086.

Bookseller and Stationer. Toronto, ON and Montréal, QC: MacLean Publishing Company, January 1904.

Boutilier, A., and T. Bruce. *Tom Thomson? The Art of Authentication*. Kingston, ON: Agnes Etherington Art Centre, 2021.

Brown, E. Letter to T. MacDonald, December 15, 1936. In *The Beaver Dam*, accession no. 4529, curatorial file. National Gallery of Canada, Ottawa, Ontario.

Buck, R.D. "Stretcher Design, A Brief Preliminary Survey." In *ICOM-CC 3rd Meeting, Working Group on Stretcher and Lining, Madrid, Spain, 2–7 October 1972: Preprints*. Paris, France: International Council of Museums, 1972. Available from: https://www.icom-cc-publications-online.org/4114/Stretcher-Design-A-Brief-Preliminary-Survey

Buffalo Fine Arts Academy. *Catalogue, Eighteenth Annual Exhibition of Selected Paintings and Small Bronzes by American Artists* [Museum catalogue]. The Buffalo Fine Arts Academy, Albright Art Gallery, April 20th to June 30th, 1924. J.E.H. MacDonald fonds., MG30 D111, 3-41, Library and Archives Canada, Ottawa, Ontario.

Canadian Art. "Buried Group of Seven Paintings Brought to Light in Major Donation." January 14, 2015. Available from: https://canadianart.ca/news/buried-group-seven-paintings-brought-light-major-donation/

Canadian National Exhibition. *Canadian National Exhibition: Catalogue of Department of Fine Arts, August 29 to September 14, 1908* [Museum catalogue]. Toronto, ON: Canadian National Exhibition, 1908. Available from: https://archive.org/details/cihm_991624/page/n5/mode/2up

Canadian National Exhibition. *Canadian National Exhibition: Catalogue of Department of Fine Arts, August 24 to September 9, 1912* [Museum catalogue]. Toronto, ON: Canadian National Exhibition, 1912. Available from: https://archive.org/details/cihm_83175/page/n3/mode/2up

Carlyle, L. *The Artist's Assistant: Oil Painting Instruction Manuals and Handbooks in Britain 1800–1900*. London, UK: Archetype Publications, 2001.

Carter, H.R. *Technical Handbook No. 9: Jute and its Manufacture*. London, UK: John Bale, Sons & Danielsson, Ltd., [1921]. Available from: https://archive.org/details/juteitsmanufactuoocartrich

Casadio, F., C. Daher, and L. Bellot-Gurlet. "Raman Spectroscopy of Cultural Heritage Materials: Overview of Applications and New Frontiers in Instrumentation, Sampling Modalities and Data Processing." In R. Mazzeo, ed., *Analytical Chemistry for Cultural Heritage*. Cham, Switzerland: Springer, 2016, pp. 261–311.

Charlesworth, H. "Pictures That Can Be Heard." *Saturday Night*, March 18, 1916.

Christensen, L. *A Hiker's Guide to Art of the Canadian Rockies*. Calgary, AB: Fifth House, 1999.

Christensen, L. *The Lake O'Hara Art of J.E.H. MacDonald and Hiker's Guide*. Calgary, AB: Fifth House, 2003.

Corbeil, M.-C., P.J. Sirois, and E.A. Moffatt. "The Use of a White Pigment Patented by Freeman by Tom Thomson and the Group of Seven." In J. Bridgland, ed., *12th Triennial Meeting, ICOM-CC, Lyon, France, 29 August–3 September 1999: Preprints*. London, UK: James & James, 1999, pp. 363–368. Available from: https://www.icom-cc-publications-online.org/2411/The-use-of-a-white-pigment-patented-by-Freeman-by-Tom-Thomson-and-the-Group-of-Seven

Corbeil, M.-C., E. Moffatt, P.J. Sirois, and K.M. Legate. "The Materials and Techniques of Tom Thomson." *Journal of the Canadian Association for Conservation* 25 (2000), pp. 3–10. Available from: https://www.cac-accr.ca/wp-content/uploads/2018/12/Vol25_doc1.pdf

Corbeil, M.-C., K. Helwig, and J. Poulin. *Jean Paul Riopelle: The Artist's Materials*. Los Angeles, California: Getty Publications, 2011.

Corbeil, M.-C., E.J. Henderson, and S. Walker. "A Survey of the Use of Cambridge White by Canadian Artists." *Journal of the Canadian Association for Conservation* 45 (2020), pp. 51–58. Available from: https://www.cac-accr.ca/download/jcac45-corbeil-et-al/

Dawe, E.A. *Paper and Its Uses: A Treatise for Printers, Stationers and Others*. London, UK: Crosby Lockwood and Son, 1914.

de Keijzer, M. "The Delight of Modern Organic Pigment Creations." In K.J. van den Berg et al., eds., *Issues in Contemporary Oil Paint*. Cham, Switzerland: Springer International Publishing, 2014, pp. 45–73.

Dix, U. Memorandum to P. McKeever, July 15, 1982. In *The Solemn Land*, accession no. 1785, curatorial file. National Gallery of Canada, Ottawa Canada.

Duval, P. *The Tangled Garden: The Art of J.E.H. MacDonald*. Scarborough, ON: Cerberus Publishing Ltd./Prentice-Hall of Canada, 1978.

E. Harris Company. *Illustrated Catalogue and Price List of Artists' Materials* [Catalogue]. Toronto, ON: The E. Harris Company, 1900. Toronto Public Library, Special Collections, Toronto, Ontario.

Ekundayo, G., and S. Adejuyigbe. "Reviewing the Development of Natural Fiber Polymer Composite: A Case Study of Sisal and Jute." *American Journal of Mechanical and Materials Engineering* 3,1 (2019), pp. 1–10. Available from: https://doi.org/10.11648/j.ajmme.20190301.11

Eastaugh, N., V. Walsh, T. Chaplin, and R. Siddall. *Pigment Compendium: Optical Microscopy of Historical Pigments*. Amsterdam, Netherlands, and Boston, MA: Elsevier/Butterworth-Heinemann, 2004.

Fairley, B. "J.E.H. MacDonald." In *A Loan Exhibition of the Work of J.E.H. MacDonald, October 30–November 13* [Museum catalogue]. Toronto, ON: Mellors Galleries, 1937.

Feller, R.L., and M. Bayard. "Terminology and Procedures Used in the Systematic Examination of Pigment Particles with the Polarizing Microscope." In R. L. Feller, ed., *Artists' Pigments: A Handbook of Their History and Characteristics*, vol. 1. Washington, D.C.: National Gallery of Art, 1986, pp. 285–298. Available from: https://www.nga.gov/content/dam/ngaweb/research/publications/pdfs/artists-pigments-vol1.pdf

Fiedler, I., and M. Bayard. "Cadmium Yellows, Oranges, and Reds." In R.L. Feller, ed., *Artists' Pigments: A Handbook of Their History and Characteristics*, vol. 1, Washington, D.C.: National Gallery of Art, 1986, pp. 65–108. Available from: https://www.nga.gov/content/dam/ngaweb/research/publications/pdfs/artists-pigments-vol1.pdf

Firestone, O.J. *The Other A.Y. Jackson: A Memoir*. Toronto, ON: McClelland & Stewart, 1979.

Flescher, S. "The International Foundation for Art Research." In R.D. Spencer, ed., *The Expert Versus the Object: Judging Fakes and False Attributions in the Visual Arts*. Oxford, UK, and New York, NY: Oxford University Press, 2004, pp. 95–102.

Gettens, R.J., H. Kühn, and W.T. Chase. "Lead White." In A. Roy, ed., *Artists Pigments, A Handbook of Their History and Characteristics*, vol 2. Washington D.C., and Oxford, UK: National Gallery of Washington and Oxford University Press, 1993, pp. 39–109.

Gettens, R.J., and G.L. Stout. *Painting Materials: A Short Encyclopaedia*. New York, NY: Dover Publications, 1966.

Grier, W. Letter from Wyly Grier to H.O. McCurry, Assistant Director, National Gallery of Canada, January 13, 1939. Curatorial file for *The Tangled Garden*, accession no. 4291. National Gallery of Canada, Ottawa, Ontario.

Grissom, C.A. "Green Earth." In R.L. Feller, ed. *Artists' Pigments: A Handbook of Their History and Characteristics*, vol. 1, Washington D.C.: National Gallery of Art, 1986, pp. 141–168.

Gould, C.S., K.A. Konrad, K.C. Milley, and R. Gallagher. "Fiberboard." In T.C. Jester, ed., *Twentieth-Century Building Materials: History and Conservation*. Los Angeles, CA: Getty Conservation Institute, 2014, pp. 89–94. Available from: https://www.getty.edu/publications/resources/virtuallibrary/9781606063255.pdf

Gunasheka, G.S., and M. Krishna. "An Overview on Powder X-Ray Diffraction and Its Current Applications." *Research and Reviews: Journal of Physics* 4,3 (2015), pp. 6–10. Available from: https://sciencejournals.stmjournals.in/index.php/RRJoPHY/article/download/468/284

Hackney, S., J. Reifsnyder, M. te Marvelde, and M. Scharff. "Lining Easel Paintings." In J.H. Stoner and R. Rushfield, eds., *Conservation of Easel Paintings*. London, UK: Routledge, 2012, pp. 415–452.

Hammond, M.O. "Down on the Old Farm." *The Lamps* (December 1919), pp. 40–43. Available from: http://www.artsandlettersprivate.ca/lampsletters/lampsletters_1919.pdf

Harbour, G. Record of work done on pictures, August 1935. In *The Solemn Land*, accession no. 1785, curatorial file. National Gallery of Canada, Ottawa, Ontario.

Harbour, G. Handwritten notes, 1935–1936. In *The Solemn Land*, accession no. 1785, conservation file. National Gallery of Canada, Ottawa, Ontario.

Harris, B. Letter to Russell Harper, 14 July 1962, file 12-4-196, vol. 1, p. 5, National Gallery of Canada fonds, National Gallery of Canada Library and Archives, Ottawa, Ontario.

Harris, L. Letter to J.E.H. MacDonald, September 1918, MG30 D111, 1-3, *Correspondence, Xerox Copies, Lawren Harris, 1916-1919*, J.E.H. MacDonald fonds, Library and Archives Canada, Ottawa, Ontario.

Helwig, K. "Iron Oxide Pigments: Natural and Synthetic." In B.H. Berrie, ed., *Artists Pigments, A Handbook of Their History and Characteristics*, vol 4. Washington, D.C., and London, UK: National Gallery of Washington and Archetype Publications, 2007, pp. 39–109.

Helwig, K., V. Monahan, and J. Poulin. "The Identification of Hafting Adhesive on a Slotted Antler Point from a Southwest Yukon Ice Patch." *American Antiquity* 73,2 (2008), pp. 279–288. Available from: https://doi.org/10.1017/S000273160004227X

Helwig, K., E. Moffatt, M.-C. Corbeil, and D. Duguay. "Early Twentieth-Century Artists' Paints in Toronto: Archival and Material Evidence." *Journal of the Canadian Association for Conservation* 40 (2015), pp. 19–34. Available from: https://www.cac-accr.ca/download/vol40_doc2/

Helwig, K., J. Poulin, M.-C. Corbeil, E. Moffatt, and D. Duguay. "Conservation Issues in Several Twentieth-Century Canadian Oil Paintings: The Role of Zinc Carboxylate Reaction Products." In K.J. van den Berg et al., eds., *Issues in Contemporary Oil Paint*. Cham, Switzerland: Springer, 2014, pp. 167–184.

Helwig, K., and K. Bladek. "Perspectives from a Conservation Institute: A Multi-instrumental Approach to Sample Analysis." In A. Vila and A. Murray, eds., *Diagnosis: Before, During, After. Conservation 360°*, no. 2 (June 2022), pp. 84–131. Available from: https://monografias.editorial.upv.es/index.php/con_360/article/view/388

Hill, C.C. *Pictures That Can Be Heard: J.E.H. MacDonald's "The Tangled Garden."* Ottawa, ON: The National Gallery of Canada, 1984.

Hill, C.C. *The Group of Seven: Art for a Nation*. Ottawa and Toronto, ON: The National Gallery of Canada and McClelland & Stewart, 1995.

Hill, C.C. Memorandum, December 5, 1997. In *Poplar and Pine*, accession no. 6462, curatorial file. National Gallery of Canada, Ottawa, Ontario.

Hill, C.C. "Tom Thomson, Painter." In D. Reid, ed., *Tom Thomson*. Vancouver, BC: Douglas & McIntyre, 2002, pp. 111–143.

Hunter, E.R. Letter to H.O. McCurry, Assistant Director, NGC, February 24, 1938. E.R. Hunter papers, MS Coll. 00318 Box 2, research materials 1937–38, correspondence re JEH Mac book. Thomas Fisher Rare Book Library, University of Toronto, Toronto, Ontario.

Hunter, E.R. Letter to N.S. Gurd, February 18, 1938. E.R. Hunter papers, Thomas Fisher Rare Book Library, MS Coll. 00318 Box 2, research materials 1937–38, correspondence re JEH Mac book. Thomas Fisher Rare Book Library, University of Toronto, Toronto, Ontario.

Hunter, E.R. *J.E.H. MacDonald: A Biography & Catalogue of his Work*. Toronto, ON: Ryerson Press, 1940.

Hunter, E.R. "J.E.H. MacDonald." *The Educational Record of the Province of Quebec, Special Art Issue*, vol. LXXX,3 (July-September 1954), pp. 157–162. Available from: https://numerique.banq.qc.ca/patrimoine/details/52327/4280044

Ireland, G.H. *Paperboard on the Multi-Vat Cylinder Machine*. New York, NY: Chemical Publishing Company, 1968.

Jackson, A.Y. Letter to J.E.H. MacDonald, August 26, 1917, MG30 D111, 1-2a, Correspondence from A.Y. Jackson (2 of 2), J.E.H. MacDonald fonds, Library and Archives Canada, Ottawa, Ontario.

Jackson, A.Y. Letter to his cousin Florence Clement c/o Lawren Harris, September 29, 1919, MG30 D351, 76–22, Naomi Jackson Groves fonds, AYJ Letters – "B" copy, 1915–1928 (2/4), Library and Archives Canada, Ottawa, Ontario.

Jackson, A.Y. Letter to J.E.H. MacDonald, March 17, 1920. MG30 D111, 1-2, Correspondence from A.Y. Jackson (2 of 2), J.E.H. MacDonald fonds, Library and Archives Canada, Ottawa, Ontario.

Jackson, A.Y. Accounts Book, 1921 to 1931, MG30 D351 75, vol. 99, Files 18-21, accounts book 1921–31, Naomi Jackson Groves fonds Library and Archives Canada, Ottawa, Ontario.

Jackson, A.Y. Transcript of an excerpt of a letter to E. Brown, January 10, 1928. In *The Solemn Land*, accession no. 1785, curatorial file. National Gallery of Canada, Ottawa, Ontario.

Jackson, A.Y. "J.E.H. MacDonald." *The Canadian Forum* 13,148 (January 1933), pp. 136–38.

Jackson, A.Y. Letter to T. MacDonald, April 2, 1934. Thoreau MacDonald papers, MS Coll. 180, Folder 6, Thomas Fisher Rare Book Library, University of Toronto, Toronto, Ontario.

Jackson, A.Y. *A Painter's Country: The Autobiography of A.Y. Jackson*. Toronto, ON: Clarke, Irwin & Company, 1967.

Jeffries, C.W. "MacDonald's Sketches." *The Lamps* 1,2 (December 1911), p. 12. Available from: http://www.artsandlettersprivate.ca/lampsletters/lampsletters_1911.pdf

Jiménez, J.J., J.L. Bernal, S. Aumente, L. Toribio, and J. Bernal, Jr. "Quality Assurance of Commercial Beeswax II. Gas Chromatography–Electron Impact Ionization Mass Spectrometry of Alcohols and Acids." *Journal of Chromatography A* 1007,1-2 (2003), pp. 101–116. Available from: https://doi.org/10.1016/S0021-9673(03)00962-2

Joyner Auctioneers & Appraisers. *Joyner Canadian Art* [Auction catalogue]. Toronto, ON: Joyner Fine Art, May 14, 2002, lot 117.

Katlan, A. "The American Artist's Tools and Materials for On-site Oil Sketching." *Journal of the American Institute for Conservation* 38,1 (1999), pp. 21–32. Available from: https://doi.org/10.1179/019713699806113565

Kelly, J.S., and M. Angel, eds. *Forensic Document Examination in the 21st Century*. Boca Raton, FL: CRC Press, 2021.

Klempan, B., M.-C. Corbeil, J. Poulin, and P. Cook. "A Technical and Scientific Study of Two of A.Y. Jackson's Paintboxes." *Journal of the Canadian Association for Conservation* 34 (2009), pp. 29–38. https://www.cac-accr.ca/wp-content/uploads/2018/12/Vol34_doc4.pdf

Klempan, B. "Early Manufacture of Artists' Materials in Canada: A History of Canadian Art Laboratory." *Journal of the Canadian Association for Conservation* 37 (2012), pp. 41–51. Available from: https://www.cac-accr.ca/wp-content/uploads/2018/12/Vol37_doc4.pdf

Klinkhoff, A. "In Reaction to the Controversy Surrounding the Vancouver Art Gallery's J.E.H. MacDonald Donation." *Learn* [Blog], March 20, 2015. Available from: https://www.klinkhoff.ca/blog/5738/

Kronkright, D.P. "Deterioration of Artifacts Made from Plant Materials." In M.E. Florian, D.P. Kronkright, and R.E. Norton, eds., *The Conservation of Artifacts Made from Plant Materials*. Los Angeles, CA: The Getty Conservation Institute,

1990, pp. 139–193. Available from: https://www.getty.edu/publications/resources/virtuallibrary/0892361603.pdf

Kühn, H., and M. Curran. "Chrome Yellow and Other Chromate Pigments." In R.L. Feller, ed., *Artists' Pigments: A Handbook of Their History and Characteristics*, vol. 1. Washington, D.C.: National Gallery of Art, 1986, pp. 187–218. Available from: https://www.nga.gov/content/dam/ngaweb/research/publications/pdfs/artists-pigments-vol1.pdf

Laing, G.B. *Memoirs of an Art Dealer*, vol. 1. Toronto, ON: McClelland & Stewart, 1978.

Landry, P. *The MacCallum-Jackman Cottage Mural Paintings*. Ottawa, ON: National Gallery of Canada, 1990.

Language of Bindings Thesaurus. London, UK: University of the Arts London, n.d. Available from: https://www.ligatus.org.uk/lob/

Laurie, A.P. *Facts About Processes, Pigments and Vehicles: A Manual for Art Students*. London, UK: MacMillan and Company, 1895. Available from: https://archive.org/details/factsaboutproces00laur

Laurie, A.P. *The Painter's Methods and Materials*. London, UK: Seeley, Service & Co. Limited, 1926.

Laurie, A.P. *Pictures and Politics: A Book of Reminiscences*. London, UK: International Publishing Company, 1934.

Laver, M. "Titanium Dioxide Whites." In E.W. Fitzhugh, ed., *Artists' Pigments: A Handbook of Their History and Characteristics*, vol. 3. Washington, D.C.: National Gallery of Art, 1997, pp. 295–355. Available from: https://www.nga.gov/content/dam/ngaweb/research/publications/pdfs/artists-pigments-vol3.pdf

Lederman, M. "The Controversy Surrounding the Vancouver Art Gallery's J.E.H. MacDonald Donation." *The Globe and Mail*, March 14, 2015. Available from: https://www.theglobeandmail.com/arts/art-and-architecture/the-controversy-surrounding-the-vancouver-art-gallerys-jeh-macdonald-donation/article23457955/

Leone, B., A. Burnstock, C. Jones, P. Hallebeek, J. Boon, and K. Keune. "The Deterioration of Cadmium Sulphide Yellow Artists' Pigments." In I. Verger, ed., *ICOM-CC 14th Triennial Meeting, The Hague, Netherlands, 12–16 September 2005: Preprints*. London, UK: James & James (Science Publishers) Ltd., 2005, pp. 803–813. Available from: https://www.icom-cc-publications-online.org/2129/The-deterioration-of-cadmium-sulphide-yellow-artists-pigments

MacDonald, Joan. *Extract from TM's mother's diary, 1905–06*. 25 leaves. (Xerox holograph), MS Coll 180, Box 5, Folder 26, Thoreau MacDonald papers, Thomas Fisher Rare Book Library, University of Toronto, Toronto, Ontario.

MacDonald, J.E.H. Letter to Eric Brown, December 4, 1918, Series: Loans, exhibitions, and outside activities – Canadian War Artists. Box 167, file 5, National Gallery of Canada Archives, Ottawa, Ontario.

MacDonald, J.E.H. "A.C.R. 10557." *The Lamps* (December 1919), pp. 33–39. Available from: http://www.artsandlettersprivate.ca/lampsletters/lampsletters_1919.pdf

MacDonald, J.E.H. Letter to W.J. Wood, March 11, 1920. Christine Boyanoski-W.J. Wood Collection, CA OTAG SC030, file box 5, letters from J.E.H. MacDonald, Art Gallery of Ontario, E.P. Taylor Research Library and Archives, Toronto, Ontario.

MacDonald, J.E.H. Letter to W.J. Wood, March 15, 1920. Christine Boyanoski-W.J. Wood Collection, CA OTAG SC030, file box 5, letters from J.E.H. MacDonald, Art Gallery of Ontario, E.P. Taylor Research Library and Archives, Toronto, Ontario.

MacDonald, J.E.H. "A Glimpse of the West." *Canadian Bookman* 6,11 (November 1924), pp. 229–231.

MacDonald, J.E.H. Lecture Notes, Untitled, General Art, n.d. [circa 1925], MG30 D111 3-32, J.E.H. MacDonald fonds. Library and Archives Canada, Ottawa, Ontario.

MacDonald, J.E.H. "Interior Decorations of St. Anne's Church, Toronto." *Journal of the Royal Architectural Institute of Canada* 2,3 (May–June 1925), pp. 85–93.

MacDonald, J.E.H. "Art Indoors and Out." *Canadian Forum* 6,63 (December 1925), pp. 77–78.

MacDonald, J.E.H. Diaries, 1925 to 1930, MG30 D111, 1-8 to 1-11, J.E.H. MacDonald fonds, Library and Archives Canada, Ottawa, Ontario.

MacDonald, J.E.H. Lectures, Painting and Poetry, October 20, 1929, J.E.H. MacDonald fonds, MG30 D111, 3-20, 1 of 2, Library and Archives Canada, Ottawa, Ontario.

MacDonald, J.E.H. Miscellaneous notes, Endeavors After Art, November 14, 1930, MG30 D111, 3-33, J.E.H. MacDonald fonds, Library and Archives Canada, Ottawa, Ontario.

MacDonald, J.E.H. "Scandinavian Art." *Northward Journal* 18/19 (1980), pp. 9–35.

MacDonald, J.E.H. Letter to Eric Brown, April 7, 1932. Series: Art and artists – Correspondence with/regarding artists – General. Box 264, file 7, National Gallery of Canada Archives, Ottawa, Ontario.

MacDonald, J.E.H. *Sketchbook, 1915–1922: A Facsimile Edition*. Moonbeam, ON: Penumbra Press, 1979.

MacDonald, J.E.H. *The Barbados Journal, 1932*. Edited by J.W. Sabean. Kapuskasing, ON: Penumbra Press, 1989.

MacDonald, J.E.H. The Decorative Element in Art. Arts and Letters Club, n.d. MG30 D111 3-21, J.E.H. MacDonald fonds, Library and Archives Canada, Ottawa, Ontario.

MacDonald, T. Letter to E. Brown, Director, NGC, December 23, 1936. In *The Beaver Dam*, accession no. 4529, curatorial file. National Gallery of Canada, Ottawa, Ontario.

MacDonald, T. Notebook 11, 1956, MS Coll. 180, Box 25, Folder 13, Thoreau MacDonald papers, Thomas Fisher Rare Book Library, University of Toronto, Toronto, Ontario.

MacDonald, T. Letter to Mrs. R.R. Bradfield, December 1, 1966. In *Algoma Hilltop*, accession number 2102, curatorial file. Art Gallery of Ontario, Toronto, Ontario.

MacDonald, T. Notes for autobiography, 1971, MS Coll. 180, Box 5, Folder 28, Thoreau MacDonald papers, Thomas Fisher Rare Book Library, University of Toronto, Toronto, Ontario.

MacDonald, T. 25 Severn St. for Canadian Art, February 1975, MS Coll. 180, Box 5, Folder 30, Thoreau MacDonald papers, Thomas Fisher Rare Book Library, University of Toronto, Toronto, Ontario.

MacDonald, T. Notes on J.E.H. MacDonald, n.d., MS Coll. 180, Box 5, Folder 32, Thoreau MacDonald papers, Thomas Fisher Rare Book Library, University of Toronto, Toronto, Ontario.

MacDonald, T., and H. Bishop. "No Ordinary Life." In R. Stacey, ed., *J.E.H. MacDonald: Designer: An Anthology of Graphic Design, Illustration and Lettering*. Ottawa, ON: Archives of Canadian Art, 1996, pp. 1–13.

Madderton & Company. *Permanent Colours for Artists*. Loughton, UK: Madderton & Company, December 1908.

Małachowska E, D. Pawcenis, J. Dańczak, J. Paczkowska, and K. Przybysz. "Paper Ageing: The Effect of Paper Chemical Composition on Hydrolysis and Oxidation." *Polymers* 13,7 (March 2021). Available from: https://doi.org/10.3390/polym13071029

Marinach, C., M.-C. Papillon, and C. Pepe. "Identification of Binding Media in Works of Art by Gas Chromatography–Mass Spectrometry." *Journal of Cultural Heritage* 5,2 (2004), pp. 231–240. Available from: https://doi.org/10.1016/j.culher.2003.12.002

Mass, J.L., R. Opila, B. Buckley, M. Cotte, J. Church, and A. Mehta. "The Photodegradation of Cadmium Yellow Paints in Henri Matisse's *Le Bonheur de vivre* (1905–06)." *Applied Physics A* 111 (2013), pp. 59–68. Available from: https://doi.org/10.1007/s00339-012-7418-0

McCrone, W.C. "The Microscopical Identification of Artists' Pigments." *Journal of the International Institute for Conservation – Canadian Group* 7,1-2 (1982) pp. 11–34.

McCurry, H.O. Letter from H.O. McCurry, Assistant Director, National Gallery of Canada, to Wyly Grier, January 17, 1939. In *The Tangled Garden*, accession no. 4291, curatorial file. National Gallery of Canada, Ottawa, Ontario.

McFaddin, C.E. Art Gallery of Ontario, Data by Curator, 1971. In *The Junk Cart*, accession no. 70/327, curatorial file. Art Gallery of Ontario, Toronto, Ontario.

McMichael, R. *One Man's Obsession*. Scarborough, ON: Prentice-Hall Canada, 1986.

Mellen, P. *The Group of Seven*. Toronto, ON: McClelland & Stewart, 1970.

Middleton, J.E. "J.E.H. MacDonald: An Appreciation." Supplement to *The Lamps*, November 29, 1932.

Moffatt, E., A. Salmon, J. Poulin, A. Fox, and J. Hay. "Characterization of Varnishes on Nineteenth-Century Canadian Furniture." *Journal of the Canadian Association for Conservation* 40 (2015), pp. 3–18. Available from: https://www.cac-accr.ca/wp-content/uploads/dlm_uploads/2018/12/vol40_doc1.pdf

Morgan, S., J. Townsend, S. Hackney, and R. Perry. "Canvas and Its Preparation in Early Twentieth-Century British Paintings." In J.H. Townsend, et. al, eds., *Preparation for Painting: The Artist's Choice and Its Consequences*. London, UK: Archetype Publications, 2008, pp. 132–140.

Munsell Soil Colour Book. Grand Rapids, MI: Munsell Color, revised 2009, printed 2019.

Murray, J. *The Art of Tom Thomson*. Toronto, ON: Art Gallery of Ontario, 1971.

O'Conner, F. "Authenticating the Attribution of Art: Connoisseurship and the Law in the Judging of Forgeries, Copies, and False Attributions." In R.D. Spencer, ed., *The Expert Versus the Object: Judging Fakes and False Attributions in the Visual Arts*. Oxford, UK: Oxford University Press, 2004, pp. 3–27.

Ontario Society of Artists. *Ontario Society of Artists: Forty-Fourth Annual Exhibition, From March 11 to April 15, 1916* [Museum catalogue]. Toronto, ON: Held at the Art Museum of Toronto, Public Reference Library, College St., 1916.

Ontario Society of Artists. *Ontario Society of Artists: Forty-Fifth Annual Exhibition, 1917* [Museum catalogue]. Toronto, ON: Public Reference Library, College St., 1917.

Pantazzi, S. "A Picture Frame by J.E.H. MacDonald." *Canadian Art Review / RACAR: Revue d'art canadienne* 4,1 (1977), pp. 32–35. Available from: https://doi.org/10.7202/1077241ar

Plesters, J. "Cross-sections and Chemical Analysis of Paint Samples." *Studies in Conservation* 2,3 (1956), pp. 110–157. Available from: https://doi.org/10.1179/sic.1956.015

Pond, C. *The Buildings of Loughton and Notable People of the Town*, 2nd ed. Loughton, UK: Loughton and District Historical Society, 2010.

Pond, C. Personal communication, July 24, 2020.

Poulin, J., M. Kearney, and M.-A. Veall. "Direct Inlet Py-GC-MS Analysis of Cultural Heritage Materials." *Journal of Analytical and Applied Pyrolysis* 164 (June 2022). Available from: https://doi.org/10.1016/j.jaap.2022.105506

Pratt, B. "The Loughton Firm that Manufactured Artists Materials." *Essex Countryside* 28,280 (May 1980), p. 46–47.

Price, B.A., B. Pretzel, and S. Quillen Lomax, eds. Infrared and Raman Users Group Spectral Database. 2007 ed., vol. 1 & 2. Philadelphia, PA: IRUG, 2009. Accessed 20 June 2014. Available from: www.irug.org

Pitthard, V., S. Stanek, M. Griesser, and T. Muxeneder. "Gas Chromatography – Mass Spectrometry of Binding Media from Early 20th Century Paint Samples from Arnold Schönberg's Palette." *Chromatographia* 62,3–4 (August 2005), pp. 175–182. Available from: https://doi.org/10.1365/s10337-005-0595-7

Reid, D. *The Group of Seven /Le Groupe des sept*. Ottawa, ON: The National Gallery of Canada, 1970.

Robertson, N. *J.E.H. MacDonald, R.C.A., 1873–1932: [Exhibition held at] the Art Gallery of Toronto, November 13-December 12, 1965; the National Gallery of Canada, January 7 to February 6, 1966* [Musuem catalogue]. Toronto, ON: Art Gallery of Toronto, 1965.

Roberts, M., and D. Etherington. *Bookbinding and the Conservation of Books: A Dictionary of Descriptive Terminology*. Washington DC: Library of Congress, 1982. Available from: https://cool.culturalheritage.org/don/

Robson, A.H. *J.E.H. MacDonald, R.C.A.* Toronto, ON: Ryerson Press, 1937.

Rossell, L. Unpublished notes about Grip, written by L. Rossell for National Gallery of Canada files, before 1938, MS Coll. 00318 Box 2, *Research materials 1937–38 correspondence re JEH Mac book*, E.R. Hunter papers, Thomas Fisher Rare Book Library, University of Toronto, Toronto, Ontario.

Rowell, R.M., and H.P. Stout. "Jute and Kenaf." In M. Lewin, ed., *Handbook of Fiber Chemistry*, 3rd ed. Boca Raton, FL: CRC Press, Taylor & Francis Group, 2007, pp. 406–452.

Ruggles, A. Brief description of treatment, December 23, 1987. Restoration and Conservation Laboratory Request for Services, National Gallery of Canada. In *The Solemn Land*, accession no. 1785, conservation file. National Gallery of Canada, Ottawa, Ontario.

Sabean, J.W., ed. Introduction to *A Boy All Spirit: Thoreau MacDonald in the 1920s*. Manotick, ON: Penumbra Press, 2002.

Schaefer, C. Financial Records 1931–1942. MG30 D171, volume 40, file 6, financial records 1931–1942, Carl Schaefer fonds. Library and Archives Canada, Ottawa, Ontario.

Siegel, P. "Signature Identification: From Pen Stroke to Brush Stroke." In R.D. Spencer, ed., *The Expert Versus the Object: Judging Fakes and False Attributions in the Visual Arts*. Oxford, UK, and New York, NY: Oxford University Press, 2004, pp. 89–94.

Sirois, P.J., C. Stewart, K. Helwig, E. Moffatt, and K.M. Legate. "A Technical Study of the Materials and Methods Used by David B. Milne in his Oil Paintings." *Journal of the Canadian Association for Conservation* 32 (2007), pp. 17–33. Available from: https://www.cac-accr.ca/wp-content/uploads/2018/12/Vol32_doc2.pdf

Smith, B.H. "The Arsenic Content of Shellac and the Contamination of Foods from this Source." Circular 91. Boston, MA: United States Department of Agriculture, Bureau of Chemistry, 1912. Available from: https://archive.org/details/arseniccontentof91smit/page/n1/mode/2up

Stacey, R., and H. Bishop. *J.E.H. MacDonald, Designer: An Anthology of Graphic Design, Illustration and Lettering*. Ottawa, ON: Archives of Canadian Art, 1996.

Stark, N.M., and Z. Cai. "Chapter 11: Wood-based Composite Materials: Panel Products, Glued Laminated Timber, Structure Composite Lumber, and Wood-Nonwood Composites." In R. Ross, ed., *Wood Handbook: Wood as an Engineering Material*. General Technical Report FPL-GTR-282. Madison, WI: U.S.

Department of Agriculture, 2021, pp. 11-1 to 11-29. Available from: https://www.fpl.fs.usda.gov/documnts/fplgtr/fplgtr282/chapter_11_fpl_gtr282.pdf

Streeton, N.L.W. "Conservators at the Interface with History of Art: Technical Art History, Multi-Disciplinarity and Material Culture." In A. Villa and A. Murray, eds., *Diagnosis: Before, During, After. Conservation 3600* no. 2 (June 2022). Available from: https://monografias.editorial.upv.es/index.php/con_360/article/view/387

Stols-Witlox, M., B. Ormsby, and M. Gottsegen. "Grounds, 1400–1900; Including Twentieth-Century Grounds." In J.H. Stoner and R. Rushfield, eds., *Conservation of Easel Paintings*. London, UK: Routledge, 2012, pp. 161–188.

Stoney, D. A. "The Use of the Chelsea Filter and Alternative Dichromatic Effects in the Microscopical Characterization of Paint Pigments." *The Microscope* 38 (1990), pp. 67–81.

Studio Building Ledger 1914 to 1917. MG30 D351 102-21, Studio Building [1913–1915] (2 of 2), Naomi Jackson Groves fonds, Library and Archives Canada, Ottawa, Ontario.

Sutherland, K., and J.C. del Río. "Characterisation and Discrimination of Various Types of Lac Resin Using Gas Chromatography Mass Spectrometry Techniques with Quaternary Ammonium Reagents." *Journal of Chromatography A* 1338 (April 2014), pp. 149–163. Available from: https://doi.org/10.1016/j.chroma.2014.02.063

Thickens, J.H. Wall-board, US Patent 1,121,951, filed September 17, 1914, and issued December 22, 1914, lines 20–25. Available from: https://patentimages.storage.googleapis.com/80/df/31/2bb0321d3e5b7b/US1121951.pdf

Thickens, J.H. Waterproofed Wall-Board, US Patent 1,191,099, filed December 5, 1914, and issued July 11, 1916, lines 20–25. Available from: https://patentimages.storage.googleapis.com/9c/84/64/55b230caacofcf/US1191099.pdf

Thickens, J.H. Adhesive, US Patent 1,377,739, filed January 20, 1915, and issued May 10, 1921. Available from: https://patentimages.storage.googleapis.com/d5/f6/c3/27e2459cb6addf/US1377739.pdf

Thomson, S.L. "J.E.H. MacDonald." In *Canadian Art: The Thomson Collection at the Art Gallery of Ontario*. Toronto, ON: Skylet Publishing/The Art Gallery of Ontario, 2008, pp. 89–103.

Toronto City Directories. Toronto, ON: Might Directories Ltd., 1900 to 1937. Available from: https://www.torontopubliclibrary.ca/history-genealogy/lh-digital-city-directories.jsp

Town, H. Introduction to *Tom Thomson: The Silence and the Storm, 3rd ed.* Toronto, ON: McClelland & Stewart, 1977, reprinted 1989, pp. 19–30.

Tummers, A., and R.G. Erdmann. "The Eye Versus Chemistry? From Twentieth to Twenty-First Century Connoisseurship." In M.P. Colombini, I. Degano, and A. Nevin, eds., *Analytical Chemistry for the Study of Paintings and the Detection of Forgeries*. Cham, Switzerland: Springer International, 2022, pp. 3–45.

van den Berg, K.J., J.J. Boon, I. Pastorova, and L.F.M. Spetter. "Mass Spectrometric Methodology for the Analysis of Highly Oxidized Diterpenoid Acids in Old Master Paintings." *Journal of Mass Spectrometry* 35,4 (April 2000), pp. 512–533. Available from: https://doi.org/10.1002/(SICI)1096-9888(200004)35:4<512::AID-JMS963>3.0.CO;2-3

van Keulen, H. "The Analysis and Identification of Transparent Finishes Using Thermally Assisted Hydrolysis and Methylation Pyrolysis Gas Chromatography Mass Spectrometry." In M.V. Dias, ed., *Furniture Finishes: Past, Present and Future of Transparent Wood Coatings: 12th International Symposium on Wood and Furniture Conservation, Amsterdam, Netherlands, 14–15 November 2014*. Amsterdam, Netherlands: Stichting Ebenist, 2014, pp. 134–141.

Waldron, A. "The Studio Building, 25 Severn Street, Toronto, Ontario." *Journal of the Society for Study of Architecture in Canada* 31,1 (2006), pp. 65–80. Available from: http://hdl.handle.net/10222/70780

Warwick Bro's and Rutter. *On the Making of Blank Books*. Toronto: ON: Warwick Bros. and Rutter, [190?], p. 11. Available from: http://www.canadiana.ca/view/oocihm.86133/19?r=0&s=1

Weaver, S. "Beaver Board and Upson Board: History and Conservation of Early Wallboard." *APT Bulletin: The Journal of Preservation Technology* 28, 2/3 (1997), pp. 71–78. Available from: https://doi.org/10.2307/1504537

Webster-Cook S., and A. Ruggles. "Technical Studies on Thomson's Materials and Working Method." In D. Reid, ed., *Tom Thomson*. Vancouver, B.C.: Douglas & McIntyre, 2002, pp. 145–152.

Whitehouse R., and N. Eastaugh. "From Munnings to Mondrian: Studies in the Deterioration of Early Twentieth-Century Artists' Materials." In *Deterioration of Artists' Paints: Effects and Analysis: A Joint Meeting of ICOM-CC Working Groups Paintings 1 and 2 and the Painting Section, UKIC, London, UK, 10–11 September, 2001: Extended Abstracts of Presentations*. London, UK: United Kingdom Institute for Conservation of Historic and Artistic Works and International Council of Museums, 2001, pp. 61–65.

Whiteman, B. *J.E.H. MacDonald*. Kingston, ON: Quarry Press, 1995.

Wilson R., and K. Snodgrass. *Early 20th-Century Building Materials: Fiberboard and Plywood*. Facilities Tech Tips 2. Missoula, MT: United States Department of Agriculture, Forest Service, Technology and Development Program, 2007. Available from: https://inspectapedia.com/interiors/Fiberboard-and-Plywod-Plywood-USDA.pdf

Young, C. "History of Fabric Supports." In J.H. Stoner and R. Rushfield, eds., *Conservation of Easel Paintings*. London, UK: Routledge, 2012, pp. 137–144.

Zumbuehl, S., N.C. Scherrer, A. Berger, and U. Eggenberger. "Early Viridian Composition: Characterization of a (Hydrated) Chromium Oxide Borate Pigment," *Studies in Conservation* 54,3 (2009), pp. 149–159. Available from: https://doi.org/10.1179/sic.2009.54.3.149

LIST OF ILLUSTRATIONS

(all works of art by J.E.H. MacDonald unless otherwise noted)

Fig. 1.17 *Forest Wilderness*, 1921
oil on canvas, 122 × 152 cm
Gift of Colonel R.S. McLaughlin
McMichael Canadian Art Collection
1968.7.1
Photograph: McMichael

Fig. 1.18 *Old Dock, Petite Rivière, Nova Scotia*, 1922
oil on paperboard, 21.4 × 26.4 cm
National Gallery of Canada, Ottawa
Photograph: NGC

Fig. 1.19 *Cathedral Peak and Lake O'Hara*, 1927
oil on paperboard, 21.4 × 26.6 cm
Gift of Mr. R.A. Laidlaw
McMichael Canadian Art Collection
1966.15.9
Photograph: McMichael

Fig. 1.20 *Near Lake Oesa, Abbot's Pass*, 1930
oil on paperboard, 21.5 × 26.6 cm
National Gallery of Canada, Ottawa
Photograph: NGC

Fig. 1.21 *Mount Goodsir, Yoho Park*, 1925
oil on canvas, overall: 107.3 × 122.3 cm, frame: 116 × 130.5 cm
Art Gallery of Ontario
Gift of Dr. and Mrs. Max Stern, Dominion Gallery, Montreal, 1979
79/228
Photograph: © AGO

Fig. 1.22 *Goat Range, Rocky Mountains*, 1932
oil on canvas, 53.8 x 66.2 cm
Gift of the Founders, Robert and Signe McMichael
McMichael Canadian Art Collection
1979.35
Photograph: McMichael

Fig. 1.23 *Windy Sky near Pointe au Baril*, 1931
oil on paperboard, 21.5 × 26.6 cm
National Gallery of Canada, Ottawa
Photograph: NGC

Fig. 1.24 *Palms, Barbados*, 1932
oil on paperboard, overall: 21.6 × 26.7 cm
Art Gallery of Ontario
Gift of the Students' Club, Ontario College of Art, 1933
2113
Photograph: © AGO

Fig. 1.25 J.E.H. MacDonald Painting in Algoma, circa 1918–1919
A.Y. Jackson Scrapbook
National Gallery of Canada Library and Archives
Photograph: NGC

2. SUPPORTS AND PREPARATION

Figs. 2.1a and 2.1b Details of *Oaks, October Morning*, 1909
McMichael Canadian Art Collection
1966.15.15
Photographs: McMichael

Fig. 2.2 Detail of back of *View from Split Rock*, 1912
National Gallery of Canada, Ottawa
Photograph: © Government of Canada, Canadian Conservation Institute

Figs. 2.3a and 2.3b Details of *Oakwood*, 1913
McMichael Canadian Art Collection
1972.5.3
Photographs: McMichael

Fig. 2.4a and 2.4b Details of *Near Minden*, 1916 or 1917
McMichael Canadian Art Collection
1966.15.12
Photographs: McMichael

Fig. 2.5a and 2.5b Details of *Gleams on the Hills II*, 1918
National Gallery of Canada, Ottawa
Photographs: © Government of Canada, Canadian Conservation Institute.

Fig. 2.6a and 2.6b Details of *Algoma Bush, Autumn*, circa 1919
National Gallery of Canada, Ottawa
Photographs: © Government of Canada, Canadian Conservation Institute

Fig. 2.7a, 2.7b, and 2.7c Details of *Mist Fantasy*, 1920
National Gallery of Canada, Ottawa
Photographs: © Government of Canada, Canadian Conservation Institute

Fig. 2.8 *Moose Lake, Algoma*, 1920, back, UV fluorescence
McMichael Canadian Art Collection
1966.15.4
Photograph: McMichael

Fig. 2.9a and 2.9b Details of *Study, Lake McArthur (Grey Weather)*, 1924 to 1930
National Gallery of Canada, Ottawa
Photographs: © Government of Canada, Canadian Conservation Institute

Fig. 2.10a and 2.10b Details of *Near Lake Oesa, Abbot's Pass*, 1930
National Gallery of Canada, Ottawa
Photographs: © Government of Canada, Canadian Conservation Institute

Fig. 2.11a and 2.11b Details of *Mount Odaray*, 1930
National Gallery of Canada, Ottawa
Photographs: © Government of Canada, Canadian Conservation Institute

Fig. 2.12 Detail of Belgium, 1915
Art Gallery of Ontario
62/21
Photograph: © AGO

Fig. 2.13a Detail of back of *Belgium*, 1915
Art Gallery of Ontario
62/21
Photograph: © AGO

Fig. 2.13b Detail of back of *Harvest Evening Moon*, 1917
McMichael Canadian Art Collection
1978.31
Photograph: © Government of Canada, Canadian Conservation Institute

Fig. 2.14 Detail of back of *Goat Range, Rocky Mountains*, 1932
McMichael Canadian Art Collection
1979.35
Photograph: McMichael

3. PAINTING TECHNIQUES

Fig. 3.1 Detail of *Oaks, October Morning*, 1909
McMichael Canadian Art Collection
1966.15.15
Photograph: © McMichael

Fig. 3.2 Detail of *Snow, High Park*, 1909
McMichael Canadian Art Collection
1981.24
Photograph: McMichael

Fig. 3.3 Cross-section from *Snow, High Park*, 1909
McMichael Canadian Art Collection
1981.24
Photograph: © Government of Canada, Canadian Conservation Institute

Fig. 3.27a Inscription on back of *Rocky Stream, Algoma*, circa 1918
McMichael Canadian Art Collection
1966.16.45
Photograph: McMichael

Fig. 3.27b Inscription on back of *Tamarack, Lake O'Hara*, circa 1929
McMichael Canadian Art Collection
1969.14.2
Photograph: McMichael

Fig. 3.27c Inscription on back of *Rainy Weather, Algoma*, 1919
McMichael Canadian Art Collection
1966.16.34
Photograph: McMichael

Fig. 3.27d Inscription on back of *Rocky Stream, Algoma*, circa 1918
McMichael Canadian Art Collection
1966.16.45
Photograph: McMichael

Fig. 3.28a Stamp on the back of *Solemn Land, Algoma*, circa 1919
Art Gallery of Ontario
Photograph: © Government of Canada, Canadian Conservation Institute

Fig. 3.28b Stamp on the back of *Lake O'Hara Shores Stormy Weather*, 1929
McMichael Canadian Art Collection
1969.23.4
Photograph: McMichael

4. PAINTING MATERIALS

Fig. 4.1 Cross-section from *Snow, High Park*, 1909
McMichael Canadian Art Collection
1981.24
Photograph: © Government of Canada, Canadian Conservation Institute

Fig. 4.2 Cross-section from *Near Minden*, 1916 or 1917
McMichael Canadian Art Collection
1966.15.12
Photograph: © Government of Canada, Canadian Conservation Institute

Figs. 4.3a and 4.3b Cross-section from *Algoma Hills*, 1920
McMichael Canadian Art Collection
1966.15.6
Photographs: © Government of Canada, Canadian Conservation Institute

Figs. 4.3c and 4.3d Cross-section from *Old Dock, Petite Rivière, Nova Scotia*, 1922
National Gallery of Canada, Ottawa
Photographs: © Government of Canada, Canadian Conservation Institute

Figs. 4.3e and 4.3f Cross-section from *Solemn Land, Algoma*, circa 1919
Art Gallery of Ontario
Photographs: © Government of Canada, Canadian Conservation Institute

Figs. 4.4a and 4.4b Cross-section from *The Elements*, 1916
Art Gallery of Ontario
Photographs: © Government of Canada, Canadian Conservation Institute

Figs. 4.5a and 4.5b Cross-section from *The Tangled Garden*, 1916
National Gallery of Canada, Ottawa
Photographs: © Government of Canada, Canadian Conservation Institute

Figs. 4.6a and 4.6b Cross-section from *Algoma Waterfall*, 1920
McMichael Canadian Art Collection
1968.7.2
Photographs: © Government of Canada, Canadian Conservation Institute

Fig. 4.7 Madderton & Company 1908 catalogue, details of pages 10 and 21.
Photographs: © Government of Canada, Canadian Conservation Institute

Fig. 4.8 Microscopic dispersion from *Solemn Land, Algoma*, circa 1919
Art Gallery of Ontario
Photograph: © Government of Canada, Canadian Conservation Institute.

Fig. 4.9 Microscopic dispersion from *Old Dock, Petite Rivière, Nova Scotia*, 1922
National Gallery of Canada, Ottawa
Photograph: © Government of Canada, Canadian Conservation Institute

Fig. 4.10 Microscopic dispersion from *Logs on the Gatineau River*, 1914
McMichael Canadian Art Collection
1981.85.5
Photograph: © Government of Canada, Canadian Conservation Institute

Fig. 4.11 Microscopic dispersion from *Near Minden*, 1916 or 1917
McMichael Canadian Art Collection
1966.15.12
Photograph: © Government of Canada, Canadian Conservation Institute

5. APPLYING THE RESEARCH

Fig. 5.1a (front) and 5.1b (back) Unknown artist, *Sketch after The Tangled Garden*
oil on paperboard, 14.6 × 21.1 cm
Vancouver Art Gallery
2014.33.1
Photographs: © Government of Canada, Canadian Conservation Institute

Fig. 5.2a Detail of *Study for "The Tangled Garden,"* 1915
oil on paperboard, mounted on plywood, 20.2 × 25.4 cm
National Gallery of Canada, Ottawa
Gift of Arthur Lismer, Montreal, 1946
Photograph: NGC

Fig. 5.2b Detail of *The Tangled Garden*, 1916
oil on beaverboard, 121.4 × 152.4 cm; framed 140.5 H × 171 W × 9.5 cm D
National Gallery of Canada, Ottawa
Gift of W.M. Southam, F.N. Southam, and H.S. Southam, 1937, in memory of their brother Richard Southam
Photograph: NGC

Figs. 5.3a (front) and 5.3b (back) *Poplar and Pine*, circa 1919
oil on paperboard, 20.3 × 25.3 cm
National Gallery of Canada, Ottawa
Photographs: NGC

Fig. 5.4 Detail of *Falls, Montreal River*, 1920
oil on canvas, overall: 121.9 × 153 cm
Art Gallery of Ontario
Purchase, 1933
2109
Photograph: McMichael

Fig. 5.5 Detail of *Falls, Montreal River,* 1920
oil on canvas, overall: 121.9 × 153 cm
Art Gallery of Ontario
Purchase, 1933
2109
Photograph: McMichael

Fig. 5.6 Detail of back of *The Solemn Land*, 1921
National Gallery of Canada, Ottawa
Photograph: McMichael

NOTES

AN INTRODUCTION TO THE RESEARCH

1 Jeffreys 1911.

2 MacDonald, T. and Bishop 1996, p. 8; Laing 1978, p. 106.

1. LIFE AND ART

1 Bishop 1979, p. vii.
2 Hunter 1940, p. 1.
3 Middleton 1932; Fairley 1937; Rossell before 1938; Hunter 1954; MacDonald, Joan, Diary extract 1905–1906 (see entry for August 7, 1905, p. 12).
4 Duval 1978, pp. 14–15.
5 Robertson 1965, p. 6.
6 George Reid (1860–1947), in his role at the COSAD, and later as principal and instructor at the OCA, provided guidance and encouragement to many painters of MacDonald's generation. Biographer Paul Duval, who had access to MacDonald's correspondence from the 1890s, describes how Reid's influence on MacDonald is evident in MacDonald's early letters. For example, MacDonald wrote, "Mr. Reid's class began work early in January. We have had four lessons so far. I like the work immensely, and I am going forward, I think. I am weak in drawing but according to Mr. Reid, I put my 'notes' of colour true.... Mr. Reid is a good teacher, careful, ample in explanation, ready to demonstrate anything he says, with his brush." (Duval 1978, pp. 18–19).
7 Hunter 1940, p. 2.
8 Whiteman 1995, p. 18.
9 Robertson 1965, p. 5.
10 Duval 1978, pp. 16–18.
11 Ibid, p. 19.
12 Ibid, pp. 21–22.
13 Stacey and Bishop 1996, p. 117.
14 Duval 1978, p. 14.
15 MacDonald, Joan, Diary extract 1905–1906 (see entry for August 7, 1905, p. 12).
16 Canadian National Exhibition, 1908, p. 35.
17 Pratt 1980; Madderton & Co. 1908; Simon, J. "Madderton & Co." in British artists' suppliers, 1650–1950 on National Portrait Gallery website, http://www.npg.org.uk/research/programmes/directory-of-suppliers/m.php. This entry last updated March 2022.
18 Pratt 1980; Simon, J. "Madderton & Co." in British artists' suppliers, 1650–1950 on National Portrait Gallery website, http://www.npg.org.uk/research/programmes/directory-of-suppliers/m.php. This entry last updated March 2022.
19 Pond 2010, pp. 13 and 84; Pond 2020; Laurie 1934, p. 98.
20 Helwig et al. 2015.
21 Hunter 1940, pp. 4–7.
22 Duval 1978, p. 24.
23 Whiteman 1995, p. 23.
24 Jeffries 1911.
25 Whiteman 1995, p. 24.
26 Duval 1978, p. 45.
27 Landry 1990, p. 17.
28 Art Gallery of Ontario 1970, pp. 267–280; Canadian National Exhibition 1912, p. 59.
29 Duval 1978, p. 44.
30 Ibid, p. 49.
31 MacDonald, J.E.H. 1980. This is the text of a lecture given by MacDonald at the Art Gallery of Ontario, April 17, 1931. The original handwritten lecture notes can be found here: J.E.H MacDonald lecture on Scandinavian Art, April 17, 1931, MG30 D111, box 3, folder 27, J.E.H. MacDonald fonds, Library and Archives Canada, Ottawa, Ontario .
32 Waldron 2006.
33 Studio Building Ledger 1914 to 1917. Although the name on the Library and Archives Canada folder gives the dates as 1913–1915, the contents date from 1914 to 1917.
34 Jackson 1967, p. 28.
35 Harris, B., Letter to R. Harper, 1962.
36 Studio Building Ledger 1914 to 1917; Laing 1978, pp. 24–25; Stacey and Bishop 1996, pp. 119–120.
37 Helwig et al. 2015.
38 Laing 1978, pp. 24–25.
39 Duval 1978, p. 53.
40 Duval 1978, pp. 48–49; Sabean 2002, p. 19.
41 Hill 1984.
42 Ontario Society of Artists 1916, p. 18.
43 Robertson 1965, p. 28.
44 Hill 1995, pp. 55–59.
45 Charlesworth 1916.
46 Charlesworth 1916; Ahrens 1916; Hill 1984.
47 Hill 1984.
48 Landry 1990, p. 26.
49 Duval 1978, p. 58.
50 Landry 1990, p. 26.
51 Robertson 1965, p. 49.
52 Bishop 1979, p. xii; Stacey and Bishop 1996, p. 120.
53 Duval 1978, p. 141; Stacey and Bishop 1996, p. 119.
54 Our examination of *Near Minden* revealed an unsigned inscription on the back with the title and 1916 date written in cursive script using black ink. While it appears to be an early inscription, we cannot confirm that it is in MacDonald's hand.
55 Bishop 1979, plate XLIII.
56 Jackson, Letter to MacDonald, 1917.
57 Duval 1978, p. 82; MacDonald, T. and Bishop 1996, p. 3.
58 Bishop 1979, p. xiii.

59 Bishop 1979, p. xvi; Hammond 1919.
60 Stacey and Bishop 1996, p. 120.
61 Fairley 1937.
62 Duval 1978, p. 84.
63 Stacey and Bishop 1996, p. 120.
64 MacDonald, T., Notes for autobiography, 1971.
65 Duval 1978, p. 89; Whiteman 1995, p. 68; MacDonald, T., Notes for autobiography, 1971; MacDonald, T., 25 Severn St. for Canadian Art, 1975.
66 MacDonald, T., Notebook 11, 1956.
67 Jackson 1933.
68 MacDonald, J.E.H. 1919.
69 Harris, L., Letter to MacDonald, 1918.
70 Art Gallery of Toronto 1919.
71 Duval 1978, p. 87.
72 Art Gallery of Toronto 1919.
73 Duval 1978, pp. 87–88.
74 MacDonald, J.E.H. 1919.
75 Duval 1978, p. 88; Reid 1970, pp. 159–160.
76 MacDonald's sketches for *The Solemn Land* include one in the collection of the AGO (Art Gallery of Ontario 1970, p. 274), a second, signed and dated 1919, in the Thomson Collection at the AGO (Thomson 2008), and a third in the collection of the Art Gallery of Algoma (available from: https://www.artgalleryofalgoma.com/group-of-seven.html). A.Y. Jackson sketched a similar view of the Montreal River during the 1919 Algoma trip (Reid 1970, p. 138).
77 Whiteman 1995, p. 41.
78 Hill 1995, pp. 87–89.
79 Duval 1978, p. 139.
80 Duval 1978, p. 141; Stacey and Bishop 1996, pp. 119–121.
81 MacDonald, J.E.H. May–June 1925.
82 Whiteman 1995, p. 66.
83 Duval 1978, p. 139.
84 Christensen 2003, p. 6.
85 MacDonald J.E.H., Diaries 1925–1930.
86 Christensen 2003, p. 8.
87 MacDonald, T. and Bishop 1996, p. 4.
88 MacDonald, J.E.H. 1924.
89 MacDonald, J.E.H., Diaries 1925–1930 (see entry for September 9, 1930).
90 Christensen 2003, p. 98.
91 Ibid, p. 103.
92 MacDonald, J.E.H., Diaries 1925–1930 (see entry for September 9, 1930).
93 Whiteman 1995, p. 74.
94 Robertson 1965, p. 12.
95 Three sketches in the study group indicate that MacDonald was in the Coboconk area in 1926 and 1927. The sketch *Little Turtle Lake* (MCAC 1966.16.40) is signed "J.E.H. MacDonald '27" in fine black ink in the lower right corner. The back includes the artist's estate stamp and pencil inscriptions including one reading "Coboconk." The sketch *Gull River* (MCAC 2005.6.2) is signed "JM '26" in what appears to be graphite in the lower right corner. The back includes the artist's estate stamp and pencil inscriptions including one reading "Gull River/ J E H MacD," possibly in the artist's hand. The sketch *The Narrows, Gull River* (NGC 4525) is signed "JM '26" in slightly faded black ink in the lower right corner. There is an artist's inscription in ink on the back that reads "The Narrows/Gull River/J. MacD" as well as a graphite inscription of unknown origin that reads "1922?"
96 Duval 1978, p. 151.
97 MacDonald, J.E.H. 1989.
98 MacDonald, J.E.H., Letter to Brown, 1932.
99 MacDonald, T. and Bishop 1996, p. 5.
100 MacDonald, J.E.H., Letter to Brown, 1918.
101 MacDonald, J.E.H. December 1925.

2. SUPPORTS AND PREPARATION

1 The complete data for each of the examined works and a detailed description of the methods used for visual examination can be obtained by contacting CCI, https://www.canada.ca/en/conservation-institute.html.
2 Firestone 1979, p. 68; Murray 1971, p. 54; Webster-Cook and Ruggles 2002.
3 To determine the pattern in MacDonald's sketching support dimensions, it was important to use the verified data from our survey, since errors in dimensions were noted in books, exhibition catalogues, and occasionally in collections databases. These errors are particularly common regarding the 8 × 10-inch versus the 8½ × 10½-inch formats, which is a key distinction in the chronology of his sketches. The colours of the supports were matched to Munsell colour charts (Munsell 2019) to ensure consistent colour names, since descriptions of support colours in the published literature are inconsistent. The thickness of the boards was measured with a Meichan 0 to 10 mm thickness gauge.
4 The paper pulp was characterized using polarized light microscopy, described in Appendix B. The two sketches for which the support was analyzed are *Leaves in the Brook* (MCAC 1966.16.35) and *Moose Lake, Algoma* (MCAC 1966.15.4).
5 In March 1920, A.Y. Jackson wrote to MacDonald: "Ask Arthur to send me right away 35 panels. Cardboard will do and the five tubes of white he will find at the north end of my gallery." Jackson, Letter to J.E.H. MacDonald 1920. Just a few days before, MacDonald had written to fellow artist W.J. Wood with advice about sketching supports and sizes. In this letter, he described using sketching supports made from "bookbinder's mill-board of fairly heavy quality." MacDonald, J.E.H., Letter to W.J. Wood, March 15, 1920.
6 In collections databases and recent literature, the term "paperboard" is one of the more commonly used terms. Webster-Cook and Ruggles (2002) refer to Tom Thomson's supports of this type as "composite wood-pulp board" to emphasize that the boards include components in addition to wood pulp. We have not adopted this terminology since it is not in general use and could be confused with thicker, wood-pulp construction panels like fibreboard.
7 For simplicity, we refer to ground layers that appear to be artist-applied as having been prepared by MacDonald himself. However, beginning in 1918, MacDonald was sometimes assisted by his son, Thoreau. For example, there is evidence that Thoreau MacDonald sometimes sealed paperboard sketching supports with shellac for his father in advance of a sketching trip (Duval 1978, p. 89).
8 Although the term "academy board" is still in use and provides a succinct way to name these boards, a more complete descriptive name would be the preferred terminology in collections database descriptions; two possible choices of appropriate terminology would be "paperboard prepared with a ground layer by the manufacturer (academy board)" or "pre-prepared paperboard (academy board)."
9 Hill 2002, p. 132; McMichael 1986, pp. 189–190.

10 McMichael 1986, pp. 189–190; Duval 1978, p. 89; Laing 1978, p. 106.
11 MacDonald, J.E.H., Letter to Wood, March 15, 1920.
12 *Language of Bindings Thesaurus* n.d., see entries for paper board, laminated board, couched-laminate board, and pulp board; Roberts and Etherington 1982, see entries for board, binder's board and millboard.
13 McMichael 1986, pp. 189–190; Duval 1978, p. 89; Laing 1978, p. 106.
14 Warwick Bro's and Rutter [190?], p. 11.
15 Laing 1978, p. 106.
16 Art Metropole 1906.
17 E. Harris Company 1900.
18 Artists' Supply Company, *Price lists*, n.d. [1906–1936]; Artists' Supply Company, *No. 1111*, n.d. [1906–1936]. Both documents list the company's address as 77 York Street, Toronto, indicating a date between 1906 and 1936. This date range is based on our examination of Carl Schaefer's purchase receipts, which show that the Artists' Supply Company moved from their original location at 77 York Street to 35 Wellington Street West sometime between November 1935 and January 1936 (Schaefer, financial records 1931–1942).
19 Artists' Supply Company 1920.This catalogue includes various colours and thicknesses of Canadian-made "cardboard." They also sold "plain grey pulp board for mounting, at ⅛ inch [3 mm] thick" and various card-cutting machines.
20 Duval 1978, p. 89.
21 MacDonald, J.E.H., Letter to Wood, March 15, 1920.
22 MacDonald, J.E.H., Diaries 1925–1930 (see entry for August 31, 1925).
23 Painters at this time chose their sketching support sizes using imperial measurements (inches and feet). For this reason, when we discuss support sizes in a general fashion, we have chosen to use imperial measurements. When we list the measurements from our observations, we provide height and width in metric first with the corresponding imperial measurement in parentheses.
24 Roberts and Etherington 1982.
25 An earlier composition with a different colour scheme is visible in cracks and losses.
26 Art Metropole 1906.
27 Although sixteen sketches were examined, the support characteristics could not be determined for one of them: *The Junk Cart* (circa 1915, 70/327, AGO collection). The AGO curatorial file indicates that the sketch was originally painted on a larger, thicker support, with a sketch by Thoreau MacDonald on its back. In 1970, the support was split in half to separate MacDonald's painting from that of his son. The J.E.H. MacDonald sketch was then cut down in width and height and mounted on plywood. As a result, the dimensions of *The Junk Cart* are not an accurate reflection of MacDonald's practice. Based on the colour and texture visible on the front of the board, combined with the fact that it would be very difficult to split the type of thin paperboard support that MacDonald generally used, it is possible that *The Junk Cart* was painted on a type of fibreboard such as beaverboard.
28 Hill 2002, p. 123.
29 Robertson 1965, p. 13.
30 Webster-Cook and Ruggles 2002.
31 In *Near Minden*, the orange ground was applied when the green beneath was still partially wet. This has caused the orange ground to include streaks of green, leading to a duller tone. This is not the case for *Georgian Bay*, where there is no visible mixing of the green and orange.
32 One other sketch from the same summer, *Orchard at York Mills* (NGC 15848) has intermediate dimensions of 20.9 × 25.5 cm (8.2 × 10 in.). This sketch exhibits several unusual aspects. The paperboard support is uncharacteristically coated overall (front, back, and edges) with a textured, thick, grey-brown paint. It appears to have been originally used as a sign. A chalk inscription on the back reads, in part, "Will the student who removed my sketch by JWB from the door...." A nail hole shows that the board was hung with this side facing out. During the summer of 1918, MacDonald replaced J.W. Beatty as instructor at the Ontario College of Art summer school at York Mills (Stacey and Bishop 1996, p. 120). The note appears to be addressed to his students.
33 Firestone 1979, pp. 119–120; Murray 1971, p. 54; Hill 2002, p. 123; Webster-Cook and Ruggles 2002. This paintbox type was designed by A.Y. Jackson in 1914. Tom Thomson and J.W. Beatty used similar boxes. The box was designed to transport up to three sketching panels. The panels were held in slots at the left and right of the top of the box, with one of the panels acting as the lid. Because they were held in separate slots, the freshly painted surfaces of the panels were protected from contacting each other and potentially sticking together.
34 Appendix A provides detailed descriptions of the two paintboxes available for study.
35 Some sketches on wooden panel by A.Y. Jackson and Tom Thomson have vertical bands of unpainted support at their left and right edges, presumably because the edges of the support were covered by the slots in their paintbox lids. It is also common to see smeared or crushed paint at the left and right edges of their sketches from placing them in the paintbox lid or in a secondary carrier for transport while they were still wet. Our examination of MacDonald's sketches showed that his paint almost always extends completely to the left and right edges of his supports. We noted minor amounts of paint smearing, often at the lower part of the left and right edges, but this only extended a few millimetres into the painted composition. We also noted fingerprints from handling the boards while the paint was still wet on a number of sketches.
36 MacDonald, J.E.H., Letter to Wood, March 11, 1920; MacDonald, J.E.H., Letter to Wood, March 15, 1920. These letters discuss the possibility of Wood contributing to the first Group of Seven Show in May 1920. On March 11, MacDonald wrote to Wood, "You might let me know if you have anything in landscape or figure that you could send to another exhibition here in May. Several of us are getting up a small exhibition of pictures representing the modernist tendency among us. I feel well assured in extending you an invitation to contribute.... We shall be able to make easy arrangements for you in regard to shipping and we might possibly have a frame or two that you could borrow. If, for instance, you have any small paintings or sketches 8½ × 10½ inches I can easily loan you a number of frames." On March 15, 1920, he added, "If you cut your painting boards to 8½ × 10½ they will fit the frame back and front. The opening, or 'space of exposure' is 8¼ × 10¼, the rebate of the frame covering ⅛ of an inch all round.... We have a number of frames of a slightly larger size if you could work better a little larger. Your painting board for the larger size would have to be 13¾ × 10½."
37 MacDonald, J.E.H., Letter to Wood, March 15, 1920.
38 The fine, diagonal lines sometimes show a slight curvature, suggesting the use of a curved or circular blade.
39 Duval 1978, p. 89; MacDonald, J.E.H., Letter to Wood, March 15, 1920.

40 Certain sketches have an overall varnish layer on top of the painted composition. Surface varnishes can obscure the fluorescence of layers beneath, and in these cases, it was not always possible to determine whether MacDonald coated the front of the board with varnish before painting.
41 MacDonald, J.E.H., Letter to Wood, March 15, 1920.
42 The location of the thin, dark brown pulp layer is variable. While the dark layer most often appears about one-quarter of the way through the thickness of the board when viewed on edge, it is not always in the same location. In a few cases, the dark pulp layer was not visible, although the supports showed all other attributes of the Rockies Type B board.
43 *Lake MacArthur* (NGC 4530) is the only mountain sketch with a Rockies Type C support that does not date from 1929 or 1930. This sketch also has a traditional ground layer, a technique that MacDonald used commonly in his sketches from 1929 to 1932. While not directly dated on the front or back, the sketch has been given a date of circa 1925 by Duval (Duval 1978, p. 166) and Christensen (Christensen 2003, p. 47). Additional research into the date of this sketch may be warranted.
44 Although many of the supports for sketches from the Rocky Mountains showed a slight vertical or horizontal texture on the back, the texture on the Type C boards was more pronounced.
45 A double-sided sketch in the collection of the NGC (4845) has a composition entitled *Barbados* on one side and a possibly unfinished sketch entitled *Field at Thornhill* on the other. It seems likely that the Thornhill sketch was painted first and that MacDonald reused this board for his Barbados composition. Based on our study group, double-sided sketches appear to be relatively uncommon in MacDonald's oeuvre.
46 The complete data for each of the 14 studio paintings examined can be obtained by contacting CCI, https://www.canada.ca/en/conservation-institute.html.
47 Although a large-scale survey of dimensions and support types for the studio paintings was not undertaken, general trends were noted in published exhibition catalogues, biographies, and the collections databases of the MCAC, AGO, and NGC. The publications that were consulted for descriptions and dimensions of the supports include Hunter 1940; Robertson 1965; Art Gallery of Ontario 1970, pp. 267–280; and Duval 1978.
48 Hunter 1940, pp. 45–57; Ontario Society of Artists 1916, p. 18; Ontario Society of Artists 1917, p. 17.
49 Weaver 1997.
50 Beaver Board Companies 1920; Weaver 1997; Wilson and Snodgrass 2007.
51 Grier, Letter to McCurry, 1939; Brown, Letter to T. MacDonald, 1936; MacDonald, T., Letter to Brown, 1936.
52 Weaver 1997; Wilson and Snodgrass 2007.
53 For example, two paintings on beaverboard from the 1920s in the MCAC collection show a different type of trademark stamp than the 1915 to 1917 works on beaverboard by MacDonald. Rather than a shield design incorporating a beaver, *Old Barn, Quebec* by Arthur Lismer (MCAC 1970.14.10) from 1926 and *Mt. Lefroy* by Lawren Harris (MCAC 1981.85.2) from circa 1929 both show a patterned red stripe with a stylized "B" along one edge of the back.
54 Beaver Board Companies 1920; Weaver 1997; Wilson and Snodgrass 2007.
55 The MacCallum murals, now in the collection of the NGC, were not available for examination at the time of our study. A comparison of the supports and painting technique of the murals to MacDonald's studio works on beaverboard is an interesting area for future work. Further research to determine whether any of MacDonald's studio works on beaverboard predate the mural project would also be of interest.
56 Landry 1990, pp. 26–28. The largest of MacDonald's murals for the cottage, *The Supply Boat*, has a Beaver Board trademark stamped on the back of the support (information from NGC curatorial file for *The Supply Boat* 15648).
57 As in the case of the oil sketches, we established the presence of a varnish sealing layer on the front or back of the paintings by examining them with UV illumination and observing the visible fluorescence. This phenomenon is described in the glossary.
58 E. Harris Company 1900; Art Metropole 1906; Artists' Supply Company, *Price lists*, n.d. [1906–1936]; Artists' Supply Company, *No. 1111*, n.d. [1906–1936]; Artists' Supply Company 1920.
59 Artists' Supply Company, *Price lists*, n.d. [1906–1936]; Artists' Supply Company, *No. 1111*, n.d. [1906–1936].
60 Various weave types are listed in the catalogues consulted: plain weave; basket weave (described as "2 × 2 thread" by the Artists' Supply Co.); modified basket weave (described as "Roman" by E. Harris and the Art Metropole and as "2 × 1 thread" by the Artists Supply Co.); and twill weave (described as "ticken weave" by E. Harris and "twill" by the Artists' Supply Co.). According to Christina Young, "Roman" corresponds to a modified basket weave, while "ticken" is a twill weave (Young 2012). Definitions of the different weave types can be found in the glossary.
61 Harris, B., Letter to R. Harper, 1962.
62 E. Harris Company 1900; Art Metropole 1906; Artists' Supply Company, *Price lists*, n.d. [1906–1936]; Artists' Supply Company, *No. 1111*, n.d. [1906–1936].
63 Carlyle 2001, p. 179. Carlyle notes that in a Reeves catalogue from 1904, unprepared canvas was supplied at two-thirds the price of prepared canvas.
64 Art Metropole 1906; Artists' Supply Company, *Price lists*, n.d. [1906–1936]; Artists' Supply Company, *No. 1111*, n.d. [1906–1936].
65 These weave types are defined in the glossary under "Canvas weave."
66 Hunter, Letter to Gurd, 1938; Hunter, Letter to McCurry, 1938. In the letter to McCurry, Hunter wrote: "I recently borrowed one of MacDonald's paintings, *The Lonely North* from its owner… In returning it I suggested relining as it is painted on that poisonous jute so much favoured by our old masters." Assuming that Hunter is correct, this indicates that MacDonald began using jute as early as 1913. In the letter to N.S. Gurd, the representative of the owner of *The Lonely North*, Hunter specifies that jute was in regular use by 1913: "A number of Canadian artists at this time, and subsequently, used jute instead of canvas [sic: by canvas he appears to mean cotton]." Visual examination of another 1913 canvas painting by MacDonald, *Ten War Canoes* (MCAC 1985.8), indicates that the horizontal fibres are jute (examination by Alison Douglas, 2022).
67 Although a large-scale survey of dimensions and support types for the studio paintings was not undertaken, general trends were noted in published exhibition catalogues, biographies, and the collections databases of the MCAC, AGO, and NGC. The publications that were consulted for descriptions and dimensions of the supports include Hunter 1940; Robertson 1965; AGO 1970, pp. 267–280; and Duval 1978.

68 Pantazzi 1977.
69 Cusping, also known as garlanding or scalloping, was also visible at the tacking edges of the canvas. Cusping is a scalloped pattern of distortions to the canvas edges produced by tension from the nails used to hold it on the stretcher. Its presence provides further indication that the ground was applied with the painting on its stretcher.
70 Corbeil et al. 2000.

3. PAINTING TECHNIQUES

1 Jackson, Letter to Clement, 1919.
2 MacDonald, J.E.H., Diaries 1925–1930 (see entry for September 1, 1930).
3 MacDonald, J.E.H., Diaries 1925–1930 (see entry for September 12, 1930).
4 Ibid.
5 MacDonald, J.E.H. 1979.
6 Available archival photographs of MacDonald sketching were not of sufficient quality to determine whether they depict either of the two paintboxes that we studied. It is possible that he also used other portable sketching boxes during his career.
7 Firestone 1979, pp. 119–120; Murray 1971, p. 54; Hill 2002, p. 123; Webster-Cook and Ruggles 2002; Klempan et al. 2009.
8 A portable easel believed to belong to J.E.H. MacDonald was sold at auction in 2002 and described as follows: "TRAVELLING EASEL. Probably J.E.H. MacDonald's. Reeves & Sons Limited, London, maker's metal label. Circa 1912. Folding oak portable easel standing on three adjustable tripod legs. Brass fittings. 150/250." (Joyner 2002, lot 117). MacDonald's use of a portable easel was also noted by Christensen (Christensen 2003, p. 23).
9 MacDonald, J.E.H., Lecture Notes, Untitled, General Art, n.d. [circa 1925]. Reference to sketching in the mountains indicates that these notes post-date 1924. The similarity in the description of sketching as "the one great sport" in his 1925 article (MacDonald, J.E.H. 1925) suggests that the notes date from around this time .
10 Christensen 1999, p. 76. Christensen's source is Oral History Tape S 37/157 (A&B), George K.K. Link fonds, Archives of the Whyte Museum of the Canadian Rockies.
11 MacDonald, J.E.H., Diaries 1925–1930 (see entry for September 2, 1925). In this diary entry, MacDonald describes finding the oil bottle that he had left at a sketching site the year before.
12 As well as transporting freshly completed sketches in their paintboxes, some Group of Seven artists also used additional small wooden carriers. In a 1934 letter from A.Y. Jackson to Thoreau MacDonald, Jackson asked him to send a parcel of sketching panels and "also a carrier to hold a couple of wet panels.... There are a couple of them on the gallery in my studio.... Put a couple of panels in it or it will get broken in the mail." (Jackson, Letter to T. MacDonald, 1934). Jackson also described carrying wet sketches, separated by bits of matchsticks and tied together with a cord (Jackson 1967, p. 65). The McMichael Canadian Art Collection owns a sketch carrier that belonged to Lawren Harris.
13 Christensen 2003, p. 23.
14 Duval 1978, p. 141.
15 MacDonald, J.E.H., Diaries 1925–1930 (see entry for August 29, 1925).
16 MacDonald, J.E.H., Diaries 1925–1930 (see entry for September 12, 1930).
17 Jackson, Letter to MacDonald, 1920. Although the year is not included in the date of this letter, it was written from Osborne House, Franceville, March 17, and so dates from 1920 (Mellen 1970, pp. 210–211). The letter is also transcribed and dated 1920 in A.Y. Jackson's autobiography (Jackson 1967, p. 53).
18 MacDonald, J.E.H. December 1925.
19 MacDonald, J.E.H., Lecture Notes, Untitled, General Art, n.d. [circa 1925].
20 Based on observations made by Alison Douglas of works in the MCAC collection.
21 For infrared photography, CCI photographers used a Speedotron (xenon) flash system, and a Phase One (model XF IQ4) camera system manufactured without the infrared blocking filter. The camera was equipped with a Kodak IR Wratten 87A long-pass filter, which transmits between 880 and 1100 nm. This allowed only the reflected infrared light from the painting to be recorded.
22 Based on the works in our study group, it was uncommon for MacDonald to paint over an existing sketch.
23 Webster-Cook and Ruggles 2002.
24 Ibid.
25 MacDonald, J.E.H., Lecture Notes, Untitled, General Art, n.d. [circa 1925].
26 Ibid.
27 Town 1989, p. 26
28 MacDonald, J.E.H., Letter to Wood, March 15, 1920.
29 MacDonald, J.E.H. 1919.
30 Duval 1978, p. 89. Permanent blue is a commercial name for artificial ultramarine used by both Winsor & Newton (Art Metropole 1900, pp. 6–11) and Madderton & Company (Madderton & Co. 1908, pp. 10–11).
31 MacDonald, J.E.H., Lecture Notes, Untitled, General Art, n.d. [circa 1925].
32 MacDonald, The Decorative Element in Art, n.d.
33 MacDonald, J.E.H., Lecture Notes, Untitled, General Art, n.d. [circa 1925].
34 The oil-rich appearance is perhaps due, in part, to the fact that MacDonald usually sealed his supports with varnish, which would have prevented the oil medium from soaking into the support. This differs from Harold Town's description of Tom Thomson's sketches on wood panel (Town 1989, p. 27), where the paint is described as "crusty." Town attributes this to the fact that Thomson painted on bare wood panels that absorbed some of the oil medium from the paint, leading to a stiffer, crisper paint.
35 MacDonald, J.E.H., Diaries 1925–1930 (see entries for August 31 and September 9, 1930).
36 Hunter 1940, p. 34.
37 MacDonald, J.E.H., Diaries 1925–1930 (see entry for September 9, 1930).
38 MacDonald, J.E.H. 1924; MacDonald, J.E.H., Diaries 1925–1930 (see entries for August 26, 1925, and September 9, 1930).
39 MacDonald, J.E.H. 1924.
40 MacDonald, J.E.H., Diaries 1925–1930 (see entry for September 2, 1925).
41 Christensen 2003, p. 17. Christensen's source is Oral History Tape S 37/157 (A&B), George K.K. Link fonds, Archives of the Whyte Museum of the Canadian Rockies.
42 Robertson 1965, p. 28.
43 An interesting avenue for further research would be to

determine whether any of MacDonald's studio works on beaverboard predate the MacCallum mural project.

44 The MacCallum murals, now in the collection of the NGC, were not available for examination at the time of our study. However, Landry has described some of their features (Landry 1990, pp. 26–28).

45 *Belgium* was painted with a somewhat different technique than the other works, presumably because it was a poster or design for one. As such, it has a strong black painted outline to delineate foreground, sky, and other forms and a limited, dark palette. Within each area or form, the same colour is used throughout with a thin, dappled paint application. We see the use of what appears to be ink as well as oil paint. There may also be a limited use of graphite pencil on this work.

46 MacDonald, J.E.H., Lecture Notes, Untitled, General Art, n.d. [circa 1925].

47 Although the process of lining may have increased the prominence of the canvas texture in some of these paintings, *The Solemn Land* remains unlined and shows evident canvas texture, indicating that this was an intentional effect.

48 Buffalo Fine Arts Academy 1924.

49 Firestone 1979, p. 38.

50 Robertson 1965, pp. 8–9.

51 Town 1989, p. 26.

52 Jackson, Letter to Brown, 1928.

53 Duval 1978, p. 145.

54 Hunter 1940, pp. 34–35.

55 There is some variation in presence or absence of periods after the letters in the initials.

56 Kelly and Angel 2021; Siegel 2004.

57 MacDonald, T., Letter to Bradfield, 1966.

4. PAINTING MATERIALS

1 More information about the ethics and practice of sampling artworks is found in Helwig and Bladek 2022.

2 Stols-Witlox et al. 2012; Morgan et al. 2008; Laurie 1926, p. 76. Laurie specifies that an excellent mixture for oil grounds is "white lead containing some 10 per cent of barytes [i.e., barium sulfate]." While these references focus on oil grounds for paintings on canvas, several late nineteenth- to early twentieth-century sources indicate that millboards and academy boards were prepared with similar ground formulations to those used for panel or canvas (Carlyle 2001, pp. 187–189).

3 Supports with two layers of commercial ground are referred to in catalogues of the time as "double primed." See, for example, Art Metropole 1906, p. 59.

4 As described in chapter 2, an oil-based ground should be left for at least several days after application, and ideally longer, before painting.

5 As described in chapter 2, examination of *Near Minden* indicates that the yellow-orange preparation completely covers the green below and that the lower green ground has little to no effect on the final colour. This could indicate that MacDonald changed his mind about the colour choice for the ground in this case.

6 Helwig 2007.

7 Examination and analysis of more works on plywood could determine if this difference is significant.

8 Appendix B provides the Py-GC-MS analysis method and the characteristic markers that allowed identification of these components.

9 Smith 1912.

10 This differs from his oil sketches, which were normally prepared with shellac before any application of compositional underpainting.

11 Heated pine resin was identified using Py-GC-MS. Appendix B provides the analysis method and the characteristic markers used for the identification.

12 Stols-Witlox et al. 2012; Morgan et al. 2008; Laurie 1926, p. 76.

13 Ground layers based on lead white and calcium carbonate have also been identified in several of Tom Thomson's oil paintings on canvas painted between 1914 and 1917 (Corbeil et al. 2000).

14 MacDonald, T. and Bishop 1996, p. 5.

15 E. Harris Company 1900; Art Metropole 1906; The Artists' Supply Company, *No. 1111*, n.d. [1906–1936]; Artists' Supply Company 1926a; Artists' Supply Company 1926b; Artists' Supply Company 1934.

16 Helwig et al. 2015.

17 MacDonald may also have had access to other types of oil paint, sourcing them further afield, for example, during sketching trips to Nova Scotia or to the Rocky Mountains.

18 E. Harris Company 1900.

19 Helwig et al. 2015.

20 E. Harris Company 1900.

21 Helwig et al. 2015.

22 Stacey and Bishop 1996, p. 45.

23 Art Metropole 1906; Helwig et al. 2015.

24 Art Metropole 1906.

25 Helwig et al. 2015

26 Laing 1978, pp. 24–25.

27 Mr. Ken Arnott, grandson of Mr. Albert William Arnott (1870–1946), long-time manager of the Artists' Supply Company, confirmed that the company was created as a branch of George Ridout & Company to handle their artists' materials product line (Arnott 2020). At the turn of the twentieth century, A.W. Arnott worked at the Art Metropole for several years. In about 1903, he left the Art Metropole and joined George Ridout & Company (*Toronto City Directories* 1900 to 1937, see entries for 1900 to 1905 inclusive). He began as a "traveller" for Ridout, and, in that capacity, visited firms that the company represented in England and Europe. A short description of his travels is found in the *Bookseller and Stationer* (*Bookseller and Stationer* 1904, p. 91). The Artist's Supply Company was created upon his return to Toronto. A.W. Arnott is listed as manager of the Artists' Supply Company in the *Toronto City Directory* from 1906, the first year that the company appears therein (*Toronto City Directory* 1906).

28 *Toronto City Directories* 1900 to 1937. All listings for "Manufacturing Agents" and "Artists' Materials" were examined. George Ridout & Co. is listed as an agent for artists' materials for the first time in the 1903 directory. The Artists' Supply Company appears for the first time in the 1906 directory, sharing an address with George Ridout & Co. in the Nordheimer building at 75–77 York Street.

29 Artists' Supply Company, *No. 1111* n.d. [1906–1936]; Artists' Supply Company 1926b; Helwig et al. 2015.

30 Helwig et al. 2015.

31 Pratt 1980; Madderton & Co. 1908; Simon 2022.

32 Pratt 1980; Madderton & Co. 1908; Laurie 1934, p. 98; Simon, J. "Madderton & Co.," in British artists' suppliers, 1650–1950, on National Portrait Gallery website, http://www.npg.org.uk/research/programmes/directory-of-suppliers/m.php. This entry last updated March 2022.
33 Madderton & Co. 1908.
34 Helwig et al. 2015.
35 Artists' Supply Company, *No. 1111*, n.d. [1906–1936].
36 Three Cambridge Colours paint tubes that belonged to A.Y. Jackson are in the McMichael Canadian Art Collection, providing direct evidence that he used this paint brand. As well, in an artist's questionnaire, Jackson listed "probably Cambridge and Lefranc" as the brands he used for a 1914 painting in the AGO collection (Helwig et al. 2015). Finally, Jackson's account books from 1921 to 1931 include many entries for purchases from the Artists' Supply Company (Jackson, Accounts Book 1921–1931).
37 Carl Schaefer's financial records from 1931 to 1942 show numerous purchases from the Artists' Supply Company, including Cambridge Colours paints along with other materials (Schaefer, Financial Records 1931–1942).
38 In addition to these close colleagues of MacDonald's, there is archival evidence of other Canadian painters using Cambridge Colours. An advertisement for Cambridge Colours from the Artist's Supply Company includes endorsements from Canadian painters Owen Staples and Franklin Brownell. A paint box that belonged to Kathleen Munn included Cambridge Colours paint tubes (Helwig et al. 2015).
39 In all samples, the paint medium was identified as a drying oil using FTIR spectroscopy. To determine the type of oil, more precise analysis using Py-GC-MS would be required.
40 E. Harris 1900; Art Metropole 1906; Artists' Supply Company, *No. 1111*, n.d. [1906–1936]; Madderton & Co. 1908.
41 In MacDonald's paintings, the zinc soaps are most often in a non-crystalline form. This stage in their evolution is not usually associated with conservation issues like protrusions or delamination (Beerse et al. 2020).
42 Thomson's materials are described in Corbeil et al. 2000. Since publication of this article, supplementary study of several samples from *The West Wind* (AGO 784) was undertaken, and these results have also been included in CCI's data on Thomson's materials (Anema et al. 2013).
43 MacDonald, Lecture Notes, Untitled, General Art, n.d. [circa 1925].
44 Corbeil et al. 2000.
45 Laurie 1895, back matter advertisement; Madderton & Co. 1908. By a "patented process," the authors likely refer to Freeman's 1882 patent for a white pigment made from a mixture of lead sulfate and zinc oxide ground under pressure (Corbeil et al. 1999). When used as a pigment, zinc oxide is usually referred to as "zinc white," which is the name we use for this compound throughout.
46 Madderton & Co. 1908.
47 Ibid.
48 Helwig et al. 2015.
49 For samples from MacDonald's paintings composed primarily of this lead sulfate–zinc white pigment, the relative peak areas for lead and zinc in the SEM/EDX spectra are similar to the tubes of New Flake White in Kathleen Munn's paint box. The FTIR spectra and XRD patterns are very similar as well.
50 Laurie 1895; Corbeil et al. 1999.
51 Traditional lead white is composed of lead carbonate hydroxide and lead carbonate. It is known to darken when exposed to pollutants, particularly sulfur (Gettens et al. 1993).
52 Madderton & Co. 1908.
53 Artists' Supply Company 1926a; Artists' Supply Company 1934.
54 Corbeil et al. 2000. In this article, the name "Freeman's White" is used for the same lead sulfate–zinc white pigment that we refer to as Cambridge White.
55 Corbeil et al. 1999; Corbeil et al. 2020.
56 Helwig 2007.
57 Helwig et al. 2015.
58 Fiedler and Bayard 1986.
59 Ibid.
60 The type of cadmium yellow was determined using XRD. The results of SEM/EDX on MacDonald's cadmium yellow paints suggest that additives or residual starting materials containing aluminum, magnesium, and phosphorous are present in most cases. However, compounds containing these elements were not identified by XRD. The FTIR spectra showed some indication of sulfates (a broad band close to 1100 cm^{-1}) and oxalates (sharp bands at 1320 and 1380 cm^{-1}). On one sketch, *Leaves in the Brook*, cadmium carbonate was identified associated with cadmium yellow: this could be a starting material or a reaction product (Fiedler and Bayard 1986). To date, we did not note a difference in composition in cadmium yellows that showed cracking compared to those that were intact. However, as described in chapter 5, other factors such as the presence of other pigments mixed with the cadmium yellow can affect the aging of the pigment.
61 Art Metropole 1906.
62 Madderton & Co. 1908.
63 Whitehouse and Eastaugh, 2001; Leone et al. 2005; Mass et al. 2013.
64 Madderton & Co. 1908.
65 Corbeil et al. 2000.
66 Art Metropole 1906; Madderton & Co. 1908.
67 Art Metropole 1906.
68 This was not confirmed using XRD, as peak shifts among reference patterns of Mg-substituted and non-substituted varieties of cobalt tin oxide were small.
69 Helwig et al. 2015.
70 Green earth was confirmed as the celadonite type in these cases using FTIR spectroscopy. This mineral pigment has characteristic, sharp hydroxyl stretching bands in the 3610 to 3530 cm^{-1} region (Grissom 1986). Since mixtures of green earth and chromium oxide were sold by Madderton & Co. under the name "Terre Verte," it is possible that the combination of green earth and viridian in these paints is a manufacturer's mixture of this type (Madderton & Co. 1908).
71 Alizarin (Pigment Red 83) was identified using FTIR and/or Raman spectroscopy. The use of an aluminum phosphate base was inferred based on the high concentration of aluminum and phosphorous identified by SEM/EDX.
72 Kühn and Curran 1986.
73 de Keijzer 2014.
74 Toluidine red (Pigment Red 3) was identified using both FTIR and Raman spectroscopy on these two paintings.
75 Corbeil et al. 2000. The single occurrence of toluidine red listed in the article was from a painting on canvas *The Pool* (NGC 4725), circa 1915–1916.
76 Helwig 2007.
77 MacDonald, J.E.H. 1980. This is the text of a lecture given by J.E.H. MacDonald at the Art Gallery of Ontario, April 17, 1931. The original handwritten lecture notes can be found here: J.E.H MacDonald lecture on Scandinavian Art, April 17, 1931, MG30 D111, box 3, folder 27, J.E.H. MacDonald fonds, Library and Archives Canada, Ottawa, Ontario .
78 MacDonald, J.E.H. May–June 1925.

79 Art Metropole 1906.
80 Cobalt violet is listed by Madderton & Co. and by Winsor & Newton early in the twentieth century (Madderton & Co. 1908; Art Metropole 1906). Manganese violet is known to have been sold by Winsor & Newton by 1910 and has been identified in paintings by David Milne as early as 1917 (Sirois et al. 2007).

5. APPLYING THE RESEARCH

1 O'Conner 2004; Flescher 2004.
2 Streeton 2022; Tummers and Erdmann 2022.
3 Boutilier and Bruce 2021.
4 Laver 1997.
5 "Buried Group of Seven Paintings Brought to Light in Major Donation." *Canadian Art*, January 14, 2015.
6 Klinkhoff 2015; Lederman 2015.
7 The results presented here have been expanded from the original report written for the VAG in 2015–2016 to include a more thorough description of the support and preparation.
8 Hill 1984.
9 The painting has an overall surface varnish, which partially obscured the preparatory varnish below. Further analysis would be required to confirm the use of shellac.
10 de Keijzer 2014.
11 Laver 1997.
12 For UV-induced fluorescence photography, the sketch was irradiated with UV radiation (300–400 nm) and the visible light emitted (fluorescence) was recorded photographically. This technique often allows areas of overpaint to be distinguished from original paint, based on differences in their fluorescence.
13 Hill 1997.
14 In a 1938 letter, E.R. Hunter states that *The Lonely North* was painted on jute (Hunter, Letter to McCurry, 1938). Assuming that Hunter is correct, this indicates that MacDonald began using jute as early as 1913. In another 1938 letter, this one to the representative of the owner of *The Lonely North*, he wrote that jute was in regular use at the time MacDonald painted it: "A number of Canadian artists at this time, and subsequently, used jute instead of canvas [sic: by canvas he means cotton]." (Hunter, Letter to Gurd, 1938). In addition, visual examination by Alison Douglas of an early painting on canvas by MacDonald, *Warpath Canoes*, from 1913, in the collection of the McMichael, indicates that it is painted on jute.
15 Based on visual examination by Alison Douglas, several studio paintings by Group of Seven artists and Tom Thomson in the McMichael collection were determined to be on jute, including Tom Thomson's *Woodland Waterfall*. Thomson's *The West Wind* is also painted on jute (Webster-Cook and Ruggles 2002).
16 Harris, B., Letter to Harper, 1962.
17 A comparison of the thread counts for jute supports from this period for Group of Seven paintings would be an interesting area for future research.
18 Hunter, Letter to McCurry, 1938.
19 Hunter, Letter to Gurd, 1938. By "canvas (or duck)" he is referring to cotton.
20 Ekundayo and Adejuyigbe 2019; Rowell and Stout 2007.
21 Ekundayo and Adejuyigbe 2019; Kronkright 1990; Rowell and Stout 2007. As well as the inherent properties of the fibres, the processing methods may also play a role in the degradation of jute fabrics. For example, jute fibres were often treated with various oils during processing (Atkinson 1964; Carter 1921). These coatings could augment deterioration of jute by causing a higher retention of volatile degradation products within the fibres.
22 Ekundayo and Adejuyigbe 2019; Kronkright 1990; Rowell and Stout 2007.
23 Harris, B., Letter to Harper, 1962.
24 Hackney et al. 2012.
25 Ibid.
26 Barclay 2009.
27 Harbour 1935. Harbour likely used the terms "burlap" and "jute" synonymously (see the glossary).
28 Dix 1982; Barclay 1984.
29 Ruggles 1987.
30 Wilson and Snodgrass 2007; Beaver Board Companies 1920; Weaver 1997.
31 Thickens 1914; Beaver Board Companies 1920; Weaver 1997; Wilson and Snodgrass 2007.
32 Thickens 1914. The steam and pressure treated pulp used for the faces was called "cooked wood pulp" in this patent. The mechanically processed wood pulp core was called "ground wood pulp." According to the patent, the use of pressure and steam prior to mechanical processing led to a denser product with longer fibres.
33 Thickens 1914; Weaver 1997; Wilson and Snodgrass 2007.
34 Thickens 1914.
35 Banik and Brückle 2018.
36 Thickens 1914.
37 Małachowska et al. 2021.
38 Grier, Letter to McCurry, 1939.
39 McCurry, Letter to Grier, 1939.
40 While some of MacDonald's sketches have a final varnish layer, he did not likely varnish them himself. By the early twentieth century, many painters had abandoned the use of a traditional final varnish, and outdoor oil sketches are even less likely to include an artist's varnish. Laing (1978, p. 112) noted that A.Y. Jackson never varnished his paintings: "Jackson himself never varnished his paintings, nor did he like a varnished surface; he claimed, with some validity, that with the passage of time varnish oxidized and turned brown, darkening the surface of the paintings and becoming difficult to remove."
41 McMichael 1986, p. 190.
42 Whitehouse and Eastaugh 2001; Leone et al. 2005; Mass et al. 2013.
43 Art Metropole 1906; Madderton & Co. 1908.
44 Helwig et al. 2014.
45 Beerse et al. 2020.
46 Harbour 1935.
47 Jackson, A.Y. Transcript of an excerpt of a letter to E. Brown, January 10, 1928. In *The Solemn Land*, accession no. 1785, curatorial file. National Gallery of Canada, Ottawa, Ontario. Corroboration of Jackson's observations through analysis of the oil medium to determine if it was poorly cross-linked or showed residues of turpentine or other diluent was not possible because the paint was "fed" with linseed oil during the 1935 to 1936 treatment.
48 Harbour, handwritten notes, 1935–1936.
49 Barclay 2009.

CONCLUSION

1 Corbeil et al. 2000. Note that in this article, the name "Freeman's White" is used for the same lead sulfate-zinc white pigment that we refer to as Cambridge White.

2 MacDonald, J.E.H., Lecture Notes, Untitled, General Art, n.d. [circa 1925].

APPENDIX A: PAINTBOXES

1 Hill 2002, p. 123.

2 The materials inside the McMichael box were not catalogued here, as previous research has shown that at least some of them were placed in the box after MacDonald's death (Klempan 2012).

3 The box was purchased by a private collector from Joyner's auction house in Toronto on May 14, 2002 (lot 139 in that sale). Description in the auction catalogue reads: "THE ARTIST'S PAINTBOX, containing a palette, numerous brushes, palette knife, pencil, charcoal fragments, paint pot and linseed flask, the paint box and palette both certified by Thoreau MacDonald, horizontal splits in front and back panels." (Joyner 2002).

4 The Artists' Supply Company, *No. 1111*, n.d. [1906–1936].

APPENDIX B: ANALYSIS METHODS

1 Price et al. 2009.

2 Gunasheka and Krishna 2015.

3 Stoney 1990.

4 McCrone 1982; Feller and Bayard 1986; Eastaugh et al. 2004.

5 Casadio et al. (2016) provides a summary of Raman databases for cultural heritage materials.

6 Poulin et al. 2022.

7 Corbeil et al. 2011; van Keulen 2014; Pitthard et al. 2005.

8 van Keulen 2014; Sutherland and del Río 2014.

9 van den Berg et al. 2000; Helwig et al. 2008; van Keulen 2014.

10 van Keulen 2014; Moffatt et al. 2015.

11 Bonaduce and Columbini 2004; Jiménez et al. 2003; van Keulen 2014.

12 Marinach et al. 2004.

13 Plesters 1956.

APPENDIX C: SKETCHING NOTES

1 MacDonald, Lecture Notes, Untitled, General Art, n.d. [circa 1925]. Reference to sketching in the mountains indicates that these notes post-date 1924. The similarity in the description of sketching as "the one great sport" in his 1925 article (MacDonald, J.E.H. December 1925) suggests that the notes date from around this time.

APPENDIX D: ANALYSIS RESULTS

1 Fiedler and Bayard 1986.

2 Berrie 1997.

3 Zumbuehl et al. 2009.

4 Grissom 1986.

GLOSSARY

1 Beaver Board Companies 1920; Weaver 1997; Wilson and Snodgrass 2007.

2 Ibid.

3 Thickens 1914.

4 Thickens 1921.

5 Thickens 1916.

6 Beaver Board Companies 1920; Thickens 1914.

7 Beaver Board Companies 1920; Weaver 1997.

8 Roberts and Etherington 1982.

9 *Language of Bindings Thesaurus* n.d.; Roberts and Etherington 1982.

10 *Language of Bindings Thesaurus* n.d.; Roberts and Etherington 1982; Ireland 1968, pp. 6–7 and 277–289; Dawe 1914, pp. 1–7 and 35–37.

11 McMichael 1986, pp. 189–190; Duval 1978, p. 89; Laing 1978, p. 106; MacDonald, Letter to W.J. Wood, March 15, 1920.

12 Webster-Cook and Ruggles 2002.

13 Ekundayo and Adejuyigbe 2019; Rowell and Stout 2007.

14 Kronkright 1990; Rowell and Stout 2007; Ekundayo and Adejuyigbe 2019.

15 Email correspondence between Alison Douglas and Vijay Sharma, Jute Division, Birla Corporation Ltd., Calcutta, India, 30 July 1999.

16 Wilson and Snodgrass 2007; Stark and Cai 2021; Gould et al. 2014.

17 *Language of Bindings Thesaurus* n.d.

18 Roberts and Etherington 1982.

19 Ireland 1968, pp. 6–7 and 277–289; Dawe 1914, pp. 1–7 and 35–37.

20 Roberts and Etherington 1982; Ireland 1968; Dawe 1914, pp. 1–7 and 35–37.

21 Art Metropole 1906, pp. 58–60; Artists' Supply Company, *Price Lists*, n.d. [1906–1936]. The Artists' Supply Company, *No. 1111*, n.d. [1906–1936]. Buck 1972.

22 Art Metropole 1906.

23 Gettens and Stout 1966, pp. 221–222; Katlan 1999; Carlyle 2001, pp. 187–190; E. Harris Company 1900, pp. 55–56; Art Metropole 1906, pp. 58–60; Artists' Supply Company, *Price Lists*, n.d. [1906–1936]. The Artists' Supply Company, *No. 1111*, n.d. [1906–1936].

CONTRIBUTORS

Kate Helwig completed her Bachelor of Science in Chemistry at the University of Toronto and Master's in Physical Chemistry at Stanford University. To combine her interests in art and science, she then studied art conservation at Queen's University and received a Master of Art Conservation (M.A.C.). She works at the Canadian Conservation Institute in Ottawa, Ontario, as a senior conservation scientist, specializing in the analysis of cultural heritage materials. Kate has led many scientific examination projects related to attribution and authentication of paintings. These projects included the interpretation of scientific imaging, close visual examination of artist's technique, multi-instrumental chemical analysis, and the correlation of scientific results with historical information. She has presented her research at numerous national and international conferences, and she has authored over 50 peer-reviewed articles and several book chapters.

Alison Douglas completed her Bachelor of Fine Art and Master of Art Conservation (M.A.C.), specializing in paintings, at Queen's University. She has worked for 20 years at the McMichael Canadian Art Collection in Kleinburg, Ontario. For the past 18 years, she has been their only conservator. As the McMichael collects exclusively Canadian art, Alison has gained extensive knowledge of the methods and materials of the Group of Seven and their contemporaries as well as many other Canadian and Indigenous artists. Her research interests include the use of jute and its inherent conservation issues as a painting support used by early twentieth-century Canadian artists, as well as the varied uses of artist materials in contemporary painting, and preventive conservation. Alison has also continued to work as an artist in oil paint, ceramics, and various other media.